THE BOARDWALK JUNGLE

Books by Ovid Demaris

THE BOARDWALK JUNGLE
THE VEGAS LEGACY
THE LAST MAFIOSO
BROTHERS IN BLOOD
JUDITH EXNER—MY STORY
THE DIRECTOR
DIRTY BUSINESS
THE OVERLORD
POSO DEL MUNDO
AMERICA THE VIOLENT
JACK RUBY
(with Garry Wills)
CAPTIVE CITY
THE GREEN FELT JUNGLE
(with Ed Reid)

How Greed, Corruption,
and the Mafia turned
Atlantic City into . . .

THE

BOARDWALK JUNGLE

Ovid Demaris

BANTAM BOOKS
TORONTO · NEW YORK · LONDON · SYDNEY · AUCKLAND

Once more,
to Inez,
with love

THE BOARDWALK JUNGLE
A Bantam Book / April 1986

Library of Congress Cataloging-in-Publication Data

Demaris, Ovid.
  The boardwalk jungle.

  Includes index.
  1. Gambling—New Jersey—Atlantic City.   2. Crime and
criminals—New Jersey—Atlantic City.   I. Title.
HV6721.A8D45   1986   363.4'2'0974985   85-48046
ISBN 0-553-05130-X

Published simultaneously in the United States and Canada

Bantam Books are published by Bantam Books, Inc. Its trademark, consisting of the words
"Bantam Books" and the portrayal of a rooster, is Registered in U.S. Patent and Trademark
Office and in other countries. Marca Registrada. Bantam Books, Inc., 666 Fifth Avenue, New
York, New York 10103.

PRINTED IN THE UNITED STATES OF AMERICA

FG   0 9 8 7 6 5 4 3 2 1

Acknowledgments

Many have contributed to the making of this book. For reasons entirely proper, some have asked to remain anonymous. I honor their wish and extend my warmest thanks. I am equally grateful to the others: Jeffrey Blitz, Atlantic County Deputy District Attorney; G. Michael Brown, former Director, New Jersey Department of Gaming Enforcement; the late Robert L. Brown, Las Vegas reporter; Brendan T. Byrne, former New Jersey Governor; Ray Charyn, private investigator; Russell Corby, Atlantic City political worker; the late Paul "Skinny" D'Amato, Atlantic City nightclub operator; Al Delugach, *Los Angeles Times* reporter; Lt. Col. Justin Dintino, Deputy Superintendent, New Jersey State Police; Jim Drinkhall, former *Wall Street Journal* reporter; James F. Flanagan III, Deputy Director, New Jersey Department of Gaming Enforcement; Joseph A. Fusco, Atlantic County District Attorney; Dennis Gomes, Las Vegas and Atlantic City gaming investigator; Michael Hamel-Green, private investigator; Robert W. Greene, *Newsday* reporter and author of *The Sting Man;* Patrick F. Healy, Director, Chicago Crime Commission; Gigi Mahon, author of *The Company That Bought The Boardwalk;* Joseph McGahn, former Atlantic County senator; Hank Messick, author of several organized crime books; Guy Michael, former Deputy Director, Department of Gaming Enforcement; Thomas R. O'Brien, Director, Department of Gaming Enforcement; Clinton Pagano, Superintendent, New Jersey State Police; Charlie J. Parsons, Assistant Special Agent in charge of the Las Vegas FBI office; Steven Perskie, Atlantic City politician and judge; Fred Romonowski, state police investigator; Dick Ross, FBI agent, Atlantic City; Knut Royce, former *Kansas City Times* reporter; Denny Walsh, *Sacramento Bee* reporter; Charles Yeager, Atlantic City free-lance writer; Joseph Yablonsky, former Special Agent in charge of the Las Vegas FBI office.

I am grateful to the *Las Vegas Review Journal* and members of its staff, including Mary Hausch, Jean Morrison, Clyde Weiss, and Charles Zobel. And to the *Atlantic City Press* and reporters Aly Ackermann, Phil Linsalata, Joseph Tanfani, Kathy Brennan, Michael Chicchio, Daniel Heneghan, Cynthia Burton, Bret Skakun, Carla Linz, and with special thanks to *Press* reporter Michael Pollock, who worked as my research assistant. I am also indebted to other journalists who have written extensively on this subject, particularly *Philadelphia Inquirer* reporters George Anastasia, H. G. Bissinger, Marguerite Del Giudice, and Fen Montaigne.

And finally, as always, I thank my wife Inez for her enthusiastic assistance in innumerable ways.

Contents

Author's Note

It was nearly a quarter century ago that I first ventured into Las Vegas to see for myself what everyone was raving about. Even with the 15 hotel-casinos along the Strip, and the half-dozen or so sawdust joints in the downtown "Glitter Gulch" district, it was still a primitive place. A hundred yards from the Strip, in any direction, was rattlesnake country.

What was less primitive was the arrangement the politicians had worked out with the mobsters, and, of course, the fleecing machine that was already working over ten million tourists a year. Both operations had been in business a dozen years before I came along. The result of that visit and many others that were to follow, was *The Green Felt Jungle*.

After New Jersey passed the Casino Control Act in June 1977, I often wondered how things would turn out in Atlantic City. There was much publicity about the state passing tough regulations designed to protect the gambling industry from the crime-ridden image associated with the Nevada experience.

Yet Nevada was virgin territory when it legalized gambling in 1931, occupied by old cowpokes, sourdoughs, sheepherders, and a few crafty politicians. Most of the gambling was in pool halls. It puttered along this way until the arrival of Bugsy Siegel in 1946 and the opening of his "fabulous" Flamingo hotel-casino that year.

Not so virginal was New Jersey. Legalizing gambling in this

Mafia-infested and most politically corrupt of states was tantamount to dropping the chicken coop into the heart of fox country.

My first visit to Atlantic City was in the early fall of 1983. By then it was already the country's most frequently visited resort. Nine hotel-casinos were doing land-office business, with gross annual revenues of $1.8 billion—two years later, with 11 hotel-casinos, total earnings were $2.2 billion, which was a half-billion greater than the total earnings of the *sixty-odd* licensed establishments in Las Vegas.

Having started out in a pristine desert, Las Vegas had taken a few decades to become garish and gaudy. In Atlantic City the transformation was instantaneous. A stroll on the Boardwalk is a surrealistic experience. It's like stepping into another time dimension, with glitzy casinos squeezed in between sleazy fast-food stalls and carnival-type clip joints.

After forty years of corrosive decay, this blighted slum of a city is now called South Bronx by the Sea by its bitter, trapped denizens. Only one block from the Boardwalk, and just about anywhere one chooses to look, there are burned-out and boarded-up shops and homes, rubbish-littered parking lots, and beyond them more vacant lots equally strewn with weeds and garbage. It is one vast, crumbling, burned-out ghetto populated by impoverished minorities and elderly survivors clinging to lost hopes.

A 1983 study by the Twentieth Century Fund concluded that nothing had been done to improve housing conditions for the elderly and the needy. "You don't see any spillover," it said. "The casinos are walled-off universes. . . . In terms of revitalizing the city, it is a disaster. . . . The visitor to the city who passes beyond the thin layer of tinsel trappings along the Boardwalk enters a wasteland."

Since 1978 violent crimes have doubled, tripled, and quadrupled. Pacific Avenue, only a block away from the Boardwalk, is crawling with hookers, pimps, pickpockets, drug pushers, car strippers, and thieves. Loansharks are having a field day and muggers attack people in broad daylight. Everybody is chasing fast bucks, which eventually wend their way into the casinos' coffers. When I asked a cabdriver what gambling had done for him, he angrily replied that it had turned his daughter into a hooker and his son into a hustler.

Real estate values and property tax assessments have skyrocketed, driving out most small businessmen who had dreamed of sharing in the gambling bonanza. By 1985 nearly 90 percent of the city's businesses had vanished, and its population had shrunk from 45,000 to 37,000. There is only one supermarket and no department stores. Until it burned down in 1983, the town's only movie theater showed X-rated films.

Slum landlords, unable to evict tenants, are burning down their buildings to collect the insurance and with the hope of selling the land to developers. Already the casinos own more than 25 percent of the city's developable land, and much of this land was acquired from the city through convoluted transactions that investigators will never untangle.

Most visitors never leave the Boardwalk. Junket bus conductors instruct their passengers not to leave the casinos. "It's dangerous," they say. "It's rip-off city, it's a jungle out there." Of course, they are right, but it is also dangerous in the hotels. Rooms are broken into, guests assaulted, purses and wallets snatched, cars in the subterranean garages rifled.

Just getting there can also be hazardous. Buses and cars traveling the Atlantic City Expressway are often ambushed by rock-and-bottle-throwing vandals who live in slum housing near the Expressway.

There is nothing new about the business of separating a sucker from his money. That is what gambling is about. Legal larceny. What is particularly unfortunate about it in Atlantic City is that the deluge of greenbacks is not coming from high rollers, or even from the middle-class family willing to lose a set amount at the tables for a few days of holiday fun, as is pretty much the case in Nevada. In Atlantic City it is coming from the poor and from lower-middle-class senior citizens who can ill afford to lose any money. Some are so old they need walkers and wheelchairs to get around.

The real difference is that to get to gambling in Nevada most visitors have to travel long distances. Atlantic City is much more accessible. They can come for a few hours, on junket buses that pick them up on street corners in Philadelphia, 60 miles away, New York and Newark, a 100 miles—60 million people live within 300 miles—and gamble, lose what little they have, and go home financially and mentally depressed, but usually with the thought of getting more money and returning to beat the house. In the meantime, they will eat less, or somehow make do with less, to make up for what they've lost and to save enough for the next trip.

The casinos derive over half of their revenues from slot machines, which are favored by the elderly. This is repeat business, from people who come strictly to gamble. The average visitor to Atlantic City returns 23 times a year—this means nearly every fortnight. In 1984, 12,240,214 visitors were hustled into town on 384,358 junket buses.

Gambling is a game of fantasy versus the harsh reality of the house's odds, but there is another side to this story, one that is hidden from view, one that involves greed and political corruption and organized crime and murder.

That is also part of the story that resulted in *The Boardwalk Jungle*.

PROLOGUE
High Noon on the Boardwalk

June 2, 1977—it's ten o'clock on a Thursday morning under a threatening sky, and hundreds of people are dancing on the Boardwalk. Thousands more clap and stamp their feet to the Dixieland rhythms of Jerry Vigue's band. Hissing above their heads, and dwarfing all underneath, is Great Adventure's wondrously monstrous red hot-air balloon, with gay orange and green teardrop shapes along its sides.

"Good luck, Atlantic City," someone in the gondola yells into a bullhorn. People laugh and wave happily in acknowledgment.

Everywhere, fluttering in the wind, are advertisements for gubernatorial candidates. It is five days before the primaries, but that's not why these people are celebrating.

Yesterday the Boardwalk was deserted, for most of the rides, arcades, stalls, and shops were padlocked long ago. There's nothing left here for anyone to enjoy. The Steel Pier has been closed for years. Thirty and forty years ago, all the big bands played its great ballroom, and people from hundreds of miles away came to dance to the syncopated swing music. Millions more came to this resort to bathe in its sparkling surf, lounge on its broad beach, stroll along its exciting Boardwalk and piers, or ride in wicker rolling chairs under the stars. Its grand hotels entertained millionaires and Hollywood royalty. At its prime, it was touted as America's favorite playground, the Queen of Resorts.

But nothing stays young and vibrant and exciting and idyllic forever. The resort began hitting the skids as early as the mid-1950s, with the gradual decline of the railroads and the growth of cheap jet travel to more exotic places. At first the erosion was slow, then almost pellmell.

By the early 1970s the city had reached its terminal stage of urban decay. The whole area had been transformed into a massive slum, with most businesses closed, and young people had moved out, leaving the rotting remains to the elderly and minorities who couldn't afford to escape.

Now a miracle is in the offing. And the people are rejoicing. Reporters from the *Atlantic City Press* move through the throngs, recording happy words about this glorious moment for posterity. "This is Christmas, New Year's, and Fourth of July all rolled into one giant celebration." "This is the happiest moment of our life." "This is jobs." "This is everything." "This is our renaissance." "When I see buildings going up and money coming in—boom-boom-boom— then I'll be happy." "This is a once-in-a-lifetime event." "I wouldn't have missed this for the world." "This city has everything: the ocean, the beach, and now the gambling." "Las Vegas can't offer you an ocean, all they've got is a desert." "There's so much excitement in the air." "Everything is fabulous, exciting, and all the other words you use to describe something like this." "You can just feel the vibrations coming from everybody." "Atlantic City needed this badly." "Now investors will start revitalizing the city." "There's going to be a ripple effect up and down the New Jersey coast— everyone will profit from it."

Clowns cavort. People throw confetti at one another. Some release brightly colored balloons and wave gaily as the balloons soar into a grayish sky. Many wear buttons that say: "You Can Bet Atlantic City Loves You."

Russell Corby has been at it since six this morning, attending to the hundreds of little details that will make the difference between the day's being a success or a fiasco. He nervously fingers through the pages on his clipboard as he hurries to the rear of the Convention Center's West Hall, at Georgia and Pacific Avenues. It is the staging area for the marching bands.

It's bedlam. The kids from the three high-school bands are tuning their instruments, and the majorettes are twirling their batons. Everybody looks tense and anxious. Corby motions for the band directors to join him and again consults his clipboard.

"Okay, listen, I'll go over this one more time," he says, reading from his notes. "The A.C. band will wait in the middle of the Boardwalk, at Arkansas, facing south. Toms River will wait along the Boardwalk rail, northside of Missouri, facing west. And Deptford at Columbia, along the Boardwalk rail, facing west.

"Now, here's the way it's set up for the motorcade. Governor Byrne's party will enter the Boardwalk at Arkansas. The A.C. band will lead off the motorcade with a selection. I'll leave that up to you. Play from Arkansas to Missouri. Toms River will join the motorcade at Missouri, get in between the media truck and the A.C. band. Deptford will fall in at Columbia."

Corby pauses and looks up from his notes. "Clear so far? Okay, the A.C. band will play from Mississippi to the center of the Convention Hall entrance. The others will mark time at the north side of Mississippi. At the conclusion of the A.C. band's selection, it will double-time to its position directly to the left of the podium and stay at rest. Toms River will play a selection from Mississippi to the center of Convention Hall, with Deptford marking time at Mississippi. When Toms River has finished its selection, it will double-time to its position directly to the right of the podium. Then it's Deptford's turn. Play your selection from Mississippi to the center of Convention Hall, at the conclusion of which you double-time to left of the podium."

Corby looks closely at the three men. "Any questions? Okay, at the end of the ceremonies, the bands will retreat to the West Hall assembly area." Corby slaps his clipboard and begins moving away. "By the way, if the weather turns on us, I've got a contingency plan, and we'll go over it then."

And he's gone, hurrying to his next problem. This is Corby's first experience as an advance man for a governor. He's 34 and a legislative aide to State Senator John Russo of Ocean City and on assignment to the governor for the duration of his reelection campaign. He's spent weeks working to make this day perfect. But who would think that a simple ceremony could get so complicated?

First there had been the sticky problem with Mayor Joseph Lazarow, who had insisted on introducing Governor Brendan Byrne at the ceremony, though the two men were at opposite ends of the political spectrum. Lazarow was a product of the Atlantic County Republican machine, and Byrne had come through the Newark Democratic machine, both powerful political apparatuses. A personal animosity had grown between them to the point where Byrne wasn't at all sure that Lazarow would portray him in the best possible light at a time when Byrne's political career was on the line. Nor did Byrne trust Joseph McGahn, the state senator from Atlantic County, a fellow Democrat who was facing a strong challenge from Assemblyman Steven Perskie, a close friend of the governor.

Byrne wanted Perskie to introduce him, and it was Corby's job to see that the governor's wishes were carried out. But Lazarow dug in his heels. He was the mayor and this was to be his city's big day. It was incumbent on him to introduce the governor, as he would any distinguished guest visiting his city. Meetings between the mayor and some of the governor's people ended in shouting matches with nothing accomplished. Meetings between Corby and Lazarow were equally fruitless. Fed up with spinning his wheels with "this horse's ass," Corby told the governor as much.

The day before the ceremony, Byrne got Lazarow on the telephone and issued an ultimatum. Unless Lazarow agreed to defer to Perskie, Byrne would sign the bill in his office in Trenton. Lazarow capitulated and Corby got on with his work.

Not the least of Corby's problems today are the other nine candidates challenging Byrne in the primary. Most of them are here, with their troops armed with balloons, placards, buttons, T-shirts, funny hats, and bags full of political literature. Everybody is hustling votes, at the governor's expense. This is supposed to be his day in the sun. Yet even the sun is refusing to cooperate.

Governor Brendan Byrne is still in Princeton, running a half hour late. In a household with seven children, ranging in age from 22 to 7, getting out on time in the morning is never easy. This morning is no exception. As he hurries toward the limousine waiting in the driveway, he turns for a look at Morven, the grand relic that is the governor's mansion.

Morven was built by Richard Stockton, one of the signers of the Declaration of Independence. It was 201 years ago that Stockton walked from that door, the way Byrne has done this morning, and went to sign that historic document.

Awaiting Byrne in the limousine are his secretary, Jerry English, and a close adviser, Jeff Lorenti. As he settles into the back of the limousine, ready to be driven to nearby Springdale Country Club, where a helicopter is waiting to take him on the 45-minute ride to

Bader Field in Atlantic City, Byrne can't suppress a smile. What would old Stockton think if he knew what Byrne was up to today?

Russ Corby is feeling the pressure as he hurries along the Boardwalk. No question about it. Byrne's renomination is anything but certain. He's seen by his challengers as extremely vulnerable. Byrne, who did not support a state income tax in his 1973 campaign, has pushed one through the legislature and is now suffering at the polls. His campaign strategists are trying to turn the tax to his advantage by portraying him as a man of principle, not afraid to follow his convictions. His slogan is: "The courage to do what's right."

It appears that the governor's people want to milk the ceremony in Atlantic City for all the media coverage milkable. And much of what will happen here rests on Corby's shoulders. This being Corby's first venture into statewide politics, it is only natural that he's uneasy about his heavy responsibilities.

Still, Governor Brendan Thomas Byrne has a lot going for him. On paper, he looks impressive. In March 1943, at the age of 19, Byrne quit Seton Hall to enlist in the Army Air Corps. Commissioned a lieutenant, he served as squadron navigator with the "Wing and a Prayer" Squadron in the European Theater, where he was awarded the Distinguished Flying Cross and four Air Medals. Back in civilian life after the war, he graduated from Princeton, where he majored in public and international affairs. From there it was a degree from Harvard Law School, followed by a career of public service: Executive Secretary to Governor Robert B. Meyner, Deputy Attorney General in charge of the Essex County's Prosecutor's office in Newark, followed by a nine-year stint as Essex County Prosecutor. Then two years as President of the state's Board of Public Utility Commissioners, and finally judge of the Superior Court, leaving the bench in the spring of 1973 to campaign for Governor and being elected by the biggest plurality in state history, thereby calling attention to himself as a possible Democratic vice-presidential nominee.

Corby admires Byrne's credentials. But he knows there's more to a successful politician than what looks good on paper. Tall, lean, with a patrician cast to his features, accentuated by sandy hair graying in flattering streaks at the temples, Byrne looks more like a character actor playing the role of a governor than the backslapping, baby-kissing vote-getter the public has always trusted on sight.

· Politically, by temperament and practice, Byrne is considered a cold fish. This has to be an inordinate handicap in a state where politics has always been the province of wheeler-dealers. Byrne was so stiff and shy in his early public appearances that, in his own judgment, the result was "painful to watch." He not only looks like Charlton Heston but talks with the same extreme sobriety and sincerity—something like Heston's Moses reading the Ten Commandments.

Time and hard work have softened some of the stiffer edges. In a strange way, he seems to love the political fray. Perhaps not as passionately as he loves his wife, children, tennis, and the opera, but enough to put up with the masochistic rigors of political life that are so foreign to his nature. Yet his record, so far, has been one toward more quiet competence than noisy achievements. As the chief law enforcement official in a county where corruption reigned supreme for decades, Prosecutor Byrne never laid a glove on his important machine supporters. It took the federal government, under an edict from newly elected President Nixon, to come in and clean up its Democratic house.

Corby stops dead in his tracks. Up there on the Boardwalk is the "Bateman train." Raymond Bateman, a Republican state senator who will later challenge Byrne in the general election, has rigged up a flatbed float to look like a locomotive which he's been parading throughout the state.

"The nerve of the guy," Corby mumbles angrily as he hurries to a policeman, grabs his walkie-talkie, and talks to Inspector Joseph Pasquale. "Joe, you've got to get that monstrosity off the Boardwalk." When Pasquale seems indecisive, Corby boldly assumes Byrne's tactic: "Joe, you get rid of that thing in the next two minutes or I'm calling the governor and telling him you guys are out to embarrass him. He'll stay in Trenton and you'll have to tell this crowd why the star stayed home."

The Bateman train is promptly ejected and Corby sighs in relief. "My God," he tells himself, shaking his head, "a one-mile motorcade—how the hell do they do it in Pasadena?"

The bulk of the crowd has gathered in front of the platform that will serve as the podium. It's in an area of the Boardwalk, facing Convention Hall, called Kennedy Plaza. The carnival atmosphere is contagious.

Steven Perskie is at Bader Field when the governor's helicopter lands. The two men shake hands and take their seats in the back of an unmarked car that will carry them to the staging area. Seated in the middle is Jerry English, who looks hard at Perskie as she says, "After all we've been through, that introduction of yours better be good." Byrne smiles and Perskie settles back. He is young, but he moves and talks with the mature confidence of a man who has implicit faith in the quality of his work.

"Ladies and gentlemen," a voice booms over the public address system, "Governor Byrne has just left Bader Field and he'll be right here." Everybody cheers. Nobody seems to notice it's 11:45 and the governor is a half hour late. The occasion has all the makings of a political rally. Overhead, a miniature blimp sails by with Ray Bateman's name emblazoned on its sides—try to eject that if you can. Aerial banners with the names of other candidates streak across the sky. Girls, wearing Robert Roe's Angels shirts, giggle in packs.

People are bumping, pushing, prodding, and congratulating one another. "I'm thinking this town hasn't changed a bit," a man, not too pleased with the hoopla, grumbles.

Photographers click away tirelessly, capturing one another's small moment of glory, a priceless tableau for the album, to be savored at a more leisurely moment, when all becomes history.

Frank "Hap" Farley is already seated on the podium. After two massive heart attacks he's a mere shadow of his old self, a gaunt old man, a bag of brittle bones in a baby-blue leisure suit. Once he was the big boss, the one who made the Atlantic County Republican machine the most awesome in the nation. No one, anywhere, ever exercised more raw political clout than this man. He was the state's most feared politician.

Gone now are the dark three-piece suits of his power days. Gone are the six-foot-three inches and 250 pounds of Irish temperament that made him such a formidable figure on the senate floor and on hundreds of podiums like this one. Gone is the good-guy smile that perpetually split his round face like a cartooned moon.

Now, ignored by the crowd, he sits alone, dead eyes scanning faces, jaws shifting restlessly, lips moving silently—is he trying to say something, or is he rehearsing his lines for the moment when he again will address these people (for thirty years *his* people) perhaps for a last time?—his right hand resting tremulously on a cane.

Also unnoticed on the podium is I. G. "Jack" Davis, president of Resorts International, the company most responsible for what is about to take place here today. Davis has spent a fortune on lawyers and politically connected people to realize his goal, and now the moment is at hand. Still there's a dark look on his tanned face as he surveys the crowd and awaits his moment to speak his piece. Gain his brief moment in the spotlight.

It's that voice again on the public address system: "Ladies and gentlemen, Governor Byrne has arrived at the staging area and the motorcade will begin momentarily."

"I'll bet Steven Perskie will be in the governor's car," a young woman confides to her friend.

"He's so cute," the friend answers breathlessly.

Camden Mayor Angelo J. Errichetti has buttonholed a reporter and he's not letting go. Errichetti is another New Jersey politician who holds more than one elective office. A state senator from Camden County, Errichetti is proud of the role he played in the passage of the Casino Control Act, the legislation that everyone is celebrating here today. He counts himself among its founders:

"We're going to have an overnight rebuilding of Atlantic City, an overnight rebirth of Atlantic City, and we won't be doing it by begging for state or federal handouts. It's going to be accomplished through private enterprise and a rush of millions of private dollars. Given the tools of casino gaming, Atlantic City certainly has the capability of recapturing its onetime position as the world's play-ground."

His breathless barrage is followed immediately by another. "To tell you the truth, I was first opposed to it, but I'm all for it now, as long as they confine it to Atlantic City. I've mourned the decline of this great resort. I feel a sense of urgency to save it. Atlantic City needs a rebirth, a transfusion. There's no question in my mind that Atlantic City desperately needs gambling. And in the long run, not only will Atlantic City be revitalized, but the state's economy will benefit appreciably. In fact, you know, I've said as much to the governor. I told him we didn't want gambling in Camden. That's why I went on TV and blasted the first referendum in 1974 that proposed statewide gambling. And you know, I've got a pretty big mouth. Man, I destroyed it. Fuck this idea of having gambling in all our major cities. We need it right here in Atlantic City. All the talk about saving this place is a crock of shit. We don't need speeches, we need action. We've got to get these movers and shakers off their ass. What I'd like to do is escort Governor Byrne, Steve Perskie, and Joe McGahn around this fucking town, show them what's really happening here. Give them a real close look at how this place has run down, until it's one big fucking slum. It's going to take millions to rebuild it and I'm going to do everything in my power to see they get the money."

Errichetti would risk everything to get his own hands on some of the millions being poured into the resort. And he would lose. The cost: his career and freedom.

It's one o'clock, nearly 45 minutes past Governor Byrne's scheduled arrival, and the crowd is getting restless. Some older people complain that reporters, photographers, and cops are blocking their view.

Then, gradually, the deep-throated growls of police motorcycles penetrate up the Boardwalk, and there is a massive quake of excitement as the huge crowd surges forward. Jerry Vigue's band breaks into "Happy Days Are Here Again." Suddenly, even the sun decides to cooperate and shoots slivers of sunlight through a thick, blackish cloud cover.

As though they have rehearsed it, people start yelling: "The governor's here, the governor's here." The thousands seated on chairs facing the podium stand up and those in the back of the Pavilion yell, "Down in front, down in front."

The Atlantic City High School Band is blasting its way into their presence and more cheers go up. It's followed by the Indians of Toms River South High School, who perform the routine given to them by Corby, then inexplicably reverse themselves and head back uptown on the Boardwalk. Nobody seems to mind, except Russ Corby.

The green convertible carrying the governor is visible now. He is sitting on the trunk, with his feet resting on the back seat. On his right is Steven Perskie and on his left Mayor Lazarow. Seated in the front and barely visible are Senator Joseph McGahn and Assemblyman Howard Kupperman. All eyes are on Governor Byrne, the man who is about to deliver them from poverty with a bold stroke of his pen.

The dignitaries take their places on the podium. Jerry Vigue's band keeps playing "Happy Days" until it's time for the invocation by the pastor of the First Union Baptist Church. His prayer is that the rebirth of the city will lead to a town "where brother walked with brother, where human compassion negated human greed."

The atmosphere is more solemn when it's Mayor Lazarow's turn. Thirty-five years ago, as a high-school student, Joe Lazarow won the

American Legion's oratorial contest in South Jersey. He spoke on "Americanism" and how to keep its traditions of freedom alive.

On this day, Lazarow is full of promises. "We will provide for the people living in Atlantic City because they are the ones who worked for gambling and we will not let them suffer because they got it," he says in his strong resonant voice. "This is the fulfillment of a dream, the beginning of a great future, but with this great future, we know there is a grave responsibility. We know there are many battles ahead. We need the jobs. We need the construction, but we know we need the housing for our citizens."

This is welcome news. Everyone here knows that the poor are being ruthlessly evicted by landlords who are receiving kings' ransoms for their land from prospective casino operators.

Senator McGahn is more cautious. Though the legislation was rushed through both the Assembly and Senate, he says it will take time for the city's casino population to get its feet wet. "I don't want people to over anticipate the rapidity of the city's rebirth." It's his guess that the first casino will open early in 1978. "I would hope that any potential investors who might have been holding back until the bill was signed would come on in. We're ready for them."

Now it's old Hap Farley's turn. With the aid of his cane and several men, he is led from his chair to the lectern. Like a shot, everybody is up, clapping, whistling, yelling, and stamping their feet.

Supporting himself with his cane and holding on to the lectern, Farley's voice is frail as he tells the audience: "This is a day of rejoicing, the beginning of a new era, an era that challenges the businessmen, the Chamber of Commerce, the people who live and work here. It's not difficult to get people to come here. But I have to warn you that it is difficult to get people to return here, especially if you don't treat them the way they should be treated. It's incumbent upon all of us to be courteous, to be the hosts that we would expect."

He pauses, thanks Byrne, and takes a deep trembling breath. "And I thank God for being good enough to me to let me witness this occasion." Three months later Frank "Hap" Farley is dead.

Introduced by Lazarow, Steve Perskie gives Governor Byrne a rousing welcome. Again the crowd is on its feet. This is the moment everyone's been waiting for all day. The sun is again peeking through angry clouds. Tall and lean, Byrne stands before them, and, in patrician tones, speaks of renaissance, of restoring the aging dowager to its preeminent position.

"I use the term Queen of Resorts, not King of Resorts, because queen imparts a sense of dignity and gentleness, and Atlantic City meets that description." His voice softens as he tells them of his hopes for Atlantic City. "If in the legislation and in its implementation we make sure Atlantic City will be a home for all its citizens, we will be judged a success. It is not enough to create 16,000 rooms for guests if we don't provide decent housing for our citizens. Our efforts will not be deemed a success unless we carry out the constitutional mandate that the proceeds be used for senior citizens and the disabled. I've committed myself, over the next several months, to regional conferences with senior citizens and the disabled as to how the money should be spent in their behalf. Finally, the legislation will be viewed as a success if the casinos in Atlantic City are operated honestly, decently, and cleanly."

This is met with another round of thunderous applause. Byrne takes this opportunity to study the lines that he inked in after consultation with Jeff Lorenti. He wants a strong finish, something that will strengthen his image as a man of courage and principle.

Clearing his throat, he forges ahead: "I have made this pledge before to all law enforcement agencies and I will repeat it again. We will keep the limelight of public opinion focused upon organized crime." Pausing again to gaze gravely at the crowd, he raises his right hand and shakes it, his voice hardening as he says, "I've said it before and I will repeat it again to organized crime: Keep your filthy hands off Atlantic City! Keep the hell out of our state."

PART I
THE WAY IT WAS

1

In the Good Old Summertime

The Lenni-Lenape Indians called it Absegami, meaning Little Sea Water. It wasn't much more than three small sandbars, which eventually filled in and became one, now known as Absecon Island. Ten miles long and from a hundred yards to a mile wide, it is separated from the mainland by seven miles of water and wetlands.

Its early history might as well have been written in that wet sand, for little is known of the first white inhabitants. Even before the American Revolution, New England whalers, who followed the great whales to Delaware Bay, used its wide beach to carve up their catches, leaving the great carcasses to bleach in the sun.

By the early 19th century, young people from the mainland were coming to the island for picnics and beach parties. The Quaker farmers who worked the land paid little attention to them, but in time more enterprising men would recognize the area's potential as a "bathing village."

The Camden and Atlantic Railroad Company was formed, and the chief engineer, whose job it was to map the line from Camden to the island, lettered in the name "Atlantic City" on his layout, and it stuck. He also named all the streets running north and south, parallel to the beachfront, after the world's seas: Pacific, Atlantic, Arctic, Baltic, and Mediterranean, and the ones running east and west after American states.

On July 1, 1854, the first railroad train steamed into Atlantic City with 600 excited visitors from Camden. It took the train 2½ hours to cover the 50 miles—the passengers had to be rowed across Absecon Bay to a second train—which was still better than a whole day in an open stagecoach. In time the Beach Thoroughfare Bridge, followed by the Delaware River Bridge, would be built, and they would link the resort by direct rail to Philadelphia, which meant it was opened to the rest of the world.

Food stands and bathhouses began appearing on the landward side, followed by small hotels. Then a hotel owner named Alexander Boardman suggested to other hotelmen that a walkway of boards be constructed on the beach to prevent visitors from tracking sand into their hotels—it was first built in sections so it could be stored away for the winter. And from this practical suggestion, Atlantic City was on its way to gaining its exalted position as the Queen of American Resorts, a title it would jealously struggle to hold on to for nearly a century.

Grand hotels sprang up, and the sections of planks became a permanent boardwalk, which in time would become its most famous attraction. By 1880, as described in a *Harper's Weekly* article, Atlantic City and its Boardwalk was already a thriving resort:

> Its streets and avenues are broad, straight, planted with great numbers of well-grown shade trees, and bordered with the summer homes of city men. Many of the cottages are architectural gems, and all are attractive and pretty.
>
> Many of the hotels, of which there are a dozen first-class, and a hundred more of various degrees of excellence, front on the ocean, though set well back from the beach. In front of them, and offering an unobstructed view of the beach, the bathers, and the limitless expanse of ocean stretching away to its far horizon, is the Boardwalk and the great pier reaching far out over the waters. This is the promenade, the center of life and interest; everybody strolls over the two miles of Boardwalk in search of exercise or amusement, and everybody visits the pier for a few breaths of the very purest and freshest ocean air.

Two Boardwalk institutions were created in quick succession. A candymaker came up with ''saltwater'' taffy when a rising tide accidentally dampened his batch of taffy, and a hardware dealer started renting man-powered wicker rolling chairs. The Boardwalk itself grew into a 40-foot-wide avenue, carried on high concrete pillars and steel beams, and stretched out along the shore for seven miles, weaving its way through Atlantic City and the adjoining island towns of Ventnor, Margate, and Longport. Many great piers would soon push out into the sea.

The Boardwalk seemed to have a flair for excitement, ranging from the vulgar to the elegant, from the mundane to the bizarre. There were carnival rides and games on the Boardwalk and piers, dancing in open-air pavilions and in great ballrooms over the water, shooting galleries, penny arcades, snake charmers, gypsy palm readers, phrenologists, and learned pigs. Sideshows with barkers hawking freaks with two heads, iron jaws, snakeskins, Siamese twins, and premature babies in glass display cases.

There were jugglers, flagpole sitters, boxing midgets, boxing cats, Primo Carnera boxing a kangaroo, the Wild Man of Borneo (he spent his days caged in a pit under the Boardwalk, gnawing on raw bones), daredevils, and horses high-diving into tubs of water. There were balloonists, acrobats, high-wire walkers, and lots of dazzling fireworks.

There was Lucy, the six-story white elephant. Sculpted of wood and tin, it was created as an advertising gimmick to sell real estate. It later became a tavern and finally a summer cottage. Built in 1881, it has survived a century of fires and storms. It is now a National Historic Landmark.

There were beer gardens, fine restaurants, greasy spoons, and makeshift little stands offering everything from hot dogs and oysters to sea-foam fudge and free Heinz pickles. Scattered everywhere were clipjoints of every type, selling every kind of junk imaginable. As one vacationer observed, "So long as the stroller was not looking at the ocean, he was looking at something for sale." Everything from racy postcards to phony antiques. Ed McMahon got his show-biz start as a Boardwalk pitchman for kitchen gadgets.

The Boardwalk had it all. It offered everything from honky-tonk dive to penthouse suite. It was show-biz American style, complete with the variety that has always been part of our popular entertainment.

Atlantic City knew all there was to know about ballyhoo long before Madison Avenue copywriters could dream it up. It knew that it was the sizzle that you sold, not the steak. As far as the *New York Times* was concerned, it was the "apotheosis of publicity. It is the crescendo of horn-tooting."

Thousands, from all walks of life, dressed in their finest, crowded the boards, drinking in the sights and sounds. The wealthy built summer homes in Ventnor, Margate, and Longport, and there was nothing unusual about seeing women "walking the boards" wrapped in their minks. The Boardwalk became Atlantic City. It was where the action was.

As one city commissioner boasted, "To say the Boardwalk is Atlantic City's greatest asset is obvious and trite. As far as the lure and prosperity of Atlantic City is concerned it might as well lose the sea as its Boardwalk."

The building boom skyrocketed the cost of land accessible to the Boardwalk. Developers were reaping millions. It was such a lucrative game that it inspired Charles B. Darrow's Monopoly game. As in Monopoly, when a developer built on the Boardwalk, he paid. Plenty.

But nothing could deter the Boardwalk's progress. By the turn of the century, Atlantic City had about 500 hotels and boardinghouses lining the beach and was entertaining 700,000 visitors a season. Before long the Boardwalk boasted some of the world's finest hotels. Among the earliest ones which survived until the casino era were the Dennis, Seaside, Shelburne, Traymore, Marlborough-Blenheim, Breakers, Brighton, Mayflower, Ritz Carlton, St. Charles, President, Ambassador, Chalfonte-Haddon Hall, which was the largest in the world, and Claridge, the world's tallest in 1930 and the last of the big hotels to be built on the Boardwalk for nearly fifty years.

In those gentler days the hotels gave the Boardwalk class. The rich came in their own private railroad cars, rolling palaces of red plush and gilt, staffed by servants in livery. They were picked up at the railroad station by coachmen in scarlet uniforms and transported in brightly decorated coaches pulled by four horses. Rooftop pavilions provided string orchestras for decorous dancing in the afternoon. In the evening, a brass section was added for more energetic dancing— the Cakewalk would soon be followed by the Charleston.

The Chalfonte-Haddon Hall held musicals with leading singers from the Metropolitan and Chicago operas. The Shelburne was favored by such turn-of-the-century celebrities as Diamond Jim Brady, Lillian Russell, Victor Herbert, Ethel Barrymore, Ed Wynn, John Drew, Al Jolson, Eddie Cantor, and John Philip Sousa, whose brass band was one of the resort's favorite. George M. Cohan wrote many of his songs here, including "Over There."

The Ritz Carlton, a 1921 entry became the favorite of show-biz people, politicians, and gangsters. It was favored by Al Capone, New York City Mayor Jimmy Walker, and Enoch L. "Nucky" Johnson, who pretty much ran things around Atlantic County and other parts of New Jersey. It was also a favorite of Sophie Tucker and opera star Lawrence Tibbett, who once sang "Road to Mandalay" from his beachfront suite window to the delight of his Boardwalk audience.

Countless songs were written about Atlantic City, but the one most admired was "By the Sea," written by Harry Carroll in 1912. For most of the city's denizens, the first six bars said it all:

> By the sea, by the sea
> By the beautiful sea,
> You and me, you and me
> Oh how happy we'll be.

The Boardwalk developed a reputation as a sexy place. It became a swinging singles haven. A big hit by the turn of the century was "Moonlight on the Boardwalk." For its day, it had some rather provocative lines: "Honey, you make me do what you know I oughtn't to. . . ."

There was vaudeville and minstrel and opera, but more importantly there was theater, which really came into its own in the Roaring Twenties. The year 1920 saw 168 shows opening at the three main Boardwalk theaters: the Apollo, Globe, and Woods.

The year started out with Victor Herbert's "My Golden Girl," followed by George White's premiere of his "Scandals of 1920" and Flo Ziegfeld's "Follies." John Drew appeared in "The Catbird," Marie Dressler in "Tillie's Nightmare," Eva Le Gallienne in "Not So Long Ago," Chauncey Olcott in "Macushla," Helen Hayes in "Bab," Marilyn Miller in "Sally," and so it went. Any performer of any stature—singer, actor, dancer, comedian—made his appearance on the Boardwalk. Besides numerous premieres, every big show headed for Broadway had a tryout on the Boardwalk. It became a laboratory for producers, including Earl Carroll, Oliver Morosco, and David Belasco.

Important extensions of the Boardwalk were its piers. Many were built through the years. Some were washed out to sea in storms, others destroyed by fire, but Atlantic City has always had more piers than any other resort.

The ones that survived, in one form or another, to this day are the Iron Pier (1886), Steel Pier (1898), Steeplechase Pier (1899), Million Dollar Pier (1906), which became Central Pier in 1922, and Garden Pier (1913). Besides providing amusement rides of every description, the piers had their share of ticky-tacky concession shops and stalls. And they had the largest ballrooms. Every big band of the Twenties and Thirties played the Steel Pier. Harry Houdini often appeared and disappeared on the Million Dollar Pier. In 1912 Teddy Roosevelt gave a speech here and the crowd was so thick that one of his secret service men ran over and killed a potential voter.

However popular in the summer, no resort can survive the long winter months without a convention center. So when the city fathers decided to build one, they went all out for the biggest money could buy and put it at about midpoint in the Boardwalk, where it occupies two city blocks—seven acres. The main hall is 488 feet long, 288 feet wide, 137 feet high—there are no pillars, making it the largest unobstructed room in the world. It seats 41,000 and houses the world's largest pipe organ. Every fall football games were played in the big hall, and in recent years, a helicopter has flown around inside. Its formal opening in 1929 coincided with the city's Diamond Jubilee. The Miss America Pageant, created in 1921 to stretch the season beyond Labor Day, has been held in the main auditorium since its opening.

Great fortunes were made from the pennies, nickels, and dimes forked over by vacationers. Even greater fortunes were made by the hotels. Yet all of this merchandising was as nothing compared to what was really going on beyond the pale.

Were there lucrative vices hidden in the woodwork? And if so, who was running that show? Isn't there always somebody a little more devious, a little more unscrupulous, a little more ambitious, who somehow becomes a little more equal than the others? There was such a man and he owned a hotel. It wasn't the biggest hotel, or the best, but Louis Kuehnle had other irons in the fire.

2

Here Comes the Boss

What distinguishes boss rule in Atlantic City from most other places in the first seven decades of the 20th century is that its political machine was Republican. And no Big Bill Thompson, Huey Long, or Boss Crump was more corrupt or exercised more political control than the three bosses who successively ruled this tiny island during that period.

To be successful, the boss of any political machine not only has to be above the law, but able to hold his supporters up there inviolate with him. He must be able to guarantee police protection to those who wish to provide gambling, prostitution, drugs, and booze 24 hours a day, seven days a week. As well as dish out liquor licenses and variances to the right people. And he must learn to close his eyes to all kinds of infractions.

To do all this, he must control elections, and for that he must be able to deliver the votes. That was something that Louis Kuehnle understood as well as any man. Atlantic City, being a town with 20,000 hotel rooms, had a population with a large percentage of blacks, who performed the menial hotel services.

Until Franklin D. Roosevelt came along, most blacks, in gratitude to Lincoln, voted Republican. That was something else Kuehnle understood. Though he started out as a Democrat, it didn't take him long to switch parties once he learned that Atlantic County was overwhelmingly Republican. His election slogan was a "bigger and better Atlantic City," and in carrying out this pledge, he found a way—or rather a variety of ways—to pocket one of every three tax dollars spent by the city and county.

Corporations under his control expanded the Boardwalk, built a sewage system, a street railway service, all at a handsome profit for Kuehnle and his friends. At his direction, the city council gave his corporations liberal franchises, and he was later able to sell each of these companies at immense profits.

Atlantic City was a wide-open town. By 1890 gambling joints could be found on every block, from nickel-limit games on Mississippi Avenue to high-stake games on Delaware Avenue that attracted businessmen, politicians, and vice operators. Embarked on a moral crusade, the *Philadelphia Bulletin* listed the addresses of 24 brothels, including May Woodston's "pestilential hole" and one called the Sea Breeze, operated by Minnie Wiegle, "the high kicker in Fox's Theatre fifteen years ago."

On Arctic Avenue there was an interracial brothel operated by a black madam and her white husband. The *Daily Union* said that a W. H. Furney was allowed to conduct his "low negro resort" at Baltic and North Carolina because he could turn out the black vote on election day.

Election days were quite a production. Kuehnle would personally take a group of twenty or thirty blacks and march them from one polling place to another and have them vote repeatedly. His poll workers would place carbon paper between the actual and the sample ballot.

Not only was Kuehnle electing his own people to local and state legislative offices, but the Republican governors were grateful for his support, and showed their appreciation by not messing around in his bailiwick. If people on vacation wanted to gamble, drink, and fuck, that was their business. It was all nicely contained on that little island. Besides, the majority of tourists were from out of state, Philadelphians mostly.

Not long before his fall, the *New York Sun* summarized Kuehnle's reign: "If you were to take all the power ever exercised by Boss Tweed, the Philadelphia Gang, the Pittsburgh Ring, Boss Ruef of San Francisco, and Tammany Hall, and concentrate it in one man you would still fall a little short of Kuehnle's clutch on Atlantic City."

The election of Woodrow Wilson, a Democrat, to the governorship in 1910 was Kuehnle's undoing. In looking over the returns, Wilson was not amused to discover that his opponent had received more votes in Atlantic County than there were registered voters. He appointed a special commission, made up of Democratic assemblymen, to look into the matter. When the commission learned that Democratic election officials had been abducted and drugged, a grand jury was empaneled. In March 1911, 18 voters were indicted for false registration.

Governor Wilson was not satisfied. In those days grand jurors were selected by the sheriff, and in Atlantic County the sheriff was Enoch "Nucky" Johnson, the acknowledged protégé of Boss Kuehnle. To add to the governor's dissatisfaction, it was revealed that Nucky had erased proof that one of the grand jurors had voted twice in the last election. What's more, the twice-voting juror had been paying Nucky $500 a week to be allowed to operate crap games at a hotel he was managing.

The Burns Detective Agency was put to work and the result was the indictment of Kuehnle, Johnson, and the city clerk for opening ballot boxes, removing registry books, and tampering with records. Five freeholders were indicted for extorting money on road contracts, and five members of the city council were indicted after being entrapped by the Burns agency in a scheme to approve the building of a *concrete* boardwalk—which goes to show that some politicians will approve anything if the price is right.

One hundred and twenty-nine others were indicted after the new grand jury heard testimony that 3,800 of the 12,000 names on the voting lists were phony. In pleading mitigating circumstances, one defendant set the tone of what politics was like in Atlantic County. He said election corruption had been so universally accepted for such a long time that he hadn't thought he was doing anything wrong "by getting into it."

Kuehnle and Johnson were acquitted of election tampering, but Kuehnle was then indicted for conflict of interest. He had awarded a city contract to a company in which he was a leading stockholder.

Even before Kuehnle was carted off to prison, Nucky Johnson had taken over the reins, and would hold on to them for thirty years before he too would be carted off to prison. The political machine that Wilson had hoped to break was not even bent.

3

Knuckling Under Nucky

When it comes to consummate political scoundrels, Atlantic City has always carried its heart on its sleeve. In other words, it has the political skin of a rhinoceros.

The whole town turned out with a brass band to welcome Kuehnle home from jail. But though the people still loved him, politics waits for no man. Mafia bosses can run things from behind prison walls, but politicians need votes and two years away from the polling places is a lifetime. By the time he got back and tried to regroup, the Republican organization was already solidly in Enoch "Nucky" Johnson's grip. In later years Nucky permitted his old boss to become a city commissioner, a position he held until his death in 1934.

In his history of Atlantic City, *So Young, So Gay!* William McMahon says that Johnson was "not only Atlantic County Treasurer and Republican party political boss but he was the resort's official and unofficial host through the '20s and '30s." McMahon goes on to say that Johnson was "the host to some of the gayest and most elaborate parties ever held in the resort," and that he knew "virtually every celebrity of that era."

In his nostalgic portrait, McMahon says that Nucky's one fault was that his heart was too great. "Those who can trace their success to an early push from Nucky are numerous. No history of the Boardwalk would be complete without mention of the colorful personality who was symbolic of the era in which he lived—happy, restless and carefree. . . . Nucky Johnson was a huge man with a gravel voice who ruled the South Jersey political scene without challenge from 1911 to 1941. He had an amazing memory for names and faces. He was a Robin Hood in many ways. No one ever went hungry or cold in his domain if he knew about it.''

A native of Atlantic County, Nucky began his political career with a dab of nepotism. In 1904 he was appointed undersheriff by his father, who was the sheriff, and would soon succeed his father to the post. In those days, sheriff was an important political position. His control over grand juries not only made him wealthy in protection money, if he were so inclined, but it gave him enormous power over local law enforcement. The vice operators never went hungry or cold while Johnson was in charge.

As a result of Wilson's purge, a five-member commission was created to replace the cumbersome 17-member city council that ran the city's operating departments. With the new formula, one of the elected commissioners was picked by his colleagues to act as mayor— and thereby be in charge of the police department, propose ordinances, and make board appointments. The proponents of commission government believed it would end corruption and increase efficiency. It did neither.

Nucky's machine was so powerful that he could name the Democrats as well as Republicans who ran for office. His first selection for mayor was William Riddle, a Democrat. Riddle was so anxious to please Nucky that he proposed Sunday booze and zoned brothels: ''Return Atlantic City to the halcyon period of wet Sundays, and real estate will boom, prosperity will abound, and the resort will expand to magnificent proportion.''

It wasn't long before Nucky would begin spreading his wings by taking advantage of his power base in South Jersey.

In 1916 he picked Atlantic County Senator Walter Edge to run for governor—Wilson was now President—and received the backing of Frank ''I am the Law'' Hague of Hudson County, the state's foremost Democratic boss. Hague's clout added to Nucky's campaign chest (filled with protection money from the vice operators) made for an unbeatable combination. Theirs was a political marriage that would last a lifetime.

To demonstrate his gratitude, Governor Edge appointed Nucky Clerk of the New Jersey Supreme Court.

Then came Prohibition and the Roaring Twenties and Atlantic City was there to welcome both with open arms. Overnight it was Sin

City, with speakeasies and whorehouses crowding every block, and with every form of gambling invented by man, from punchboards and slot machines in grocery stores to elaborate casinos with crap tables, roulette wheels, and baccarat, to low- and high-stake poker games, numbers banks, and horse parlors where a bettor could place wagers on tracks anywhere in the country. The rackets were said to gross $10 million a year, a substantial sum in those days. There was never any secret about Atlantic City's back rooms. They were there for everyone to enjoy.

Through sheer blind fate, a little nepotism, and plenty of grits, Nucky had inherited this best of all possible worlds. There he was, a widower with a red carnation in his lapel and a beautiful showgirl on each arm, gay and carefree as he lavished his generosity on the era's great celebrities. And they in turn showered him with gifts. In 1929, at the height of his career, he received 5000 Christmas cards and 7500 telegrams. Squads of mail carriers and Western Union boys staggered to his suite at the Ritz Carlton with bales of messages from well-wishers. He became affectionately known as the "Beau Brummell of the Ritz Carlton." He rode around in a chauffeur-driven, powder-blue Pierce Arrow limousine and wore a $1200 raccoon coat.

Forty years later, an obituary writer for the *Atlantic City Press* would note that Nucky had ruled "in the manner of le grand seigneur. . . . In another age, he would have been the mutton-munching baron on the hill, or the Roman pro-consul who ruled from his bath."

Johnson helped Warren Harding get into the White House. For his troubles he was invited to sleep in Lincoln's bed and given two interstate highways—Routes 30 and 40—for Atlantic City. There was nothing he wouldn't do for his constituents. No wonder they loved him so.

By 1925 Atlantic City was bursting at the seams. It had 1000 hotels and rooming houses that could accommodate 400,000 visitors, 99 daily trains in the summer and 65 in the winter, and three airports. It had the world's longest Boardwalk, stretching seven miles, with five piers, and fabulous beach. Some 400 sailing and power boats were moored in its marina. The city had 21 theaters, three country clubs, four newspapers, the Miss America Pageant, and an Easter Parade as famous as Fifth Avenue's.

Everything was running smoothly. Between 1924 and 1928 the voter registration jumped 98 percent, with the result that 70 percent of the entire population, kids and all, were eligible to vote. When he was caught again with his hand in the voter registration till, Nucky trimmed 2379 names from the voting list, including a parrot named "Johnny Talk."

It was at the height of Johnson's reign that the country's top racket bosses decided to use Atlantic City as the site for an underworld conference. Arranged by Al Capone and Lucky Luciano, the conference was an attempt to restructure the rackets on a nationwide basis.

"Seated in a rolling chair at Kentucky Avenue and the Boardwalk yesterday afternoon, puffing on a big black cigar and surrounded by half a dozen henchmen, 'Al' took in the sights of the famous strand and breathed deeply and freely of the ozone with apparently not a care in the world," the local press reported.

None of the visiting mobsters seemed to have a care in the world. They were spotted cavorting on the beach in the daytime and in the local nightclubs at night. The way they acted it was as though Atlantic City had been declared a DMZ for the week of the conference. That was how powerful Johnson was in his bailiwick.

Included among the conferees were the bosses of New York City's five Mafia families. Representing Atlantic City was Herman "Stumpy" Orman, who one day would become known as the "King of Rackets" in Atlantic City, beholden, of course, to the political powers that be.

New Jersey was represented by Abner "Longie" Zwillman, who was known as the Al Capone of New Jersey. Tall, ruggedly handsome, and tough, Zwillman was brought up in a slum tenement in Newark. He started out as a pushcart peddler but soon discovered that numbers running was more lucrative. But he would find his real niche in bootlegging.

According to testimony before the Kefauver Crime Committee, Zwillman's group was responsible for nearly 40 percent of all the illegal alcohol funneled into the United States between 1926 and 1933. He had a fleet of 30 ships running booze from the French islands of St. Pierre and Miquelon off the coast of Canada, and most of it was being unloaded on the wide beaches of Absecon Island.

The ships would heave to a few miles out at sea where small fast speedboats raced out to rendezvous with them, returning loaded to the gunwales. To add spice to the nightly forays, the Coast Guard would occasionally give chase but not enough to deter a conscientious smuggler. In fact, when four Coast Guardsmen became too excited and fired on rumrunners who refused to obey their command to stop, they were arrested and charged with "intent to kill." The law was none other than Atlantic County Sheriff Al Johnson, Nucky's brother.

From scattered points along the beach, as many as fifty trucks would pick the liquor up and haul it to distribution centers. Longie used cops to escort his cargos, but he didn't hesitate to apply a bit of muscle himself against rival bootlegging mobs. In a period of two years, he was arrested five times on assault and battery charges, and convicted once, serving six months in 1928 for viciously beating a policy runner: by then he also controlled the numbers racket in Newark. It was the only time he ever served.

He had others to do the rougher stuff. Among some of the tougher boys around him were Joseph "Doc" Stacher and Gerardo "Jerry" Catena, a close friend of Luciano. For out-of-state murder contracts, he used the Bug and Meyer mob, which carried out executions for gangs operating on the East Coast. This alliance between Benjamin "Bugsy" Siegel and Meyer Lansky predated Murder, Inc., by seven years.

Once Zwillman was a millionaire, he tried to clean up his act—on the surface, at least—by branching out into legitimate business. His financial interests included steel, barium, scrap iron, and used machinery. The *Wall Street Journal* would eventually recognize him: "How Abner Zwillman Clicked in Business After a Rough Start," was the story's headline.

And he polished his political act. Besides buying cops, judges, and other public officials, he founded the Third Ward Club in his old Newark neighborhood. It was nonpartisan—that is, it sided with whomever could do Zwillman the most good.

Zwillman and Johnson were close friends, which perhaps explains why the racket bosses chose Atlantic City for their conference. Being the congenial host that he was, Nucky Johnson provided the boys with bonded booze, thick steaks, and juicy showgirls to help them wind down after hard negotiation sessions. Rest periods, one writer noted, "found the gangsters strolling along the beach with their trousers rolled up around their knees, their shoes and socks in their hands, their feet washed by the lapping surf of the Atlantic Ocean." Just like ordinary folk.

One enterprising photographer from the *New York Evening Journal* snapped a picture of Nucky and Capone strolling down the Boardwalk, but the local papers never acknowledged Nucky's hosting chores during the conference.

Nothing lasts forever. Two quick body blows knocked Atlantic City to its knees. The Depression and the repeal of Prohibition. The city's wealth turned to dust. Unable to pay its employees, in February 1933 the city started issuing scrip, a practice that lasted four years.

Looking for a way to lure back the tourists, Nucky tried to sell the state on a 25-year plan. The mayor spelled out his program for a "Monte Carlo" to the *New York Times*. The idea was to build a "super resort" that would provide something for everybody. "Segregation is not a fair description of our plans," the mayor told the *Times,* "but we feel that when groups come here, some seeking rest and quiet, others hilariously celebrating a hurried holiday, it is absurd to have them trampling on each other's toes and spoiling each other's fun. There should be facilities for every person—and every desire—in Atlantic City. And if visitors want merry-go-rounds or a gambling casino, Atlantic City should give them what they want."

By the end of the thirties, the city's real estate base had shrunk one-third and the tax rate had climbed from $2.88 to $6.43. Yet despite the economic reversals, Nucky retained his popularity with the voters.

But his political popularity ended when William Randolph Hearst, then a strong supporter of President Franklin D. Roosevelt, persuaded the President to send the federal boys in to clean up the Republican party in South Jersey. While FBI agents were counting towels laundered for local brothels, Treasury accountants were going over the records of numbers bankers. The result was an indictment for income tax evasion. It was charged that Nucky's income from vice alone amounted to more than $500,000 a year.

Convicted in July 1941, he was sentenced to ten years in Lewisburg prison and fined $20,000. Flamboyant to the end, he married his showgirl sweetheart 12 days before the prison doors closed behind him.

He served only four years, but by the time he got out he was a relic. He couldn't even fix a parking ticket. His protégé and successor, Frank "Hap" Farley, had waited in the wings long enough. Now it was his turn at the public trough.

4
Smiling Hap Farley Crowns Himself

With Nucky Johnson behind bars, Hap Farley lost little time in establishing himself as the boss of Atlantic County. Besides being a senator, chairman of Atlantic County's Republican committee, and a practicing attorney, Farley appointed himself county treasurer. This not only gave him control of the purse string, but made it clear to county employees who was signing their paychecks and to welfare recipients who was responsible for their checks. And he let the judges know who was boss. Once a month, he had his nephew deliver their paychecks.

If anything, vice operations became more rampant under Farley's reign. He made sure the police were underpaid so that vice payoffs would be more palatable. And to make sure the police understood their role, Farley demanded that they sign "loyalty oaths" to the Organization, as his Republican Club was called. So when Farley or one of his flunkies told a cop to lay off a vice operator, he laid off, or else.

By 1951 the stench of vice in Atlantic City was so ripe that U.S. Senator Estes Kefauver decided to bring his Crime Committee, which was investigating political corruption and organized crime in the nation's major metropolitan centers, to Atlantic City. Kefauver would later write in his report: "When this committee moved into Atlantic City at the height of its tourist season, numbers runners and bookies ran for cover and a storm of protests arose from the politicians and racketeers (both of whom seem to think alike in Atlantic City)."

Among the conclusions reached by the committee was that Farley was head of the city's rackets, that the Republican party assessed members of the police force $30 a year, that the police department showed "signs of deliberate laxity" and could never find any gamblers to prosecute, despite the fact that about 200 bookmakers were operating there.

As a state senator, Farley garnered more power than his two predecessors. In those days there were only 21 senators, one from each county, and Farley served as chairman of the "21 Club" for over twenty years. He would also serve twice as senate president, twice as majority leader, and six times as acting governor during his 33 years at the State House, which is the longest stint in New Jersey history. In the heyday of the Republican Senate caucus, in the 1940s and 1950s, no bill could get through the legislature without his approval. That was the measure of his power in the state. Which was still far less than he wielded in Atlantic County.

The city commission underwent so many state and federal probes that they became routine. The commissioners spent more time testifying under oath than they did on city business, but Farley was never called to testify on anything.

Vote fraud remained as rampant as ever. The Organization got the votes from wherever it could, whether the address was a boarded-up tenement, a leveled home, or a vacant lot. County and municipal employees were forced to pay tribute to the Organization, and merchants and contractors doing business with the city and county kicked back 10 percent to Hap Farley and his minions. No one thought twice about it. It was the accepted practice, not only in Atlantic County, but just about everywhere else in the state.

There's no question that Farley's methods were good for certain businesses. Like Kuehnle and Johnson, his goal was always a bigger and gaudier resort. In Trenton he became the champion of special interest legislation. In his effort to make Atlantic City the leading convention town, he enlarged the already mammoth Convention Center and made possible the Garden State Parkway and the low-toll Atlantic City Expressway. He kept the town free of the state's sales tax and managed to get a luxury tax for Atlantic City only.

A tall, heavyset man who walked with a slight stoop because of a chronic back problem, Hap Farley was an ordinary-looking man, the kind easily lost in a crowd. His only distinguishing feature was the smile that almost permanently creased his moon-shaped face. As one old-timer recalled: "Hap can twist your arm until it's almost broken off and you give in. But he always keeps smiling and when the battle is over—when you've finally given in to something he wants—he'll put his arm around you and you suddenly think you're the best of pals."

Like all political bosses, Farley had a lot of pals. One of them was Public Safety Commissioner Mario Floriani, head of the Fourth Ward Italian American Club. A strong supporter of Floriani was Paul "Skinny" D'Amato, who never had any problem running prostitution and gambling in the 500 Club which he fronted for a succession of Mafia bosses. The 500 was a hangout for Mafiosi and politicians. That is where many of the deals were cut while Skinny acted as genial impresario.

Not all entertainment in Atlantic City was on the Boardwalk. What kept the city going in the fifties and early sixties was the side avenue nightclubs that offered top entertainment. The Club Harlem, with Larry Steele's high-kicking chorus line, featured black stars like Moms Mabley, Sammy Davis, Jr., Billy Daniels, Slappy White, Billy Eckstine. Grace's Little Belmont featured organist Wild Bill Davis and his jazz trio, and LeBistro booked Jack Jones, Belle Barth, Vic Damone, Jackie Mason, and a young comic named Lenny Bruce.

But the 500 Club, 50 yards from LeBistro, became the Big Daddy of them all after Skinny took over in the early forties. Its showroom was gradually expanded until it seated a thousand, and his backroom housed a plush casino. At one time or another the lineup included all the top headliners on the nightclub circuit from Sophie Tucker to Patti Page, from Jimmy Durante to Joe E. Lewis and Jackie Leonard. Jerry Lewis and Dean Martin teamed up for the first time at the 500 back in 1946. But the biggest draw ever at the 500 was Frank Sinatra, whose five engagements over a period of a half-dozen years literally became historical events.

What is amazing about Sinatra's appearances at the 500 is that he performed free of charge, doing as many as four shows a night. Skinny D'Amato says that it was because Frank loved him "like a brother," but then Skinny seemed to feel that way about everybody he knew. And he acknowledged with pride that he knew all the important politicians in New Jersey and every Mafia boss in the country.

The 500 was built by Marco Reginelli, underboss of the Philadelphia family, who lived and operated out of Camden. His successor,

Angelo Bruno, also loved Skinny like a brother. Skinny was so proud of his new boss and partner that he named his only son Angelo. Through the years, Skinny turned the Five, as the club was known to its devotees, into a local institution and had himself crowned "Mr. Atlantic City."

In the late 1930s Skinny had done a stretch in Lewisburg after being convicted as a "white slaver," and was still there, in fact, when another brotherly friend, Nucky Johnson, arrived at the federal pen to serve his time.

It was after Skinny's release from prison that Reginelli picked him to front the Five. Skinny put the club on the map and made millions for his friends.

According to Skinny, his managerial abilities so impressed another close friend, Chicago Mafia boss Sam Giancana, that when Giancana and Sinatra bought into the Cal-Neva Lodge at Lake Tahoe they picked Skinny to manage the place. But that was short-lived. Sinatra was forced to surrender his Nevada gaming license because Giancana, who was blacklisted in Nevada, came to visit his sweetheart, singer Phyllis McGuire, who with her two sisters was headlining the Cal-Neva showroom.

In recalling that event, Skinny told me that he and Sinatra had advised Giancana not to come. "We died when we saw him drive up. But he was in love, what are you going to do?"

During the 1960 presidential campaign Giancana sent Skinny D'Amato to West Virginia to get votes for Jack Kennedy. He was to use his influence with the sheriffs who controlled the political machine of that state. Most of them had been customers at his 500 Club, and according to Skinny, loved him like a brother. Whether he helped turn the tide for Kennedy in that crucial primary state is not as important as the fact that Giancana sent him there on Kennedy's behalf.

Sinatra made only one more appearance at the 500 after his Nevada debacle. That was the one in August 1964. As *Atlantic City Press* columnist Sonny Schwartz would note in later years, "Sans Sinatra, summer business in '65 and the following years took a decided downhill turn."

It was a pointless tribute. But then an army of Sinatras couldn't have solved the city's problems. However powerful the political machine, however diligent the effort to keep America's Playground afloat, by the early 1960s time was running out. The economic prosperity of the 1950s, combined with low-cost jet travel, had seen Americans looking for new playgrounds for their vacations—Miami, Las Vegas, Caribbean islands, Europe, anyplace that promised something different. The makeup of tourists coming to Atlantic City changed dramatically. They were poor, elderly, black—sometimes all three—and they came for one day and brought a picnic lunch. Which meant that they weren't using the hotels or the restaurants or paying for any of the other pleasures that cost money. They were there for a free day at the beach. The great Boardwalk was rapidly dying before everybody's eyes and no one knew what to do about it.

In an article on the resort, *Time*'s quote of a third-rate comic playing a local club told it all: "This town really swings. Every Friday night we shop till ten at the supermarket. Listen, the typical couple visiting Atlantic City these days is a very old lady . . . and her mother."

By 1960 Atlantic City had the second-highest percentage of people 65 or older in the country. The large hotels became refuges for senior citizens. The percentage of blacks grew from 23 percent to 45 percent and the total population decreased from 60,000 to 45,000.

The city's federally funded antipoverty agency reported that "no other area in the state can match this one for poverty, substandard housing, broken families, and infant mortality." Considering the pervasive blight of urban rigor mortis that affected most of New Jersey, this was an awesome indictment. Large families were jammed into one-room firetraps while children, lacking playgrounds, played in the streets where drugs were openly peddled. "And no one seems to care," a local clergyman complained. "Atlantic City is dying, the victim of an unholy alliance between crime and politics." Those who cared, and could afford it, moved out, abandoning the sinking ship while there was still time to build a future elsewhere.

Hap Farley seemed unaware of the insidious erosion. He talked of "progress" at a time when the city was regressing faster than the South Bronx and of "prosperity" when the county's unemployment rate was one of the highest in the nation. He seemed unaware that the Boardwalk was nothing more than a collection of shabby stalls peddling cheap junk, that the beaches were filthy and the city itself a no-man's-land of flophouses, boarded-up stores, burned-out buildings, and streets abandoned to derelicts, drug pushers, muggers, and whores.

When the Democrats decided to hold their 1964 National Convention in Atlantic City, Farley called a meeting and told a cheering crowd that the eyes of the world would be focused on the resort for a whole week. It would be, he said, the "pinnacle of prestige" for the city if everybody pitched in and gave it their best effort. The whole world would be impressed. In fact, there was a good chance the Republicans would come in 1968.

If ever a city took a pummeling from the press, it was Atlantic City that August. Farley's dream was pounded into the ground and into the heads of the millions who viewed it on network television and read about it in the print media. NBC News' David Brinkley presented a special segment on the city's deterioration, with similar footage shown on the other networks.

It gave reporters something to do during the long hours of rhetoric. They inspected the Boardwalk, the hotels and restaurants, the city's streets, and their most frequently used adjective was "tawdry."

"Early arrivals are dubious, inspecting rooms without TV or air conditioning and with puzzling dark stains on the dingy wallpaper," wrote a reporter for the *Indianapolis Star*. The *Washington Star* was less generous: "As a convention town, this is strictly Endsville. Now I know this is a resort left over from the early 1900s, but they could clean the room. . . ." The *Cincinnati Enquirer* described it as "paying for poverty at peak prices. Our room looked like something out of a Charles Addams cartoon book."

Farley refused to believe that the resort had been harmed by the adverse publicity and even produced his own poll which showed that of 750 men and women interviewed, 532 said they would like to return to Atlantic City for future vacations. Whether he actually believed his own figures is not known. But what was obvious to anyone who took time to look around was that Atlantic City was finished as a resort. No dubious poll or pep talk could change that fact. Nearly nine decades of political corruption had reaped its inevitable reward.

Farley was facing even more serious problems. For the first time, the city was feeling racial tension. Farley was losing his grip on black voters. In an effort to neutralize the black vote, voter registration cards were marked to denote race. This became important in picking grand juries and in letting precinct captains know which voters to get out on election day, for it had become clear that the Republican machine could no longer depend on black Democrats.

Still Farley persevered in the 1968 election. He did more than that at the Republican National Convention when he threw his weight behind Richard Nixon. Going into the convention, it was still a horse race. Nixon, Governor Nelson Rockefeller, and Governor Ronald Reagan were there to do battle. All surveys showed Nixon 15 votes short of nomination on the first ballot. If he failed to win then, it was believed that his northern supporters would move to Rockefeller and his southern supporters would go for Reagan.

The New Jersey delegation was pledged to a favorite son, U.S. Senator Clifford Case, who the Nixon forces regarded as a stalking horse for Rockefeller. But Farley met with Bergen County Republican boss Nelson Gross and between them they mustered enough votes to put Nixon over the top. This move so pleased Nixon that he would later save Farley from the fate suffered by his two predecessors. But a new era of power politics would dawn in Atlantic City.

5

New Jersey's Extortion Industry

Back in the 1960s Anthony "Tony Boy" Boiardo was used to dealing with guys like Paul W. Rigo. He dealt with them every day of the week and always it was the same story. They tried to hold back, pleading poverty, until he laid down the law. Then they wet their pants.

He knew all he had to know about Rigo. Rigo lived in a mansion in snooty Tewksbury Township, had a yacht, and not only flew around in his own helicopter but had his own fucking heliport in his backyard. Ten years ago he had been a lousy $8000-a-year state engineer, and now he owned two engineering firms, Capen-Rigo and Constrand, Inc., and what was more important to Tony Boy, Rigo had a contract for a Newark sewer project. So Tony Boy was in no mood for any bullshit when he put the bite on him.

Besides, Tony Boy knew that Rigo had been briefed on him. Hell, everybody in New Jersey knew that Tony Boy ran all the political shit for the Genovese Mafia family in Newark. His own father, Ruggiero "Richie the Boot" Boiardo had been a caporegime in the Genovese family going back to the days of Lucky Luciano and though he was 80 years old, he was still active, and still a power in the family. In fact, Richie the Boot bossed the numbers racket in Newark.

The meeting had been arranged by Anthony LaMorte, who was Newark's director of public works. "You're going to meet the real boss of Newark,'' LaMorte had told Rigo, ''the man who runs this town.''

Tony Boy gave Rigo his standard hard, unblinking stare. He liked doing it—it never failed to make people cringe. ''I've got only one thing to say to you,'' he said, keeping the evil eye on him. ''You kick back ten percent.''

''That's too much,'' Rigo said. ''I can't afford it on the bid I made for this job.''

Tony Boy shook his head in disgust. ''Hey, you'll pay, and in cash. Everybody in Newark pays ten percent—or he doesn't work in Newark. There's a lot of mouths to feed in city hall.''

And Rigo had paid. Later, when he was not paid for a second city contract, he slowed down his kickback payments, and complained to the ''Pope,'' the nickname for Newark Mayor Hugh Addonizio.

''The city council has to approve the contract,'' Addonizio told Rigo, ''and they're not moving on it.'' Then barely pausing, the mayor said, ''Boiardo has to move it. Why not see him?''

Rigo went to see Boiardo at his palatial home in exclusive Essex Fells. But Rigo was soon made to realize that the luxurious ambience had nothing to do with the way Tony Boy conducted business.

''You'll pay your ten percent,'' Tony Boy threatened, ''or I'll break both your fucking legs.''

Tony Boy seldom made empty threats. Federal agents had earlier bugged a conversation in which he was entertaining his colleagues with a story of how he and his father had handled a stubborn victim: ''The Boot hit him with a hammer. The guy goes down and he comes up. So I got a crowbar this big . . . eight fucking shots in the head. What do you think he finally said to me? He spit at me and said, 'You motherfucker.' '' Which were probably the victim's last words.

Rigo had seen enough television and had read enough news stories to know that people like Tony Boy actually did break legs. Without further protest, Rigo went to his office, put $30,000 in a brown paper bag, and gave it to Ralph Vicaro, one of Tony Boy's enforcers. Other payments were made at the offices of Valentine Electric, a company that listed Tony Boy as a salesman, a company which had a knack for getting public contracts, with $11 million worth of work on the city courthouse, the federal building, and other public buildings.

Gradually, Paul Rigo was sucked into a system he couldn't escape. Tony Boy's message to him was ''Keep up the payments and keep your mouth shut.'' One day he found a note in his car that said: "This could have been a bomb." For Paul Rigo, this was an introduction into the netherworld.

By 1969 New Jersey was mentally and physically drained, on the very edge of moral and financial bankruptcy, devoured internally, as it was, by racial riots, rampant vice, political corruption, and Mafia domination.

Nothing moved in New Jersey because the government had become the people's enemy. Services were at the level of a backward country. One mental hospital in Hudson County had over a thousand patients and not one psychiatrist. Mass transit hardly existed. The state's form of government was arbitrary. Only the governor and legislators were elected by the people. All state officials—Secretary of State, Attorney General, Treasurer, etc.—were appointed by the governor, who also appointed all judges and local prosecutors, in most cases deferring to the "courtesy" of the local boss. Its system was described as 21 counties in search of a czar. And it usually managed to find one, and in most cases he wasn't someone elected by the voters. Greed was at the core of its decay. The result was mismanagement on a diabolical scale that shackled all progress.

A prime example of this malaise was New Jersey's largest city, Newark, which could have been its queen city. With its great port location and nearby airport, it had the world's market at its front door and the industrialized wealth of its northeast corridor in its backyard. Yet the city became the state's example of urban decay. Its unemployment rate was double the national average and it had more people in public housing than any city in the country, with more than 10 percent of its 400,000 population on welfare. In 1965 it was cited by the President's Crime Commission as having the highest crime rate for cities of more than 250,000 population.

Port Newark, the immense waterfront complex that moved $9 billion worth of goods each year, was under the undisputed control of Jerry Catena, the Genovese family underboss, whose lieutenants were officers of the International Longshoremen's Association. What went on at Port Newark every day was like a rehearsal of *On The Waterfront:* illegal shape-ups, gambling, loansharking, pillage running into the millions, and extortion that bled more millions in "sweetheart" contracts at the expense of the union members, not to mention the embezzlement of union dues. To keep all this working smoothly took the kind of violent discipline that often led to beatings and murder.

Early in 1969 the Nixon administration decided to fulfill its campaign pledge of an all-out war on organized crime by zeroing in on New Jersey's Democratic machine. Through the good offices of Senator Clifford Case, Nixon appointed Frederick P. Lacey as the new U.S. Attorney in Newark and gave J. Edgar Hoover carte blanche in the use of electronic surveillance. By the fall of 1969 Lacey had three federal grand juries sitting in Newark and the politicians were getting nervous. At one point Lacey told the press that "Organized Crime is taking us over, callously, brazenly, and ruthlessly."

In mid-December that year, Lacey announced the indictment of Mayor Addonizio and 14 others on charges of widespread corruption at city hall. Included were three members of the city council, four former councilmen, the public works director, and two former corporation counsels and a sitting municipal court judge. Also indicted were two officers of the Valentine Electric Company, Tony Boy Boiardo, and a contractor named Mario T. Gallo, who later became a government witness. Among the charges were 65 counts of getting kickbacks through "fear of financial injury or under color of official right." Addonizio also faced charges of income tax evasion.

In a separate indictment, Simone "The Plumber" DeCavalcante and 54 others were charged with operating a $20 million-a-year numbers racket. DeCavalcante was the boss of the only Mafia family based in New Jersey. In all 62 people were charged with crimes involving corruption. During the investigation, the FBI uncovered a graveyard in a South Jersey chicken farm which had been used to deposit victims of Mafia executioners. DeCavalcante was convicted of extortion and sentenced to 15 years in prison.

Lacey released transcripts of FBI electronic surveillance that involved gruesome conversations among Tony Boy, Catena, DeCavalcante, and others about gangland murders.

Mario Gallo died the morning after he agreed to be a government witness in the Addonizio trial. His car veered off the road and struck an abutment. Four months later, another government witness in the Addonizio trial, Paul Anderson, a vice-president of the First Jersey National Bank, was killed the morning he was to testify. His car veered off the road and smashed into a tree. Both victims were alone in their cars and there were no witnesses to the accidents. Both accidents took place in West Orange, not two miles apart.

The next government witness, Paul Rigo, was kept under tight security until after he had testified. The result was that all defendants were convicted. Addonizio was sentenced to ten years in prison.

But that was just the beginning for Lacey and his chief prosecutor, Herbert Stern, who would later take over as U.S. Attorney when Lacey was appointed to the federal bench. Their next target was Angelo "The Gyp" DeCarlo, another high-powered Mafioso maneuvering around Newark.

DeCarlo was convicted and sentenced to 12 years for loansharking and extortion. A little over a year later President Nixon commuted his sentence, raising a controversy that brought Frank Sinatra into the picture. A Senate committee looked into allegations that Sinatra had engineered the gangster's early release through or by virtue of his close friendship with Vice President Spiro Agnew. The probe got nowhere.

The next on Prosecutor Stern's list to fall was Jersey City Mayor Thomas Whelan and his co-conspirators, including the president of the city council, a Port of New York Authority Commissioner, the treasurer of Hudson County, a Hudson County freeholder who was also the Democratic County Chairman, the city's purchasing agent, the county's police chief, and the city's business administrator.

The Little Guy, John V. Kenny, the boss of the Hudson County machine, which was characterized by Stern as "the most venal, long-run corrupt organization which has ever appeared on the American scene," temporarily escaped justice due to ill health.

All on Stern's list were convicted, with Mayor Whelan sentenced to 15 years for extortion, conspiracy, bribery, and tax evasion. In a separate trial, Kenny was sentenced to 17 years for tax evasion, but died before prison doors were to close behind him. The only politician to escape a prison term was one who pleaded not guilty for reasons of insanity and received a ten-year suspended sentence.

Stern would soon join Lacey on the federal bench, to be replaced by Jonathan Goldstein, who continued the forays through the muck of New Jersey corruption. The three of them bagged ten mayors, a congressman, leaders of the state Democratic and Republican parties, two secretaries of state, two state treasurers, an assembly speaker, a president of the senate, and two U.S. Senate candidates. Scores of lesser politicians, bureaucrats, contractors, bankers, and hoodlums also found themselves prison-bound.

In a little over two years Lacey and Stern had virtually convicted the entire governments of the state's two largest cities and had transformed the Lewisburg federal penitentiary into a New Jersey "jailhouse cabinet." What had begun as a Democratic purge had soon become bipartisan in scope.

Before joining Lacey on the federal bench, Herbert "Herb the Hawk" Stern had directed his attention to what he termed the "third of the long-range objectives of our office": Atlantic City. That it was a Republican stronghold helped to persuade some Nixon critics that this was a crusade against corruption, not a witch hunt. But for those convicted, it was of little solace.

6

Götterdämmerung in Atlantic City

There was something weird about the 30-year cycle in Atlantic City. It was becoming virtually generational in concept. Boss Kuehnle's 30-year reign had ended in 1911 with his incarceration. His successor Nucky Johnson's 30-year reign ended in 1941 with his incarceration. His successor Hap Farley came a cropper in 1971, losing his senatorial seat, but at least incarceration was not in the cards he was holding. There was that Nixon ace up his sleeve.

When contractors and low-level city employees began appearing before a federal grand jury sitting in Camden, there was speculation in the *Press* that the investigation was really aimed at Farley and his "influential GOP machine through which he has flexed awesome political muscle throughout the state for decades."

There was a lot of breath holding until the indictment came down on May 4, 1972, five days before a city commission election. Of the three indicted commissioners who were candidates, only Arthur W. Ponzio was reelected. Mayor William Somers and Karlos LaSane went down to defeat. Others indicted were former Mayor Richard S. Jackson, Airports Supervisor Robert Glass, public works department aide Germaine Fisher, and Purchasing Agent Florence Clark.

Each defendant was charged with 17 counts of extortion and 9 counts of using interstate facilities to commit bribery. Convictions on all counts carried a maximum sentence of 385 years for each defendant.

In his opening remarks to the jury, federal prosecutor Goldstein said the defendants ruled Atlantic City as if it were their private kingdom. "They enforced a total feudal system of corruption upon that society and they acted as lords of corruption." He described Jackson as standing "at the pinnacle of this conspiracy."

The irony was that the chief lord, Hap Farley, whose fingerprints were on every crooked deal cooked up by anybody in that county in the past 30 years, escaped with a whole skin. Farley had laid low during the city commission election. It was the end of an era, marking the demise of the old coalition ticket of three Republicans and two Democrats handpicked by Farley. More than 30 candidates threw their hats in the ring and when the votes were counted Ponzio was the only survivor and he by a hair.

There was talk that the county prosecutor was about to conduct his own inquiry into local corruption. In addressing that possibility, the *Press* forecast that "Atlantic County residents who bleed easily whenever the news media prints anything unfavorable about Atlantic City or the county will feel they are sitting on a rash of boils this fall. . . . Some solid citizens found it difficult to respond with fervor when the business community sought to start to crusade in favor of casino gambling in Atlantic City, because they had heard too many whispers about prominent persons here being linked with organized crime."

The whispers had been loud enough in 1970 during Angelo "The Gyp" DeCarlo's trial when FBI transcripts of taped conversations that involved Farley, Stumpy Orman, and corruption in the Atlantic City police department were made public.

In a taped conversation with DeCarlo, Frank Ruggieri, a Mafia associate, described how in 1963 Joseph Pasquale, a sergeant in the Atlantic City police department, took him to the homes of both Hap Farley in Ventnor and former Mayor Richard S. Jackson in Chelsea Heights, whom Ruggieri identified as the man who would succeed Farley. Farley is quoted as promising to intercede for Ruggieri, who had been convicted of bookmaking and was barred from the local racetrack. Ruggieri said he told Farley he didn't want to be embarrassed by being arrested at the track. Farley, Ruggieri said, told him, "Don't worry about it. Tomorrow, send your name with Joe [Pasquale]. I'll call Ryder up myself. Don't worry about it." Jesse Ryder was head of the security force at the racetrack.

In describing Pasquale's position on the police force, Ruggieri said: "What a job he's got. On top of it, he's president of the PBA [Patrolmen's Benevolent Association]. You want [to place] a bet—

call him at headquarters. He takes it right on the phone. He goes out when he wants—goes to the track when he wants. They don't bother him at all. All they got to worry about is the [state] troopers. . . . They [police department] won't pinch nobody. Owners, trainers, jockeys—when the track comes in there—they can do anything they want, they won't pinch them. They [the police] grab them and say they won't pinch them. They grab them and say, 'Give me a horse.' That's all they want—a horse.''

Ruggieri then ventured the opinion that, except for Union City, the Atlantic City police department is "unique in that the police sell baseball tickets, book horses, and work on percentages.'' He explained that he had a special detective's badge and a key to the city, "both in little black leather cases.''

When the tapes were revealed in 1970, Pasquale was working out of the office of the police chief, who in turn reported to Public Safety Director Mario Floriani. By 1977 Pasquale was an inspector. In early 1984 he became police chief, at a time when his old boss, Floriani, was not only county sheriff but again had been appointed Director of Public Safety. According to one newspaper report, the DeCarlo tapes were "discarded as unsubstantiated chatter.''

The federal trial, scheduled for October 1972, was delayed until February. The proposed county prosecution was delayed into oblivion. Testimony at the federal trial sounded like a replay of Newark and Jersey City. Businessmen and contractors testified, almost verbatim, that it was common knowledge that to do business in Atlantic County they had to kick back about 10 percent.

"If I didn't pay, someone else would, so what's the point of my riding a white charger,'' one contractor reasoned bluntly. Robert Glass was quoted as having told a businessman that his company wouldn't get any city contracts because "that Bible-singing ho-hum boss of yours refused to pay off.''

The seven defendants received sentences ranging from two years probation to six years in prison.

Outside the courtroom, Ponzio, recipient of the longest sentence, told the press that he was the victim of a "definite vendetta and I can put the blame on no one else but the McGahn brothers.''

Patrick "Paddy'' and Joseph McGahn were the sons of a local tavern owner whose influence in the local Republican party had been significant enough that both Nucky Johnson and Hap Farley were honorary pallbearers at his funeral in 1949. Paddy was a lawyer and what he called a "real" Democrat, on the verge of becoming a political power in Atlantic County. Joseph was a gynecologist and the man who was to unseat Farley in the 1971 election. Though Joseph became the senator, it was Paddy who exercised its political clout through a sort of brotherly proxy.

Paddy McGahn's strength lay in the black community. As the attorney for the Atlantic City NAACP, he had tried to get black policemen promotions but the city had refused to give them Civil Service examinations. This had culminated in a referendum drive to abolish the commission form of government in favor of a mayoral one. Though the drive had failed, it further weakened Farley's power base when it was revealed that the voting process had again been corrupted via forged signatures, nonexistent addresses of voters (300 voted from an apartment house that had been demolished), out-of-state and deceased voters, and again some from a home for the feeble-minded.

In his campaign for state senator in 1971, Joseph McGahn had made effective use of the DeCarlo tapes. He called for the removal of what he termed "this corrupt Republican machine."

But it was something even more fundamental that led to the downfall of Hap Farley.

For several years powerful forces had been pressing for the legalization of gambling in Atlantic City. There had been the now infamous Acapulco meeting on February 15, 1970, which was monitored by the FBI, the IRS, the Illinois Racing Commission, the U.S. Customs Service, and the Royal Canadian Mounted Police. Officiating at the meeting, attended by top-level mobsters from the United States and Canada, was Meyer Lansky, the underworld's gambling ambassador, the man who had pioneered legalized gambling in pre-Castro Cuba and the Bahamas. It was at this meeting that Lansky proposed a campaign to legalize casino gambling in Atlantic City and the methods by which they could infiltrate the casinos.

In 1973 Farley, who was still reeling from the DeCarlo tapes and the federal grand jury investigation of his minions in Atlantic City, was given the task of getting enabling legislation through the senate for a statewide referendum that would legalize gambling in Atlantic City. But Farley, afraid of a backlash, refused to be identified with the bill, getting one of his senate cronies, Union County Senator Frank X. McDermott, to become the bill's sponsor while Farley met privately with advocates of the bill.

The chairman of the New Jersey State Commission of Investigation testified before the senate committee holding hearings on the bill that "organized crime figures as far west as Chicago are meeting and arguing over how to whack up casino gambling in Atlantic City."

Their hopes were premature. The referendum was soundly defeated in 1974. Farley's feigned reticence outraged many of his most influential supporters. Even Skinny D'Amato, who to this day still professes his love for Farley, offered his support to Joseph McGahn and Steven Perskie when they promised to make legalized gambling their first priority. In fact, the new Democratic team of McGahn and Perskie based their campaign partly on the platform that they would be better able than Farley to bring casino gambling to Atlantic City because they had no taint of organized crime.

Not long after their election, Skinny was telling the press that what Atlantic City needed to get back on its feet was legalized gambling. He was so certain that McGahn and Perskie could pull it off that he began making alterations at the 500 Club, tripling the size of the kitchen and increasing the seating in the showroom—this at a time when the government was holding a $150,000 lien on his club for nonpayment of federal corporate income taxes and when Skinny had applied for protection under Chapter 11 of the Bankruptcy Act!

The way he saw it, legalized gambling was the answer to all his problems. He would convert the showroom into a casino and add a new room for shows and dinners on property he owned adjacent to the club. The way out for Atlantic City was to turn it into another Las Vegas. "It's not hard to do," Skinny told the *Trenton Times*. "You get your license, then get a group of guys. You get $500,000 from this one, $500,000 from that one, $500,000 from another, and you build. It's got to be done right."

By now forces far more powerful than Skinny D'Amato wanted legalized gambling and the politicians who opposed it were writing their own political obituaries.

7

"The Man Who Couldn't Be Bought"

When Gyp DeCarlo was overheard on a wiretap saying that Essex County Prosecutor Brendan Byrne was a man "we can't make," he inadvertently contributed the campaign slogan that ten years later would lead Byrne into the governor's mansion. It became Byrne's golden badge of integrity at a time when Watergate and the local federal prosecutions had riveted the voter's attention on corruption.

Having been cleansed of taint by DeCarlo, Byrne could campaign vigorously for legalized gambling without having to look over his shoulder to see if organized crime was gaining on him. During his 1973 campaign Byrne promised to push for a public referendum to legalize casino gambling, but the bill "should not and cannot turn Atlantic City into a Las Vegas." He favored a law similar to Puerto Rico's, where hours and operations were restricted. He wanted it to be "properly" handled and not "subject to the pitfalls and distortions" of Las Vegas.

Yet he was not sure the voters would approve it. There could be "some trouble because the image that exists in North Jersey of politics in the Atlantic City area is not the greatest." He felt that there "would be some reluctance" to approve the referendum in areas outside of Atlantic City unless the people have "confidence" in the governor. What they needed to inspire this confidence was a governor with a law enforcement background, such as his own.

The big question mark raised by his opponent, Congressman Charles Sandman, the boss of Cape May County, whose rule over his dominion was every bit as iron-fisted as Farley's, was that Byrne had never done anything to impede the power and corruption of the state's political bosses during the ten years (1959–68) he was chief law enforcer in Newark, a period when corruption there was unmatched throughout the whole sad history of New Jersey. On four occasions Byrne had issued grand jury presentments critical of police and official corruption, but had never pinpointed the blame through indictments. Yet, former Police Director John Redden had called one Newark precinct the "hellhole of the world. Mob people walk in and out of there like they own the place. They even use the police telephones. The whole place stinks from top to bottom."

In his defense, friends of Byrne explained that his inability to deal with the Newark cesspool stemmed from his indisposition to grasp the filthier tangles of life.

Meanwhile, the New Jersey legislature had set up a gambling study commission, made up of members who generally opposed a state income tax. The commission's most evangelistic proponent of gambling was William V. Musto, a senator and mayor of Union City, and an old friend of the Atlantic City machine. It was Musto's theory that legalizing gambling would not only increase revenues but would reduce organized crime. (In 1977 Musto was charged with using his mayoral power to protect an illegal baccarat game operated at a bar owned by the wife of the city's police director. Though the case was dismissed because the prosecution refused to name a key informant, four years later Musto was found guilty of racketeering and sentenced to seven years in prison. The next day he was reelected mayor of Union City.)

The flames shot through the roof and smoke belched skyward. The 500 Club was giving its final performance. Watching from across the street on this Sunday afternoon, June 10, 1973, Skinny D'Amato was being consoled by his two daughters, Paulajane and Cathy, and his son, Angelo. Reporters surrounded them.

Fighting back tears, Skinny pointed to the second-floor living quarters above the nightclub. "That's where my kids were born— where they grew up." The tears started running down his sunken cheeks. He lowered his head, wiped at his face, and looked up. "I'll rebuild," he said. "I don't know how, but I'll try. I'm going to keep going. I was born on this street." Then he shook his head. "People can't afford it anymore.'' What he meant was that the 500 had been in the bankruptcy courts.

A moment later Skinny was entertaining the reporters with stories about Dean Martin and Frank Sinatra. ''They each called on Christmas and spoke to the whole family—to the kids,'' he said, now ignoring the flames that were ravaging the club. ''Sinatra appeared here five times and never charged me a penny.''

After the fire was brought under control, Skinny toured the smoking ruins. The roof had caved in, the rear wall had collapsed. He moved through the muddy debris, shaking his head in disbelief at the skeletal remains. Then he stopped and stared in astonishment at a charred wall where he had hung a lifesize photograph of Sinatra. There it was, untouched by the flames. He took faltering steps toward it to make certain. How was it possible? The heat had been so intense that steel girders lay twisted in the ruins. He reached up and touched the photograph. Yes, it was true. It had survived. This had to be a good omen, God's way of assuring him that the future was secure. It was a miracle.

Testifying in favor of legalized gambling was I. G. ''Jack'' Davis, president of Resorts International, which operated a casino on Paradise Island, off the coast of Nassau, in the Bahamas. It was Davis's opinion that it was ''possible to operate a casino honestly and make it a business contributing to the economic well-being of the community.'' Davis talked at length on the merits of a gambling operation, but was never asked to comment on his company's connections with Meyer Lansky and his Mafia associates.

The commission, which was bipartisan and had citizen members, decided that the issue should be resolved by referendum, but the Assembly rejected three separate measures, leaving the matter in abeyance until after the election, which Brendan Byrne won by a two-to-one margin.

In his speeches endorsing casino gambling, Byrne said he agreed with U.S. Attorney Jonathan Goldstein that it could mean a resurgence of organized crime. ''But I know that organized crime has always been in those areas where we have prohibited some form of commerce that the public endorses, makes illegal, and [then] doesn't want enforced,'' he said. He recognized the problems, but ''I think we can handle them.'' In fact, he maintained that ''problems become more difficult'' for law enforcement ''when you have gambling under cover. Where you have it open and regulated and accounted for, I think the ability to deal with those problems is there.''

As governor, Byrne disapproved of an open-ended referendum that would legalize gambling throughout the state, subject to local approval. He wanted to test it first in Atlantic City. Calling it a "morale booster" for the deteriorating area, he went on to make what has to rank as one of the most ingenuous remarks on record: "I think if it's tested in Atlantic City and if it doesn't work, it's easy to get rid of it.''

But Goldstein asserted that casinos would provide economic aid for criminals, not for Atlantic City. Having only recently cleaned house in the resort, he pointed out that "for over two decades, both government officials and the business community have been involved in the all-encompassing corruption that has struck at the heart of its governmental process. Atlantic City's governmental and business leaders who have permitted an omnipresent fabric of corruption in Atlantic City, who have allowed Atlantic City to deteriorate and have made few if any meaningful investments to rebuild that city, are those people who now want the state to entrust to it legalized gambling." Then hitting the target a direct blow, he said, "The very same interests which have allowed Atlantic City to deteriorate will be the sole financial beneficiaries of casino gambling.''

It became a contest of evil versus good. Crime versus revenue. The referendum on the November 1974 ballot permitted statewide gambling of all kinds. The opposition, "Casinos, No Dice," played on the state's fear of organized crime. "Gambling dens in your own backyard," was the catchphrase that fall. Disapproving of the vague language in the bill, Governor Byrne refused to campaign actively for it. When it was soundly defeated by better than a three-to-two margin, the *Atlantic City Press,* which had supported it, editorialized: "They warned of prostitutes and loan sharks and the public apparently bought their arguments.''

There was a lesson in the defeat. Next time around it would be a different story.

8

Seducing the Electorate

Within a year of the referendum's defeat, Senator Joseph McGahn and Assemblymen Steven Perskie and Howard Kupperman had devised a new plan for a referendum to be placed on the 1976 ballot that would limit casino *gaming* (as in Nevada, the word "gambling" became verboten) to Atlantic City.

Remembering that the opposition of church and law enforcement had been most effective among the state's army of elderly citizens, they came up with the most inspired gambit of all: tax revenues derived from casinos would go into a fund to be "applied solely to reduce property taxes, rentals, and telephone, gas, electric, and municipal utilities charges of eligible senior citizens and disabled residents of the state."

The real wizardry of the new referendum was what it left unsaid. Whereas the 1974 referendum had indicated a state-owned operation, the new version omitted all wording as to ownership, leaving the door open to the private sector, which attracted campaign money from prospective casino operators. As for the elderly and handicapped, eligibility was never defined, and even the most liberal estimates placed the maximum individual benefit at less than $20 a year.

In a speech before the Atlantic County Democratic Club, Perskie proposed a new approach. "Last time the question was casinos-yes versus casinos-no," he said. "If we in this community allow ourselves to defend casinos as an idea, we are going to lose again. We must talk about the position of Atlantic City in the state's economy. I do think we can sell Atlantic City to the people of New Jersey.''

In April 1976 hearings were held before a joint committee of Senate and Assembly members at the statehouse in Trenton. Again the same church groups and law enforcement officials voiced their disapproval and vowed the same vigorous opposition.

Clinton Pagano, the newly appointed superintendent of the State Police, testified that legalized gambling would attract organized crime and increase trade in narcotics, loansharking, prostitution, and street crimes. "It will bring to New Jersey more problems than it will cure.''

But by now the formidable forces of backroom and corridor politics had joined hands to pull the secret levers of power politics. Even old Hap Farley, ailing and feeble, came out of retirement. "All the talking in the world, all the meetings mean nothing at all unless personal contacts are made,'' he advised. "Your contacts can't control the vote, but they can be the deciding factor.''

The power brokers were recruited. From Cumberland County, Assemblyman James Hurley not only reversed himself, but followed Perskie's strategy: "At a time when the Governor is cutting out such Medicaid items as physical therapy in hospitals, we should look seriously to casino gambling as a way of financing these worthwhile services.''

Camden Mayor and Senator, Angelo Errichetti, was quick to catch on to Farley's backscratching politics: "Let's generate enthusiasm so people will be able to say, 'I helped Atlantic City.' Let's work together and help each other. I'm working for what's good for your community. You must work for what is good for my community.'' Also falling in line were Newark Mayor Kenneth Gibson, U.S. Senator Harrison Williams, and Governor Brendan Byrne.

Bergen County Sheriff Joseph Job, who had not backed the 1974 referendum, came out to help his "old pal" Farley. He felt that "the people of Atlantic City deserve the chance to recover economically. I'm for it myself because it's a better break for the people, offering a lot better odds, like 37 to 1 at roulette as compared with 1100 to 1 in the State Lottery.''

Though politicians are quick to support certain causes, money must come from the private sector. In this case the goal was a million dollars. An organization called the Committee to Rebuild Atlantic City (CRAC) was formed under the leadership of Joseph Lazarow, the city's newly elected mayor. By far the most generous contributor to CRAC was Resorts International, which was already buying land bordering the Boardwalk, paying $2.5 million for the Chalfonte-Haddon Hall Hotel, and promising to spend another $15 million to add a casino and refurbish it. Resorts not only contributed nearly $200,000 to CRAC, but spent another $100,000 on its own media campaign.

Resorts President Jack Davis understood power. Resorts added to its legal stable possibly the most powerful political lawyer in the state, Joel Sterns, a major fundraiser and campaign adviser to Governor Byrne and a former counsel to Governor Richard Hughes. And Resorts added Richard Weinroth, a former aide to Governor William Cahill.

Unable legally to hire Senator Joseph McGahn and Assemblyman Steven Perskie, Resorts did the next best thing. It hired Joseph McGahn's brother, Paddy, and Perskie's uncle, Marvin Perskie, both lawyers, and asked them to write the gaming act that would be submitted for enactment once the referendum was approved.

Steven Perskie admitted during a September 1976 press conference that another relative, his cousin Philip, had "spent the summer" drafting the proposed casino legislation. Philip, he hurried to explain, was a law-school graduate and like Steven, only a nephew of Marvin, not his son.

Philip worked on the project on a volunteer basis, but his uncle Marvin, as everybody knew, was being paid $10,000 a month by Resorts International to write the casino law. Senator McGahn and Assemblymen Perskie and Kupperman were slaving over the act's language, but Marvin was a sharp old lawyer—his talents were sought by organized crime figures who could afford his services—and he was used to dealing with the kind of intricate language it would take to make the law the strongest in the world. Besides, he knew precisely what his client needed, which was more than the legislators could say about their constituencies.

Patrick "Paddy" McGahn's contribution was equally important. Although not in Farley's old power broker class, Paddy often boasted to colleagues that he controlled the City Commission and that his clout extended throughout the state and the nation. An ex-Marine who had retained his flattop haircut, Paddy's connection to Resorts was to make him one of the wealthiest lawyers in the state.

"In selecting any attorney, you look to the law firms that are able to deal with dispatch with government on the state and local level," said H. Steven Norton, executive vice-president of Resorts, in explaining why his company had hired McGahn.

Paddy McGahn was so convinced that the referendum would pass that he bought an estimated 100,000 shares of Resorts stock at a bargain price of about $2 a share in 1976 and in less than two years sold a large portion of it for about $200 a share. This was in addition to his handsome monthly retainer and the bonus he received when the referendum passed.

What Paddy lacked in charm he made up in vocal pluck. The image he strove to present was that of a tough ex-Marine who had earned the nickname "Piano Wire Paddy" while serving in Korea. The way he told the story was that he used to penetrate enemy lines in North Korea and decapitate enemy soldiers with piano wire. Detractors said there was more fantasy than reality to this story, but it was the way Paddy wanted others to perceive him. A hardheaded, hot-blooded Irishman, he was in many ways the typical pol—loyal to his friends and unforgiving to his enemies.

"The image of the oily, slick, inside wheeler-dealer does not fit," one lawyer explained. "He's about as slick as sandpaper, about as smooth as a battering ram. His style is that when he walks into a room, he kicks everyone where it hurts, turns out the lights, and breaks all the windows. He likes to be the only one who knows what's going on. Hit 'em fast and move on."

In his own inimitable ass-kicking style, Paddy McGahn served Resorts well, getting it most of what it wanted in terms of variances and exceptions to planning and zoning from the city, as well as the kind of casino law it demanded from the state.

Marvin Perskie also had powerful political connections. His father had been a state Supreme Court justice and his brother was a Superior Court judge. Steven Perskie would later admit that he felt uncomfortable having an uncle in the employ of Resorts. "If Joe McGahn or I had ever attempted to discourage them from getting involved, they would have told us to go pound sand," Perskie would later tell the *Press*. "It was perfectly legal and perfectly ethical—even if it was politically unfortunate."

Big money came pouring into CRAC. Even the *Atlantic City Press* contributed $40,000. Once the $1 million was raised and the political forces marshaled, it became a question of finding someone who could reshape realities, turn a negative into a positive. Attitudes had to be altered, appearances manipulated, the bitter pill sugar-coated. It was time to summon a professional persuader, a packager of candidates and causes, a seducer of the electorate.

They reached all the way to San Francisco. As a political strategist, Sanford Weiner had an almost flawless record, having lost only 13 of 172 campaigns in the past 18 years, and all 54 issues he had orchestrated had been endorsed through referendum.

With opposition areas pinpointed by demographic surveys and voter polls, Weiner drew up a game plan to neutralize them. Noted speakers, entertainers, athletes, and charismatic out-of-state politicians were recruited for the seduction. Blacks and Hispanics were appealed to by ethnic champions. Sound trucks, canvassers, brochures, and media ads blitzed the state.

All the bases were covered. The direction of the entire campaign can be seen in the wording of one CRAC brochure:

Help
Yourself
Help
Atlantic City
Help
New Jersey

A ''yes'' vote for
Casino Gaming in Atlantic City
will help . . .

---

balance taxes
create jobs
boost the economy
cut down on street crime

''YES'' CASINOS
Atlantic City Only

On the reverse page was this copy:

Respectability
   New Jersey has learned from Nevada's mistakes. This time the controls will be built-in right from the start.

Who will be applying for licenses? Large hotels and corporate chains—public corporations subject to stringent control by the Securities and Exchange Commission (SEC), Internal Revenue Service (IRS), and other federal monitoring agencies.

Less Violent Crime

Here's an accepted fact in law enforcement: the more jobs available, the less likelihood there is that the community will be victimized by rape, armed robbery, murder. It's been demonstrated, time and again, that places with legalized casinos have a sharp reduction in violent crime statistics. And there are good reasons.

More police surveillance for one thing—especially in the vicinity of the casino hotels. And with more people working, there is less need to commit crime for profit.

Legalized casino gaming is hardly a cure for crime. But it can—and will—help.

It worked. CRAC had turned the rationale upside down. A vote against casinos was not only a heartless rejection of aid to the aged and disabled, but a stand against all the ills of society that casino gambling would cure, a vote against the anticipated economic benefits that would accrue to Atlantic City, to New Jersey, and to the voters themselves.

Senator McGahn and Assemblyman Perskie assured the voters that the Casino Control Act would be the "strongest in the world." It would create a classy operation, along the lines of Monte Carlo or the Bahamas. Nothing, certainly, as glitzy and vulgar as Las Vegas would be tolerated.

Gambling, McGahn maintained, would become "an element of a resort, tourist, and entertainment hospitality package" rather than "an end unto itself."

The campaign's most relevant issue became money. The state was flooded with hundreds of thousands of billboards, posters, and bumper stickers bearing the campaign's slogan, "Help Yourself," against a money-green background. The other slogan was "Atlantic City Only." To emphasize the benefits to the elderly and disabled, an old man or woman, usually seated in a wheelchair, would plead for help in television commercials.

Jonathan Goldstein called the senior citizen benefit plan "one of the most manipulative, cynical plots I've ever witnessed.'' But few people were interested in negative comments.

As for the organized crime issue that had been so damaging in 1974, Weiner defused it with personal attacks on Goldstein. ''It's a shame that the United States Attorney has used something as important as the casinos are to the future well-being of Atlantic City and New Jersey to get name recognition for himself and his ambition to run for Governor.'' Weiner played rough: ''Mr. Goldstein apparently does not care about the people of Atlantic City who are out of work, hungry, and living in substandard housing.'' Every time Goldstein talked about the campaign's ''economic smokescreens,'' Weiner would label him a demagogue.

In fact, organized crime was no longer a relevant issue. Public feeling on the matter was summed up by Albert Marks, Jr., of the Atlantic County Improvement Authority, when he said, ''New Jersey already has organized crime.'' Which was certainly true. ''Nobody likes to see tainted money come in, but if it stays in the background there is no harm. It isn't good maybe. But it's better than nothing.'' Senator McGahn was already espousing the Nevada rationale: ''The only people who can run casinos profitably are people with experience in that line of work.'' And who has more experience than the Mob?

Everything was going Weiner's way. Yet there was still the problem of getting out the vote. Politics has always been a cash-on-the-barrelhead proposition in New Jersey. ''It's a political fact of life in New Jersey that you have to pay people to work on Election Day,'' Weiner would later complain. ''The measure of a county leader's power is how much he pays his Election Day workers—and if you don't pay, they don't work.''

To help the bosses get out the votes in the large counties where the populace was more or less apathetic, CRAC earmarked $168,670 for ''street money'' to pay workers to canvass their districts. The Atlantic County NAACP was given $10,000 and told to round up its people. CRAC even brought in a charismatic black legislator from California and paid him $15,000 to come in and weave his magic spell over his brothers and sisters. In all CRAC spent more than $1.3 million, as opposed to $21,250 for the No Dice group.

It was no contest. On November 2, 1976, the people of New Jersey voted three to one in favor of legalized gambling. There was dancing in the streets in Atlantic City. The old bums crawled out from under the Boardwalk to sample the free booze. The celebration lasted through the night. More than the sun would rise that morning, a new era was dawning. The casinos were coming. There would be jobs and new buildings, and visitors by the million would toss money around like confetti. Hallelujah. The years of long, dark winter nights were over. Lights would once again glow on the Boardwalk.

Long live the Queen of Resorts.

9

Hurry Up and Deal

The writing of the Casino Control Act was an exercise in political horse trading unsurpassed in New Jersey legislative history, which makes it something that probably belongs in the *Guinness Book of Records*. But even before the ink had dried on the final referendum count, Steven Perskie was acknowledging that there was "a slight possibility" that the basic outline of the measure drawn up for the referendum would be altered before final passage, and Joe McGahn considered changes more than likely. Perskie indicated that the vast tier of what he labeled the "second-level decisions"—the rules governing operation, hours, credit for gamblers—had yet to be resolved.

As for the more than a quarter million elderly and disabled who voted for the measure, Perskie was conceding that he didn't know when or if they would receive aid, or how much it would be should they get any. This too would be determined at a later time. In fact, Perskie termed the plan an "ancillary issue," noting that "casinos were never intended to help the seniors—they were designed expressly to aid tourism in Atlantic City." What Perskie seemed to have forgotten was that the support of the elderly had been anything but ancillary to the success of the referendum.

"When a locality becomes economically dependent upon casino gambling, politics that might otherwise seem prudent and reasonable become a threat to the industry," sociologist Bernard Skolnick pointed out. "The only value strong enough to challenge the puritanism that opposes gambling is capitalism.'' And what can oppose capitalism? Not the New Jersey legislature certainly.

Governor Byrne appointed a Staff Policy Group on Gambling which came up with some rather prescient ideas: ''[Casino] profitability is . . . not a direct function of a quality of gaming or environment in and around the casino. Corporate corruption, cheating, loansharking, overextension of credit, insobriety, prostitution, and a honky-tonk atmosphere are not antithetical to a desire for profit, and in the industry are occasionally viewed as legitimate societal overhead so long as they encourage or at least do not interfere with, the vitality of the gambling market. . . . The interest of the state and the success of casino gambling are not conterminous with the interests of the entrepreneur.''

The policy group's report envisioned the creation of a gracious atmosphere in Atlantic City that would appeal to family vacationers and convention groups without becoming so expensive as to be exclusive. Its proposals limited all gaming operations to 112 hours per week (16 hours per day), prohibited the serving of alcoholic beverages, free or otherwise, on the casino floor, the tipping of dealers and other casino employees, the comping—perks—of high rollers, free junkets. And in an attempt to protect gamblers from losing more than they could afford and at the same time to close the area of greatest ease in skimming and of infiltration of organized crime, it allowed credit only in the form of checks that had to be deposited within two business days.

All these recommendations were defeated. In the end, it was free booze while gambling, easy credit, tipping to one's heart's content, and gambling 18 hours daily on weekdays and 20 hours on weekends.

Much of Resorts' victory belongs to Paddy McGahn, Marvin Perskie, and Joel Sterns, the journalist-turned-lawyer who became Resorts' most active lobbyist. A former counsel to once Governor Richard J. Hughes, who was by then the chief justice of the state supreme court, Sterns was a skilled legislator and a crackerjack lobbyist in Trenton. Sterns had also been counsel to ''Democrats for Byrne'' in the governor's reelection campaign.

When push came to shove, Sterns proved most persuasive in the key areas of credit, tipping, alcoholic beverages, and related issues. His focus was on how they would impact on the casino industry. Resorts' interest was in the economic issues, and Sterns talked dollars and cents. The way he evaluated the situation, the state was ''almost embarrassed'' that it had legalized gambling and was fearful of the unknown damage it would wreak. It was this that made Sterns decide to steer clear of the stickier issues of casino security and integrity.

As for Paddy McGahn, he guided his brother with dramatic signals during the public sessions in Trenton. For example, when Paddy wanted a speaker cut off, he would make a choking motion with his fist and Senator McGahn would quickly interrupt the speaker and change the subject. It was the old shell game that legislators and lobbyists know how to play so well. And Resorts, which stood to gain the most, would not forget its friends. When Joe McGahn was defeated by Steven Perskie in his reelection bid, the former senator, a gynecologist, became house doctor at Resorts.

One sticky issue that was curiously overlooked by the legislature was ethics. There was nothing in the act to prevent any public official, legislator, or judge for that matter, from enjoying a close relationship with the casino industry. Conflict of interest was something that never occurred to these lawmakers. In fact, many received lines of credit at casinos, stayed in casino hotel rooms at reduced prices, owned stock in casinos, received pay for various services, and when they left office found employment in the casino industry, particularly if they had been helpful to the industry during the performance of their public trust.

But there were limits. The Committee on Ethics ruled that Assemblyman Kenneth Gewertz's attempt to sell slot machines to Resorts was a conflict of interest and decreed that he had to sell his 25 percent interest in the slot machine distributorship. Gewertz charged that the ruling was arbitrary and politically motivated. ''I'm not one of their favorite people,'' he complained. Besides, his dealings, he felt, were no more unethical than countless others in the state. ''It would appear that it's a horrifying type of situation. But you go back through the history of this country, money was always power. This state was run by railroads, then farmers, then insurance companies.'' The only one he omitted was banking, which today is the most powerful institution in the state, and one very much involved with the gambling industry, having extended enormous loans to casino corporations.

(After the death of Marvin Perskie, Gewertz would bring conflict-of-interest charges against Steven Perskie, who had become executor of his uncle's estate and trustee of several thousand shares of Resorts stock. Perskie was also the beneficiary of land that was in an area zoned for casinos. But Gewertz lost again. Perskie was cleared of the charge and Gewertz was voted out of office in 1979. To compound matters, he was rolled by three prostitutes in Atlantic City.)

Nothing is perfect. There were a few minor inconveniences in the casino act that irked the industry. After all, legislators have to serve many masters. Yet not to worry. So do administrators. So with time there would be a steady erosion in the state's power to control the industry. Irksome requirements that became part of the Casino Control Act signed by Governor Byrne on June 2, 1977 would be whittled down, some deleted entirely, others diluted, and others that remained were conveniently ignored.

Resorts International, and the other casinos that would soon come on line, would lose little time in mounting a massive campaign designed to reshape the public's attitude toward deregulation, so that the changes they wanted made would be more palatable to legislators.

By using their connections gained from politically oriented law firms and from other former state employees now on their payrolls, they succeeded in securing the following changes, all designed to increase their profits: the $2 minimum bet at all table games was increased to a $5 minimum; the early "surrender" rule in blackjack was eliminated, which increased their take by about 2 percent (about $11 million per casino annually); blackjack dealers no longer had to draw additional cards if all decisions for or against players had been reached; casinos could eject players who counted cards in blackjack— this was later disallowed by the state supreme court; drinks could be served in casinos until 15 minutes before closing time to any customer unless his "apparent" intoxication might impair his judgment; mandatory nightly live entertainment was left to the discretion of each casino; the ban on the display of female areolas (topless dancers) was modified to permit "pasties"; the prenotification of the Casino Control Commission was no longer required for advertising copy, which was to depict gambling "as an activity conducted in an atmosphere of social graciousness"; and there were drastic changes in the requirements for security personnel.

Affirmative action requirements, and many other rules that remained on the books, were ignored if the casinos found them cumbersome or unprofitable. Within five years of the law's enactment, the locus of power to regulate casino gambling would shift to the hands of the industry. The rationale was profits. The greater the industry's profits, the more investors it would attract, and the more casinos licensed, the more people would be employed.

U.S. Attorney Jonathan Goldstein characterized the legislation as the "child of special interests who hope to reap tens of millions of dollars in profits at the expense of our working citizens."

In some ways, the casino industry's greatest victory was in the molding of its own tax structure. Proposals for taxing gross revenues had ranged from Nevada's 5.5 percent to 20 percent, with Byrne asking for 16 percent. "The formulation process for the taxation provisions was preempted, thoroughly and effectively, by the industry," said one legislative aide. "They were their own patronage machine—their argument carried the day so easily that you could hardly describe it as a struggle."

The figure arrived at was 8 percent, with the casinos permitted to deduct bad debts up to 4 percent of gross revenues, which made the state bear the burden of their poor credit practices. To appreciate how good a deal this was, compare it to what Resorts had to pay in the Bahamas: a $3.5 million annual fee, plus 22.5 percent gaming tax on the first $20 million gross win and 15 percent on gross win over $20 million.

Another tax victory for the industry was its defeat of a proposal by the state treasury department that asked for an excess profits tax to be used for rebuilding Atlantic City, more specifically, housing for the poor who were being uprooted by the "land rush" created in the wake of the referendum. This was to be the revitalization promised by Perskie and other politicians. In the end, a vague clause known as the reinvestment tax called for a 2 percent tax of gross win after a casino's gross revenue had exceeded its cumulative investment, which meant that it would be years before the city saw a penny of that money.

Meanwhile, the Atlantic City Commission, demonstrating its usual ineptitude in the art of governing, had decided to update its 1921 Master Plan and had hired Angelos Demetriou. New Jersey Public Advocate Stanley Van Ness issued a scathing critique of the new Master Plan, pointing out that for a million dollars, Demetriou gave them 130 pages on bikepaths, but only three on the relocation of displaced residents. Demetriou's solution to the parking problem was to concentrate it in two areas: one in the protected Wetlands, the other on top of a public utility generating station.

As for the housing problem, complained Van Ness, Demetriou

recommended that blighted residential neighborhoods be cleared, but he never took the time to count the number of people who would be left homeless. The plan called for the preservation of the wealthier areas along the Boardwalk and permitted casinos to build where the poor and minorities lived.

Even a month before Byrne signed the act, some 2000 of the city's 13,000 on welfare had been evicted or faced eviction and had no place to go. And it was only the beginning. A year later the housing shortage became so critical that health inspectors were prevented from closing down unsanitary housing. Lack of utilities or plumbing or sewage were no longer valid complaints—a building had to pose an "imminent hazard" such as the threat of immediate collapse.

Perhaps the most fascinating part of the Casino Control Act was the creation of a two-tier system of enforcement: the Casino Control Commission and the Division of Gaming Enforcement.

It was left to the commission to implement the act's complex set of rules, many of which were, at best, ambivalent and, at worst, conflicting. To ensure the integrity of casino gambling, the commission was given the power to license corporations and individuals involved in the industry and to set up internal financial controls to prevent skimming or other illegal practices. It would also act as an economic regulator by setting up the rules and percentage odds of the various gambling games, with an eye toward striking a balance between fairness to the player and to the casino's profits, and, at the same time, oversee the revitalization of Atlantic City.

Yet, because tax receipts depended on casino profits, the state and the casinos had a mutual interest in the success of the games, including the 50 percent house odds on the big six wheel. It was the casino industry that was laying the golden eggs, and the primary responsibility of the commission would soon become the protection of that fat goose.

The division's role was to investigate applicants and submit its finding to the commission. The division was placed under the jurisdiction of the state attorney general, who was appointed by the governor. The five commissioners were also appointed by the governor, which meant that gambling in New Jersey was the governor's show. And it wasn't long before the show got on the road. Although New Jersey had promised to enact much stricter rules and safeguards than those practiced in Nevada, "in the end," as the *New York Times* editorialized, "New Jersey hurried up and dealt."

PART II
THE WAY IT IS

10

The Docile Don and His Merry Men

Angelo Bruno hated the State Commission of Investigation (SCI). He had waged a seven-year court battle against the SCI's efforts to force him to talk about his role as boss of the Philadelphia Mafia family and its influence in Atlantic City.

His first encounter with the SCI in 1970 had cost him three years at Yardville for refusing to testify after he was given immunity from prosecution. He would have been there longer if he hadn't developed a bleeding ulcer that was described as "leaking like an old crankcase." He was released for an indeterminate period because of his medical condition.

After his release, Bruno, a native of Sicily, had made tracks for his homeland and an indeterminate vacation. But in 1977 he had returned and now, after a platoon of doctors had pronounced him fit, a judge had ruled that Bruno would either testify before the SCI or go back to Yardville.

It was August 8, just two months after Governor Byrne had signed the Casino Control Act. With television lights blinding him, Angelo Bruno, accompanied by four lawyers, took faltering steps to the witness stand. His expression was pained and he seemed bewildered by all the attention. Cameras whirred and clicked as he carefully lowered himself in the chair.

Besides being great theater and a sure way for the commission members to gain wide public attention, the hearings offered the hope that Bruno might be so intimidated by the commission that he would tell them what he knew about his family's plans for Atlantic City. Or might let something slip in his confusion that would provide the commission with the kind of leads it was looking for in its efforts to expose organized crime in New Jersey.

In setting the purpose of the hearings, SCI Chairman Joseph H. Rodriguez had explained: "The record will show an obvious presence of organized crime figures, associates, allies, kinfolk, and namesakes in and on the periphery of Atlantic City casino and casino-connected deals. . . . The door of Atlantic City is presently ajar and it is now that government should lay its collective shoulder against it."

The SCI had been created in 1969, at the height of the federal purge of official corruption, and was patterned after the New York Commission. Its mandate was to "conduct fact-finding investigations, bring the facts to the public's attention, and make recommendations to the Governor and the Legislature for improvements in laws and the operations of government."

It was obvious that at 69, and ailing, Bruno didn't want to return to Yardville. In his various court pleadings, he had emphasized that he was too ill to be punished by another jail term, that he would never survive the ordeal. Of course, the alternative, if he should break his oath of *omertà,* was even less attractive than Yardville and definitely more determinate.

His only remaining option was to talk but not reveal anything not already on the record. That would require some fancy wordplay and a good memory. It wouldn't do for him to trip himself and end up with a perjury conviction. It was a delicate situation, but not one beyond the capabilities of the man who had earned the title of Docile Don for his ability to avoid violence through peaceful negotiations.

Bruno had come to power in the late 1950s when the boss, Joseph Ida, had fled to Sicily following his arrest and indictment after he was caught at the Apalachin meeting in upstate New York. For his temporary replacement Ida had picked Antonio Pollina, who in an attempt to consolidate his power, had plotted the murder of his principal rival, Angelo Bruno. But Pollina's underboss had informed Bruno of the plot and Bruno had taken the problem to the Mafia's national commission, which ruled in Bruno's favor. As the new boss, he was given the privilege of having Pollina murdered, but he declined and kept Pollina as an inactive member of his family.

During Bruno's rule no initiated member of his family ("made guy," or in East Coast slang, "wiseguy") was murdered.

Bruno adjusted his thick glasses and stared at the microphone in front of him. He leaned forward, a perplexed expression on his round face, as SCI Executive Director Michael Siavage explained that he had to answer all questions because he had been given a grant of immunity for any crimes except possible perjury before the commission.

After consulting with his attorneys, Bruno nodded, but when he tried to speak, his voice was scratchy and he had to struggle to clear his throat. Once he had, he lost little time in pointing out that his memory was defective, that details often failed him, that he was even worse with faces, meeting people one night and forgetting them the next. Hardly the qualities of a star witness.

He would have been a lot less worried had he known beforehand that the commissioners interrogating him would never mention the terms "Mafia" or "Cosa Nostra" or even "organized crime" in his presence. All they seemed to care about was that he earned $51,000 a year as a salesman for John's Wholesale Distributors, which operated cigarette-vending machines in Atlantic City, and that one of his chauffeurs, Raymond "Long John" Martorano, who was the company's president, earned less than Bruno.

Even when they questioned him about the late Carlo Gambino, the boss of the country's largest Mafia family, they were only interested in how long Bruno had known him and whether he had vending machines in restaurants owned by Carlo's nephews, Giovanni (John), Giuseppe (Joey), and Rosario (Sal) Gambino.

The only question that was at all tricky concerned Bruno's meeting in April with Paul Castellano, the new boss of the Gambino family, at Valentino's Restaurant in Cherry Hill, which was owned by the Gambino nephews.

But Bruno was ready for it, having read stories in the press that said the meeting had been monitored by federal agents. Monitored, Bruno knew, meant observed, and not tape-recorded. From the speculation in the press, it seemed obvious they had nothing. In the news stories it said that Castellano had tried to persuade Bruno to allow the Gambino family to set up shop in Atlantic City, until now Bruno's exclusive territory. The meeting was deemed a success when the Gambino nephews were seen visiting Bruno's South Philadelphia home on Easter Sunday. The conclusion reached was that the visit had sealed a mutual cooperation pact between the two families—that Atlantic City was carved up during the holiday dinner.

Playing on his failed memory, Bruno conceded that it was possible that Castellano was Carlo Gambino's brother-in-law, but he wasn't sure when he had met him.

"I don't remember if it was before I went to Yardville or after Yardville. I don't remember."

After more tedious questioning, Bruno admitted that he had dinner with Castellano at Valentino's.

"What did you discuss at that time?" Siavage asked.

"General conversation. I don't remember."

"Did you discuss Atlantic City?"

"I don't remember. He may have asked me what I thought of Atlantic City. General conversation. I have nothing to do with Paul Castellano in anything in Atlantic City or any business anywhere. This way you got the whole answer."

"Your answer is you do not conduct any business—"

"No."

"—with Mr. Castellano?"

"No business of any kind."

"Did you discuss in Valentino's doing business separately in Atlantic City?"

"I don't know what you mean by separately."

"Well, did he tell you what business he was going to go in, perhaps, and you tell him what business you were going to go in?"

"I don't recall it, but I don't know what his intentions are. I have a pretty good feeling about what my intentions are with Atlantic City. Would you want me to tell you that?"

"What are your intentions with Atlantic City, Mr. Bruno?"

"Stay away from it. That's my intentions."

Bruno was not asked about all the years that he and members of his crime family had spent their summers vacationing in Margate and Ventnor, Absecon Island's two most exclusive residential areas. Or about Nicodemo "Little Nicky" Scarfo, who lived there year-round and watched over the family's rackets in Atlantic City.

Back in 1970, the *Press* had run a feature story with the headline "Mafia Figures Come to Resort for Summertime Fun," in which the reporter had concluded that "the only business interests the Mafia has here are recreational, except for reportedly loosely strung gambling rackets. . . . Regardless of their activities, the family that plays here throughout the summer is known as the 'nicest' Mafia family in the country. Bruno, the leader, is a quiet, bespectacled man whose kingdom runs from northern New Jersey over to Trenton, through Philadelphia, and to Atlantic City. The 60-year-old chieftain is known as a man who runs his business quietly and shuns the bloody intra-fighting that has marked Mafia activities in New York and other cities.''

At the conclusion of his testimony before the SCI, Bruno put it all in a nice, tidy little package: ''I got nothing to do with Atlantic City as far as gambling's concerned. I'm not interested in any hotels; I'm not interested in any casinos, directly or indirectly. If they were to give me a hotel with a casino for nothing, I wouldn't take it.''

That was it, all they wanted to know. To Bruno, it was incredible. And, to think, for this nonsense, he had served three years in Yardville, which had nearly killed him. Who would believe it.

Nor was anything said about Nicodemo ''Little Nicky'' Scarfo, a soldier Bruno had exiled to Atlantic City years before when there was nothing worth carving up in that town. Now with the casinos coming in, Scarfo suddenly found himself sitting in the catbird seat. Despite his diminutive size (five feet five), Scarfo was a man to be feared. He had a long history of gratuitously violent behavior, which had gone against the grain with Bruno.

Back in 1963, Scarfo had fatally stabbed William Dugan, a 24-year-old longshoreman, in a squabble over who would sit in a restaurant booth. The charge was downgraded to manslaughter and Scarfo served 6 months of a 23-month sentence. A co-defendant in the case, Salvatore ''Chuck'' Merlino, a close friend of Scarfo, was acquitted. It was upon Scarfo's release from prison that Bruno, tired of his underling's hot temper and brashness, had shunted him to Atlantic City.

Still, Scarfo's credentials were impressive. His late father had been a member of the Genovese family and three of his mother's brothers, Joseph, Michael, and Nicholas ''Nicky Buck'' Piccolo, were members of Bruno's family. One of Scarfo's closest Mafia associates in Atlantic City was his sister's son, Philip ''Crazy Phil'' Leonetti.

As for Bruno, he hadn't become boss because he was weak. Violence, and the fear it instills, has always been the Mafia's most powerful weapon. It has been the most vital part of its modus operandi, a management tool that has ensured its growth and survival both here and in Sicily. Bruno was never opposed to violence when it was used to protect the family or in the successful conduct of its business.

For example, take Frank Sindone, Bruno's chief loanshark, who was feared for good reasons, as FBI wiretaps have revealed. In a 1970 telephone call he warned one of his customers: "You better bring me that fucking money here, you cocksucker, and stop all that bullshitting. You understand? I ain't going to tell you no more. I'll come up to your fucking house. I'll pull your eyes right out of your head. I had enough of you. You understand?"

By April 1976 Sindone had had enough of the business and wanted out. He wanted to go west for his twilight years: "I'll get out of here one day. You watch, I'll get the fuck out. Get a fucking ranch. I want to get a nice ranch, with some grapes on it, you know. Make a little bit wine. Sell the wine, get a couple of horses, oranges. About forty or fifty acres. I've got to get out. This business is gonna make me steal all my life. I'll get out. Change my name. This way they can't call me no more. If I stay here, I'll end up like Little Nicky. Nuts." This was a reference to Scarfo.

Sindone was discussing his problem with the Merlino brothers, Salvatore "Chuck" and Lawrence "Yogi." They were in his restaurant, Frank's Cabana Steaks, and talking into hidden FBI microphones.

"I want to go out there, but, I told him. He [Bruno] says, 'What do you want in Vegas? What do you want in California?' I said, 'Ange, you want me to tell you the truth or do you want me to lie to you?' He says, 'You know, that bothers me. What do you want with that big house of your own?' I said, 'I'll try to tell you, maybe you'll understand. I was poor all my fucking life. I didn't have nothing. My mother and father wasn't rich people. Whatever I have, I had to steal. I had to make it on my own. My father used to sell fish, like a fucking Indian. So now, I got money. I'm getting old fast. I'm almost fifty. I want to enjoy the fucking money.' "

Salvatore agreed with him: "What's the good of having it if you can't spend it?"

"If I don't make no money for the rest of my fucking life I'd never be broke. I can't spend what I've got. . . . So I got a right to enjoy myself. I've lived my fucking life in one lousy place."

"Sure. I agree with you," said Lawrence.

"Sure, you can see the writing on the wall," said Salvatore.

"Sooner or later they're gonna knock my fucking socks off," Sindone said, not really realizing how prophetic his words were.

"See, this guy [Bruno] is . . . I love this guy. This guy, this guy has been good to me. But he's got them old fucking ways. He ain't getting out of them, you know what I mean? Those guys, I don't know. I don't understand them. It's just get the money. Get the money! Get the money! Don't spend it. What the fuck good is it? I mean, you know, I mean, that's all he says to me . . . Oh, man, was he mad. 'Forget this trying to get out of town,' he says. 'Now you don't bring it up no more.' "

Docile or not, Bruno had his ways of keeping his men in line. No one was leaving town without his blessings. The younger members of the family were unhappy with his conservative ways but without assassinating him there was nothing they could do about it.

According to FBI wiretaps there was a great deal of complaining in the ranks. For one thing, Bruno was stingy. He had made his fortune and wouldn't share it downward. And he was sanctimonious. "We got to agree with him [Bruno]," Sindone told the Merlinos. "He don't want nobody that drinks around him, and nobody that gambles. He wants all priests around him!"

Yet Bruno seemed unaware of what some of his men were doing behind his back. For example, Scarfo was already in the gambling business with the Gambino family, as revealed in excerpts from FBI taped conversations which had taken place at the Tyrone Denitas Talent Agency in Philadelphia on November 4, 1977. Participating in the conversation with Scarfo were Harry "Hunchback" Riccobene, Frank "Chickie" Narducci, and Bruno's underboss, Philip "Chicken Man" Testa:

SCARFO: And now Atlantic City! You know them guys from North Jersey opened up crap games, card tables, and everything.
RICCOBENE: Uh-huh.
SCARFO: They're cautious because all the law is around Atlantic City. I swear to God. The guys in Trenton, they got two games going. That was their excuse for opening them.
TESTA: I don't blame them.
SCARFO: He [a reference to Nicholas Russo, a Gambino family member] said I was all over Atlantic City, they [Gambino's] notify us [about the games].
TESTA: There is a game in Trenton?
RICCOBENE: In Trenton?

TESTA: Who has a piece of it? Do you have a piece of it for downtown?

SCARFO: Fifty percent.

TESTA: Who's got that?

SCARFO: Pappy's [Carl Ippolito] got the other fifty percent.

TESTA: Oh, I see.

SCARFO: In other words, Philadelphia and New York, they made an agreement. If either one of them open a game—

RICCOBENE: Give the other—

SCARFO: Give the other fifty percent, if they accept it. If they don't want it there, they keep it for themselves.

TESTA: This is Trenton?

SCARFO: Yeah, this is Trenton. In other words they have an agreement for card games and crap games. Say like you're from New York and I want to open up this game. I say, "Look, I want to open up. You've got fifty percent." Now say I don't want it, you know. But the way it stands now, Pappy's got fifty percent and, ah, Nick Russo and them guys [from New York] have got fifty percent.

Meanwhile, State Police Superintendent Clinton Pagano had issued a warning: "Our intelligence indicates an upsurge of interest in Atlantic City. We have always had an organized crime problem in Atlantic City. We are identifying organized crime figures coming into Atlantic City. Organized crime will concentrate its efforts in areas that are lucrative."

Pagano estimated there were more than 5400 reputed members and associates of organized crime "now active" in New Jersey and that 7 of the 24 nationally recognized Mafia crime families had active organizations in New Jersey. The seven families were Bruno, Gambino, Genovese, Lucchese, Bonanno, Colombo, and DeCavalcante. The FBI would later include Chicago, Kansas City, and the family of Russell Bufalino, based in Pittston, Pennsylvania.

Testimony of law enforcement officials before the SCI confirmed rumors that Atlantic City, like Las Vegas, was an "open city" for the underworld, which meant that different families could operate in the area as long as their efforts were coordinated. Though many were jockeying for position, the Bruno and Genovese families were believed to be wielding greater influence in the area of ancillary businesses that would provide services and products to casinos such as garbage hauling, trucking, laundry, junket operations, limousine service, security personnel, vending machines, linen, silverware, liquor, cigarettes, food, coffee, and the like. Not to mention construction companies, and some labor and service-related unions historically associated with organized crime.

And the Mob was infiltrating local businesses in anticipation of the expected boom casinos would bring to the resort. There were frantic efforts to invest in Atlantic City real estate, bars, restaurants, motels, a janitorial company, security firms, and even a croupier's school.

Then there were the institutional rackets that organized crime has always thrived on: extortion, bribery, bookmaking, numbers game, prostitution, loansharking, narcotics, labor racketeering, hijacking, pornography, and the violence it took to keep it all in line.

How many of these activities were already in motion and how much they would increase when the casinos started coming on line was something that only time would tell, but even then, never the full story.

At least ten law enforcement agencies were gearing up for the opening of the first casino. Those involved on the local and state levels included the state police, Atlantic County prosecutor's office, Atlantic City police force, Atlantic County sheriff's office, New Jersey attorney general's office, and State Commission of Investigation. The federal agencies were the FBI, Attorney General's Strike Forces in Camden and Newark, Drug Enforcement Agency (DEA), and Internal Revenue Service (IRS). They could have been a formidable network if only they had trusted one another. Instead they were disorganized, competitive, and mutually antagonistic. They kept vital intelligence from one another, making investigations unnecessarily repetitious.

While the cops were jealously protecting their information and the local hoods were maneuvering on the periphery, getting ready for the deluge of dollars that would soon be floating across gaming tables, the real sharks, the multinational gambling concerns that would inherit this bonanza, were sharpening their legal and political arsenals for their assault on the Casino Control Commission. The engagement would be no contest.

11

The Governor's Man

During his 1977 campaign for reelection, Governor Brendan Byrne made effective use of the warning he had given organized crime the day he signed the Casino Control Act in Atlantic City. His battle cry "Keep the hell out of our state!" was repeated ad infinitum.

As "The Man Who Couldn't Be Bought," he made many speeches that projected a crime-free future for the casinos, and in moments of great exhilaration, he even dared the mobsters to show up. The more he talked about them, the more confident and daring he became in his speeches.

However, there was nothing novel about Byrne's warning. In fact, there was a faint echo of plagiarism. Some twenty years before it had worked at the polls for Nevada Governor Grant Sawyer, who had declared in speeches that gangsters weren't welcome in Nevada. "I agree with any measures to keep hoodlums out of Nevada. We might serve notice on underworld characters right now. They are not welcome in Nevada and we aren't going to have them here." The world knows how well the underworld heeded that dictum.

To demonstrate his good intentions, Byrne appointed Joseph P. Lordi to the chairmanship of the newly created Casino Control Commission. What was remarkable about this appointment was that Byrne named Lordi even after State Police Superintendent Clinton Pagano told him that Lordi had failed their background check because of serious questions about his past associations and actions. Some of the information had been obtained from illegal FBI wiretaps of conversations involving Lordi. Other information came from police intelligence files.

Since Byrne was in the midst of his reelection campaign, it was pointed out to him that, at the very least, the appointment could become a major embarrassment. But the governor was adamant and would later tell the press, "I think I got the best man available."

It was at this point that the state police decided to review the 1965 homicide of Richard Brody. On the night that Rona Brody shot and killed her husband, Essex County Prosecutor Brendan Byrne, a friend of the Brody family, personally appeared at the police station and took charge of the case. The killing occurred shortly after Brody had taken out a substantial new life insurance policy with a double-indemnity clause in the event of accidental death. Byrne listed the shooting as "accidental" and personally presented the evidence to the grand jury, which agreed with his findings.

In 1974, when the state police had first looked into the Brody homicide, the file was not with other homicide reports. The state police investigator was told: "No one gets that file. It's in the boss's office." The boss was Joseph Lordi, who had been Byrne's first assistant when he was Essex County prosecutor and had succeeded him in the post. The investigator was later given the file, and in 1978 Lordi would tell two *New York Times* reporters, "I looked into the file and saw what it was about. As far as I was concerned, it was just another case that was presented and everything was in order. . . . I never discussed the Brody affair with Mr. Byrne."

In trying to explain his role in the Brody murder to the two *Times* reporters, Byrne, to quote the *Times,* "offered several conflicting explanations for his appearance at the station house," even though the *Times* had submitted the questions to the governor's office five days before the interview. "At first he said," the *Times* reported, " 'On a Sunday night I might have been covering homicide.' Later he said that the police 'called someone else [in the Prosecutor's Office] and when he didn't answer, they called me.' Later still he recollected, 'I called an assistant that night to handle the case, and when he couldn't be reached, I went to the station house.' Does Governor Byrne have something to hide, or are the discrepancies simply the result of the difficulty of recalling, 13 years later, the normal actions of a suburban prosecutor-politician confronted with a potential scandal?" Byrne didn't think so. "The Brody case is clean," he insisted. "They can look at that case six ways to Christmas and they'll never find anything."

Whatever review the state police made of the Brody case in 1977 was never publicly disclosed. What is known is that State Police Superintendent Pagano, who served at the governor's good graces, soon recanted and publicly endorsed the Lordi appointment.

The Senate Judiciary Committee, whose chairman, Martin Greenberg, was a former law partner and close adviser of Byrne, routinely confirmed Lordi without seeing the report.

The existence of the state police report was first made public in October, when Ray Bateman, Byrne's gubernatorial opponent, brought it up in a campaign speech. The story was then picked up by the *New York Daily News* and given wide coverage. It reported that when John Bartels became director of the federal organized crime task force for New Jersey, he was warned by U.S. Justice Department officials to "stay away from Prosecutor Joseph Lordi and his office." Bartels said the Justice Department considered Lordi too close to the Catena brothers. The FBI and the New York-New Jersey Bistate Waterfront Commission had "illegal tapes" that compromised Lordi and showed him to be untrustworthy.

New Jersey Mafia boss Gerardo "Jerry" Catena, underboss of the Genovese Mafia family, had for years been the most powerful mobster operating in New Jersey. While he was Essex County Prosecutor, Joseph Lordi had approved a gun permit for an old friend, who happened to be a Catena soldier. Back in 1964, while serving as director of the State Alcoholic Beverage Commission, Lordi had hired a Catena associate as a commission investigator, and one of Lordi's brothers had worked as a bartender in a Catena restaurant. And Lordi himself had frequented bars and restaurants that were reputed hangouts for mobsters.

Even more damaging was the disclosure that his law firm, in which he was a full partner, though most of the work was done by his brother James, had represented the Catena family in setting up Best Sales, a food brokerage business fronted by Jerry Catena's brother, Gene.

What ensued could be characterized as a textbook example of what happens when the Mafia branches out into the legitimate marketplace. In the spring of 1964 the Catena brothers contracted with the North American Chemical Company and its subsidiary, Ecology Corporation of America, both of Paterson, New Jersey, to wholesale a detergent that was sold under two labels, Ecolo-G and Bohack. For salesmen the Catenas used members of their crime family and representatives of the Amalgamated Meat Cutters and Butcher Workmen and of the Teamsters. Both unions had workers in food chain stores in New Jersey.

This sales force began moving the product into food marts. The sales pitch was that there were "good people" in Best Sales, and "they're friends of ours." Most store managers got the message and laid in an ample supply of the detergent.

Delighted with their initial success, the Catenas decided that their next step would be to persuade the Great Atlantic and Pacific Tea Company to handle the product. At first it seemed A & P was seriously considering it, but after tests disclosed that the detergent was inferior to other brands, it refused to stock the product.

When the Catenas heard rumors that A & P had rejected their detergent because the food chain had learned that the Catenas controlled Best Sales, Gene Catena swore to "knock A & P's brains out." That's when the trouble began.

On a spring night in 1964 a fire bomb was tossed into an A & P store in Yonkers, New York. The store burned to the ground. A month later, a Molotov cocktail destroyed an A & P store in Peekskill, New York. In quick succession, A & P stores in Manhattan and the Bronx were gutted.

When executives of the food chain failed to get the message, a more direct approach was taken. On the evening of January 23, 1965 Manager James B. Walsh closed his Brooklyn A & P store and headed home in his car. A few blocks from the store, one of his tires went flat, and he got out to fix it. A moment later a car pulled up, three men emerged, and shot Walsh to death. On February 5, Manager John P. Mossner left his A & P store in the Bronx and got as far as his own driveway before a gunman stepped out of the shadows and killed him. Two months later, another A & P store in the Bronx was destroyed by a fire bomb.

To increase the pressure on A & P, the butchers' union, which had begun negotiations on a new labor contract, threatened to strike after the chain rejected what it considered "outrageous" demands, and the Teamsters announced they would not cross the picket lines.

In desperation, the A & P sought help from the Justice Department. In less than a month, federal investigators, working with informants, had linked the terrorism to the Catenas' detergent sales campaign. U.S. Attorney Robert Morgenthau summoned Jerry Catena before a federal grand jury. That was the day the terror ended.

Even the butchers signed the contract they had earlier rejected. When a federal investigator ran into Jerry Catena a few days later, he asked how the detergent business was going. "I'm getting out of detergent," Catena replied.

Two innocent men were murdered and property valued at $60 million was destroyed by arson, and yet, because the government wouldn't jeopardize its informants by bringing them into court, the cost to Jerry Catena was nothing more serious than the minor inconvenience of appearing before a grand jury. Meanwhile, the consumer, too, was affected: In March 1970, the Food and Drug Administration ordered Ecolo-G and Bohack off store shelves and charged that the products should have been labeled as dangerous to users. The lesson of this case is twofold: it shows what can happen when mobsters get into legitimate business, and how inadequate the law is in dealing with the problems they create.

In response to the state police report, Joseph Lordi called the charges politically motivated. "The mere fact that you rub shoulders with somebody or eat in his restaurant doesn't make you an associate," he said at a news conference. While not denying the allegations, Lordi said, "If you lived in the Ironbound section [of Newark], it was a hopping area. You lived in a completely different era in the 1950s. . . . This was the environment that I was born and raised in. I am sure that there are other bars that I went to that might be controlled by organized crime. . . . Don't ask me to identify them."

As for Best Sales, he pointed out that his law firm had represented a member of the Catena family but only on civil matters. No one asked him if he were aware of Best Sales's record in the marketplace. In fact, no one in the media seemed to know about it, for it was never brought up.

Then Lordi gave the media something to ponder. "There is nothing in that article that would in any way prevent me from doing my job completely and with integrity," he said. "Is there anything in that article that charges I committed a crime, did anything improper, or had a conflict of interest?"

The press conference was held at Morven, the governor's mansion in Princeton, and was attended by Byrne, state Attorney General William F. Hyland, and Superintendent Pagano, all of whom vigorously endorsed Lordi.

After Lordi was sworn in at the state house, he told cheering legislators, "Who would have believed that when I was shooting craps on the sidewalks of Newark, someday I would control gambling?"

As established by law, the Casino Control Commission was composed of five members, with a full-time chairman paid $60,000 a year and four part-time members paid $18,000 each. Two of the part-time members were Republicans: Kenneth MacDonald, the commission's vice-chairman, was the mayor of Haddonfield and the owner of a Ford dealership; Albert Merck was a director of and heir to the Merck pharmaceutical empire. The Democrats were Prospero DeBona, an attorney who served on the state Board of Higher Education, and Alice Corsey, a housewife who fulfilled Byrne's desire for a representative mix: she was a woman and she was black.

None of the four part-timers knew the first thing about gambling, nor of the complexities of operating a casino, nor of how to implement the mind-boggling set of rules devised by a horse-trading legislature. MacDonald said gambling was "too fast" for him; Mrs. Corsey said she knew little about it; Merck had voted against the referendum; and DeBona said he once visited a casino in Venice but "couldn't understand what anyone was saying." DeBona was so little interested in serving on the commission that it was only Byrne's dangling a judgeship that kept him on it after his first year.

All the better for Lordi in his role of *primus inter pares*. By virtue of his twenty years in law enforcement, his street-smart upbringing, his dominating personality, his umbilical tie to the governor, and the fact that he was the only full-time member, he was in position to assume total control of the commission, taking action without bothering to consult his colleagues. His first move in that direction was to handpick the commission's staff, making it responsible to him and no one else. His first two appointments were Joseph Fusco and Benjamin Cohen, both of whom had been assistant prosecutors under him.

The media would soon be praising him as "Casino Czar," but Lordi was the governor's man, and no one knew whose man Byrne was. Still, it was a catchy title and made for good copy. But when it came down to it, there was only one real czar of gambling, and that was the industry itself. Resorts International would prove that soon enough.

12

The Man from Nevada

Resorts International filed the first application to operate a Boardwalk casino in Atlantic City. On December 22, 1977, Resorts Board Chairman James Crosby handed Joseph Lordi a check for $100,000, a nonrefundable deposit that would finally put the wheels in the licensing process into motion.

Although the meeting in Lordi's temporary office in Trenton was amiable enough, with Crosby's attorney, Joel Sterns, asking in jest if he could use his credit card, there was a sense of urgency in the air. Advocates of legalized gambling appeared to be gaining headway in Florida, New York, Hawaii, Connecticut, Massachusetts, Vermont, Maryland, and even in the Poconos, which was not all that far away. Not to be ignored was the Bahamian government which was on the verge of expropriating Resorts' Paradise Island casino-hotel.

And to top it off, others in Atlantic City were anxiously waiting in the wings. Caesars World, Inc., which owned Caesars Palace in Las Vegas, was planning an extravaganza on the site of the old Traymore Hotel; Bally Manufacturing Corporation of Chicago, the world's largest manufacturer of slot machines, had taken a long-term lease on the Marlborough-Blenheim Hotel; Playboy Enterprises, Inc., was going to build a $69 million establishment on a site near Convention Hall, and Penthouse was to follow suit with a $50 million operation on the site of the old Mayflower Hotel. At least a dozen others were waiting to see how Resorts fared in its licensing hearings before undertaking a final commitment.

So right from the start, a lot was riding on the commission's performance, and Resorts was to be the lucky benefactor of this pressure play. To gain more time on its competition, Resorts decided to restore the 1000-room Chalfonte-Haddon Hall instead of putting up a new hotel. Not only would it save millions, but it would give them at least a year's head start—in corporate terms, a monopoly that would make possible revenues of $200 million from a captive marketplace.

Also of great help in giving Resorts a clear field was the amendment to the Casino Control Act proposed by Senator McGahn. It increased a hotel-casino's required minimum number of rooms from 400 to 500, which meant that Resorts was the only company with a hotel large enough to qualify. The others, stuck with smaller hotels, who thought they could build additions, were told to tear them down and start from scratch. Governor Byrne had decided he wanted new buildings, no more "patch-and-paint" jobs. Even historic landmarks like the Marlborough-Blenheim Hotel, with its lovely rotunda, would soon vanish in great blasts of smoke and dust.

In the meantime other forces were coming into play. The Division of Gaming Enforcement was gearing up for its role in the investigation of applicants. The newly appointed director, Robert P. Martinez, was sent halfway around the world to visit casinos. "He learned more about the intricacies of casino gambling than anybody else in the state," his boss, Attorney General Hyland, assured the press.

That may have been true in New Jersey, but what did Martinez really know about putting together an investigative team that was sophisticated enough to delve into the background and operating procedures of multinational corporations? What did he know about the day-to-day operation of a casino? What did he know about skimming—the taking of money from the top without reporting it as income—that could be done in a hundred ways, from outright stealing from the counting room to phony credit, falsified markers, bogus fill slips, and countless other ways, many still unknown to law enforcement? What did he know about the ways employees ripped off the casinos, or how mobsters and drug dealers conspired with casinos to launder illegal money? And what did anybody in Trenton know about the awesome task of policing an operation of this magnitude?

To get some of the answers, Martinez went to Las Vegas and hired Dennis Gomes, who was chief of the audit division of the Nevada Gaming Control Board, the investigative arm of the gaming commission. Gomes had six years of expertise in auditing casinos which knew how to hide hoodlums in the woodwork and defraud the government out of its fair share of their gross revenues.

By the time Martinez got to him, Gomes had pretty much worn out his welcome in Nevada. His hard-nosed methods were resented by the casino industry, which has always run the show in that state. Except for sporadic intrusions by the federal government and nosey reporters, the marriage of state and industry was the kind that used to be made in heaven. The control board and gaming commission had a silent agreement with the governor not to rock the boat.

Twenty years ago Governor Sawyer articulated his philosophy: "Our attitude toward life, save under the most urgent provocation, is relaxed, tolerant, and mindful that if others are allowed to go on their way unmolested, a man stands a chance of getting through the world himself with a minimum of irritation."

Either Gomes was unaware of this golden rule, or he had ignored it when an informant tipped him off that the Stardust, owned by the Argent Corporation, was skimming money from slot machine returns. After two raids by his men on the Stardust cashier's cage and counting room drew blanks, Gomes led his own team of investigators in an evening raid and discovered that bags of quarters had been secreted in the Stardust's auxiliary vault without being recorded. A search at another Argent casino, the Fremont, yielded similar unrecorded caches. After a lengthy investigation, Gomes reported that the skimming of the slot machines at both casinos—accomplished by rigging the scales to underweigh the coins—amounted to $12 million.

Gomes had then turned his attention to the Aladdin hotel-casino. The investigation revealed that Detroit and St. Louis mobsters were skimming money through lines of credit.

The gaming commission's new chairman, Harry Reid, chose to ignore Gomes's report, only to be embarrassed in 1979 when the federal government convicted four Detroit mobsters of illegally managing the Aladdin. In handing down the sentences, Federal Judge John Feikens said he "was surprised to hear counsel argue that these men have committed no crime under Nevada law. The state of Nevada seems to be reluctant to prosecute offenses committed under its own laws." Feikens noted the lack of case references on any similar offense.

A lawyer and politician, Harry Reid was casino-industry-oriented. He not only rejected Gaming Control Board reports of wrongdoing but didn't hesitate to criticize publicly the board's investigation. There began a mass exodus of board investigators, some joining law firms, others going to work for casinos. For them, it was a case of switching sides and getting the money, for they knew they couldn't beat the industry working for the state.

It was at this point that Dennis Gomes decided to give New Jersey a try. His new boss, Robert Martinez, placed him in charge of the Special Investigations Bureau of the Division of Gaming Enforcement. His salary of $40,000 was nearly double his old one. Even more encouraging, he was given the freedom to hire his own agents, allowed a meaningful budget, and given enthusiastic assurances that it was going to be his baby, to operate as he saw fit.

He was told he could forget about political pressure, for New Jersey was not like Nevada where gambling was *the* industry and everything else was ancillary to it. New Jersey was an industrialized state and gambling revenues were going to be minuscule by comparison. Therefore, the casino industry's political clout would be too weak to pressure unduly the forces of state government. Here was Dennis Gomes's chance to really fight the bad guys, be a crusader.

The first inkling that there was more to these promises than a sweet dream came when Resorts International realized that builders, with the proper incentive, work faster than investigators.

By the first of May, 1978, the thousand rooms of the old Chalfonte-Haddon Hall had been reduced to 566 to allow for the casino, restaurants, shops, and the required minimum space of 325 square feet in each room. The casino was ready, the gaming tables and slot machines in place, two of the six restaurants already open, along with an arcade of exclusive shops. A truckload of chips had been delivered, and 400 trainee dealers and croupiers were anxiously awaiting their debut. All that remained before the hotel could open its doors to the public were a few finishing touches. A little paint here and there, corridor ceilings lowered to cover water pipes, and the sprinkler systems required by new fire codes.

The commission had already ruled on questions dealing with the hotel's decor, size of outdoor signs, size and color of gambling chips, number of tables and slot machines it could operate, and even the amount slot machines would pay back—83 percent, which meant that every time a bettor dropped a coin in a one-armed bandit, the house took 17 percent.

Resorts was aiming for a Memorial Day opening date. All it

needed was a license from the Casino Control Commission. And all the commission needed was for the Division of Gaming Enforcement to complete its numerous and seemingly endless investigations, not only of Resorts itself, but of the nearly 2500 employees who had to undergo careful background checks, along with the 300 vendors who had applied for casino service industry licenses.

That was when Dennis Gomes heard the first shoe drop. Back in March, at Resorts' request, Governor Byrne had pushed a bill through the legislature that gave the commission the power to issue a temporary license that would allow Resorts to open its casino before the division completed its investigations.

To prod the commission along in its decision, Resorts began a campaign of publicly criticizing the division's investigation, charging that it was taking too long and costing too much—by law, Resorts had to reimburse the state for its cost, which eventually would total nearly a million dollars.

Resorts apparently began concentrating on the governor through its formidable legal and political connections, because Byrne's new attorney general, John Degnan, soon was lobbying in favor of the temporary license as the answer to everybody's problems. It would give New Jersey a leg up on any other state that was considering casino gambling; Resorts' early success would demonstrate to potential but still hesitant investors that Atlantic City was the place for them; it would take the heat off the governor; give the division more time to complete its probe; and the state could start taxing that golden goose. Best of all, this premature opening would in no way compromise law enforcement safeguards in favor of economic benefits.

While this was going on in the spring of 1978, other matters were being decided by the commission in heated discussions with Resorts executives and attorneys. They involved the number and kind of gaming tables, the size of the staff needed, security measures, and where Resorts could buy its slot machines: the commission waived a rule that prohibited a casino from buying more than half of its slot machines from any one source and allowed it to buy all of them from Bally. The licensing requirements on hundreds of ancillary companies were also waived, and the commission licensed pit bosses and other key casino employees, even though they had not filed the required financial statements. For the time being, Resorts wasn't required to use percentage payout meters on its slot machines, as long as they promised that their payout would exceed the required 83 percent, but it would later be shown that it didn't live up to the state's requirement.

The most heatedly contested issue involved minimum and maximum bets required at certain games. Resorts wanted high minimums at blackjack and crap tables, arguing that it would keep the inexperienced players from mixing with high-stake gamblers. Commissioner Al Merck, who would become the panel's gadfly, pointed out that since there was no competition in Atlantic City, as there was in Nevada, players would be forced to play high-stakes games they couldn't afford. Or be driven to "sucker" games like big six wheel and the slots.

On the other hand, Resorts wanted low maximums to prevent a gambler on a hot streak from making a quick kill. What they wanted was the best of both worlds: small maximums that would allow time to take its toll on anyone on a hot roll, and high minimums that would force players to lose their money in a hurry, so they could make room for the next loser.

Finally it was decided that half the tables would carry one- and two-dollar minimums. Resorts President Jack Davis and attorney Joel Sterns jumped up and announced they were shocked, then proceeded to advance their favorite argument: if they were forced to have such low minimums, no other casino operator would invest in Atlantic City. In fact, Davis declared, if they had known about this rule, they never would have invested $50 million themselves. At this point, Resorts Chairman James Crosby leaned toward Sterns and said, "I have serious reservations about opening with dollar minimums."

It was the commission's turn to be shocked. And the waves would stun the governor, legislators, and the good people of Atlantic City who had been waiting with bated breath since the passage of the referendum. It was unthinkable. Crosby's remark, in contract terms, was a deal breaker, or, in this case, a deal maker, for the commission's opposition promptly collapsed. On opening day, there wouldn't be a single dollar-minimum sign in view, and 90 percent of the tables would require a five-dollar minimum or more. In practice, the five-dollar minimum would be abruptly jacked up to twenty-five—against the law, of course, but jacked up nonetheless—if players at a certain table suddenly got too lucky.

On May 14 Lordi announced that the commission would decide the issue of a *temporary* license at its May 25 hearing, a Friday, and one day before Resorts' projected Memorial Day weekend opening. All that was needed was a majority of three votes. At this late stage of the game, it was unthinkable that the license would be withheld.

The crowd that gathered at Resorts' doors on May 26, 1978, was not disappointed, although thousands had to stand in line for three and four hours for their chance to make a run at the house. All pretenses to Monte Carlo had vanished. People were dressed for action: Levis, T-shirts, Bermuda shorts, Hawaiian shirts, cheap polyester leisure suits, all the trappings of a working-class clientele.

Inside the casino, pandemonium reigned. Customers were jammed twenty deep at the tables, aisles and slot machine areas were jammed, the casino was blue with smoke. The noise level of the 900 slot machines, of gamblers exhorting their dice, and of music blaring from the cocktail lounge had reached a numbing crescendo, but no one wanted to leave. An army of breast-and-buttock-baring cocktail waitresses, their high-heeled shoes sinking into the deep carpeting, stumbled along with trays of drinks for the tables. People with money clutched in their fists pushed and shoved and fought for a chance to get at a table. Before the day was out, they would lose nearly a million dollars.

The "land rush" was on again in Atlantic City. Resorts' stocks crashed through the ceiling. In fact, all casino stocks skyrocketed during the summer of 1978, gaining a billion dollars' worth of market value. It was like a turn-of-the-century gold rush. Fly-by-night operators, with options on land already optioned by someone else, saw their stock double and triple overnight. It was the kind of gold fever that infects small investors, the poor people who raid their saving accounts or cash in perfectly safe stocks and bonds for get-rich-quick pie-in-the-sky deals.

Overnight, Resorts' Class A stock, selling at just $2 in 1976, skyrocketed to $210 and its Class B shares from around $2 to $185. It soared for a while, then split three for one, and still hovered around $60 before crashing to earth.

The people who were to make Resorts richer in its first year of operation by $200 million in revenues were again the losers. At its annual meeting in 1979, Resorts rejected the pleas of its stockholders for a dividend. And the stockholders, who were holding 2,954,832 Class A shares, which had only one hundredth the voting power of the 332,415 Class B shares held by Resorts' close-knit board of directors, were powerless to do anything about it.

It wasn't long before Resorts was in trouble. During the 1978

Fourth of July holiday, Giuseppe and Rosario Gambino and their party were treated to four days of free rooms, food, and drink by Resorts. The *Press* was the first to learn of their visit, which came as news to commission inspectors assigned to the casino and to Intertel, the Resorts subsidiary which provides security for the casino.

In June Resorts had been charged with 20 violations of credit regulations and improper procedures in the "count" room. Several Resorts employees, including Jack Davis, entered the vault when the count of money was under way. It appeared to the state police that "everyone could walk into the counting room as he saw fit." Credit violations included the granting of credit before proper forms were filled out.

Resorts asked for a hearing to discuss the "streamlining" of regulations pertaining to credit, the handling of cash and chips, the counting of gambling receipts, authorized personnel and clothing worn in the room and storage of both money and cashboxes. The hearing officer, Commissioner Kenneth MacDonald, reduced the fines from $195,000 to $39,000, but Joel Sterns still wasn't satisfied, arguing that any fines would be setting a precedent. "I'm not talking as if $39,000 is a lot," he said. "I'm talking because it is the beginning of a long road."

That long road would soon become a well-traveled one. On the eve of its permanent licensing hearings that were to begin in January 1979, Resorts was back before the commission responding to more serious charges. Both Crosby and Davis were there to deny that their corporation had ever attempted to mislead the commission. Though they had known that $179,000 was missing from their slot machine operation in July 1978 when they had received permission from the commission to nearly double the size of their casino and had added 158 slot machines, they hadn't told the commission of the missing money because they hadn't fully investigated the loss themselves. Crosby said he couldn't see any relationship between the two events. Davis was more direct. "It was our money," he said. "It wasn't anybody else's. In fact, we may have overpaid the public."

There was also the question of somebody making off with a tray of chips valued at $14,260. And allegations that Resorts employed unlicensed casino and hotel workers and violated internal accounting controls procedures, and that the executive in charge of the casino had lied to the commission concerning his duties in the casino. Resorts, said the division report, "abused the privilege granted to it by the commission to operate a casino in New Jersey,'' and it called for ''severe sanctions.''

In Resorts' defense, Jack Davis said he had told Robert Martinez, the division's director, that the firm couldn't follow the ''letter of the law'' and handle the overwhelming crowds. The conversation had taken place in the baccarat pit during the first days of operation.

''He [Martinez] said,'' Davis told the commission, '' 'Well, you have to do what you have to do, and if you commit some violations, you will, down the road a couple of months, get'—I don't remember if he said traffic violations or speeding tickets—'you'll get some minor discipline and it will all be in the past.' It was certainly clear to me from his answer that the proper course to follow was to meet the demands of business. There was no indication that we should close up if we couldn't live up to the letter of the law.''

In all there were eight major violations with possible fines of nearly $1 million, but in the end they were reduced to $144,000, which Vice-Chairman Kenneth MacDonald termed ''severe monetary sanctions.'' But Joel Sterns was delighted, calling the reduction a ''significant finding in our favor.''

By then Resorts could well afford any fine the commission saw fit to impose. In June 1978 the casino's average daily win had been more than $750,000, which set a new worldwide record in gambling revenues. In the first three months of operations, its total wins were $62.8 million. To get a perspective on this figure, the MGM Grand in Las Vegas, which was the nation's biggest volume-producing casino in 1977, had a gross win of about $84 million *for the entire year*, and the gross earnings of Resorts' Paradise Island casino for that year were $22 million.

Of the 75,000 people who passed through Resorts' casino on an average day in the summer of 1978, more than 11,000 people gambled at the 84 tables and the rest played the slots. In dividing the take, 55.3 percent came from the slots and the rest from the tables.

In September Joseph Lordi went before the Assembly's State Government Committee to ask for amendments in the casino act. He wanted the commission to be made more self-sustaining and for the chairman, not the entire commission, to have the authority to issue licenses to casino employees not directly related to gambling, such as cocktail waitresses.

His proposals, Lordi said, were designed so that ''the goals of the act may be more expeditiously achieved without unduly affecting the basic concept of strict control.'' He also wanted the commission to be granted the powers of discretion in deciding whether people formerly convicted of certain crimes could be licensed to work in a casino or casino-related industry. The present law automatically disqualified anyone with a criminal record. Lordi cited several cases where he believed the applicant had been rehabilitated. ''There's no question in my mind,'' he said, ''that the tools are there [in the Casino Act] to keep out organized crime.''

For Special Investigations Chief Dennis Gomes, the sweet dream was turning into a nightmare. He'd had his fill of Martinez and his assistant, Pete Richards, who was called ''Repeat'' because he followed Martinez around like a puppy dog and re-said everything he said.

Martinez had unprofessional habits that disturbed Gomes. His idea of a good time was to take a carload of agents and tour the red-light district in Trenton. On an investigative trip to Florida, Martinez wanted another investigator to go with him to Paradise Island to pick up women. Another time he was drunk on the casino floor. Some mornings he would come to work with his clothes rumpled as if he had been out all night. This was not the kind of behavior expected from the head of the division. It was not the kind of behavior that Gomes would have tolerated from any of the agents in his Special Investigations Bureau.

It had taken Gomes nearly six months to find and train the 28 men who formed his unit, which he thought was the best ever assembled anywhere. He had created teams to investigate specific areas: financial stability, organized crime associations, stock manipulation, and the most dangerous of all, political corruption. But hovering over his shoulder were Martinez and Repeat, who always wanted to know what he was doing, which was contrary to the promises that he would have complete control of his unit. The more nosey Martinez became, the more secretive was Gomes, and the more nervous in turn was Martinez.

Still Gomes was making progress. In the summer of 1978, when he thought he was ready, Gomes picked ten agents, and they raided Resorts' casino on Paradise Island. Knowing that customs officials were paid off in the Bahamas, Gomes cooked up phony identifications and they went through customs in pairs. The raid came as a total surprise. First they raided the casino and the cashier's cage, then they headed for the corporate offices and seized some twenty file cabinets. All hell broke loose. Executives were calling New York and Atlantic City for help. Gomes was told he couldn't go into the files until the next morning. Gomes agreed and promptly sealed all the cabinets so nobody could get into them.

The next morning, Gomes and his men were up bright and early. What they found was so politically explosive that it sealed their doom instead of the people they were investigating. Gomes was reluctant to go into detail, but admitted that what he found concerned the possibility of bribes having been paid to New Jersey officials and politicians who were involved in the enactment of the referendum and the Casino Control Act. He found numerous memos concerning Patrick McGahn and Marvin Perskie that indicated continuous discussions with their politician relatives.

When he returned to Trenton, he wanted to start an investigation to determine if any financial transactions had taken place between the politicians and their relatives employed by Resorts. "That's when the shit hit the fan," Gomes recalled.

Not only was the investigation dropped, but Martinez disbanded Gomes's Special Investigations Bureau and placed him under the supervision of a state trooper, with a different organization structure. Gomes's agents, with their sophisticated expertise in casino controls, found themselves doing background checks of casino employees not directly related to gambling. Investigations that had been pursued for months were dropped or permanently "put on the back burner," which became a popular euphemism at the Division of Gaming Enforcement. When questioned about it later, Martinez's stock answer was that it was a matter of judgment, that time and money were better utilized elsewhere.

To make matters worse, from the beginning there was a built-in acrimony between the accountants and the troopers. The troopers resented the accountants because they earned more money, and the accountants resented the cockiness of the troopers who were always bragging about how fast they could drive to Atlantic City without getting a speeding ticket.

Meeting in secret, Gomes and his men decided to hire a Trenton attorney to represent them before Attorney General Degnan. Their demand was naive: unless Martinez was removed they would tell the press how the investigation was being sabotaged. If they had any hopes of ever working again in the state of New Jersey, the Trenton attorney told them, they had better forget it.

Gomes decided to return to Las Vegas. In September he packed his bags and said goodbye to New Jersey. Within weeks most of his investigators had left. None were ever debriefed on what they had learned about Resorts in the months they had worked with Gomes.

Back home Gomes decided it was time that he used his expertise, which qualified him as one of the country's leading experts in casino controls, to his own advantage. In no time he was executive vice-president of the Frontier Hotel, a subsidiary of Howard Hughes's Summa Corporation, where he increased profits by 400 percent, adding $24 million in incremental profits.

Meanwhile, tremendous economic and political pressures were being exerted in Trenton to get the commission to begin its hearings. In late November Governor Byrne took a hand in the matter and told Attorney General Degnan to get the division's investigation report to the commission.

"The best thing you can do is recommend they get a license," Byrne allegedly told him. "The next best thing is recommend they don't. Either way, get the damned investigation over with."

Less than a week later, on December 4, the commission had the report and Degnan had issued a press release stating that it had 17 exceptions to the licensing of Resorts to operate a casino in Atlantic City. And it recommended that Resorts be denied a permanent license.

Shock waves permeated the Trenton bureaucracy and Atlantic City. No license for Resorts? Who would believe it? Not Resorts certainly. Nor Dennis Gomes.

If there was one thing Gomes knew, it was that the temporary license had corrupted the licensing process by throwing the burden of proof back on the state.

Here was a company, employing 4000 people and doing incredible business, paying millions in taxes, and all it was asking was to be allowed to carry on its good work. Not only that, but a dozen other prospective casino builders were awaiting the outcome of the hearing before deciding on whether or not they would invest in the city. When it came right down to it, the Casino Control Commission was not voting on Resorts International's right to operate a casino, but rather on whether or not casino gambling itself would survive in Atlantic City.

The only way Resorts could lose was for the division to produce the most heinous direct evidence of criminality imaginable, and to prove it beyond the slightest doubt. And nobody at the division, Gomes knew, had anything like that. There were no videotapes of casino executives handing bags of money to Mafia bosses, nor were there any signed partnership contracts between Resorts and Meyer Lansky. If any such evidence ever existed, it never came into the division's possession.

There was something almost farcical about the situation that recalled a statement Brendan Byrne had made when he was stumping for gambling during his reelection campaign: ''I think if it's tested in Atlantic City and if it doesn't work, it's easy to get rid of it.''

13

From Paradise to the Boardwalk

Resorts International was doing land-office business on the Board-walk and nobody knew the first thing about its past. Here was a company that had not only been instrumental in the passage of the gambling referendum but had through its contacts with politicians pretty much controlled the language of the legislation that was to govern its operation in Atlantic City, and all that was known was that it operated a casino on Paradise Island in the Bahamas. And the way the boys from Paradise were telling it, integrity was the name of the game down there and the primary reason for their great success in the gambling business.

It was inevitable that the media would start digging into the company's background. Meanwhile, the gaming division had started its investigation which would take a year and cost a million dollars. The result would be a 115-page report that was almost devoid of hard facts and a 13-page Statement of Exception that was even more innocuous.

To understand Resorts and what later transpired during the commission's hearings, it is important to go back in time and examine its performance in the Bahamas. First of all, gambling in the Bahamas was not all that different from gambling in Nevada. In fact, a lot of the same people were involved.

In a way, casino gambling in the Bahamas owes its success to Fidel Castro, who ousted the capitalistic racketeers, gamblers, pimps, prostitutes, hustlers, hoodlums, and the rest of the American road-show from his shores in 1959.

Before then, with the blessings of his good friend dictator Fulgencio Batista, Meyer Lansky had run the show in Cuba from his casino in Havana's Riviera Hotel. He had developed a first-class operation. His team included Dan "Dusty" Peters, the courier who shuttled the money from Cuba to Miami; George Sadlo, his old Las Vegas partner; Dino Cellini, his top lieutenant, and Dino's brother, Eddie, who called himself the world's best croupier; and Frank Ritter, Max Courtney, and Charles Brudner, sports bookmakers who had gained their casino experience at an illegal casino in Saratoga, New York. Lansky's brother Jake was the manager of the "competing" casino in the Hotel Nacional. Untold millions were funneled into the coffers of organized crime in the United States. In Batista's Cuba the Americans had enjoyed the best of all possible worlds: legitimate casinos in which the didn't have to hide behind fronts.

Deprived of this vast income by Castro, Lansky began looking for another haven. He didn't have to look far. There, some sixty miles east of Palm Beach, were the Bahamas, an archipelago of 700 islands and 1800 rocks and cays that fan out from the southern coast of Florida. It was a fortuitous substitute for Cuba: lovely beaches, plenty of blue skies and gentle breezes, close to the mainland, and a corrupt government. The only catch was that casino gambling was forbidden by law. But laws that were made by men could be unmade by the same men, given the proper incentive. In fact, exceptions had been made for a small casino on Cat Cay and the Bahamian Club on the outskirts of Nassau.

The colony was one of the last remaining fragments of the British empire. The political base for the islands' 140,000 people was the United Bahamian party, made up of rich white merchants who ruled from their offices and mansions on Bay Street in the capital city of Nassau on New Providence Island.

By the mid-1960s the Bahamas were the top tax haven in the Western Hemisphere. Bay Street was touted as the Wall Street of the Caribbean. It boasted nearly 300 financial institutions. There were nearly a hundred mutual funds, many of them serving as vehicles for foreign investment in U.S. securities and real estate.

The islands were a tax dodger's paradise. Besides secrecy and freedom from taxes—income, sales, capital gains, dividends, corporate excess profits, you name it—the Bahamas offered U.S. banks a major international market for Eurodollars. As an extra convenience, the registering process for users of Nassau bank shells took place in New York.

The political functionaries, Her Majesty's Loyal, governed the islands more as a plantation than a colony. The premier was Sir Roland Symonette and the Speaker of the Assembly was his son Bobby. But the most powerful functionary was Sir Stafford Sands, the minister of finance and tourism, a millionaire lawyer who exacted whopping legal fees. A loose-jowled, hulking man, Sands has been described as a Sydney Greenstreet character, the movie actor who portrayed the antique collector in *The Maltese Falcon*.

The second most powerful man was an American named Wallace Groves. Also large, jowly, and a lawyer, Groves was a Wall Street high-roller in the late 1930s who came a cropper in 1941 when he was convicted of stock manipulation and mail fraud, and served two years of a four-year sentence. Upon his release he made tracks for the Bahamas and settled on Grand Bahama, one of the northernmost of the islands, uninhabited except for a few natives. During Prohibition it had served as an exchange point for smugglers.

In time Groves and Sir Stafford became close business associates. Another associate was Louis Chesler, a flamboyant hustler who would soon be meeting with Meyer Lansky, who had offered Sir Stafford $2 million worth of "legal fees," to be deposited to his credit in a Swiss bank account in exchange for exclusive gambling rights on the islands. At that time casino gambling was prohibited in the islands. But Lansky's visit got Sir Stafford to thinking about it and he discussed it with his two American friends.

In the winter of 1961, according to a statement Chesler would later give to the Justice Department, a secret meeting was held at the Fontainebleau Hotel in Miami Beach to discuss the implementation of gambling on Grand Bahama. It was attended by Groves, Chesler, Meyer and Jake Lansky, George Sadlo, the Cellini brothers, and several caporegimes of the Genovese family.

Groves and Chesler laid out their plans to build a luxurious hotel, to be named the Lucayan Beach Hotel. Bahamas Amusements Ltd., was formed as the operating company for their new hotel and its casino, the Monte Carlo Room. For his services, Sir Stafford was paid $1,091,900, and five of the nine members of the governor's Executive Council, including Sir Roland Symonette and his son Bobby, became paid Grove consultants.

In its first full year of operation Groves grossed an estimated $20 million, but the amount was not disclosed. He spent $1.5 million on junkets for high-rollers, and though Lansky was not visibly on the scene, his men were in charge of the casino and looking out for their boss's interest. Each was raking off salaries and bonuses that amounted to $330,000, most of it kicked back to Lansky as part of the skim.

The Monte Carlo Room was such a smashing success that Bahamas Amusements was soon building another one, which was called El Casino. By then, however, Chesler, whose wealth and various expertises had made Groves's dream possible, had had a falling out with Groves and was sent packing, poorer in money by some $12 million, but richer in experience.

Grand Bahama was a smashing success. Big American industries moved to take advantage of Freeport's tax-free guarantees. By the end of 1966 it was estimated that $480 million had been invested in Groves's fiefdom.

Early in 1967, Chesler bluntly told the Royal Commission of Inquiry—appointed to investigate political corruption—he had sought Lansky's advice in setting up the Monte Carlo Room because he was a "dean of gambling." Organizing a large-scale gambling operation was "no easy job." They needed the advice of an expert. As for George Sadlo's duties, Chesler said, "George Sadlo was in complete control of the hiring and firing of employees" in the casino.

There was no question that Meyer Lansky was the premier expert of legal and illegal gambling. But Lansky, born Maier Suchowljansky in Poland, began as a contract killer, having formed the Bug and Meyer Mob with Benjamin "Bugsy" Siegel in the early 1930s. Yet Lansky's record shows only seven arrests, on charges ranging up to murder, and only one conviction—for a minor gambling charge. He served three months. The closest he came to a serious charge was in 1926 when a man named John Barrett was taken for a gangland ride, shot in the head, and dumped from the car. He survived and named Lansky as his assailant, but later refused to sign the complaint when someone tried to poison him with strychnine as he lay in his hospital bed.

It was Lansky who ordered the murder of his partner Bugsy Siegel after Siegel, with Lansky's backing, had built the Flamingo, Las Vegas's first plush gambling joint. But the Flamingo was not the end of Lansky's involvement in Las Vegas. Through George Sadlo, both Meyer and Jake Lansky controlled the Thunderbird Hotel, which had

Cliff Jones, a former lieutenant governor of Nevada, as one of its major stockholders. Lansky's influence was felt from one end of the Vegas Strip to the other. He was the Mob's adviser in the construction of the Desert Inn, Sands, Tropicana, Stardust, Riviera, Caesars Palace—and the Fremont, the first high-rise in the downtown Glitter Gulch section.

In 1959 Huntington Hartford, the A & P heir, bought a little island just across Nassau Harbor and changed its name from Hog to Paradise. His dream was to transform it into the Monaco of the Caribbean. In his enthusiasm, he poured several millions into its development before realizing that he had made a serious miscalculation in the matter of "legal fees," having contributed $15,000 to the Progressive Liberal Party (PLP) and its leader, Lynden O. Pindling, a black activist, and the archrival of the Bay Street Boys' United Bahamian Party.

Besides a gambling permit, Hartford needed a bridge to connect his little inlet to Nassau. Assisting him in this endeavor was Seymour "Sy" Alter, who had been with the eccentric heir through thick and thin for decades. Burly, with a smashed nose, he looked more like a movie thug than a millionaire's alter ego. Someone once said he looked "as if somebody had stepped on his face."

When Alter's dealings with Sir Stafford for a gambling permit reached an impasse, Hartford took his problem to Sam Golub and Alvin Malnik at the Fontainebleau Hotel in Miami. Golub was said to have good connections with Sir Stafford. And Malnik, a lawyer, was recognized by anyone who knew anything about organized crime as Meyer Lansky's heir apparent.

Hartford signed a contract with Golub and Malnik, calling for a substantial fee if they could get him his permit. When nothing happened and he heard that Groves was building a casino, he again importuned Sir Stafford and was told to get a suitable partner. That was when Alter was approached by Malnik and told that he had a potential partner for Paradise Island. Malnik took Alter to a restaurant in Miami and introduced him to Lansky. Alter would later say under oath that he had told Lansky that Hartford wouldn't deal with him. Malnik has denied the story.

It was not long after this incident that the Mary Carter Paint Company came into the picture. Based in Tampa, it was a small company with big ideas. Its board chairman, James M. Crosby, was anxious to diversify his holdings.

By 1963, Crosby and Irving George "Jack" Davis, the company's president, having agreed that paint offered a limited future, decided to branch out into land development. They came to Grand Bahama and purchased 3500 acres from Groves and went on to build a residential development called Queens Cove.

As luck would have it, Huntington Hartford was looking for someone to bail him out. Despite the $30 million the supermarket heir had supposedly plowed into his Paradise playground, he was no closer to attaining gambling and bridge permits than he had been the day he bought the island.

In 1965, after Hartford indicated his interest in selling the island, Crosby met with Sir Stafford who presented him with another form of partnership. For $750,000 Mary Carter would get the Certificate of Exemption that belonged to the small Bahamian Club in Nassau, which Mary Carter could operate until the Paradise Island hotel-casino was ready to open, at which time the certificate would be transferred. Approval for the bridge was granted by the government, which had now decided that the span across the harbor would not pose a hazard to shipping.

The negotiations were going along painlessly until Sir Stafford announced that the paint company would have to yield four-ninths of the casino and all of its management to Groves's Bahamas Amusements, which would hold the license. Crosby reluctantly agreed to the terms and Sir Stafford received $240,000 in "legal fees." Within weeks Mary Carter was in the gambling business at the Bahamian Club. The manager was Eddie Cellini, who ran the place with personnel sent by his brother Dino. Eddie and his crew were slated to run the Paradise casino when it opened and had been cut in for a flat 15 percent of the gross gambling profits.

After having been deported from the Bahamas as a result of complaints by U.S. agencies, Dino Cellini had opened a croupier school in London to train Europeans for work in Bahamian casinos. Then when the British banned him from their country, he returned to Miami to operate Lansky's international gambling junket business. Since two-thirds of all casino profits in the Bahamas came from junkets, it was not too difficult to assess Dino's importance to casino operators.

In January 1966 the U.S. Justice Department sent Robert D. Peloquin, a lawyer in the Organized Crime and Racketeering Division, to the Bahamas to check out some of the reports they were receiving from Florida informants. Upon his return, Peloquin reported that "Mary Carter Paints will be in control of Paradise Island with the exception of the casino which Groves will control. The atmosphere seems ripe for a Lansky skim."

Slowly at first, then like an avalanche, stories about gangsters and corrupt politicians in the Bahamas started breaking in the press, which resulted in the overthrow of the Bay Street Boys and the election of Lynden O. Pindling and his Progressive Liberal party.

The Americans running Pindling's political campaign were David Probinsky, a bankrupt Miami nightclub operator, and Mike McLaney, who financed the campaign almost single-handedly. To some, it was a mystery where McLaney got the money. However, it was known that McLaney was a former Lansky gambling associate in Cuba and later in Haiti, and that Lansky wanted to back a leader with grass-roots support.

Stafford Sands retired to Spain to spend his remaining years in luxurious exile. Groves received $80 million from Benquet, a Philippines mining corporation, for his interests on Grand Bahama, and $1 million from Mary Carter for his interest in Paradise Island.

In his campaign Pindling had often said, "How long will it be before we have a Mafia-run casino in every hotel? It could be Las Vegas all over again—but at least in Las Vegas a good deal of the money gets back to the people." But now, ensconced in the seat of power, he preached caution. "There will be no compromise on the undesirable element. They must go. But I don't want to close the casinos right away. That might be disastrous to the economy of the islands."

In May 1968 Crosby dumped Mary Carter for $9.9 million and three months later Resorts International was born, with a mandate that envisioned a gambling cartel with casinos in all the glamour capitals of the world. Resorts visited Tunisia, Greece, Yugoslavia, the Philippines, and Haiti—years later, a *Washington Post* story charged Resorts offered Papa Doc Duvalier a bribe for the rights to open a casino, but Resorts denied it.

How Resorts financed its new operation was something that had greatly interested Dennis Gomes. Some of the machinations were later outlined in the gaming division's report: "In order to commence casino operations in the Bahamas, Mary Carter Paint Co. raised approximately $24,000,000 during a two-year period, and a substantial amount of these funds were received by or through the efforts of persons or organizations of unsuitable character and nature.''

The report went on to name nearly a score of brokers, dealers, bankers, or lawyers who had been suspended, disciplined, or had their license revoked by the Securities and Exchange Commission, had pleaded guilty to violations of criminal banking laws, maintained associations with at least seven persons convicted of criminal offenses, or were close friends of Meyer Lansky.

It was at the time of Resorts' founding that Crosby decided to hire Robert Peloquin, who had since left the Justice Department. He created International Intelligence, Inc. (Intertel), which would soon become known as the world's most mysterious private superspy organization. Peloquin recruited chiefs and directors of the government's most sophisticated intelligence agencies, from the National Security Agency to the IRS, FBI, Narcotics Bureau, Secret Service, State Department experts on different areas of the world, Interpol, Customs Bureau, SEC, CIA, and even J. Edgar Hoover's only nephew. On the business end, Intertel directors included men who were, or had been, president of the Dreyfus Corporation, publisher of *Life*, president of Carte Blanche, board chairman of the Royal Bank of Canada Trust Company, vice-chairman of R. H. Macy, and director of the Prudential Life Insurance Company.

In the words of Jim Hougan, an expert on private intelligence agencies, Intertel ''is nothing less than the legal incorporation of an old-boy network whose ganglia reach into virtually every nerve cell of the federal investigative/intelligence community.'' However noble its declared intentions, the firm was for hire and its clients were secret.

Yet, with all that expertise concentrated in Intertel, Peloquin's advice was that Eddie Cellini be retained to manage the new Paradise casino when it opened in December 1967. ''I told the company to keep him as manager because I knew nobody to substitute for him who had adequate experience.''

However, in time, Eddie found himself the subject of a growing media storm of criticism. Not only had Eddie worked for Lansky in Havana, but also in illegal Mob joints in Ohio and Kentucky. His reputation was bad enough that in 1968 he was banned from entering Britain, a procedure known as ''stop-listing.'' That same year his brother Dino, acting as a salesman for Bally, the Chicago slot machine manufacturer, received a commission of $28,200 for selling slot machines to Resorts.

In November 1969 the Bahamas government also stop-listed Eddie and ordered him off the island. Resorts told the press it had fired Eddie before he was banned, but, as it turned out, Eddie only shifted his base of operation to the Miami office of Travel Resorts Enterprises, a Resorts subsidiary, which packaged junkets to Paradise Island. That job lasted two more years before the press tumbled to it.

The philosophy at Resorts seemed to be that black governments could be seduced as easily as white ones, and more cheaply. The man Resorts selected for this "public relations" work was Seymour Alter, whom the company had inherited from Hartford when it purchased the island.

As luck would have it, Alter belonged to the Coyaba Club, whose membership consisted mostly of Bahamian customs officials. Since a hotel stuck on a little island had to import everything it needed through customs, Jack Davis decided they should do something nice for the men who, in a three-year period, had allowed Resorts to import 150 million pounds of what Davis called "everything from peas and carrots to steel girders."

Why not give these poor devils a breather? Davis reasoned, and Alter agreed. The customs officials were flown to Las Vegas for a little wining, dining, gambling, and fucking. When Davis later questioned Alter about a $650 voucher for "girls," Alter explained that it was the least he could do for the boys after they had lost their gambling chips and still had time to kill. The trip was such a hit that it was followed by more trips to Las Vegas and to Acapulco. Thousands of dollars diverted to a slush fund—unrecorded on the books—were used for gifts and cash payments to government officials.

Premier Pindling got more than his share of gratuities. Within days of his election, he moved from his humble abode to a million-dollar mansion, allegedly a gift from Robert Vesco, a mutual fund swindler who would soon need a friendly haven safe from the clutches of American justice. To go along with the mansion, Pindling got a Rolls Royce, a gift from Resorts and other grateful foreigners.

Instead of "legal fees," Resorts gave Pindling hundreds of thousands of dollars in "political contributions," either in cash personally delivered by Jack Davis, or in funds laundered through a local law firm and employees' paychecks. Other times the payments were carried on the company's books as "legal expenses."

What had stood David Probinsky in good stead with Pindling during his election campaign was the expertise he had gained in New Jersey politics. A high-school dropout from Wildwood, New Jersey, where he tended bar and dabbled in real estate, Probinsky's faltering career had taken an about-face when he arrived in the Bahamas via a bankrupt nightclub in Miami.

Probinsky was once chairman of the Young Democrats in the Republican stronghold of Wildwood and Cape May County. Probinsky also knew Marvin Perskie. Not long after the defeat of the 1974 gambling referendum, Probinsky had learned in a telephone conversation with Marvin Perskie that his nephew, Assemblyman Steven Perskie, was sponsoring a bill for a referendum that would limit gambling to Atlantic City.

With Crosby's approval, Probinsky flew to Atlantic City, and after an encouraging talk with Assemblyman Steven Perskie did a survey of the area, including aerial photographs of Boardwalk hotels. Probinsky recommended that Crosby come look for himself. When Crosby agreed, Probinsky told Perskie that the top brass was coming and the assemblyman made the arrangements for a royal welcome. Crosby, Peloquin, Davis, and others were met at the airport by a contingent of limousines and driven up and down the Boardwalk to inspect various hotels and piers. Later they met with influential politicians, including State Senator Joseph McGahn, Perskie's cosponsor of the casino legislation.

Afterward they met with the real political string-pullers, Marvin Perskie and Paddy McGahn, and immediately put them on the payroll. From the Housing and Redevelopment Authority, they picked up an option on a 55-acre Boardwalk-front track of land that had already been optioned to a Philadelphia company, which then sued and settled out of court. Resorts kept the land and later an HRA official left the agency and entered into land deals with Resorts executives.

Probinsky took an instant dislike to Paddy McGahn. "He turned me off, like one of those nickel-and-dime lawyers, a real wheeler-dealer," Probinsky said. "I didn't like the way McGahn was sort of taking charge of this Atlantic City thing." Probinsky urged Crosby to sever the lawyer from the company. Crosby consulted Davis and Peloquin and their response was that Probinsky was a "troublemaker."

Next thing Probinsky knew, Marvin Perskie had convinced Crosby to dump *him*. But that was a little more difficult than Perskie realized. Besides being a troublemaker, Probinsky had a big mouth. What was even worse, he knew more than was good for Resorts.

Resorts finally managed to separate itself from Probinsky but the price was a cool million dollars (plus options on stocks that could make him millions more), to be paid over a ten-year period, during which time Probinsky agreed to "remove himself from the State of New Jersey and not to have any contact directly or indirectly therein during the term of this agreement or until the corporation shall have determined not to pursue its objectives therein whichever shall first occur."

Nor would Probinsky take action of any kind "inimical to the best interests of the corporation." He further agreed not to utter any statement critical of the corporation. To make sure he stayed out of town, a clause in the contract stipulated that at the company's request, Probinsky would have to embark on business trips to Europe and Central and South America, and "in connection therewith to immediately undertake a trip to the south of France for the purpose of exploring business opportunities of possible interest to the corporation." With the request came two first-class, round-trip tickets.

For David Probinsky, silence was golden. For Resorts International, that silence meant that it could go about its business of getting a gambling license without being shot down by an irate employee who knew too much.

As for any other employee who might be tempted to talk with division investigators, Resorts printed a poem "On Loyalty" in its October 1978 inhouse publication. It read:

If you work for a man, for heaven's sake work for him. Speak well of him and stand by the institution he represents. Remember, an ounce of loyalty is worth a pound of cleverness. If you must condemn and eternally find fault, resign your position and when you are on the outside, damn to your heart's content. But so long as you are a part of the company, do not condemn it. If you do, the first high wind that comes along will blow you away, and you will never know why.

But something had to be done about Seymour Alter. He was number 16 of the 17 exceptions the division had listed in its report against Resorts' license application. The language read: "Resorts International, Inc., has engaged in extensive business relationships with and presently employs an individual, Seymour Alter, who has admitted in sworn testimony an attempt to bribe a judge and supplying paid female companions to Bahamian public officials.'' Resorts' response was to suspend Alter pending the outcome of the hearings.

This was Resorts' big chance at the gold ring and nothing and no one was going to stand in its way.

The hearings on Resorts International's application for a permanent casino license lasted seven weeks, with the players going through the motions for the stenographic record and television cameras.

The attorney presenting the state's case was G. Michael ''Mickey'' Brown, a stocky, 35-year-old prosecutor who was chief of the trial section of the Division of Criminal Justice. He was presented with the assignment the day before the report was made public, which didn't allow him much time to bone up on what the division had learned during its yearlong investigation. His assistant, however, was Guy Michael, who had written the division's 115-page report. (Today Mickey Brown and Guy Michael have their own law firm in Atlantic City.)

A savvy prosecutor, Mickey Brown knew how the odds lay. ''A corporation has shareholders,'' he told me in a recent interview, ''and it says, 'Think about the public that's invested in our company.' How can you question the suitability of a corporation? A corporation is only made up of the predominate parts of the people who happen to fill the positions at the time. So no corporation is unsuitable—maybe an individual is. And we can cleanse the corporation by getting rid of individuals or moving individuals around.

''Then you get the excuse that they were dealing with another country at another time, and that conduct was perfectly acceptable. I mean Gulf Oil bribed people all around the world. So how can you question Resorts' conduct as being improper when Congress hadn't yet passed the Foreign Corrupt Practices Act. The attitude is, 'Who in hell do you think you are creating this level of integrity that we have to meet when the federal government says that we can do this without any problem?' And when they had trouble with the SEC, it was handled with consent decrees, which says we don't admit anything, but we promise not to do it again.''

In terms of the division's investigation, Brown understood the problem. ''You go to investigate this company in a foreign country and you have no subpoena power outside of New Jersey. So any information you get, you develop as a beggar. So you wind up with a state agency that's a David fighting a Goliath, with the banks on its side saying, 'What are these guys, crazy? We have $20 million of New Jersey residents' money on loan to that Goliath. You're not going to let that company open a casino? What's going to happen to our investors?' And the banks in this state are powerful.

"In the end, nobody liked the Division of Gaming Enforcement, except for some of the press. The politicians didn't like us because it caused them problems with constituents. The banks didn't because of their loans to Resorts and to a lot of other casinos that were just waiting for the outcome of the hearings before going on with their own plans. The citizens of Atlantic City didn't because we were trying to take jobs away from them."

In Resorts' corner when the hearings opened was Raymond Brown, a tall, courtly, light-skinned black man of 63 whose skills as a defense attorney had made him one of the most effective in the state. He had earned his gold stripes defending organized crime figures. A superb tactician, Ray Brown cleverly used his color to influence juries, seeming to imply in his summation that a vote against his client would be a racist act, that the jury could only reach a guilty verdict because Ray Brown was black.

This was not to be a battle of legal giants, of shrewd courtroom tactics and antics, of shrill dramatics and grand theatrics, of clever shenanigans and verbal pyrotechnics. Ray Brown's strategy was to make the hearings so dull and boring and repetitive that the press would lose interest and drift away.

Under casino law, the burden of proof supposedly rests with a casino applicant to demonstrate "by clear and convincing evidence [its] good reputation for honesty and integrity." The law also provides that evidence concerning applicant's "habits, character, criminal and arrest record, business activities, financial affairs and business, professional and personal associates covering at least the ten-year period preceding the filing of the application shall be considered in determining suitability for a license." In other words, its officers as well as the corporation had to pass the test.

"In theory, the statute sounds good," Mickey Brown said, "that an applicant should have the burden of proving his suitability, but as a practical matter, because of the court system people are accustomed to, you're innocent until proven guilty. It ended up we had to prove they were unfit. They all got on the stand and told what great people they are and before they stopped talking they went over all their mistakes and offered their explanation for them.''

With Ray Brown at the helm, the 115-page report of improprieties vanished in thin air. The established procedure was for Ray Brown to present Resorts' case first, and in any fashion or order he chose, at the conclusion of which Mickey Brown would get his turn. By then, however, Ray Brown had long since stolen not only his thunder but his time.

There was a seven-week limit on the hearings because Resorts' temporary license expired at the end of that time. Ray Brown used six of those weeks, which left Mickey Brown and the commission one week to wrap up the state's business. Otherwise, Resorts would have to close its doors, which meant that 4000 people would find themselves on the street without a job—an intolerable prospect.

Following his plan to lull the press to sleep, and at the same time eat up the clock, Ray Brown began by producing witnesses who had nothing to do with any of the allegations against Resorts. For days on end, witnesses droned on about the architecture and construction of Resorts' Atlantic City hotel. They babbled about plumbing and air conditioning and wiring and interior decoration.

One architect expounded at great length on the efficiency of the ''extra-special'' toilets imported from Italy. ''What's an extra-special toilet?'' Ray Brown encouraged. ''One that fits very well,'' the architect responded, going on to explain that they provided ''extra-flush'' power. ''Perhaps I should say they're particularly pleasing,'' he added, smiling proudly.

When Mickey Brown offered to stipulate that the hotel fulfilled legal requirements, Ray Brown disdainfully waved the offer aside.

His strategy worked. After a few days, most of the out-of-state reporters and even some of the local ones were gone. By now even the commissioners had a hard time keeping awake. Vice-Chairman Kenneth MacDonald's head seemed too heavy for his neck and Lordi had momentarily given up trying to keep his pipe going. Pete DeBona, the aspiring judge, whose frail body and beaked nose gave him the appearance of a hawk ready to take flight, seemed to have pulled in his wings. Alice Corsey nodded off from time to time, and Al Merck, while awake, seemed to have something more interesting on his mind.

The only ones who seemed fully awake, beside Ray Brown and his witness, were the brass from the 14th floor of Resorts' plush executive suites who were seated in a roped-off section reserved for them and their guests. Crosby's young girlfriend was there a lot, and Davis, Peloquin, Steve Norton, Joel Sterns, Paddy McGahn. For the most part, they remained wide awake and delighted with Ray Brown's deftly executed choreography.

At least it was warm inside the hearing room. Out on the Boardwalk, a frigid January wind was blasting sand against the ramshackle buildings facing the ocean. The wind was so powerful that people had to hang on to the metal railing and pull themselves along.

In Florida another drama was taking place. Two division investigators had located Donna Wilson, a former girlfriend of James Crosby who they believed—rightly or wrongly—was a "bag lady" for Resorts.

After interviewing her in Miami, they asked her to come to New Jersey for further interrogation. She agreed because her mother felt it was the right thing to do.

Donna Wilson had met Crosby at Hartford's house. Like Sy Alter, she was someone else Crosby inherited from Hartford. "We all had dinner together, Crosby and Sy and a bunch of other people," she told the investigators. "But then I didn't see him again for a long time. He never remembered me, anyway. He [Crosby] was always drunk. Every time he kept getting introduced to me, he'd say, 'You're a beautiful girl, why haven't I met you before?' I'd say, 'Because you're too drunk to remember.' "

He must have sobered up at some point because she became his mistress and the relationship lasted five years. She said she was his companion every night except when he was out of town. She often traveled with him to Miami and New York. But being Crosby's mistress didn't wrap her in a luxury package. To support herself, Donna Wilson gambled for Bahamian residents, who were banned by law from gambling. Her cut was 10 percent of the winnings, which had to be a slim living, except that Sy Alter, also banned from gambling, gave her a couple of hundred dollars whenever she gambled for him.

In the meantime, Hartford, who had found himself at the short end of the stick in his deal with Crosby, had filed a lawsuit and Donna was asked to help Peloquin try to pin something on Hartford that would force him to drop his legal action.

She accompanied Peloquin to New York, she said. "I went up there, went to the Pierre Hotel and met a narc [narcotics agent] there—I can't remember his name anymore—and I went up with him . . . We sat and parked on the West Side and watched somebody make a drop or pickup or something, some sort of small-time dope thing, and then I went into the club and I was supposed to find out— they were also bringing in this girl, too, who is an agent, but nothing was happening. . . . When I went to the Show Club, there was no more drug deals, it was dead. I failed my mission." The purpose of the mission, she said, was "to discredit Hartford, by proving he was involved with drugs or his club [the Show Club] was a big sort of dealing place."

When asked if someone from Resorts had contacted her during the Resorts hearing, she replied, "Peloquin. The last three days, he's been calling . . . I hung up on him."

While she had been on Paradise Island, she was hired to help find out who was ripping off the casino. "Who was head of whatever— you know, they had agents and all sorts of things—getting them to inform, to have meetings with Peloquin, and he in turn guaranteed green cards [aliens need green cards to work in the United States] for a lot of these guys. Some of the biggest thieves up there all have green cards, and they own restaurants in Washington and New York." According to her unverified statement, Peloquin was getting green cards for the ex-dealers, setting them up in businesses, and taking a part of their profits.

The investigators asked if anyone had told Donna to keep her mouth shut. "Yes," she said, "Tom did. Tom Blum [a Resorts executive]. . . . He said this would be my big chance to get paid off, and I'd be an idiot to say anything." Asked when Blum had promised the payoff, she said, "Last night." Blum had promised her $20,000. Blum, she said, had a lot of stock in Resorts he wanted to protect. If the gambling license were denied the stock would be next to worthless. Resorts had coached Blum on what to say to investigators. "They gave him a ten- or fifteen-page memorandum about what to say before he was questioned by your people." It was Crosby, she said, who gave Blum the memo. This was interesting to the investigators, because when Blum was first contacted by them on the phone, he had indicated he knew plenty and was willing to talk. But when they arrived in Florida, they found a reticent Blum, who had nothing but kind words for the company.

Donna didn't know of anyone else who had been coached because "they got rid of me really fast, so I'm not in contact with anyone.

They were in a real hurry to get rid of me. They wanted me to pull my son out of school in the middle of a term and ship my stuff over. They wanted to give me a couple of days and I wanted to find a decent area, and they said that once I get over there I could find another place. I'm not a gypsy. I can't keep moving.''

The subject then turned to Robert Vesco. Resorts officials had said that they had nothing to do with Vesco after he was indicted and the questioner wanted to know if Donna knew if it was true.

"He was over at Crosby's house regularly, having meetings . . . I guess up until the time he went to Costa Rica."

But she had no knowledge of what had gone on at the meetings. "They would never allow me. It was always 'Get lost.' ''

But she knew Vesco personally. "Oh, yes. I flew down on his plane and everything. I used to hang out with his kids . . ."

As for politicians being on the payroll, she said, "I never saw their paychecks, but I know they were on the payroll because Crosby was always in a fit and threatened to take them off the payroll because he was getting so much grief.'' Asked about American politicians, she said, "I know they wined and dined the whole FBI and congressmen and everyone else from New Jersey. They had them all down—I don't know, congressmen, whatever . . . Resorts picked up the bill.''

Thus ended Donna Wilson's interview. She was never called to testify before the commission nor was the commission advised of her testimony. "It was my decision not to call her," Mickey Brown told me. "For a number of reasons, I didn't feel comfortable in putting her up there as a witness and vouching for her credibility. Ray Brown would have murdered her. It would have been an embarrassment to put her in the public light as a witness for the state of New Jersey.''

While Donna Wilson was painting one picture of Resorts and its chairman of the board, James Crosby, with Ray Brown's artistic guidance, was painting quite another.

Of the reporters remaining, *Barron*'s Gigi Mahon best summarized Crosby's performance on the witness stand: ". . . he was an excellent witness, if you didn't count the numerous I-don't-knows and I-don't-remembers at crucial junctures. He was a combination of humor, self-deprecation, outrage, offense, and, perhaps most important, sickness. There was no measuring the sympathy effect of the coughing, or the ten-minute breaks built into the program so he could take his oxygen, or the rumors that he was testifying so early because they thought he was going to die. He was frail and pale and looked like an old man, which he was not. Once when everyone was milling about during a break, Crosby came and leaned over the railing in the hall, just sort of hung there, seeming to gasp for breath. It was a pitiful sight except to those cynical enough to wonder why he was gasping there, not in the private Resorts quarters down the hall, and why no one was with him if he was so sick. Some wondered if it was a bold pitch for sympathy. Others sympathized.''

Besides the I-don't-knows and I-don't-remembers, there was a lot of shifting of responsibility to Jack Davis: "Jack was in charge of that." And when it was Davis's turn in the witness box, he pushed a lot of it on Peloquin and other executives, who in turn reciprocated. If followed to its logical end, the blame would have ended up on the shoulders of the most recently employed chambermaid.

Ray Brown's chartered course was to steer Crosby through the troubled waters of the report without losing control of the tiller. By the time he surrendered his witness to Mickey Brown, he wanted those waters calmed for clear sailing ahead. The idea was to cover all the allegations and surgically remove the sting before the state got its chance to operate on his witness. In other words, take the play away from the state.

Besides, said Mickey Brown, "It's hard to cross-exam somebody when they're up there dying before your eyes and have to take a fifteen-minute break every forty-five minutes to go breathe oxygen.''

For a man supposedly in the last stages of emphysema, Crosby had a long and minutely detailed story to tell, weaving it over a seven-day period. He said he put $1 million of his own money into the purchase of Paradise Island and at another time advanced it $250,000 when the company was short on funds.

As for the shady bankers and brokers who had arranged some of Mary Carter's largest stock sales and had subsequently run into trouble with the federal government, Crosby explained that such violations were no reflection on the company itself. "I just didn't know it happened and it wasn't because of Mary Carter,'' he said. "It could have been General Motors or any other company.''

Suddenly, Crosby veered widely from Ray Brown's tight choreography: "That's why I'm so distressed about this implication that there is something improper about this—because I handled it. If there is something wrong, it is wrong with me, and every one of those people were the type of people I thought then and I still think now were the kind of people that should have been buying stock." Ray Brown quickly cut him off.

Ray Brown's choreography was maintained even during Mickey Brown's cross-examination. He positioned himself so he had eye contact with his witness and coached with an assortment of head and hand signals. When Mickey Brown realized what was going on and moved the podium to block that eye contact, the choreography was picked up by Peloquin, who literally moved his chair to the front area of the room occupied by the commissioners and witnesses.

Crosby claimed that prior to the release of the report he knew nothing about Sy Alter's attempt to bribe a New York judge. (In his testimony, Peloquin said, "It appeared that Mr. Alter had been the victim of a shakedown.") Crosby knew nothing about Alter supplying Bahamian officials with prostitutes, but admitted he was aware that Alter had taken the officials on junkets; that Alter's suspension a few days after the issuance of the division's report was in no way a condemnation of the executive.

Perhaps not, but it certainly was a clever stratagem. Sy Alter was never called as a witness. Since Resorts claimed he was no longer a member of the company, it followed, they argued, that he had nothing to do with their license application, and the commission agreed to sever him from Resorts' hearings. Asked if he didn't think that was a rather strange move on the commission's part, Mickey Brown said, "Yeah, lots of strange things were done. I could have subpoenaed him but I just went along with the commission's decision."

Crosby vehemently denied that the contract with David Probinsky was an attempt to silence him; it was because Probinsky is "sensitive, high-strung, and emotional" and prone to arguments with Davis and other officials: "It didn't make sense for him to be holding press conferences."

During cross-examination, Crosby discussed the new contract he had given Probinsky two days before the hearings opened. The contract now called for more than $1 million in cash and stock option and a similar amount *if Resorts gets its license*. This language sounded better than the blatant demand for silence required in the first contract but the aim was the same. At current stock prices, the new deal was worth $2.61 million if the license was issued.

Crosby's greatest performance was his version of his relationship with Sir Stafford Sands and Wallace Groves. He had not been forced to hire Sir Stafford to get his gambling permit. The plain fact was

that Sands was "far and away the most gifted [lawyer] at that time
. . . the most brilliant man in the Bahamas," and that he, Crosby,
never considered any other attorney.

As for his various associates in the Bahamas, Crosby was unaware
of anything derogatory about them until 1967 when he had read an
article in *Life* that had linked Mary Carter to Wallace Groves, Louis
Chesler, and others in business with Lansky and Cellini. All he had
known was that Groves had a conviction in the 1930s. But Sir Stafford
Sands had told Crosby a "heartwarming story" about how Groves
"had come out of a short stint in prison and had gone to the Bahamas
and settled on a remote island and gone into the logging business,
really to the point where he was, according to Sands, chopping the
trees down himself and living in a tent for many years and that's how
he came upon Freeport, actually." Now, a man who would do all
that had certainly rehabilitated himself. So Crosby was shocked to
read that Groves et al. were involved with Lansky. Three or four
days after reading the article, he tried to get permission to buy out
Groves.

Eddie Cellini was also a revelation. "All I knew him as was
Eddie. Just a pleasant guy named Eddie." Crosby didn't know about
Cellini's background and had let other Resorts executives handle who
would run the casino. "Mr. Davis worked out [Eddie's] contract,"
Crosby said, "and Mr. Peloquin." In explaining why he kept Cellini
and approved a three-year $450,000 contract after the *Life* article,
Crosby said it was "because I heard primarily about Groves and
Sands. They were the ones I was concerned about." In fact, he had
no personnel discussions before the contract was signed, but later
learned that Eddie had been put on a Bahamian "stoplist." "The
government didn't want him to come in," he said. "They said it was
because he had a brother named Dino." Eddie continued as a Resorts
employee in the Miami office until his contract expired, he said.

Crosby said that between 1970 and now, Resorts had given about
$700,000 in "political contributions," primarily to the Progressive
Liberal party that had been in power since 1967. Many of the
payments were made in cash after checks were written to executives
such as Alter and Probinsky. The cash payments were made "because they didn't want the people within the company to know how
they were being distributed." Of course, cash is also handy when
politicians want to pocket contributions. He defended the practice as
necessary to keep the political system funded, despite his decision in

1972 to make payments only to the party in power. "Well, you know, it's legal down there and if companies don't support the parties, they really might wilt."

In another exchange, he said the contributions were intended for "general good will and hopefully to preserve the two-party system"—this triggered laughter in the hearing room and Lordi remarked, "Mr. Crosby, nobody is laughing at you. They are laughing at our own two-party system."

The vast amount of money Resorts spent in New Jersey to support the referendum and the writing of the Casino Control Act was never brought up in the hearings. Nor were the names of local politicians and their relatives ever raised.

Dennis Gomes had wanted to pursue that investigation. Going through Resorts' file cabinets in Paradise Island, he had found evidence that money was illegally transferred from the Bahamas to influence key New Jersey politicians. After Gomes returned to Nevada, division investigators made a superficial check of Mayor Lazarow's CRAC group, but made no effort to determine whether any committee money went covertly to politicians. It also gave short shrift to reports that some of the "street money," nearly $200,000, went directly to politicians.

On the seventh day of the hearings and his last day on the stand, Crosby was at his sickly best as he made his final pitch for a license. "I think we're pretty poor at presenting ourselves very well," said Crosby, who had hired Ray Brown, Joel Sterns, Paddy McGahn, Marvin Perskie, and a gaggle of former state officials, reporters, and public relations experts. "But I think we compare very favorably. When we arrived in Atlantic City, we really got caught up in the whole principle of the idea, which is that if a gambling referendum is passed the city could rebuild itself. We got involved and frankly I thought we could do some good here. That the city could have a comeback, that's really what fascinated me."

Also fascinating was that in just one year, Resorts had almost doubled its net worth and total assets: from a net worth of $102,196,000 to $198,580,000, and from total assets of $48,279,000 to $86,355,000. The casino's earnings that first year were $200 million.

When James Crosby left the witness stand, he had set the tone that would carry for the rest of Ray Brown's presentation. Twenty-six witnesses took the stand, praised the company at every opportunity, and defended their actions in unctuous tones. Their words filled 7000 pages.

On October 20, when Resorts rested its case, there were only eight days before Resorts' final temporary license expired. At this point, Governor Byrne started applying pressure for a swift conclusion. He publicly criticized the commission for not working longer hours.

Lordi's reaction was to flail away at Mickey Brown. He didn't care what the state had left up its sleeve, he wanted the hearings concluded before the license's expiration.

It was just as well. Mickey Brown, as one of his aides said, had a water pistol instead of a smoking gun. It took him only three days to present his case. His last witness was James Russell Hawthorne, an ex-con from Florida with a rap sheet, as Ray Brown would gleefully demonstrate, longer than his arm.

Considering Mickey Brown's attitude toward Donna Wilson, it's hard to understand the reasoning behind this move. Claiming to have been an undercover agent for Scotland Yard, Hawthorne's sole contribution was that he had seen Eddie Cellini in Resorts' Miami office a full year after the company claimed to have severed all ties with him. It was hardly an earth-shaking disclosure. The record was already replete with Eddie's connections to Resorts.

Ray Brown argued contemptuously that Hawthorne's testimony was riddled with lies. And that was the way the state's case ended. It wasn't that Mickey Brown hadn't already made his case in his cross-examination of Resorts' witnesses. All the salient points covered in the report were painstakingly gone over time and again. It was just that in the scheme of things, Mickey Brown was a man pitted against an invincible tide—a tide of greenbacks crashing against the Boardwalk with the frenzied power of a surf maddened by winter storms.

Whatever anyone may have thought of Mickey Brown's performance, Governor Byrne was more than satisfied. Robert Martinez "retired," and Mickey Brown became the new Director of the Division of Gaming Enforcement, a post he held during the licensing of the next eight casinos.

On Monday morning, February 26, 1979, the commission ruled unanimously to grant Resorts International a permanent and unrestricted gambling license.

Reading from his 86-page opinion, Lordi said, "Viewing each of the seventeen exceptions noted by the Division, separately, the commission has found no facts which suggest that this applicant is not qualified for licensure. Now viewing all of the exceptions collectively, the commission is of a like opinion. While some of the practices engaged in by the applicant in the past and in another jurisdiction might not pass muster in this jurisdiction under the strict regulatory system established under our statute and regulations, the circumstances of prevailing law, custom and environment must be considered in placing such practices in their proper perspective . . .

"In light of these facts and in light of all of the facts and conclusions which have been found, the commission is satisfied that the applicant, Resorts International Hotel, Inc., has established by clear and convincing evidence its financial stability, integrity and responsibility; the integrity and reputation of its financial backers; its good reputation for honesty and integrity; and its business ability and casino experience, so as to qualify it for a casino license."

Later that day Mickey Brown met with Lordi. "I just told him he'd made a very grave mistake, that I thought he had damaged the state's reputation by granting them an unqualified license. And it would take a long time to overcome it."

But Senator Steven Perskie, soon to be a judge, was incensed that Resorts had been put through the ordeal of the hearings on such flimsy evidence. "I think we are going to have to get an answer as to why the attorney general took the position that he did . . . To recommend denial of the basic license on the basis of what they had was in my judgment inexplicable."

Most of the media was of a different mind. In an article titled "Surrender in Atlantic City," in *New Jersey Monthly*, Michael Dorman wrote: " . . . there was a plethora of evidence—which the commission chose to ignore—establishing that Resorts was a mismanaged, unscrupulous, mob-tainted company with the morals of an alley cat."

In an editorial, CBS-TV summarized what it said one should know to operate a casino in Atlantic City: "You should know it's okay to have employees who gained their experience in illegal gambling operations . . . to have given payments to officials of a foreign country where you had a casino, and to have improperly recorded these payments on your company's book. . . . The trick is to admit these things and say sure, you did them, but that you don't do them anymore."

The message was out, loud and clear: if Resorts could get a gambling license, anybody could, and gambling entrepreneurs lined up in a frenzy. Gambling stocks went soaring into that wide blue sky yonder and the little people, like lemmings rushing blindly into the sea, descended upon that decrepit old Resort Queen with the same incomprehensible urgency for extinction.

In a way, though, Atlantic City, New Jersey, and Resorts got what they deserved: each other.

Seven years later, in February 1985, during Resorts' annual license renewal hearings, the division presented information detailing how Resorts and Crosby had concealed payments of $431,000 to Prime Minister Pindling in 1980 and 1981. An investigation of Pindling's finances by a Commission of Inquiry in the Bahamas revealed that $91,000 of a legal fee paid by Resorts had gone to Everette Bannister, who was building a new house for Pindling, "on behalf of the prime minister." In addition, $340,000 of a $580,000 finder's fee Crosby paid a law firm when he sold the Paradise Island Bridge had also gone to Pindling through Bannister, who was a Resorts consultant and a business partner of Pindling.

Resorts protested: "Whatever fees we paid for professional services were for services that were actually rendered to Resorts." Yet at the time the fees were paid, Resorts was negotiating to purchase a Holiday Inn near the site where it planned to build a new hotel. The negotiations were conducted with the Hotel Corporation of the Bahamas, of which Pindling was chairman and president.

The division again claimed that Resorts was unfit for licensure, and Joel Stern argued that the company had done some "silly, stupid things," but "By God, they are stupid, not criminal. They don't add up to passing a bribe." The commission agreed with Stern, voting 3 to 1 to renew the license, observing that "the evidence presented at this hearing reveals a degree of general corporate laxity and imprudence which, while not so serious as to provide a basis for denying relicensure, is clearly inappropriate for a company operating in this most regulated of all industries."

During the hearings it was also revealed that Nicaraguan dictator Anastasio Somoza had contacted Peloquin after fleeing to Miami. Intertel had arranged asylum for Somoza in the Bahamas, and from there to Honduras and Paraguay, where he was assassinated in September 1980. The man Peloquin had picked to assist Somoza was Everette Bannister. According to the findings of the Bahamian Commission, Bannister had visited Somoza's yacht shortly after it docked at Georgetown. One of the two customs officers accompanying Bannister testified that Bannister was carrying a "shoulder bag with long straps on it that appeared to be empty" but it "bulged out" when he left the yacht. The customs officer said that Bannister gave him $5000 but the other officer denied that Bannister attempted to bribe him.

Division Director Thomas O'Brien said he was disappointed with the commission's decision to renew Resorts' license. "I will definitely favor an appeal because I think the record favors our position," he said, but no one at Resorts was losing sleep over it.

Four months later, Premier Pindling, who had been reported on the verge of revoking Resorts' casino license, reversed himself. He extended Resorts' management contract until December 31, 1997, and granted it approval to increase by 50 percent the size of its Paradise Island casino and to build another 250 hotel rooms.

"Right now, we just can't accommodate the crowds that are currently visiting our casino on Paradise Island," a Resorts official said by way of explanation, "and there are many times when our tables are just jammed to capacity."

14
Little Pussy's Jolly Trolley

Between 1977 and 1979, wherever Anthony "Little Pussy" Russo went, the FBI were sure to go—with their hidden microphones and tape recorders. In less than two years, they amassed 1800 hours of court-authorized tape recordings that provided fascinating insights into the workings and lifestyle of Mafia members.

Both Russo and his brother John, known as "Big Pussy," got their colorful cognomens because of their considerable expertise as cat burglars in their youth. They were members of the Genovese family, part of a group supervised by Ruggerio "Richie the Boot" Boiardo, an 88-year-old caporegime who represented Genovese family interests in North Jersey. Big Pussy was Boiardo's adviser. Little Pussy began his mob career as a driver for Vito Genovese.

According to the state police, Boiardo's "network has become a conglomerate of illicit enterprises (i.e., gambling, stolen property, loansharking, labor racketeering, and infiltration of legitimate business), operating primarily in the Essex County area of New Jersey and in Caribbean Island gambling casinos."

Little Pussy lived in Long Branch, a beach town some fifty miles south of Newark, and was known as boss of the Jersey shore. In a taped conversation, Little Pussy told his brother that Jerry Catena had asked him to see what he could do to arrange slot machine deals with the casino developers who were then lining up to move into Atlantic City. He said that Catena and his partner Abe Green were "going to find out if I can throw them into the machines."

This revelation came at a time when the Bally Manufacturing Corporation, the world's largest maker of slot machines, had itself filed a license application to operate a casino in Atlantic City. During Bally's early years as a slot machine manufacturer based in Chicago, Catena was one of its major stockholders. When his connection to the firm became known in 1965, Bally bought him out. But Runyan Sales Co., owned by Catena and Abe Green, remained Bally's pinball machine distributor in New Jersey for at least six more years, until pressure from the Nevada Gaming Commission forced Bally to end its ties to Runyan Sales. And now, in 1978, Catena was still angling behind the scenes to sell Bally slot machines in Atlantic City.

In the same taped conversation, Little Pussy mentioned men who were ready to "front" a casino for him in Atlantic City. "Now I got this guy, Kelly, and Joe Sunken [a Hollywood, Florida, restaurateur] when I was in Florida, sat down with him. Kelly said, 'Anything you want to do, Anthony, here's the guy.' The guy said to me, 'Anything, forget everybody, come to me direct, and I'll guarantee you anything you want, license and everything—not you, any name you wanna come up with.' "

His second front was Allan Sachs, who had just taken over the Las Vegas Stardust from Allen Glick, after the Nevada Gaming Control Board had discovered a $12 million slot machine skim engineered by the Chicago Mafia. Sachs too would lose his license because of skimming violations.

Little Pussy's big dreams about owning his own casino were not realized when he became the hidden owner of the Jolly Trolley, a sawdust joint off the Strip in Las Vegas. It turned into more of a nightmare than a dream. On January 13, 1978, in a conversation with one of his partners, Paul Bendetti, Little Pussy displayed his disgust with the whole operation.

"Christ, I just did the count," Bendetti told him. "There's no money. We lost $20,000 and I can't pay the customer. I got no place to put my hands on two cents. I swear to God!"

Little Pussy gruffly answered, "Total disorganization down there."

In discussing his problems at the Jolly Trolley with a friend, Little Pussy said, "They destroyed me with this." He described the customers as "all niggers and pimps and junkies" and complained that he'd have to incur more losses by buying a pornography shop next door because "that dirty rotten joint with all the fags hanging out" had driven away gambling business.

As for skimming, he said, "I'm making that kid [Bendetti] take a hundred out of the drawer every day." When Bendetti failed to follow his instructions, he called to remind him: "What the hell youse think you came up with? . . . Take it off the top. Anywhere gangsters go they take it right off the top. Am I right or wrong?"

When the Jolly Trolley needed more operating capital, he called Anthony Provenzano, a Mafioso and de facto head of Union City, New Jersey's Teamsters Local 560, the largest in the country. Provenzano was a suspect in the disappearance of Jimmy Hoffa and is presently serving a life sentence for murder. "I got Tony Pro to come in to see if he can go through another union to give me a half million." He also spoke of approaching Jerry Catena, whom he described almost reverently as having "more fucking money than God."

Little Pussy was blacklisted in Las Vegas but he had no trouble moving around the city. Nor did he have any trouble getting a credit line at Caesars Palace—the casino eventually wrote off $45,000 of gambling losses, which is the safest way to skim a casino.

Although Little Pussy had gotten 200 slot machines from Bally on credit, getting a legitimate loan for the casino was about impossible, Bendetti told him: "Our financial statement ain't so good because it's, uh, you know, we been rip—you know what we've been doing. When we take it away and then it don't show up. I mean it's a bad situation."

Little Pussy, who had been loansharking most of his life, eventually found himself in the hands of a Chicago loanshark named "Sarge." When Bendetti heard that gaming authorities were planning a surprise audit, he borrowed $30,000 from Sarge so the Jolly Trolley could meet the $150,000 minimum reserve a casino was required to have in its cashier's cage to pay off winnings of customers.

"He was able to lend it to us for an hour," Bendetti told Little Pussy. "And we were able to get it in and get it out without them [auditors] seeing it."

Little Pussy was not impressed. "I don't give a shit about the law," he shouted. "Tell me about that thousand a week for the $30,000." The interest, he complained, should have been only $600. They did more business with Sarge, getting another $20,000, but Little Pussy still wasn't satisfied with the interest rate.

When it came to loansharking, Little Pussy knew his business.

Richard Bohnert, a New Jersey building contractor, learned that lesson the hard way. He owed $200,000 at one time and was paying $4000 a week in interest. Several times Little Pussy told Bohnert that he sympathized with his money problems: "I'm in worse shape than you." But if he ever found that Bohnert was making money on his construction jobs and not paying off promptly, "I'll break your fucking head." Bohnert kept coming up short and finally was forced to sell his $100,000 Monmouth Beach house as part payment to Little Pussy and his associates, who then leased it back to Bohnert. Realizing that he was way over his head, Bohnert sought federal protection.

Little Pussy was also working on a proposal for building a Ramada Inn with four towers in Atlantic City, each with 350 rooms, with a casino running like a walkway between them. And he had a deal to build another Ramada Inn, this one in Highlands, and had already received a $3.6 million loan commitment from the New Jersey Economic Development Authority.

Both the EDA and the state Housing Finance Agency were being used to bankroll Mafia investments in real estate and housing. Another state loan agency, the Urban Loan Authority, which was later merged with the EDA, lost 82 percent of its loans from 1971 to 1978 because they were made to companies owned by, or connected to, Mafia figures.

During those years the Mafia had pressed for some of the big pools of money dispensed through these agencies. Loans went to convicted burglars, bookmakers, robbers, dealers in stolen property. And to lawyers and businessmen who represented them. One notable attorney was George Franconero, who had worked for Brendan Byrne as an assistant district attorney in Essex County, and later had become a partner in Byrne's law firm.

When Byrne was elected governor in 1973, Franconero's sister, singer Connie Francis, campaigned for Byrne. Not long after Byrne was in office, Franconero received a $165,000 loan from the Urban Loan Authority for a furniture store he co-owned in Bloomfield. *New Jersey Monthly* magazine charged the loan was made for political reasons. "No loan illustrates the corruption of the ULA better than the Best Furn," the article asserted. "It takes very little imagination to construe the loan as possibly a gesture of gratitude from the Byrne administration to the singer's friends and brother."

Franconero was soon in trouble with banks. As the lawyer for a leasing corporation that arranged for phony documents used as collateral to obtain loans from banks, he was named in a seven-count federal indictment charging conspiracy to misapply bank funds and conspiring with union officials to receive the kickbacks. Companies set up by Franconero received loans to buy nonexistent industrial equipment—one bank alone lost $4.7 million. The scheme eventually scuttled four New Jersey banks.

To avoid a prison term, Franconero agreed to cooperate with the FBI and his information led to the conviction of Ernest Palmeri, Sr., a Mafia soldier and business representative for Teamsters Local 945 in Paterson, a local dominant in New Jersey's garbage collection business.

At nine o'clock on Friday morning, March 6, 1981—one month before Palmeri was to surrender to federal authorities to begin serving his seven-year sentence—Franconero was brushing snow from his car parked at the foot of his driveway. Two gunmen concealed in shrubbery stepped out and shot him twice in the head from 20 feet away. Franconero's murder remains unsolved.

In a conversation with an associate, Little Pussy said that his brother was after him to come up with the $6700 from the Jolly Trolley he paid periodically in tribute to Boiardo. "I said to Johnny, 'tell 'em to wait until after the first of the year. When we get the money from the bank, I'll give it to him.' He says, 'Oh, jeez, the holidays.' I said to John, 'Why don't you go fuck yourself.' I said to myself, 'You'd think they were starving.' "

While the FBI were listening to almost his every word in Las Vegas, the New Jersey state police had planted bugs at his West Long Branch real estate and construction office—one inside a desktop telephone, the other in the ceiling above the bathroom doorway—and more bugs in his home. The one under the living-room rug often picked up the sound of the toilet flushing, a phenomenon police called "the Archie Bunker effect."

A tape recorded at his West Long Branch office on June 12, 1978, shows that Little Pussy was in trouble with his boss, Ruggiero "Richie the Boot" Boiardo, for not observing proper protocol channels and for getting involved with Mafia members in other cities. The Boot was also unhappy with the way Little Pussy was handling his affairs in Monmouth County. Present were Big Pussy and four others:

LITTLE PUSSY: I'm like a fucking fool down there, everybody runs down for favors, favors, favors and I got to be a fucking jerkoff. I'm there, all these guys from Brooklyn and everything—I got to jerk off there. . . . Boot, they're looking to grab every fucking guy. Where could I be, ninety fucking places at one time?

THE BOOT: Who's trying to grab you?

LITTLE PUSSY: I just got done telling you. You got Albie's crew in there. You got this Bobby Basile [Robert Occhipinti] and Sam the Plumber [Simone DeCavalcante], they come in. They're coming in, they're picking here, they're picking there.

THE BOOT: Then you haven't got them. If you have them they can't pick them. Can they pick them if you got them? They're looking for them. I had money they do it to me. Wiseguys. I've taken wiseguys out [killed] because I distrusted them.

LITTLE PUSSY: Every argument I had down there, the kid can tell you that. What am I going to say?—

THE BOOT: What was the argument about?

ANTHONY: I argue with them to make them run to you. I never hear nothing. It's forgotten.

THE BOOT: That means they're no good.

LITTLE PUSSY: I punched Mike Stavolla in the fucking mouth and everything. Now they're looking to make a move on Mike Stavolla.

THE BOOT: Did they own this guy? Does he know them? Done favors for him? How can they come and get him like this?

LITTLE PUSSY: They don't come and get them, Boot. They look for business, they got the [slot] machines and everything. I'm not in the contact. I don't know machines, so in the meantime.

THE BOOT: So you tell them this guy's with me. If they're not with you, they can have them. Ask them, "This guy ever with you?"—

LITTLE PUSSY: Boot, if I don't find out, after a while they come up with the story, ah, "How come a month, two months pass and now you're claiming them?" That's the old bullshit.

THE BOOT: I want to know who's claiming them, you say.

LITTLE PUSSY: If I'm here, if I'm in Florida, if I'm in Vegas, what am I going to say? Hey, these guys are all with me?

THE BOOT: How come you're with me? I don't think they'd switch if they were with you. I can't see it. These guys grab them, they grab everybody they can, not only here, it's all over the United States, this business, and you don't know?

The argument grew more heated, with Little Pussy giving more examples of treachery in the ranks, and the Boot showing more contempt for his lack of leadership.

LITTLE PUSSY: Then the guy Riccio turned around and said, "All these guys in this type of business with Cicalese"—

BIG PUSSY: They collect so much a month.

LITTLE PUSSY: They got it because of this guy Richie.

BIG PUSSY: Yeah, I know the lawyer for them, they pay so much a month.

LITTLE PUSSY: Cicalese got nothing to do with the concessions, so forget about it. But he had told me that, remember that the Boot okayed it, to help him out with the unions. And these guys are coming to me, Boot, concerning Johnny Riggi—anybody of the other crews and all. I always tell them two words. "Go up and see the Boot. Don't do this to me." They say, "OK." There's no problem. Now, I'm all fucked up with this hearing. I threw Vito in there. I said, "Declare yourself for twenty-five percent of all the joints they've got." Now a week passed, the guy never calls Vito. Now last night when I came back I said, "Go in and declare yourself." I said, "When we go up there I tell the Boot." Now they give the kid a name, a guy by the name of Robbie give him a call. These guys must have been reaching out all week.

THE BOOT: Robbie who?

LITTLE PUSSY: I don't know. That's the only name they mentioned. This Robbie turned around, according to Vito, this Robbie with these two other Syrians supposed to have said to Vito, he told me, that they turned around and said to him we got a message to come down there and open up. That everything was straightened out. Straightened out by who? Now they want to buy the Paddock for a $150,000 and they want to buy the Surf for $400,000, these two Syrians.

THE BOOT: What are they, Jewish?

The more he tries to explain, the deeper in trouble he gets, until finally Little Pussy cries out:

LITTLE PUSSY: I'm always wrong.

THE BOOT: No, you're not wrong, you're right.

LITTLE PUSSY: No, you are. As far as you're concerned, I'm always wrong.

THE BOOT: No, you're right. I've got to make a list.

LITTLE PUSSY: Boot, I don't give a fuck, I'm ready. I'm dying now.

THE BOOT: What did he say?

LITTLE PUSSY: I want to make all these fucking guys push me [inaudible] fuck them. What am I going to do? At this stage I've got to turn around and listen to all this bullshit down there, for what reason? If I'm wrong, I'm wrong.

THE BOOT: Now maybe it's bullshit. Maybe it ain't no bullshit.

LITTLE PUSSY: It's bullshit.

THE BOOT: Then you're bullshit.

LITTLE PUSSY: If they think that I'm bullshitting them, then let them do what they want to do with me.

THE BOOT: I can't see it. If a guy is with you, how can he go with somebody else? Can't hop from one to the other.

LITTLE PUSSY: Boot, if you had this here all by yourself.

THE BOOT: You got it?

LITTLE PUSSY: Yeah, I got it.

THE BOOT: Well, who the hell is going to take it away from you?

LITTLE PUSSY: How am I going to go to Bricktown . . . I'm one guy. What, am I going to travel the whole shore?

THE BOOT: Ain't you got a phone? Call him.

LITTLE PUSSY: I'm going to call him on the phone?

THE BOOT: Yeah, say, "Come over here, come and talk to me."

LITTLE PUSSY: You know these guys better than me. So come on . . . I ain't going against them. They got the union. This guy got the union. He's close to all the union people.

THE BOOT: Well, he's got the unions. That's why he's trying to make people, he's in the union.

LITTLE PUSSY: But, Boot, don't you understand . . . They're afraid to come near me because they feel if they're seen with me, their reputations—they get in trouble with the law. That's the shit they give me. Stay away, what am I supposed to do, stay away?

THE BOOT: No, you don't.

LITTLE PUSSY: After I turned around and made them [initiated them into the Mafia], now I've got to back away from them? . . . That's because I always shove my tongue up my ass. I never made a beef. I never had a sitdown. I'm fucking telling you how many of them are with these people, pushing.

THE BOOT: I can't see how they're pushing you. I don't see nobody pushing you, you're one of them people. You're no help yourself. You have to lead. If you no lead, you shoot. Leave them with ten cents.

LITTLE PUSSY: That's right. Everybody—who don't know that? How could I've lived with you, from when I was sixteen years old.

THE BOOT: Ah, for Christ's sake.

LITTLE PUSSY: I lived on North Street when I was a kid. You raised me. What have I got to worry about, don't I know better?

THE BOOT: You don't know better, without getting mad, without getting hot.

LITTLE PUSSY: I got nobody down there with me that you could sit down with if I'm gone. . . .

THE BOOT: When I was young, I had nobody.

LITTLE PUSSY: If there's a beef, who's going to sit down for me, who's going to go against twenty guys?

THE BOOT: Well, what the hell you think I was.

LITTLE PUSSY: When I'm in Vegas, when I'm in Florida, what do I know what's going on there? . . .

THE BOOT: You're over here, you're over there, you're all over the United States, so then you call up a guy, "Hey, that guy doesn't belong to you? That guy belongs to me." And that's it. I mean this guy doesn't fight over people. After five years, two years, we'll find him and bring him back . . .

The conversation turned to someone called Jimmy Higgins.

LITTLE PUSSY: You remember Jimmy Higgins.

THE BOOT: He said, "I hate my son, go ahead, but don't hit him here." They hit him there anyway, 'cause he hit the guy with the [inaudible]. He said, I'm going to leave town, to do it while he was away.

LITTLE PUSSY: But Pinky hit him.

THE BOOT: These things are very delicate.

LITTLE PUSSY: Oh, sure.

To reduce thefts in employee ranks at the Jolly Trolley, Little Pussy sent an enforcer: "If anybody gets outa line, he'll whack 'em," he told Bendetti. "He's that type of kid. He was in the can with me. This kid'll jump over a table and go to work on a guy."

As an additional step to cut overhead costs, Little Pussy told Bendetti to get rid of his bodyguard. "You need a bodyguard? I got ninety million guys looking to kill me, and I'm all by myself."

On the night of April 26, 1979, a few months after this call, Little Pussy arrived early at his luxurious apartment at the plush Harbor Island Spa in Long Branch and was in bed by nine o'clock, as was his habit, being an early riser.

There were reasons for his feeling that he was "all by myself." His brother, Big Pussy, who had served as a buffer between him and the Boot, had died of natural causes just before Christmas, and Little Pussy's problems with the Boot had worsened. And a joint state and federal investigation of Boiardo's group, called Operation Omega, was presenting its information to a state grand jury which was said to be within two weeks of returning indictments against nine members of the group, including Boiardo and Russo.

Besides the electronic surveillance, the most damaging evidence was the testimony of Patrick Pizuto, a turncoat soldier in federal protective custody. Pizuto had been sponsored into the family by Little Pussy after Pizuto had murdered Paul Campanile on orders of the organization. In one of the taped conversations, Little Pussy refers to Pizuto as having "earned his bones" with that murder. In another conversation, Little Pussy is overhead saying he had received "permission from New York"—showing he was again skipping channels—to kill certain persons, and that rather than bury them, he would leave their bodies out in the open "as a signal that if anyone gets out of line that's what's gonna happen to them." Pizuto, who once worked as Little Pussy's chauffeur, was said to have placed his former boss in a precarious and vulnerable situation.

Little Pussy's apartment was filled with stuffed toy cats and a three-foot porcelain statue of a tiger, proud reminders of his youth as a cat burglar. He lived alone, behind a door with a double lock and a steel bar.

Around eleven-thirty that evening, a group of women staying at the spa saw three men loitering on the fourth floor. One of the men knocked on a door and when a woman answered, he excused himself, saying he had the wrong room. She would later describe him and his two companions as men with dark complexions. About fifteen minutes later, another woman heard what sounded like a truck backfire, and remarked to a friend that "this is very noisy."

The next morning the body of Anthony "Little Pussy" Russo was found sprawled across a bed, his head resting in a pool of blood. He had been shot three times in the right side of the head and once behind the left ear, at close range with a large caliber pistol. He was dressed in his bathrobe and there was no sign of forced entry; a key to his apartment was found inside an elevator. His new Cadillac was in the parking lot with all the doors locked. Money and jewelry valued at close to $50,000 was missing, but robbery was not the motive. The weakest link in the Mob's chain had been eliminated. No one was ever prosecuted for the murder.

Eight Mafiosi were later indicted on 24 counts alleging that they had conspired "to enter into a continuous relationship of affiliation with a secret nationwide organization." They were alleged to have conspired to engage in loansharking, bookmaking, extortion, armed robbery, and to murder four people, including Philip "Brother" Moscato, the owner of a Jersey City dump where the FBI once believed former Teamsters boss Jimmy Hoffa was buried. Boiardo and Anthony DeVingo were further charged with the murder of Paul Campanile, who, according to the indictment, allegedly "shot someone affiliated with the family."

As he had done so often in the past, Boiardo escaped the police net. During the pretrial hearings, he was severed from the case because of his age and health. He would live another five years, dying in 1984 at the age of 93.

15

The Man Who Loves Murder

Ever since he had first read about the Mafia as a boy in South Philadelphia, Joseph Salerno had been intrigued by the secret criminal organization. For years he had longed to be a member, as he would later tell investigators and a jury.

Ironically, it wasn't until his plumbing business in Brigantine (a small beach town some ten miles north of Atlantic City) had gone into bankruptcy and his marriage was on the rocks that the opportunity he had been waiting for presented itself.

His business troubles had started in the spring of 1978 when a contractor defaulted on a $32,000 contract. Salerno needed money to pay suppliers as well as back rent to his father-in-law in whose apartment house he lived with his wife Barbara and their three children. He hadn't paid the rent in months, and it was creating a problem with his in-laws and his wife. So he had gone to Philip "Crazy Phil" Leonetti for a $10,000 loan at the loanshark interest rate of $250 a week—the going rate was supposed to be $500 a week, but Leonetti said he was giving him a break because of their friendship.

Salerno had met Leonetti on a job site. As president of Scarf, Inc., a concrete business he fronted for his uncle, Nicodemo "Little Nicky" Scarfo, Leonetti was well known in the construction business around southern New Jersey. He was also well known as a notorious Mafia enforcer and sidekick of his uncle who ran the rackets in South Jersey for Angelo Bruno.

Eleven months later, Salerno, who by then had paid $9000 in interest and still owed the $10,000, plus another $3000 in back interest, was approached by Leonetti and warned that if he didn't start paying the back interest "the guys I got the money from are going to get rough on you and I don't want that to happen." Salerno's only recourse was to turn to his father, Joseph Salerno, Sr., who borrowed the money from a bank.

By June 1979 Salerno's plumbing business had slipped into bankruptcy and his marriage was headed for the divorce court. The only thing that was going right for him was his relationship with Leonetti and Scarfo, which had progressed to the point where Salerno was being invited to Sunday dinners at Scarfo's second-floor apartment at 26 North Georgia Avenue where he lived with his wife Dominica and their three sons, ages 5 to 17.

The dinners were usually attended by Leonetti, Lawrence "Yogi" Merlino, Vincent Falcone, a concrete contractor, Frank Gerace, president of Local 54 of the Hotel and Restaurant Employees and Bartenders International Union, the largest labor organization in Atlantic City, and Robert Lumio, secretary-treasurer of Local 54. Lumio lived in a third-floor apartment at 26 North Georgia Avenue and Gerace's mother lived in a ground-floor apartment.

The building was owned by Catherine Scarfo, Little Nicky's mother, who also lived in a ground-floor apartment. Merlino lived with Leonetti and his mother, Nancy, who was Scarfo's sister, in a ground-floor apartment in an adjoining building also owned by Catherine Scarfo. Their apartment was behind the offices of Scarf, Inc., and Nat-Nat, a steel-rods business owned by Yogi Merlino and his brother Salvatore, also known as Chuckie, who lived in Philadelphia. Scarfo listed his occupation as a maintenance man for his mother's properties.

Salerno liked his new friends and when he decided to leave his wife that summer, Leonetti told him he could move into a Margate house owned by Yogi while it was being renovated. Instead of paying rent, Salerno did some plumbing work at his new residence.

In September a third-floor apartment became vacant at 26 North Georgia Avenue and Salerno moved in. It was the big move that could free him from his financial straits. During several conversations with Nicky Scarfo prior to his moving in, Salerno had been told that Scarfo would get him lucrative plumbing contracts with the new casinos then under construction. When Salerno asked how Scarfo was going to get rid of the plumbers who already had the contracts, Scarfo pointed his forefinger and cocked his thumb, simulating the firing of a gun, and said, "You let me worry about that." And when Salerno, who ran a nonunion shop, asked about the unions, Scarfo laughed. "Don't ever worry about the unions," he said. "We own the unions."

Salerno's confidence in Scarfo's assertions was bolstered by Scarfo's superior manner in the presence of Gerace and Lumio. Gerace often came to Scarfo for advice, and though the two men would walk away to speak privately, there was no question in Salerno's mind that Scarfo was the man in charge. On one occasion, Scarfo had bawled out Lumio for laughing about a newspaper article linking Scarfo to Local 54. Scarfo had screamed at Lumio. "I got you that job and I got that big fat jerk downstairs his job and don't you ever forget it." The "fat jerk" referred to was Gerace, who was six-feet-three and weighed 280 pounds.

This was heady stuff for a man who had secretly aspired to be a mobster all of his adult life. After moving into his new apartment, Salerno spent most of his days in the office of Scarf, Inc., answering the phone and taking messages. In the evening he went bar-hopping with his new friends. It didn't take him long to realize that he was being closely observed and he became convinced they were testing him to determine if he was worthy of membership.

One night when they were alone at a local bar, Scarfo said, "Hey, Joe, would you ever like to be a gangster?"

The bluntness of the question took Salerno by surprise. "What do you mean?" he asked.

"Listen, Joe, there are three types of criminals. There's gangsters, there's racketeers, and there's junkies. We're gangsters. The junkies, we never bother with them. The racketeers, they come to us, we do their work. But us, Joe, we do things ourselves. When we want somebody killed, we do it ourselves." He again simulated the firing of a gun with his hand.

Another time Scarfo asked Salerno if there was anyone in his family who had anything to do with the law. When Salerno told him no, Scarfo patted him on the shoulder. "You know, Joe, I like you. You're like me. We have the same bloodlines. We're Calabrese people. We're good people."

During these private conversations, Scarfo always told him that what they discussed was to be held in strict confidence. And as time went on, Scarfo's revelations became more daring. Referring to William Dugan, the longshoreman he had killed in 1963 in an argument over who should sit in a booth at the Oregon Diner, Scarfo told Salerno, "I took a knife and stuck it into an Irish motherfucker named Dugan and twisted it into his guts." Scarfo said he pleaded guilty to manslaughter and served only three months in jail.

At times like these Scarfo would get excited, his thin voice rising to a high pitch. It didn't take Salerno long to discover that Scarfo had a wild and uncontrollable temper. When anything displeased him, he started yelling at the top of his voice, no matter where he was. In restaurants and bars, the patrons would look away in fear. At home his wife would huddle in the kitchen. His temper outbursts were frequent and unpredictable. When anything displeased him, he reacted quickly and violently. Once at a Sunday dinner when a steaming platter of spaghetti served by his wife displeased him, he hurled it against the wall.

Police portrayed him as a Napoleonic figure compensating for his 5-feet-5 with violence. He loathed the nickname "Little Nicky" and never tolerated any reference to his size.

He wanted the people around him to admire and emulate him. When he drank Scotch and water, he wanted everybody else to drink it. And he wouldn't allow anyone around him to wear cologne. "It's for faggots," he would say.

One day Scarfo handed Salerno a copy of *Philadelphia Magazine* and pointed to a story about the unsolved murders of Judge Edwin "Eddie" Helfant and Giuseppe "Pepe" Leva, a gambler and professional tailor. "Read this," Scarfo commanded. "See, this is what we can do and this is what we can get away with."

Salerno knew the stories all too well. Leonetti had been a suspect in both gangland-style executions. Actually, Leonetti, who was only 25 years old, had already been a suspect in still a third gangland-style murder. The first victim, Louis DeMarco, an associate of the Bruno family, was shot to death in front of the Ensign Motel in Atlantic City.

A year later, on July 3, 1977, Pepe Leva was found beside his car on Atlantic Avenue in Farmington, with four .32-caliber slugs in his skull. Eight days before his death, Leva had been in the cocktail lounge of the Flamingo Motel when Leonetti and Vincent Bancheri, an associate of Leonetti in Scarf, Inc., had entered and asked Leva to step outside. An argument followed and Leonetti knocked Leva down with his fist, then began kicking him. The attack was stopped by Helfant, who owned the Flamingo. Two days later, Leva filed a municipal court complaint charging Leonetti with assault. Six days later he was dead.

For a moment, the police had thought they were going to solve the Leva murder. An eyewitness to the shooting, Earl DeVault, a garbage truck driver, had identified Leonetti as the man he saw leaning over and emptying a gun into Leva's head the night of the slaying.

Leonetti was indicted and two detectives were assigned to protect DeVault at all times. But three days before the murder trial was to begin, DeVault recanted his testimony. The prosecutor learned that the witness had met "secretly" with attorney Harold Garber, Scarfo's personal lawyer, who in the past had also represented Leonetti. The indictment against Leonetti was dropped and no one bothered to explain how it was possible for DeVault to have met secretly with Garber with two detectives protecting his life. For the Mob, it was the kind of message it loved to send out.

(Seven years later, Garber was suspended from the practice of law for one year by a unanimous ruling of the state supreme court. The court found his representation of both Leonetti and DeVault constituted a conflict of interest. "These personal ties [to Scarfo and Leonetti] were so close that [Garber] claimed to be able to assure safe passage to DeVault, implying that because of his connections to Leonetti and Scarfo, he was DeVault's only possible source of aid," the court said. "Presumably, this refers to some kind of threatened harm that might befall DeVault if his metamorphosis into a full recanting witness was incomplete or too slow.")

Eddie Helfant was another story entirely. Helfant, who worked out of a ramshackle courtroom in Somers Point, was likened to a modern-day Roy Bean. He was a brash, coarse-mouthed wheeler-dealer who served as a link between gangsters and politicians. At the time of his death, he was under indictment on a case-fixing charge that dated back to an incident in 1968 which he had appealed all the way to the U.S. Supreme Court.

For years Helfant's cocktail lounge, the Green Lantern in Somers Point, was the place where Scarfo, Leonetti, and their associates watched football games on Sunday afternoons.

Helfant knew where the fronts were buried in real estate deals and who was doing what to whom in politics and the Mob. He not only knew about real estate deals and liquor license transfers, but was often the one who provided the legal expertise in transactions that placed crime factions into positions for quick profits in that casino boom town.

But with the indictment Helfant was in trouble. He had exhausted his legal options and his trial was imminent. His greatest fear was of losing his license to practice law. It was this fear that led him down the dangerous path of informing against his Mob and political friends. He became a prize informant for the State Commission of Investigation, then the FBI, and finally the Atlantic County Prosecutor's office.

Once Helfant started talking, there was no holding him back. It was Helfant who told the SCI about Angelo Bruno's connection with John Wholesale Distributors and the pizzeria operation of the Gambino family and how the Genovese family was buying into the Ambassador Hotel through a front. He even told them about Frank Jock, a nephew of Herman "Stumpy" Orman, a lifelong friend of Helfant— Orman and Helfant shared offices in the Guarantee Bank Building. Jock, who was negotiating to purchase the Mayflower Hotel, was involved in narcotics distribution, a charge for which he was later indicted, the charge dropped when the two witnesses against Jock were murdered. But something went wrong with Jock's plans, for a few years later he too was murdered.

Helfant refused to talk about Orman, from whom he had purchased the Flamingo Motel on Pacific Avenue, one block from the Boardwalk, and he was careful when he talked about Scarfo and Leonetti. It was obvious that he was fearful of these men. Still he revealed important information. So much so, in fact, that some of the investigators became worried that he was talking too much and to too many people. In that town, it was inevitable that sooner than later he would talk to the wrong cop.

On the night of February 15, 1978, as a handful of customers at the Flamingo bar watched the Ali-Spinks fight on television, a man wearing a black ski mask and carrying a dented snow shovel trudged through a week-old crust of snow toward the Flamingo's bar. Setting the snow shovel next to the door, the masked figure slipped inside unnoticed and moved swiftly to a table occupied by two men and a woman. The killer stopped behind one of the men, placed a hand on his shoulder, and aimed a .38-caliber revolver at the man sitting across the table from him. Four shots were fired, one into the man's forehead and three across his chest. Marcine Helfant screamed and reached to catch her husband, but Eddie Helfant was dead before his body hit the floor. When she looked up, the killer had vanished.

An hour later, attorney Raymond Brown received a call from the judge who was to hear Brown's motion for directed acquittal the next morning. "I guess you won't be coming in to court tomorrow morning," the judge told him. "I just heard from the state police that your client is dead."

Brown, who had been putting the final touches on his motion in a motel room in Trenton, called his co-counsel, Carl Poplar, and together they drove to Helfant's Margate home. "There was a cop at the front door," Brown would later tell the *Press*. "When we went inside, there was his wife, Marcine, sitting on the couch, her dress covered with blood. And you know who was sitting next to her, the only other person in the room? Steve Perskie and shaking like a leaf." Helfant's original attorney in the case had been Marvin Perskie, who had recently died.

In commenting on Brown's statement, *Press* reporter Michael Checchio wrote: "It was a moment of undeniable irony: The politician most responsible for casino gambling was sitting next to the shocked widow of the man many law enforcement officials suspected knew the blueprint for the Mob's invasion of Atlantic City."

Scarfo's dark eyes never left Salerno as he read the magazine article. Like so many other times since he had moved to the third floor at 26 North Georgia Avenue, Salerno felt that he was "going through a test."

At a restaurant the evening before, Scarfo had started talking about hunting and had suddenly asked Salerno what kind of guns he owned. When Salerno said he had a Browning 30.06 rifle and a pearl-handled .32-caliber Colt revolver that had belonged to his father's grandfather but had been restored, Scarfo said, "Why don't you bring them down and show them to me?" Salerno explained that because of the children he had left them with his father in Philadelphia.

Nothing more was said about the guns until a few days later. Salerno, who was doing some plumbing work for Scarfo's mother, was going to Philadelphia in a Scarf, Inc., truck to pick up some cabinets. When he was ready to leave, Scarfo came into the room and said, "Why don't you bring those chandeliers back with you?"

"Chandeliers?"

"Yeah," Scarfo said, indicating guns with his hands.

Salerno caught on. He knew that Scarfo was worried about listening devices in the room. Since their conversation at the restaurant, Salerno had had second thoughts about the guns and wished he hadn't admitted owning them. Now he tried to find an excuse for not bringing them. "You know," he said, when they were in the hallway, "suppose I get stopped with the guns inside a Scarf truck."

"Good thinking," Scarfo said. "Don't bother with them today."

A few days later, Scarfo asked Salerno to drive Lawrence Merlino to Philadelphia because his car had broken down. "While you're there, why don't you pick up those guns?"

Salerno knew it was too late for excuses. He picked up the guns at his father's house, telling him he was going hunting, and delivered them to the Scarf, Inc., office where Scarfo, Leonetti, and Merlino looked them over. Scarfo smiled with satisfaction. "They're really nice," he said, handing the rifle to Merlino and holding on to the revolver. "I'm going to stash these for you."

During lunch at the Brajole Cafe the next day, Scarfo said, "We're going to need shells for the Colt. Get shorts. Longs cut right through people and damage property."

Salerno tried to mask his consternation but Scarfo caught something in his expression. He leaned forward in his chair. "You know, Joe," he said, "anything we talk about is between us. This is bad," he said, indicating moving lips with his fingers. "You do this," again he moved his fingers next to his mouth, "and you get this," and he simulated the firing of a gun, "here," tapping his head, "and in here," indicating his chest.

Salerno hardly needed this warning. He was already apprehensive enough. He was positive that he knew more than was good for him. The idea of becoming a Mafioso was quickly losing its appeal. He spent most of his free time trying to think of some plausible excuse for getting away from there. For the time being, however, he decided it was best to go along with their game, try to pacify them in any way he could.

On the morning of December 15, Lawrence Merlino came into the office and told Salerno: "He wants to see you upstairs."

Salerno hurried to Scarfo's apartment and found him alone. His wife and children were away. Scarfo took him into the kitchen and turned on the radio. "I'll tell you why we wanted the gun," he said. "There's this guy we want to hit, Tony DePasquale." Scarfo looked closely at him. "Listen, Joe, if something happens in front of you, if you see anything at all, will you be okay?"

Salerno swallowed hard. "I'll be okay."

"You sure you can stand up?"

"Yes."

"Good, now I want you to hang around Phil [Leonetti] between four and six o'clock every day. Now, don't you say a word about this to Vince Falcone—or anybody else."

On his way back down the stairs to the office, Salerno thought his legs were going to collapse under him. He knew that Scarfo had lied to him. The hit was going to be Falcone, who dropped by between four and six every day after work. Although they pretended to be good friends with Falcone, Salerno had noticed a cooling off ever since Scarfo and Leonetti had returned from a trip to Italy in November.

Around six that afternoon, after Falcone had left, Lawrence Merlino said to Salerno and Leonetti, "Let's take a ride."

They walked down Georgia Avenue to Merlino's black Thunderbird. Salerno noticed that Merlino had a brown paper bag in his hand, which he placed under the front seat. Salerno was told to get in the back. Merlino drove toward Egg Harbor Township, with Leonetti sitting next to him.

Salerno's mind was occupied with the possible content of the brown paper bag. After a while he became convinced that it held his Colt and that they were going to use it to kill him. Killed by his own gun. But why would they want to kill him? He hadn't harmed them. He had done everything they had asked of him.

Salerno caught Merlino's eyes in the rear-view mirror and tried to smile. "Hey, sit back there, relax," Merlino said.

All Salerno could think of saying was "Let's go get something to eat," which he repeated until they finally stopped at a restaurant.

Later that evening, after they had returned to Atlantic City, Merlino and Salerno went to a bar. After a few drinks Salerno couldn't hold it back any longer. "Today, when we went for the ride, you know, I thought you guys were going to kill me."

"Oh," Merlino said, "what makes you think that?"

Salerno scratched his head and tried to turn it into a joke but couldn't think of anything funny to say. "I don't know. Forget about it. But let me ask you something: If anything did happen inside a car, what would you do with the body, the evidence and stuff like that?"

"You can always get rid of a car or a body," he said, standing up. "Let's get out of here."

Early the next morning, before anybody was up, Salerno called his wife Barbara and told her he wanted to come see the kids. When she said she was on her way out to take the boys to cut firewood, he told her to wait for him.

It was a Sunday morning and Salerno left the Georgia Avenue house without seeing anyone. In Brigantine, he picked up his wife and children and drove to Galloway Township. While the boys looked for firewood, he took his wife aside and said, "Barb, I'm scared to death that something is going to happen to me or to somebody else."

"What's the matter?" she said. "What do you mean?"

"I think somebody's gonna get killed today."

"Who?"

"I don't know. I'm not sure. It could be Vince Falcone, but I doubt it because they've been good friends for years. Except, you know, lately it's been a little different. I can't explain it. Something's just not right." And he told her the whole story, about the guns, and being asked if he could stand up, and to hang around Phil between four and six, and not to mention it to Falcone. "There's something funny going on," he concluded, "but I just can't put my finger on it."

It was a little after two when they got back to the house with the firewood. A few minutes later the phone rang, and it was Lawrence Merlino. "He wants you over here."

"Can it wait a while?" Salerno asked. "I want to trim the tree."

"He needs you," Merlino said and hung up.

Salerno turned to his wife. "I have to go back," he said. "If anything happens to me, you know who I'm with."

Back at the Georgia Avenue office, he found Merlino, Leonetti, and Falcone. "Come on," Leonetti said, "we're going to the Ivory for drinks."

"Phil, I'd like to go home and help the wife and kids trim the Christmas tree."

"Look, Joe, do me a favor and come with us," Phil Leonetti said, grabbing his arm and pulling him toward the door. "Today we're going to party and drink. It's a Christmas celebration."

They all got into Merlino's Thunderbird and he started driving toward Margate. When they drove past the Ivory, Falcone said, "Where are we going?"

"We're going to pick up my uncle at Phil Disney's house at the end of Decatur Avenue here," Leonetti said.

Disney, whose real name was Phillip "Disney" McFillin, was a contractor and close friend of Scarfo. When they arrived at the house, Merlino pulled up next to Scarfo's black Cadillac and all four men went inside. Scarfo was sitting on the living-room couch watching a football game. He stood up and everybody shook hands.

"Hey, Vince," Scarfo said, "help yourself, make some drinks."

Falcone went into the kitchen, got some ice out of the refrigerator, got some glasses out of a cabinet, and began mixing the drinks. He brought a couple in the living room and went back to mix more.

What happened next was like something in slow motion for Salerno. He saw Leonetti come up behind Falcone, pull the pearl-handled Colt out of his pocket, and extend his arm until the gun barrel nearly touched the back of Falcone's head. Salerno had a glass of wine up to his mouth, watching in stunned disbelief, as Leonetti pulled the trigger.

Falcone sank to the floor, his hands on his stomach, in a sitting position, then slowly slumped onto his back. He seemed to be staring into space.

Salerno's first reaction was to bolt but he stood still. He felt a hand on his shoulder and heard Scarfo say, "Don't be afraid, Joe. Take it easy, everything's under control."

Scarfo then walked over to the body, looked down, and said "Let's wait five minutes."

Leonetti stared directly at Salerno and shouted, "He was a no-good motherfucker, Joe."

Vince Falcone was only 35 years old, Salerno's age, and a minute before he had been alive. Salerno was sure he was going to be next. "I didn't know it was going to be him," he said lamely.

Scarfo knelt beside the body and placed his ear against the chest to listen for a heartbeat. He looked up and shook his head. "I think we should give him another one, Phil. Want me to do it?"

"No, where do you want it?"

Scarfo opened Falcone's leather jacket and Leonetti placed the gun against the chest and fired. Scarfo reached into Falcone's jacket pocket and removed his car keys. He stood up and nodded approvingly. "Okay, wrap the gun in a towel and wipe it off good, then get rid of it. Phil, I want you to take Yogi to get Vince's car and Yogi you bring it back here, but first you two go home, shower good, change your clothes and get rid of them too."

After they had left, Scarfo came up to Salerno and grabbed him by the arms. "Are you okay, Joe?"

"Yeah, I'm okay."

"Great, you're doing a good job, Joe. You're one of us now," he said.

Salerno nodded, not knowing what to say, and Scarfo said, "I'm going to need your strength now to tie this guy up. There's a blanket and rope in that cardboard box. Bring it in the kitchen."

To give them working room, they moved the kitchen table out into the living room and went back into the kitchen. "Okay, Joe, let's turn him over. We're going to tie him up, like old times, tie him like a cowboy."

Following Scarfo's instructions, Salerno tied the hands behind the back, tied the feet, then pulled the feet and hands and tied them together.

"Good," Scarfo said, "now let's tie this blanket around him."

After that was done, Scarfo leaned over the body, raised the head and let it drop. He closed the eyes and pulled the blanket over the face. Then he tied the blanket around the head, stood up, and clapped his hands in satisfaction.

"I love this," Scarfo cried out. "I love this. The big shot is dead." He looked straight at Salerno and his eyes hardened. "He was a dirty motherfucker. If it wasn't so messy I'd cut his fucking tongue out."

It was difficult for Salerno to believe that what was happening was real. "Does Phil Disney know about this?" he asked, not knowing what else to say.

"No, we've got to clean up the place real good. Start in the kitchen. Put your gloves on and wipe everything clean."

After he had finished, Salerno joined Scarfo in the living room and they started drinking. "Phil [Leonetti] is the best," Scarfo said. "Already was the best."

Salerno nodded. "I wonder what's keeping Yogi?"

"Yeah, Joe, you're one of us now," Scarfo said. "When the old man [Bruno] goes, I'm going to be right next to Phil [Testa]. We're going to own Atlantic City someday."

Even with a couple more drinks, Salerno was very nervous. "I don't think Yogi's ever coming back. Maybe I should call him. See what he's doing. Hustle him up a little bit. What do you think?"

"Yeah, okay, give him a call."

When Salerno headed for the phone in the kitchen, Scarfo stopped him. "No, don't use that phone. Use the pay phone down the street, across from the Ivory."

Once out of the house, Salerno felt a great urge to run down the street, but he controlled it. His first call was home and his son Michael answered. Barbara was out shopping and Salerno told him, "Tell Mommie everything's okay." Then he called Merlino who said he was ready to leave. Reluctantly, Salerno returned to the Disney house and the body of Vincent Falcone.

They had more drinks and watched television until Merlino returned. He backed Falcone's Cougar up to the steps of the deck and Salerno helped him carry the body out of the house. But before they could place it in the trunk, Scarfo stopped them. "Wait, there's something in Vince's trunk I've always wanted." He removed a box and they dropped the body into the trunk and closed the lid.

"I'm going to drive Vince's car to Madison in Margate," Scarfo said. "You guys follow me in my car. Stay about a block or so behind. When I get out, let me walk about a block before you pick me up."

Merlino followed the instructions and when they picked Scarfo up on Madison Avenue, he was carrying the box. The moment he got into the back seat of his Cadillac, he opened the box and took out a jogging suit and a bank currency bag. "This is what I wanted all this time," he said, taking a handgun out of the bag.

But Scarfo was not yet finished with the Disney house. They went back and Salerno and Merlino wiped everything in the kitchen— floors, cabinets, appliances—with cold water until Scarfo was satisfied that it was clean.

Back at the Georgia Avenue house, Salerno was given a large plastic bag and told to go to his apartment, take a shower, and put all his clothes in the bag—sport jacket, pants, shirt, underwear, socks, shoes, belt—and bring the bag to Scarfo's apartment, which he did. When he returned to Scarfo's apartment, Salvatore Merlino was there. Scarfo stuffed Salerno's plastic bag into a larger trash bag which Leonetti and Salerno later disposed of in a dumpster trash container behind a restaurant. The box of bullets and empty shells was dropped into a storm drain.

At dinner in Scarfo's apartment that evening, Lawrence Merlino looked at Salerno and said, "Lights out."

"But why?" Salerno asked. "Why was it Vince?"

"I'll tell you why," Scarfo said. "When me and Phil went to Italy last month, Vince told Larry [Merlino] that Phil shouldn't be in the concrete business and that I was crazy. See, the guy was just jealous."

"If I could bring him back to life," Leonetti said, "I'd kill him again."

"Yeah, Joe, like I told you," Scarfo said. "Vince was a dirty motherfucker. I'd have cut his fucking tongue out if it wasn't so fucking messy."

"Yeah, and there's another motherfucker that's going to get hit," Leonetti said.

Scarfo banged the table with his fist. "Alfredo Ferraro," he shouted. "But I don't want to use no gun on him. I'm gonna stab him and cut his guts out and fry them."

Later Scarfo said, "Tomorrow, nobody works. We're going to have a day off, a vacation. We all go to Philadelphia, to the Camachs, take some steam, have dinner, celebrate. Joe, you go to your mother's house in Philly and wait for us to call you there."

After dinner everyone got girls and went to Caesars except Scarfo. He said he had to baby-sit for his wife Dominica, who had gone to a union party at Convention Hall. They partied until four in the morning, and after dropping off his date in Ventnor, Salerno drove to his wife's home in Brigantine and told her what had happened at Disney's house.

"I know why they wanted me there," he said. "Vince trusted me. He was afraid of those guys but he was sure they wouldn't do anything to him in front of me. They just used me and when they think about it they're going to get me too. So I better get back there and not give them cause for suspicion."

When he returned to Georgia Avenue, he was completely confused. He didn't know what to do next. He sat up the rest of the night. The next morning he drove to his mother's house in Philadelphia and waited for the promised call. It came in midafternoon. It was Leonetti, saying that his uncle was ill, and for Salerno to return to Atlantic City. When he arrived at Scarfo's apartment, he found the usual group plus Salvatore Testa and Frank Narducci, Jr.

He had a couple of drinks, excused himself, and drove to Brigantine. Life at home with his wife was looking better all the time, but after two days without any contact from Scarfo, he became worried that they might become suspicious, and he called the house. The phone was answered by Nancy Leonetti. She said that her son and brother were at Scannicchio's Restaurant.

By the time Salerno arrived at the restaurant, he was in a frenzy.

Scarfo asked him why he looked so worried.

"Well, the cops will know he was killed by .32-caliber bullets."

"So what?" Leonetti said.

"If my father reads that in the paper I'm afraid he might get suspicious. You know, I took the gun, and he knows I know Vince. So I don't know. What do I say to him if he asks me? What if he wants the gun back?"

Scarfo gave him an icy stare. "Don't worry about it, you can handle it. The world is full of .32s."

After Scarfo had left, Leonetti berated Salerno. "What the hell's the matter with you?" he said. "You never should have said that about the gun to my uncle. See, now you've got him all upset."

The next day, Scarfo called Salerno. "They found our friend," he said. "You better come to the house." But when Salerno arrived at Georgia Avenue, Scarfo greeted him outside. "Everything's going smooth," he said. "But you better not come in because there might be a lot of heat around here. Stay home for a while."

That Saturday, December 22, Salerno was visited by three investigators from the Atlantic County Prosecutor's office. They told him the word out on the street was that he was next to be killed. That evening Salerno gave them a complete statement and a few days later was taken into the Federal Witness Protection Program.

Early on the morning of December 23, Atlantic County investigators armed with a search and arrest warrant broke into Scarfo's apartment through a window when repeated knocking at the door was not answered. They were met by Dominica, wearing her husband's pajama top and waving a kitchen knife. Roused from sleep by the crashing window, Catherine Scarfo rushed up to her son's apartment and began screaming at the men who were going through the room "like rabbits," as she would later put it.

They were looking for Salerno's pearl-handled Colt and Falcone's jogging suit. Instead they found a derringer inside a makeshift holster and a photocopied list of names and telephone numbers written in a secret code to shield the identities of persons with residences in New Jersey, New York, Pennsylvania, Massachusetts, Florida, and Nevada. It would take the police 18 months to break the code. The investigators also found a bulletproof vest with a .22 slug lodged in it and a pair of jogging pants. Scarfo, who wasn't home, was arrested later that morning at the apartment of a woman friend.

Leonetti and Merlino were picked up and all three were charged with the murder of Vincent Falcone. In a few days they were released on bail that allowed the substitution of property for cash. Statements from scores of witnesses were taken by the defense lawyers in Scarfo's apartment, in the presence of the three defendants. The defendants had no trouble finding friends to provide alibis for the time of the murder and to impugn the character of Salerno. In all, over fifty witnesses would testify for the defense.

Salerno was described as a violence-prone man who had threatened to kill four persons. Debbie D'Amato testified that Salerno had threatened to shoot her boyfriend in the head. Under cross-examination, D'Amato admitted that she gave her statement to attorney Harold Garber at Scarfo's apartment with Scarfo and Leonetti present but denied discussing her testimony with the defendants. Lucy Campbell said Salerno threatened to shoot her husband who worked for Rick Casale, a close associate of the three defendants. Saba Pullella, owner of the Brajole Cafe and a friend of the defendants, testified that Salerno had threatened to shoot his bartender but under cross-examination said he never notified police about the threat. Maria Pullella, a waitress at the Brajole Cafe and a girlfriend of Leonetti's, offered phone toll receipts that she claimed showed she had talked with Leonetti at the time of the murder, providing him with an alibi, and further testified that she saw Scarfo's Cadillac parked outside his home that afternoon.

Three other defense witnesses placed the defendants in the Country Squire Diner in Egg Harbor Township shortly before the time of the killing. A waitress, Gertrude Willoughby, testified she didn't know the defendants by name but "Well, anyone would notice anyone that good looking. The gentleman in the middle [Leonetti] is an extremely good-looking man. Anyone would notice him."

This characterization of Leonetti was nothing compared to the one given to the press by Pamela Higgins, a member of Scarfo's defense team. A former prosecutor for the U.S. Organized Crime Strike Force in Philadelphia, Higgins described Scarfo as "charming, very handsome, very modest, extremely polite, courteous and respectful to me. He's got a great sense of dignity about him." She sang his praises in several interviews. In one she described him as "the kind of person you'd expect to meet at a dinner party . . . quiet . . . and deferential, with a lot of personal dignity."

Dominica testified that her husband was home at the time of the murder. Under cross-examination, Mrs. Scarfo repeatedly denied ever discussing the case with either of the defense attorneys or her husband.

Leonetti's 17-year-old girlfriend, Gina Barbella, who lived next door to Leonetti, testified she had been dating him since she was 15, and had seen him at the time of the murder. She had also dated Falcone. Her father, John, appeared as a character witness for Leonetti.

Even Falcone's wife was a witness for the defense, testifying that her husband had warned her to be careful of a group of men other than the three defendants. The leader of this group, she said, was Alfredo Ferraro. At the time of the murder, the Falcones were separated.

Others testified that they had seen the defendants at Scarf, Inc., that Sunday afternoon and still others had seen Scarfo in his apartment watching television. According to the witnesses, the defendants had been just about everywhere that day except at Phil Disney's house. Disney was questioned by investigators, but because he was a close friend of Scarfo, he was not called as a prosecution witness and was completely ignored by the defense.

The icing on the defense cake was provided by Detective Sergeant William Gary Breland, an investigator in the case, who was called as a defense witness. He testified that he had passed the Disney home at the time of the murder and had not seen Scarfo's black Cadillac parked there.

Under cross-examination Breland said that the previous March he had moved into a house owned by Rick Casale. It was that same month that he first reported his observation to Harold Garber. He gave this information to Scarfo's attorney because it was the first time anyone had asked him if he had spotted the Cadillac the day of Falcone's murder. But when the prosecutor inquired if Breland had been instructed during the investigation to ask if any police officer had spotted Scarfo's Cadillac in the area that day, Breland replied that he understood he was only supposed to ask officers if they had been parked near the scene of the crime that day.

Pitted against the formidable battery of defense witnesses was the uncorroborated testimony of Joseph Salerno. It took the jury 5½ hours to find the three defendants not guilty. As the verdict was read, Scarfo and Leonetti smiled, nodded knowingly, and clasped their hands as if in prayer.

"Thank God for the American jury system," Scarfo told the reporters. "It's the greatest in the world. They found innocent men not guilty. Thank God for an honest jury."

So thrilled were they by the verdict that they went home and painted a Liberty Bell on the white concrete walls of a shed behind 28 North Georgia Avenue. Above it, in red, white, and blue letters they wrote the words GOD BLESS AMERICA.

Sergeant Breland left the police force and his wife, and with his girlfriend in tow, moved to New Orleans, never to be heard from again.

"Everything that Salerno said was a lie," said one juror, who asked to remain anonymous. The theory, proposed by the defense, that Salerno alone had killed Falcone was a popular one with the jury. "You can't tell me one person couldn't have carried the body alone," said the juror. "And why didn't they put Phil Disney on the stand to say he gave the key to Scarfo? Or to Salerno?" said the juror. "How the hell do we know?"

Two years later, a man wearing a hooded jogging suit, a ski mask, and ski goggles knocked at the office door of the El Reno Motel in Wildwood Crest. When Salerno's father, Joseph, Sr., opened the door, the man pulled out a pistol and fired twice, hitting him once in the throat before he could slam the door shut. The assailant ran off and Salerno was rushed to the hospital where he recovered.

The attack came one month after Salerno, Jr., had testified before the Casino Control Commission, repeating, in even greater detail, what he had said to Atlantic County investigators on December 22, 1979, in his trial testimony, and before a U.S. Senate committee. His testimony before the casino commission stressed Scarfo's relationship with Frank Gerace, Robert Lumio, Frank Materio, and other officials of Local 54.

For several days after the motel attack, Scarfo, Leonetti, Merlino, and Nicholas "Nick the Blade" Virgilio paraded around town in jogging outfits. This brazen demonstration so outraged authorities that Scarfo was arrested for associating with known criminals, a violation of the conditions of his bail following his conviction for possession of the derringer. But this was in August 1982 and much had to transpire before this came to pass.

16

Arabs, Bagmen, and Pigeons

Angelo J. Errichetti had personally booked Kambir Abdul Rahman's party into complimentary rooms at the Holiday Inn in Atlantic City. This was to be his second meeting with Abdul's emissaries. At the first meeting, held in the Long Island office of Abdul Enterprises, Errichetti had felt he had really impressed them.

Errichetti was a tough guy who dressed, looked, and talked like a hood. And he was a thief. At that first meeting, he hadn't minced any words. "I'll give you Atlantic City; without me, you do nothing."

The three emissaries in the office with him—Tony DeVito, Jack McCloud, and Mel Weinberg—appeared impressed by his offer. Abdul, they said, wanted someone who could guarantee a casino license. Abdul didn't want to buy land or build until he had that assurance. And he wanted to buy the right state and Atlantic City officials.

"If you people do the right thing, if you do it our way, there'll be no trouble," Errichetti promised. "I'll be your rabbi." The mayor of Camden and a state senator serving on key committees, Errichetti liked to boast that he was the most powerful political leader in South Jersey.

To impress Weinberg further, Errichetti said, "I'm a very dear friend of the governor. I call him a cocksucker, but he likes it. Very close to the governor. Very close to his people. The attorney general is very close to me. I spoke with him, like it was you, on a business basis." The governor, he added, had promised that Errichetti would "be allowed to name the next member of the Casino Control Commission and two members of the South Jersey port authority."

After that first meeting, Errichetti and Weinberg had spoken on the phone several times. Now, alone with McCloud in the Holiday Inn, Errichetti gave him the bottom line: $25,000 up front to start the right wheels turning on Abdul's license, then a total of $400,000 for the license itself, assuring McCloud that he owned the comission's vice-chairman, Kenneth MacDonald, and through him three more votes, including Lordi's.

Later that evening, Errichetti told Weinberg that he had arranged for Abdul's group to meet Alexander Feinberg, an attorney and the "bagman" for Harrison Arlington Williams, Jr., the senior U.S. senator from New Jersey and chairman of the Senate Labor Committee.

The meeting was at Feinberg's office in Cherry Hill. With Feinberg was Henry Williams III, no relation to the senator, who explained that they were in partnership in a titanium mine with Senator Williams and George Katz, a garbage contractor who became a millionaire through kickback deals with corrupt politicians over a thirty-year period. Indicted once for fraud on state highway contracts, Katz refused to testify against the politicians involved, earning himself a solid reputation as a stand-up guy. The case was later dismissed due to the expiration of the statute of limitations. Katz also had solid Mob connections, including a long-time friendship with Meyer Lansky, whom he visited on trips to Florida. For Katz, paying bribes was, as he explained to Abdul's men, "doing the right thing."

All that this strange collection of business partners needed to get into the titanium business was a loan of $100 million. They could make a killing because the government was in desperate need of titanium.

As Abdul's men were leaving that day, Errichetti whispered to Weinberg. "Push this one. We can make a lotta bucks with the senator."

Mayor Errichetti paid another visit to Abdul Enterprises, received the $25,000 in up-front money he had demanded, and again repeated that he could deliver Kenneth MacDonald, hinting that he was doing the same for Resorts, which was then in the midst of its hearings.

Since everything was moving along smoothly, Errichetti suggested that Abdul should look ahead to the day he would need an expert casino manager. As it happened, he had convinced a friend, Tony

Torcasio, to leave Las Vegas to work for Penthouse's planned casino. Torcasio would make an ideal casino manager for Abdul.

Tony DeVito made Errichetti's day. Abdul, he said, had definitely decided to build a casino and wanted the mayor to select the site. Even more exciting, Abdul wanted to buy every choice site in town, which he would then sell at inflated prices and share the profits with the mayor.

Errichetti was ecstatic. "I sit here and tell you without any fucking bit of imagination or whatever have you . . . the fucking town is ours."

However, DeVito said, Abdul wanted them to get personal assurances directly from MacDonald that the license was guaranteed or the deal was off.

Errichetti grabbed a piece of paper and scribbled the figure $100,000. That, he said, was the amount needed to bribe four of the commissioners. He had already discussed the figure with MacDonald, who had cleared it with the others. But, he said, "you couldn't hand them anything, because that would be the end of it. I'm their bag guy. They're gonna deal with me. I'm gonna deal with you."

They argued and finally, after DeVito angrily pronounced the deal dead, Errichetti, with visions of a fortune slipping through his fingers, relented. "Okay," he said, "but the conversation's gonna be nothing but how are you, I'm fine, and goodbye. That's it."

The confrontation had visibly shaken Errichetti. As he was leaving, he became wistful: "Always, every time I've looked at something, there's always been a missing link. This is the most fucking unbelievable thing I've ever seen in my whole life, and I'm fifty years old. I've seen a lotta things, and heard a lotta things, and dreamed a lotta things, but this thing just seems to be coming up."

Errichetti could hardly believe his good luck. Weinberg had told him that Tony DeVito had been promoted to board chairman of a company headed by Yassir Habib, a close friend of Abdul who held the title of Emir.

"Don't worry about Tony," Weinberg had told him. "He's just like me; he'll steal a buck."

Not only that, but DeVito had told Yassir about Errichetti and now the Emir was giving a party in the mayor's honor on his yacht moored in Fort Lauderdale, Florida. As a token of his friendship, Yassir was to present Errichetti with an ancient ceremonial knife that had been in his family for centuries. Of course, if Errichetti preferred a gold watch, Yassir would understand. After all, it was an old American custom.

Errichetti opted for the knife. "I will treasure it," he assured Weinberg. "Friendship is everything."

Errichetti and his nephew, Joseph Di Lorenzo, who worked as his chauffeur but was carried on the Camden city payroll as Director of the Bureau of Energy, arrived in Fort Lauderdale two days early. With them was Tony Torcasio.

All three were booked into the Spanish River Inn in Delray Beach as guests of the sheik. Alone in his suite with DeVito and Weinberg, Errichetti agreed to bring Kenneth MacDonald to Abdul's Long Island office to collect the $100,000 bribe. But MacDonald would stay outside in the car while Errichetti came upstairs to accept the money.

Once he had the money, Abdul's casino license application "should move like lightning," he said. "If it's fucked up, I wanna know. You're buying the whole fucking town. You got four fucking guaranteed commissioners . . . Ken MacDonald, that's his job. Whether he keeps all his profit, whether he splits it up, I don't give a fuck."

In another session, the three men listened in fascination as Torcasio described the many ways he could skim as much as a third of the casino's profits without the owner's being aware of it. If Abdul agreed to finance the Penthouse casino, Errichetti had promised that Torcasio would split the skim with the three of them on a weekly basis.

Torcasio reinforced that promise. "I never lie to my friends," he said. "When we break bread, hear, you guys will never have to work. If you come up to me and say, we gotta have $80,000 taken off, it'll be there. You know what that is? Eighty thousand without any taxes!" Grinning slyly, Torcasio hinted at secret links to Mafia chiefs.

On several occasions, Errichetti had done more than hint about his Mafia connections. He'd assured Abdul's men that his Mafia links reached to the very top. In fact, his man was none other than Paul Castellano, the new boss of the Gambino family, whom he described as the "boss of all bosses." "Big Paul" had given Errichetti his personal blessings in Atlantic City.

And there was more. In New Jersey, Errichetti's Mafia connection was Gerardo "Jerry" Catena, for years the underboss of the Genovese family. Although Catena was semiretired and now spending a lot of time in Florida, Errichetti assured them that he still represented his Cosa Nostra family's interest in Atlantic City through his control of Lordi, whom, the mayor said, Catena "owned."

Senator Harrison Williams, Jr., had cancelled an important political affair to attend Yassir's yacht party. It was an impressive affair. One by one, the forty guests were escorted to the seated Emir, who greeted them with the Arab words of welcome: *"Selam Aleycum."* The emotional moment was the presentation of the ceremonial knife to Errichetti, who, with eyes glistening and a voice choked with emotion, again observed: "Friendship is everything."

Afterward, the important guests were asked by the royal photographer to pose individually with the Emir. Senator Williams looked straight into the camera and tried desperately to smile. Errichetti had no problem smiling. Dressed in a business suit and wearing a burnoose and sunglasses, the Emir never smiled.

A few minutes later, the Emir departed with a regal wave of his hand, bidding his guests remain and enjoy the party.

That evening, Errichetti agreed that MacDonald would accompany him when he came to collect the $100,000, but the money should be handed to the mayor. Later that evening, Senator Williams again expressed his personal interest in the titanium mine but asked DeVito and Weinberg to deal directly with attorney Alexander Feinberg.

A week later, on March 31, 1979, Errichetti and MacDonald visited Abdul Enterprises and were greeted by Jack McCloud, who had the $100,000 in a briefcase. While Errichetti and McCloud talked, MacDonald walked to the window and stood there quietly gazing out. McCloud twice opened the case to expose the bills stacked inside but made no effort to hand it over. Each time Errichetti reached for it, McCloud pulled it back.

Turning from the window, MacDonald assured McCloud that if Abdul had no criminal background and followed the prescribed procedure, he'd have "no trouble" getting his license. Satisfied, McCloud handed over the case, and Errichetti and MacDonald left, making a beeline for the Holiday Inn and a prearranged meeting with Weinberg and DeVito.

MacDonald was furious at the insulting way McCloud had displayed the money and the cat-and-mouse game he seemed to have enjoyed playing. Errichetti swore that he wouldn't deal with McCloud again. DeVito assured them that he soon would be taking over the entire Abdul-Yassir operation and would give MacDonald a high executive position at Abdul's casino.

Leaving DeVito and MacDonald in the hotel's restaurant, Errichetti and Weinberg went outside for a private talk. Errichetti took out a brochure with the names and pictures of all the members of the New Jersey Legislature and carefully checked off 13 names. Grinning proudly, he said they all were key members of important committees and all were for sale. Handing the brochure to Weinberg, he said he'd be glad to introduce him to all of them.

The next day Errichetti called Weinberg. "Thank God for you and Tony," he said, "because, very honestly, he [MacDonald] was quite shook up. There's no question about it."

The previous day, Weinberg had told Errichetti that DeVito could be in trouble with Yassir because of a fire in the yacht's engine room that was due to his negligence. He needed $25,000 to make secret repairs.

Now, Errichetti was saying, "Just to show you what kind of guy [MacDonald] is, when he had the case in his hand [on the ride home] and he started counting it, and I explained to him Tony's plight with the boat, that he needed the $25,000, he didn't hesitate one little second. Just whipped it right out and said, 'Give it to Tony,' and, uh, I've got it right here and I wanna know what to do with it."

Weinberg thanked him and lost no time in sending someone over to pick it up.

Errichetti was a politician of many parts. No matter what the problem he was presented with, he usually came up with an answer. For example, DeVito told him that Yassir was having problems freeing his money from his native country. What he needed were certificates of deposit, gold certificates, anything that could be sent to the Emir's banks in exchange for the money. Then the sheik would have no problem transferring his funds to the Chase Manhattan Bank, where he wanted to keep a balance of $400 million.

In no time, Errichetti delivered $435 million in counterfeit Chemical Bank certificates of deposit to DeVito. His source for the bogus CDs, he boasted, was his good friend Mafia boss Paul Castellano— which proved once and for all the quality of the mayor's connections.

Senator Williams was a product of the old John V. Kenny Democratic machine. Kenny, now long dead, had fashioned a web of corruption that was still very much a part of New Jersey politics. Kenny men were congressmen, legislators, judges, prosecutors, mayors, councilmen, sheriffs, police chiefs, and the list probably ran all the way down to dog catcher.

In the fall of 1979, after attending a New York Giants football game, Williams and his attorney, Alexander Feinberg, met with DeVito and Weinberg in Yassir's Plaza Hotel suite and presented them with another package they wanted Yassir to finance—Williams had already agreed to use his Senate position to help secure government contracts for the titanium mine and had received corporate stocks valued at $17 million from Yassir.

Now all they needed was $70 million to turn the old Ritz hotel into a dazzling casino. The Ritz had been bought by Hardwicke Companies, Inc., operator of the Benihana chain of Japanese restaurants, and Williams's wife, Jeanette, had served on Hardwicke's board of directors from 1976 to 1978 and was still employed as an $18,000-a-year consultant. Mrs. Williams also received $35,000 as an employee of the Senate Committee on Labor and Human Resources, which was chaired by her husband.

For his meeting at the Plaza, Williams brought artist sketches of the Ritz's proposed Oz-like facade designed by Great Adventure creator Warner Leroy. For the $70 million, Yassir would receive a first mortgage on the building and land.

DeVito seemed interested as he examined the sketches. But he was worried about the same old problem: What assurances could the Senator give them about the license?

"We're in excellent shape for a license," Feinberg said. "Absolutely. It's better than the average because of what's already taken place."

Smiling proudly, Williams explained that he had used his influence with Joseph Lordi to secure a declaratory ruling from the commission that allowed Hardwicke to renovate the old hotel, thereby circumventing tough casino regulations that required casino operators to build new structures. That had saved the Ritz $30 million.

The gaming commission's vote on the Ritz had been unanimous, Feinberg boasted, "Five zero." At the time of their application for the Ritz, Ramada Inn had also sought a declaratory ruling allowing them to renovate an existing structure and had been rejected unanimously. Ramada and Ritz had "comparable problems," Feinberg said.

Williams laughed. "Five zero, zero five."

"That's right," Feinberg agreed. "Five zero, zero five."

DeVito wanted to know who had arranged it.

"The two of us," Williams said, indicating Feinberg. "There's no two ways about it. We did it."

Feinberg said he had talked to MacDonald and Williams to Lordi. "MacDonald and Lordi happened to talk. Obviously, those two sold the others on the commission the bill of goods."

DeVito asked if Lordi had told him he would take care of it.

"Well, no," Williams said. "He didn't tell me that. You know, he doesn't talk that way."

"You know they don't talk—" Feinberg started to say when Williams interrupted.

"He'd go to work on it," Williams said.

Everybody laughed. "It's another way of saying it," Feinberg added.

(The man who recommended the Ritz's declaratory ruling to the commission was Joseph A. Fusco, head of the licensing division of the Casino Control Commission. Fusco had served under Lordi as an assistant prosecutor in Essex County from 1970 to 1977. When Lordi was appointed to the commission in 1977, he took Fusco with him as his chief assistant. Then when Lordi left the commission in 1982, Governor Byrne appointed Fusco prosecutor of Atlantic County. Fusco would later deny in testimony that his recommendation had been influenced by Williams.)

Senator Williams's next meeting with Yassir was on January 15, 1980, again at the Plaza. Williams arrived with George Katz, the garbage entrepreneur, and Alexander Feinberg.

For some inexplicable reason, Yassir's English improved remarkably when he asked the senator if he'd sponsor legislation that would give him citizenship or permanent status.

Williams was emotionally touched by the request. And when Yassir graciously offered to pay for the legislation, Williams wouldn't hear of it. This one was on the house—or the Senate. "I give you an absolute pledge I will do everything in my power to advance your permanency."

In the year that he dealt with Abdul's men, Errichetti offered or provided them with hot diamonds, guns and munitions, forged CDs, counterfeit money, stolen paintings, leasing contracts, municipal garbage contracts, unregistered boats for dope-running, use of Port Camden as a narcotics depot, Atlantic City zoning changes, a score of bribable state and local officials, the chairman of the New Jersey State Democratic Committee, five U.S. Congressmen and a Senator, not to mention Lordi and MacDonald, and a meeting with Alvin Malnik, the man most likely to succeed Meyer Lansky, the Mob's aging financial wizard.

In arranging the meeting with Malnik at the Hemisphere Apartments in Hallandale, Florida, Errichetti was assisted by George Katz and Howard L. Criden, a Philadelphia lawyer who boasted of his close friendship with the Miami attorney.

The meeting was set for October 27, 1979, some six months after Caesars Boardwalk Regency had received its temporary license to operate a casino on the Boardwalk. In the interim, there had been a flurry of speculation in the media about the problem Caesars might encounter in securing a permanent license because of past business connections between Malnik and Caesars board chairman Clifford Perlman.

Errichetti and Katz used this as an argument to stress the importance of Lansky's approval for anyone venturing into legalized gambling in Nevada or Atlantic City. Already it had been demonstrated that the two operational casinos on the Boardwalk had links to Lansky. Without his protection, they argued, casino operators would be victimized by uncontrolled mobsters trying to muscle into their operations. Malnik was Lansky, said Criden, and nothing happened in Atlantic City unless Lansky was part of it.

Of even greater importance, Errichetti suggested, was Lansky's ability to steer Yassir to the Aladdin in Las Vegas, which had recently gone on the market because its former operators had lost their license after it was discovered that the Detriot Mafia family had a hidden interest in it.

This was a rare opportunity to buy into a going proposition. At the moment Edward Torres and Delbert Coleman, backed by the shadowy Sidney Korshak, the same trio who had nearly bankrupted the Stardust through a boiler-room operation nine years earlier, were trying to take over the Aladdin. Haste was of the essence.

When Weinberg and DeVito arrived at Criden's condominium at the Hemisphere House, Criden was waiting with Malnik. The Aladdin was the topic foremost on Malnik's mind that night. The price was $105 million, but nearly half was an assumed Teamster mortgage.

The kicker was an under-the-table payment of $10 million to buy out the interest of the Detroit Mob.

"Well," said DeVito, "what's your opinion, as to whether they [Coleman and Torres] can fulfill the contract [raise the money], if we let it go till December fifteenth?"

Malnik smiled. "I can arrange it so that they can't."

Weinberg scratched his head. "The other, the other problem is, let's say we come, take the fifty-million-dollar mortgage over, come up with fifty-five million cash. Can we get a reduction on that?"

"Uh, it's possible," Malnik said, "yeah, uh, I don't know the answer, but I can find out the answer. The people waiting for my call, yesterday, you know I've had everything held up, pending where we're going."

Weinberg nodded. "Now, our other problem is, the ten million dollars cash. We're going to run into a problem there. Who will be getting paid that ten million cash?"

Malnik shook his head. "There's no way I can tell you."

"Well, see, we ain't going to be able to work that then," Weinberg said, " 'cause how the hell are we going to explain it to Yassir?"

Malnik waved his hands impatiently. "Nobody's going to volunteer that they're receiving it because the people that are going to receive it will never under any circumstances be identified or acknowledged as having received it."

No matter how much they protested that Yassir wouldn't blindly hand over $10 million, Malnik was unshakable. When Weinberg suggested that Malnik explain it to Yassir, he replied, "Let me tell you something. If I were going to get eight million dollars I'd consider going up front and giving him the story, okay? But I'm not. So I mean it ain't worth it for me to have a guy later on, at some conceivable time, say I gave Malnik ten million dollars because Malnik can't say that anyone else ever got a portion of that ten million dollars."

"How about the lawyer?" Weinberg asked.

"The lawyer isn't even going to be aware of it."

It went around in circles until Weinberg came up with a Swiss bank account and Malnik thought it was a good solution. "This way we can make arrangements through Yassir's European office, deposit money in Joe Smo's name, such and such bank in Switzerland. These guys must have accounts over there already—"

"I can arrange it," Malnik interrupted, "it's no problem."

With that out of the way, DeVito was interested in the kind of casino management Malnik had in mind. After all, they were charged with protecting Yassir's investment.

"We were told," Weinberg said, "there's six guys out there that got their hands in the till and you can't get rid of them unless you want a war on your hands. Now how much truth is there to that story?"

"I'm going to deliver to you a package," Malnik said, "and that's why you got me. I'm going to deliver to you a package where there is going to be nobody's hands in any till. Okay? And any hands that go in any till, will only be with your authorization, and with your authorization if it can be done, you will then direct what is to get out and what is customary to do for who, and who are taking the risk."

"And you will also arrange that we get the pit bosses, the people to run it?"

"There will be nobody that will steal anything from you. I mean that's presumably you're going to be taking care of everybody. There is nobody that is going to be taking off scores out of that place, nobody. You don't have to worry about anybody. I mean from the top down, when you have that place, no one's going to take off anything. The people that you have, that are going to come into that place, are going to be for all intents and purposes your people through me. You've got to trust somebody. So what I'm telling you is you're going to have to trust me."

Weinberg laughed. "Well, that's why we came to you."

"Right, you trust me, uh, you're going to have a group of people that aren't going to take off anything—nobody is going to be taking scores out of that place without—"

"Your permission," Criden said.

"Your permission," Malnik repeated. "Now there are certain things that are customary, that are done. There are certain obligations that are taken care of, that are on-going, uh, that's not for people, it's really for things that you'll find out about. None of it is mandatory, do you follow me? In other words, if you say, fuck it, no, there's going to be no fund for this political situation, you don't have to, it's up to you."

"You advise to go along with the tradition," Weinberg asked, "the way they run it?"

"Absolutely."

"Most of the casinos," said Criden, "make certain contributions in a group, okay."

"Absolutely," Malnik confirmed.

"To various political guys in the state, okay," Criden continued. "If you want to contribute, fine. If you contribute you get the benefits, okay. If you decide you don't want to be a part of it, you say, look, pass."

The biggest problem, Malnik told them, was getting Yassir a license. "I'm not going to have a problem making the deal for you. I'm not going to have a problem making favorable terms. I'm not going to have a problem in the operation for you. I'm not going to have a problem in the people for you. The problem is going to occur in the licensing. I'm telling you, it's going to be a problem."

Although there was no law against licensing foreigners, Malnik felt it was imminent. As soon as Yassir applied for a license they would legislate against it. Still, licensing was not impossible. "I don't view now, at this point, any major hurdles, except this one, to sit down and work out."

Weinberg wanted to know if there was "anybody you can reach out for."

"Sure."

"Well, that could be our way then."

Malnik nodded wearily. "But I mean it's not even with that, I mean there are a few things that we have going, but it's still a problem, 'cause you don't have everybody going in unison, you know, you got a couple here, couple there, and no one is going to push, if, uh, if the push is going to lose, or if the push is going to embarrass—you know, I don't have to tell you how politicians are—they'll take what you've got as long as there's no heat. Once there's a little bit of heat, hey, well, shit, you know, I don't like these guys anyway."

As the meeting broke up, Malnik's parting words were a warning that others, including Johnny Carson and Wayne Newton, had expressed interest in the Aladdin. They would have to move quickly if they wanted to take advantage of his offer.

As it turned out, the gaming commission rejected the license application of Delbert Coleman and Edward Torres. Commissioners spoke scathingly of the two applicants' past association with underworld figures, especially Sidney Korshak.

Then Torres teamed up with singer Wayne Newton, a close friend of Nevada Governor Robert List. The board expedited its investigation, climaxed by special meetings of the board and gaming commission on successive days, a procedure that ordinarily takes months.

Torres sailed through an interrogation about his federal indictment for "skimming" revenues at the Fremont in the 1960s and about a list of underworld figures he admitted knowing over the years, including Jerry Catena, Charles "Charley the Blade" Tourine, Vincent "Jimmy Blue Eyes" Alo, John Pullman, a courier of "skim" money for Lansky, Alvin Malnik, and Lansky himself. But he denied ever doing business with them or sending them "skim" money from Las Vegas casinos.

Newton was questioned about associations with several underworld figures, including Guido "Bull" Penosi, a member of the Gambino family, whom Newton said he had met when he was a teenager performing at the Copacabana nightclub in New York but had not seen more than four times in 21 years. The application was approved.

Days later, NBC-TV broadcast a "special segment" report on its evening TV news show anchored by John Chancellor, titled "Wayne Newton and the Law." It identified Guido Penosi as a "New York hoodlum from the Gambino Mafia family" and the family's West Coast representative in narcotics and in show business.

Then it dropped a bombshell: Penosi was a key figure in a federal grand jury probe of Gambino family activities in Las Vegas and of "the role of Guido Penosi and the Mob in Newton's deal with the Aladdin." Just before he announced he would buy the Aladdin, the report said, Newton had called Penosi for help with a problem that was "important enough for Penosi to take up with leaders of the Gambino family in New York." It went on to say that Frank Piccolo, a cousin of Penosi and the Gambino family's boss in Connecticut, had "told associates he had taken care of Newton's problem and had become a hidden partner in the Aladdin hotel deal."

The next day Newton called a press conference in Las Vegas and announced he was filing a $6.4 million libel action against NBC for defaming him. Newton said the problem he had discussed with Penosi concerned death threats delivered by anonymous telephone calls in the spring of 1980.

Eight months later, a federal grand jury in Connecticut indicted Piccolo and Penosi on extortion charges. But before they could be brought to trial, Frank Piccolo was gunned down outside a telephone booth on a downtown street in Bridgeport, Connecticut. At Penosi's trial, Newton testified that the death threats had come from a former business associate and that he had called on Penosi for help and was told to call Penosi's cousin "Frank," which he did, and shortly thereafter the threats halted. But he testified that he knew nothing about Penosi's alleged planned extortion of an interest in the Aladdin. Penosi was acquitted.

Newton and Torres received a better deal in their purchase of the Aladdin than the one offered Yassir's men by Malnik. They didn't have to put up any cash. They assumed the existing loans, agreed to a long-term payout to the former owners, and received the necessary "up front" money from the Valley Bank of Nevada. The price was $85 million.

Anything is possible in this world if you know the right people. A shining example of that axiom was Clifford I. Perlman, the man who promoted a little hot-dog stand in Miami into a gambling empire.

17

Caesars Captures the Boardwalk

In the spring of 1977, when Steven and Marvin Perskie were putting the finishing touches to the Casino Control Act, Clifford Perlman and members of his board spent two days in Atlantic City, meeting with state and county officials. The rumor was that Caesars World was ready to lease two Boardwalk properties for a new casino hotel.

The honor of announcing this happy news fell to Steven Perskie. "They are talking about a major new facility," Perskie told the *Press.* "I mean substantially in excess of the minimum standards [of 500 rooms] in the bill."

Perskie was described as guarded in discussing Caesars' property arrangements, but was enthusiastic about the prospective licensees. "I think it will be a major piece in the rebuilding of Atlantic City, a major contribution," he said, quickly adding, "my only involvement is as a legislator. They asked me the same type of questions other people are asking such as when will the state be ready."

Asked his impression of the meeting, Perskie said, "I was very enthused. These are first-class people who have a proven track record of quality operations from an economic as well as from a law enforcement point of view."

Perlman's visit to Atlantic City came just eight days after Nevada Governor Mike O'Callaghan signed a law allowing casino owners to invest in gambling establishments outside the state. After having met with Governor Brendan Byrne, Harry Reid, the new chairman of the Nevada Gaming Commission, said, "I think New Jersey will, in fact, have real effective control and there won't be any problem.'' Caesars World, he said, would have to run its Atlantic City casino "in the same standards of honesty and integrity required by the state of Nevada.''

Instead of starting from scratch, Caesars World leased the 11-year-old Howard Johnson Regency Motor Hotel on Pacific Avenue, between Arkansas and Missouri avenues, which placed Caesars in the very heart of the Boardwalk, and announced that it would transform the existing 425-room structure into a modern facility, adding 123 guest rooms in a five-story tower and a 52,000-square-foot casino, plus extensive recreation, convention, and shopping areas.

What it ended up with was a 527-room hotel, a 48,630-square-foot casino, 8 bars and restaurants, 1358 slot machines, 65 blackjack tables, 22 craps, 12 roulette, 4 Big Six, and 3 baccarat. The real cost was anybody's guess, with the figures ranging from $50 million to $100 million. Whatever it cost, Caesars World saved millions and precious time by being allowed to renovate and expand what the commission called "a substantially new construction,'' a commission decision that was contrary to Governor Byrne's edict against the conversion of existing hotels into casino complexes.

It was christened Caesars Boardwalk Regency.

On May 30, 1979, after a one-day hearing, the Casino Control Commission granted Caesars a temporary gambling license after Clifford Perlman voluntarily agreed to relinquish most of his New Jersey activities. But it would still be another three weeks before the grand opening, because most of its employees had yet to be licensed.

To speed up the licensing process in the future, Governor Byrne approved a 57-page amendment to the Casino Control Act. It gave the commission power to issue temporary licenses to casino workers, except dealers, and discretionary power to license people with criminal records and to issue licenses generally. Chairman Lordi could now issue employees licenses unilaterally without waiting for a commission meeting, as long as the investigation found the applicant qualified. The amendment also gave the commission power to exempt ancillary companies serving casino-hotels from licensing requirements.

As for Perlman, Gaming Enforcement Director Robert P. Martinez felt he had isolated the state "from any possible, or any theoretically possible influence. If the worst is found in the future, at least, we have protected ourselves.''

Caesars attorney Morris Brown stressed that Perlman wasn't admitting any wrongdoing in his dealings with Alvin Malnik and Sam Cohen. Martinez agreed. "No judgment has been made one way or another," he said.

There was Alvin Malnik again. And who were the Perlmans? Well, back in 1956, Clifford and Stuart Perlman had invested $12,000 in a Miami Beach hot-dog stand and within five years had bankrolled it into a fast food chain called Lum's. Eight years later Lum's bought out Caesars World, Inc., and within another decade it had mushroomed into a half-billion-dollar gambling empire.

The move to Las Vegas, which came in 1969, was more a rescue operation than an ordinary business deal. Caesars Palace, a Mob-controlled casino from the day it opened its doors, was in bad need of an image cleansing. Stories about skimming and Mob links were getting out of hand.

For the purchase of Desert Palace, Inc., the parent-owner of Caesars Palace, Lum's paid $48 million in cash, $12 million in Lum's common shares, and assumed $24 million in long-term debts to the Teamsters pension fund.

Caesars Palace, a stucco-over-chicken-wire Roman monolith, was the creation of Jay Sarno, a short, obese, bombastic gambler who succeeded in creating an edifice in his own grandiose image. It opened in 1966, when Jimmy Hoffa was still in circulation. There is no record of what the Teamsters boss thought of the building, but he was sufficiently impressed with its two primary promoters, Sarno and Nathan Jacobson, to advance $10.5 million from the pension fund.

There were reports that Jacobson, a Baltimore insurance executive, had slot machine connections back East, but that did not discourage the gaming commission from issuing a casino license. It didn't get curious even when Sarno and Jacobson hired Jerome "Jerry" Zarowitz to run the casino, though Zarowitz had served a 20-month prison term on a conspiracy conviction growing out of an attempted fix of an NFL championship game and had since operated as a sports bookmaker in the Miami area.

As his assistant, Zarowitz picked Irving "Ash" Resnick, a bookie with close connection to organized crime. Resnick had been arrested several times for bookmaking in Florida and New York and had been barred from many racetracks. As the executive in charge of casino credit, Resnick would become known as the Caligula of Caesars Palace. Before long enemies would start putting bombs in his car.

The host at Caesars was Elliot Paul Price, identified in Senate hearings as an associate of New England Mafia boss Ray Patriarca, and named in Los Angeles County grand jury testimony as a mastermind of national bookmaking operations.

Only a year after Caesars opened its doors, it was revealed through federal grand jury proceedings that both Zarowitz and Price had attended a Little Apalachin meeting in Palm Springs in 1965, along with two New York Mafia figures, Vincent "Jimmy Blue Eyes" Alo and Anthony "Fat Tony" Salerno, both Genovese family caporegimes.

The FBI and IRS were convinced that Zarowitz and Price had been planted in Las Vegas to protect the hidden interests of the real owners of Caesars Palace. Evidence would show that the hidden owners included Tony Accardo and Sam Giancana of the Chicago family; Ray Patriarca, Joseph Anselmo, Jerry Angiulo, and Joseph Palermo of the New England family; and Jerry Catena, Vincent Alo, Tony Salerno, and Jimmy "Nap" Napoli of the Genovese family. Together they skimmed millions from the casino.

The IRS had managed to infiltrate an undercover agent into the casino's cashier cage. The agent soon became intrigued by the frequent phone calls to layoff bookies and visits to lock boxes in the vault by Zarowitz, Price, and Sanford Waterman, the hotel's executive vice-president. Zarowitz's presence in the vault was particularly intriguing, since the casino had announced his resignation in May 1970. The agent gave his information to a federal strike force that was conducting a nationwide investigation of illegal sports betting operations. Twenty-six cities, including Las Vegas, were singled out for a simultaneous raid on December 12, 1970, a year after the Perlmans had taken over. A prime target was their casino vault. When agents seized the lock boxes maintained by Zarowitz, they found $1,120,000 in neatly stacked hundred-dollar bills and another half-million in boxes belonging to Price and Waterman. All three men were arrested and charged with using the telephone in aid of an illegal bookmaking operation.

Early in 1971 the Securities and Exchange Commission brought an action against Lum's charging that some of its key executives had leaked "revised" financial information to a stock portfolio manager, enabling the firm to unload its stock before the stock nosedived.

Other SEC charges accused Lum's and various executives of fraud and deceit against its shareholders in connection with its purchase of Caesars Palace: the original purchase price appeared excessive and may have been based on revenue previously skimmed by the former owners.

Among other things, the SEC sought to prevent Lum's from completing the purchase of Caesars Palace and asked the court to order the defendants to surrender all their profits and other considerations received as a result "of their unlawful activities." The defendants included Sarno, Jacobson, Zarowitz, William S. "Billy" Weinberger, Sr., president of Caesars Palace, Harry Wald, then secretary-treasurer and later executive vice-president, Albert Faccinto, later promoted to senior vice-president, and other key personnel of the casino-hotel, both past and present.

The SEC charged that even Lum's amended statement had failed to disclose the actual result of operations of Caesars Palace for the settlement period—failed to tell why the hotel-casino had a decrease of nearly $3 million and why it also had a material decline in its working capital during that period. Also omitted were the circumstances surrounding the role played by Zarowitz in operating the casino.

Information kept from stockholders included "any [of Zarowitz's] undisclosed interest in Caesars Palace," and his receipt of $3.5 million of the purchase price although he wasn't an owner of record.

Although Zarowitz wasn't qualified to be licensed as a key casino employee because of his criminal background, he was retained by Lum's as Caesars' Chief Casino Executive. And his employment continued even after his arrest and indictment for conducting an illegal bookmaking operation at Caesars Palace, not to mention the $1.5 million he and his pals had secreted in lock boxes.

His salary was set at $300,000, commencing January 13, 1971, one month after the FBI raid, for a period of five years, that sum being in addition to any other salary or bonus accruing to him in connection with his normal duties. During this period he was prohibited from engaging or associating with any other casino in Nevada.

After his arrest, of course, things got a little too hot for Zarowitz to continue his presence at Caesars. Yet he continued to receive his $1.5 million in salary. Zarowitz was also the beneficiary of a special clause in the purchase agreement that permitted the former owners to designate certain employees to receive deferred compensation from Lum's up to a maximum of $2.2 million. When the names were submitted by Billy Weinberger, Zarowitz's topped the list. His share was $300,000.

As for the SEC's complaint, all the principal owners and key casino employees of Lum's took the Fifth Amendment and refused to answer questions on the possibility of improper removal of funds from the casino. It was settled with a consent decree—that is, without admitting or denying the charges, the defendants agreed not to violate securities laws in the future. A federal court issued a judgment of permanent injunction which enjoined Lum's and Desert Palace, Inc., the operating company of Caesars Palace, from violations of the Securities Exchange Act with respect to all future acquisitions. The defendants were further ordered to pool $1.1 million in cash toward an overall settlement of stockholders suits.

Another Zarowitz aide, Jerry W. Gordon, received some notoriety early in 1971 when a federal grand jury returned indictments against him, Meyer Lansky, and two old Lansky fronts, Morris Lansburgh and Samuel Cohen, for conspiring to operate illegally the Flamingo Hotel in Las Vegas. The conspiracy involved the skimming of at least $36 million from the Flamingo between the years 1960 and 1967.

The FBI had known about the skimming at the Flamingo since 1962 and had sat on this intelligence nine years. The information came from a bugged conversation between Anthony "Little Pussy" Russo and Ray DeCarlo, a member of Jerry Catena's crew:

"Jerry's [Catena] got an income bigger than anybody around— except Meyer Lansky . . ." DeCarlo said. "Meyer owns more in Vegas than anybody—than all of ours put together. He's got a piece of every joint in Vegas. They were over in New York about a week ago, I hear, Jerry and Meyer . . . and Blue Eyes [Vincent Alo]. They were cutting up the pie from that joint out there—the joint they're robbing all the money out of. What's the name of it?"

"The Flamingo," Russo said.

"Flamingo, that's it. Harry James took six percent of it. I was going to take three percent off Harry but Jerry said, 'Don't do nothing with him because the joint is being robbed.' "

Both Samuel Cohen and Morris Lansburgh, the official owners of the Flamingo, pleaded guilty to conspiracy charges in the skimming case and were sentenced by U.S. District Judge Roger Foley to one year in prison. They were released after serving four months—for stealing 36 million tax-free dollars. Gordon became a cooperating witness and was never prosecuted. He continued working for Zarowitz at Caesars.

Foley, the chief federal judge and a product of the local political machine, wanted the government to dismiss its case against Lansky because his medical records showed "it is almost a certainty the defendant will never be well enough to undergo the rigors of the trial of this complex case." The judge refused to dismiss the case himself but said it "will lie dormant on the calendar . . . until either the defendant dies or government counsel acts responsibly and dismisses the indictment."

Four years later Judge Foley did dismiss the case and the Justice Department decided not to appeal.

Yet Lansky's health was good enough to sustain him for another decade. He died a natural death in 1983, at the age of 81.

Upon his release from prison, Cohen would continue to serve Lansky, joining forces with Alvin Malnik in several lucrative deals involving Caesars World and the Perlmans.

Cohen controlled the Miami National Bank, which funneled millions of Mob dollars into Swiss banks. He was also a part owner of the plush Eden Roc Hotel (Lansky's son-in-law was the hotel's resident manager) and six others along Miami Beach's exclusive hotel row. Cohen owned at least seventy apartment buildings in New York City alone. Much of this property was obtained through loans from Swiss and Bahamian banks—that is, illegal money coming back in the form of loans—and Cohen could then deduct the interest he paid on the loans in his tax returns.

One of the Florida real estate companies owned by Malnik and Cohen was the Comal Corporation. In February 1971 Comal bought Sky Lake North, which consisted of 320 acres of developable land, lakes, and a country club in Dade County, Florida. In making the purchase, Comal assumed a mortgage held by the Teamsters pension fund and obtained an additional $8.6 million from the pension fund to close the deal.

The ink had barely dried on this deal before Clifford Perlman had offered to purchase for Caesars World the Sky Lake North property, except for the country club, for $13 million plus picking up the existing pension fund mortgage of $10 million.

To avoid tax problems for Comal, Caesars World entered instead into a 20-year lease of Sky Lake with the provision that it could purchase all of Comal's outstanding stock between November 1, 1974, and July 31, 1975. The stock purchase option also provided for warrants to be issued to Malnik and Cohen allowing them to purchase a total of 600,000 shares of Caesars World stock on or before December 31, 1980, at prices ranging from $8 to $16 per share, for the purpose of completing a public sale of the stock.

In February 1974, with Comal having been in business the required three years and its capital gain tax status assured, Caesars World exercised its option and purchased Sky Lake North. Malnik and Cohen retained title to the country club and its 18-hole golf course, which they leased to Caesars, Comal's new owners, for $120,000 per year until 1993, with an option to purchase for $2.4 million. In addition to retaining the country club, Malnik and Cohen came away with a net profit of $14.7 million in the Sky Lake deal. The aggregate cost to Caesars World was $30.8 million.

Back in 1972, when the Nevada Gaming Commission had learned of the Sky Lake transaction, it warned Perlman not to associate with Malnik and Cohen again. But it wasn't long before Perlman was back in business with them.

In 1972, when the Jaynor Corporation ran into trouble with its high-rise condominium complex in Miami, Malnik and Cohen moved in quickly. Jaynor's president, Norman Peetluk, had served a two-year prison term for passing bad checks. His partner in the deal was Dominick Alongi, president of Vindom, Inc., and a member of the Genovese family, who had gained national publicity in 1966 when he was arrested in a New York City restaurant with four Mafia bosses: Joseph Columbo, Carlo Gambino, Joey Gallo, and Santo Trafficante.

Jaynor and Vindom received a $10.3 million loan from the Carner Bank of Miami Beach (now called Intercontinental Bank) and began constructing its condominium complex, which Malnik would later name the Cricket Club. Soon Jaynor and Vindom were in default on the mortgage and subcontractors were clamoring for their money, which they would never receive. By now the Carner Bank had disbursed $4.6 million of the $10.3 million loan and contractor liens amounted to over $1 million.

That was when Malnik came on the scene, on July 10, 1972, entering into a purchase agreement with the builders and the Carner Bank which agreed to advance him the remaining $5.7 million balance of the loan, plus an additional $1 million. All Malnik had to do was agree to guarantee the remaining portion of the mortgage note. And for that he turned to Clifford Perlman and Samuel Cohen, who was represented by his two sons, Joel and Alan Cohen. Although Perlman invested only $350,000 in a personal loan at less than 5 percent interest, he became liable for one-third of the guaranteed mortgage debt.

Malnik's first move was to renegotiate the loan with the Carner Bank, which increased the amount to $12.5 million, providing for 100 percent of the financing, and lowered the interest rate. Cricket Club, Inc., was set up as a "subchapter S" corporation, which meant that anyone making a loan to it could have a tax "writeoff" to the extent of their investment. Through this device, Malnik received an additional $15.4 million in personal loans from seven private investors.

The general contractor Malnik chose to complete the complex was Calvin Kovens, who in 1961 was convicted for receiving loans under false pretenses and placed on probation for five years. In 1964 he was convicted, along with Jimmy Hoffa, on charges of fraud and conspiracy involving $25 million in Teamsters pension fund loans, of which $7 million in kickbacks was received by Kovens, Hoffa, and four other defendants. He served 13 months of a three-year prison term.

When the story of Perlman's involvement in the Cricket Club broke in the Miami press, Perlman was again chastised by Philip Hannifin, chairman of the Nevada Gaming Commission, for associating with Malnik and Cohen. Perlman's explanation was that he thought the commission's first warning had been to the company and not to individual corporate officers. Hannifin demanded that Perlman divest his interest in the Cricket Club, but his shares were virtually worthless and impossible to sell.

While the matter dragged on for six years, Perlman made three more personal loans to the Cricket Club. Finally, Perlman's method of divesting his interest was to sell his stock back to the Cricket Club corporation for one dollar, but he remained a guarantor for one-third of the mortgage loan, which totaled $13.5 million in 1978.

To make matters perfectly clear, the gaming commission ordered that "Caesars World and Perlman cease and desist, from among other things, associating with, either socially or in business affairs, persons of notorious or unsavory reputations or who have extensive police records."

The SEC was likewise perturbed. On three separate occasions it brought civil actions against Caesars World and its officers or employees, charging among other violations that Perlman had concealed material information from shareholders with regard to Caesars' series of real estate transactions with Malnik and the Cohens. Two of the actions were settled with the defendants consenting to entry of a final judgment of a permanent injunction. The third case, a 53-paragraph complaint charging inter alia failure to disclose information in its various filings and offerings or made misleading statements, was tried without a jury and resulted in the entry of a final judgment of permanent injunction against Caesars World, Perlman, and others. The SEC required Caesars World to correct and amend all reports filed for the fiscal year 1972 to the present. A three-member audit committee was appointed to review for fairness every transaction exceeding $40,000.

Five months later Perlman and Malnik, along with Sam Cohen's two sons, were embroiled in another business deal. According to Perlman, it was he who approached Malnik to see if Malnik could work out a tax shelter for him.

Cove Haven, Inc., a subsidiary of Caesars World, operated two honeymoon resorts in Pennsylvania's Pocono Mountains called Cove Haven and Paradise Stream. It was these properties that Perlman and Malnik decided to exploit in February 1975.

Comal, Inc., owned by Malnik and Cohen, borrowed $15 million from the Teamsters pension fund, which they switched to Cove Associates, a new partnership between Malnik, who owned 69 percent, and Cohen's two sons, who owned 15.5 percent each. With the $15 million, Cove Associates bought the two resorts and leased them back to Cove Haven, Inc., for 20 years, with Caesars World as guarantor of its subsidiary's obligations under the lease. A month later Caesars World agreed to construct additional units at Cove Haven at a cost of $3.7 million, which it borrowed from two banks.

What it boiled down to was the kind of deal that mere mortals never see. Malnik agreed to repay the Teamsters fund at $126,000 a month, and Caesars agreed to lease the same property from Malnik at $177,000 a month. For being, in essence, loanbrokers on a loan that was 100 percent financed, Malnik and his partners would share a $51,000-a-month profit for 20 years. Or, in other words, a 20-year windfall of $12,240,000, not counting the interest that money would earn, and the fact that they would still own the resorts when the lease expired.

Without disclosing any of the details of the Pocono transaction or the identity of the purchaser, Caesars World president William H. McElnea, Jr. told the press, "We think we made one hell of a deal." Later, after Malnik was revealed as the purchaser, McElnea said that at the time of the sale-leaseback, Caesars World was at the top of its bank credit line, "with no ability to go in and borrow long-term money." This puzzled the gaming commission. It questioned why Caesars World, which had "inherited" multimillion-dollar Teamsters loans when it bought Caesars Palace and the Sky Lake properties, couldn't itself have gotten the Teamsters loan for the Pocono resorts.

When questioned about it, Perlman threw up his hands in exasperation. "We haven't bribed any foreign government lately," he said, his voice rising. "We haven't contributed to the Nixon campaign in cash. I mean, think about it. There are a lot of things we could have done. But what's happening is that we're being accused of associating with a guy who's accused of associating with a guy. And we are getting more newspaper coverage out of that than the Second World War. Isn't there some missing sense of balance in this thing?"

Caesars Boardwalk Regency opened its doors June 26, 1979, ending Resorts International's 13-month, $220 million monopoly on legalized casino gambling in New Jersey. Thousands of anxious bettors lined up on the Boardwalk for a chance at the green felt tables. The first unhappy gambler was a blackjack card counter who was ejected from the casino before he could make his first bet. Nobody messes with the odds, even on opening day.

"This is like a dream come true," said Stuart Perlman, explaining that his brother Clifford was in Wimbledon, England, for the British Open tennis championship. "I hope Clifford will be able to come back in a couple of weeks."

Caesars Boardwalk Regency's gilded, mirrored, modernistic facade, squeezed within the ruins of the old Boardwalk, looked like something salvaged from a Hollywood backlot. Or, to be more specific, something plucked from Las Vegas's Glitter Gulch. Another tinseled grind joint.

The fire department was opposed to the glitter for a more practical reason. It was dangerous. During the summer the angle of the panels had to be changed after it was discovered they were acting as giant sun reflectors and were setting patches of the Boardwalk on fire. Then, after high winds blew rain water onto two electrical boxes that controlled neon signs on the building's exterior, the boxes shorted out and began smoldering, setting the adhesive and the panels on fire, giving off "extremely toxic" fumes. The fire department asked Caesars to erect a safer facade and the company promised to give the suggestion consideration.

The Division of Gaming Enforcement, which spent 17 months investigating Caesars World, issued a 25-page "statement of issues" and a 121-page report that questioned the applicant's "suitability" in the following general areas: business and professional associations that "reflect adversely on the character of the individual [Clifford Perlman] and corporate entity," including leases in Philadelphia and Atlantic City with criminal figures and business investments in Florida and the Poconos with Malnik and Cohen, "associates of Meyer Lansky"; skimming allegations at Caesars Palace; the present practice of giving gambling credit through a separate set of accounts to organized crime figures, termed "mustache accounts" by Caesars' New York credit office.

In a way the report was a carbon copy of the one issued on Resorts, with both companies being faulted for perpetuating corporate and personal ties with unsavory characters, both in trouble at various times with the Securities and Exchange Commission, both with records of sloppy casino operations, loose accounting, possible skimming operations; and both with executives the state strongly objected to licensing.

What was different about the report this time around was the tone. Whereas Attorney General John Degnan had listed 17 exceptions to the licensing of Resorts, taking the active position that the license be denied, he now merely listed the negative "issues" without taking an adversary position on Caesars' license application. Having been burned by the commission which had voted unanimously to license Resorts, he seemed to be hedging his bet this time. Besides, nobody in the state of New Jersey truly believed that the commission would ever deny a license to an applicant already operating on a temporary permit.

The date set for Caesars' hearings was February 28, 1980, but three weeks before it could get under way an FBI sting operation called Abscam (short for "Abdul scam") became the media event of the year. Camden Mayor Angelo Errichetti, U.S. Senator Harrison Williams, Jr., Joseph Lordi, and Kenneth MacDonald, along with seven congressmen, Howard Criden, and other spear carriers were caught in the FBI net.

Yassir Habib was not an Arab sheik but special agent Richard Farhardt, and his underlings were agents Tony Amoroso and Jack McCarthy, who posed as Tony DeVito and Jack McCloud, respectively. Mel Weinberg, a professional con man, played himself.

Kenneth MacDonald resigned from the Casino Control Commission to preserve its integrity. He admitted having been in the room when the $100,000 was passed to Mayor Errichetti, but denied any wrongdoing. His resignation, however, did save the Executive Commission of Ethical Standards from having to rule on whether Mac-Donald's son-in-law's job with a subsidiary of Resorts constituted a conflict of interest.

Given the glare of the media spotlight, the other commissioners decided to save the ethics panel another decision by announcing that they would no longer stay at casino hotels at reduced rates when visiting Atlantic City. Not because they felt it was a violation of their code of ethics, but "because people are seeing things here that don't seem right to the public and to the press," a spokesman said. "We are sensitive to appearances."

Governor Byrne's response to Abscam was to introduce a bill dissolving the four part-time commission posts and calling for a full-time commission, a move that brought Lordi out of seclusion.

"We are here today not because of any established facts, but because of vague innuendos and suspicions concerning the integrity of the Casino Control Commission," Lordi told a legislative committee. Although he didn't directly oppose the full-time commission, he predicted that the commission's independence "would be seriously eroded, both in reality and in appearance. Might not such a precedent be used again in the future to dissolve this agency merely to effectuate the replacement of the incumbents? No one man now has or should ever have the power to control the fate of this industry."

Attorney General Degnan was in favor of a full-time commission and for provisions requiring the public disclosure of all casino credit, discount and complimentary services provided to legislators, top state officials, and officials of Atlantic County and the city. "They give free drinks and rooms to loosen the inhibitions of public office holders," he said. "Will history say that New Jersey invited a notorious industry under promises of strict controls only to have its own public officials embarrass it by their insensitivity, and the cooperative insensitivity of this seductive industry, to ethical considerations?"

Degnan warned that if the legislature didn't strengthen its ethics provisions to curtail the casino industry's pervasive influence, "the day will come when casinos in New Jersey have the same impact as they do in the state of Nevada. At that point I leave."

The legislative squabble over the ways to revamp the commission and impose stricter ethical standards delayed Caesars' hearings seven months. The bill finally enacted reconstituted the commission into a full-time regulatory agency and allowed Lordi to continue as its chairman. Salaries of commissioners were set at $60,000 and of the chairman at $65,000. The ethics measure prohibited part-time state employees from representing casinos or working for them as key employees. Legislators, judges, Atlantic City and state officials were prohibited from accepting casino-related jobs for two years after they left public service.

On the same day Governor Byrne said he would sign the ethics legislation, Herbert Wolfe, who had been Byrne's press secretary and was now assistant executive director of the Election Law Enforcement Commission, announced that he had accepted a position with Caesars World as director of corporate relations.

On his last day as a commissioner, Albert Merck, noted in the media as the panel's gadfly, got a few things off his chest. He called the casino industry "the toughest and greediest bunch of people I've ever seen. They want to squeeze the players for every last nickel. They want to run the casinos twenty-four hours a day just so they can get those people staggering around at four o'clock in the morning. Look at all the high-minimum tables. It's seven times greater than in Las Vegas. That's no church party."

Merck called Atlantic City Assemblyman Michael Matthews "overly sympathetic to casinos," and added, "Find out what he owes Resorts and whether it's been paid off. If you want to see what the casinos want, get a copy of all of Mr. Matthews' legislative bills."

Lordi didn't escape Merck's blast. "The former statute and the present one—but not to quite the same extent—give the chairman huge powers in relation to the other commissioners. The chairman is essentially a czar and is created as such. It is a concentration of power that leaves the other commissioners pretty helpless."

Nor did the governor. "All I can say is that the past history of Mr. Lordi has been as a loyal, effective follower of the governor. I find it hard to believe that the contact wasn't fairly intimate and fairly ongoing when, for instance, the legislation to approve the temporary licenses was presented to the commissioners the day before we were asked to approve it, and it was in its final form. I just can't believe that the chairman wasn't aware of that long before then. And I never did find out why he waited so long to give it to the commissioners."

Lordi rode over the Abscam scandal. He denied having given Ritz Associates preferential treatment at Senator Williams's request. "I have not been in his [Williams's] company or met with him since I joined the commission," Lordi told reporters. As for saving Ritz Associates $30 million when the commission approved plans for the renovation of the existing hotel for a casino complex, Lordi said, "The first time I heard about $30 million is when I read it in the paper." And MacDonald, Lordi said, was "being suckered into a position of not knowing what was going on. I personally relied on what he said. He did absolutely nothing wrong, and I believe him."

Also mentioned in the Abscam tapes was Steven Perskie. In a conversation with Mel Weinberg, Errichetti had revealed that he had arranged for a $1 million deposit in the Atlantic National Bank. The deposit, he said, would give him "an entree to talk to" Perskie because the bank's board president, James Cooper, was Perskie's "under the rug" partner. A former associate in Cooper's law firm, Perskie denied the charge, calling it a "matter of self-puffery." Cooper said he "didn't even know the account was open" until after the Abscam revelations.

On September 9, after 14 months of operating with a temporary license, Caesars was finally going to have its day before the commission, which turned out to be six weeks long. This time, to represent the division at the hearings, Attorney General Degnan picked Michael Cole, whose expertise was in civil matters. Cole took his lead from Degnan in playing close to the vest what restrictions the state would request at the hearings.

Caesars World's first choice for legal representation was Peter Echeverria, who had been chairman of the Nevada Gaming Commission for four years, retiring in April 1977. Seven months later he became a director of Desert Palace, Inc., the subsidiary that operated Caesars Palace. While chairman of the commission Echeverria had issued a number of warnings to Caesars officials advising them not to do business with individuals of unsavory reputation. The New Jersey gaming commission sidelined Echeverria because he had helped formulate administrative rulings against Caesars World that would be at issue at the licensing hearing.

In his opening statement at the hearings, Michael Cole, after detailing the company's past transactions with Malnik and Cohen, charged Caesars World and Perlman with "insensitivity" and "callous indifference" to warnings from the SEC and Nevada gaming authorities about his dealings with "questionable characters."

Cole recommended against granting Perlman a license. "We simply don't trust that it won't happen again." As far as Caesars World was concerned, he wanted it to sever all financial ties with "unsavory characters." "As long as Caesars World has an ongoing relationship—arm's length or otherwise—with Malnik, Cohen, or Cohen's sons, we do not consider Caesars World to be suitable for licensing."

Caesars' attorney, William Glendon, charged the Division of Gaming Enforcement with tarnishing the company with "guilt by association . . . based on hearsay twice removed." Glendon vowed to show the commission that Caesars is "an honest company run by honest people. We welcome the opportunity to tell this story, for it is truly an American success story."

The first witness was Caesars World President William McElnea, Jr., who was convinced the commission would find his company worthy of a license. "We look forward to the hearings as a forum to dispel some of the myths and misconceptions which have circulated in the press over the past two years."

Under questioning by Glendon, McElnea found nothing wrong with Perlman's relationship with Malnik and Cohen. Their real estate transactions were "perfectly normal" and formed "no basis for questioning Mr. Perlman's qualifications as chairman of Caesars World."

Under cross-examination, Clifford Perlman admitted he knew of the Lansky-Cohen indictment for skimming at the Flamingo four months before the Sky Lake deal, but he felt the problem had been "resolved."

Cole pressed Perlman to explain why he had not discussed the indictment with Caesars' directors. "We had dispensed with that problem," Perlman insisted, denying he had made a "conscious decision" to keep the information from the board.

That was pretty much the way it went for six weeks. A platoon of businessmen, former prosecutors and FBI agents testified to Perlman's excellent reputation and sterling character.

Somehow Cole got stuck in the Lansky morass and a lot of other unsavory allegations in the division's report got lost in the shuffle.

For example, in checking Caesars' security files, division investigators discovered numerous memos dealing with prostitution over a period of years. They referred to "security people demanding money from prostitutes in return for allowing them to solicit customers in the casino-hotel area." Jack Manis, Hotel Security Chief, was referred to as "having knowledge and possibly control of these operations." According to the division's report, "these activities were investigated by [Caesars'] corporate security office under the direction of H. E. Campbell [the former FBI chief who had conducted the raid on Caesars' vault]. During a discussion with Campbell, he stated to division investigators that he had been investigating allegations regarding Manis for two to three years, but to no avail. He stated, furthermore, that he familiarized Harry Wald with the situation. According to Campbell, Wald advised him that he would look into the matter, but to Campbell's knowledge took no action."

When Wald was questioned by division investigators, his reply was that he "would not know a hooker if he bumped into one." But he added that "prostitution is a way of life, and it would virtually be impossible to stop prostitution in any casino." He further felt "that if someone went to Las Vegas and gambled and desired female companionship, he should have it."

Manis denied that hookers were paying him off to prevent being arrested. However, if he had his way, he would allow prostitutes to work as in the old days, when they were "an excellent source of information. If they did not cooperate they were ejected from the hotel." Manis' philosophy was that men came to "gamble and fool with girls and that's what makes Vegas."

The term "Mustache Account" to denote Mafia customers was discovered by the division during the course of reviewing the credit records of Anthony "Little Pussy" Russo, whose credit form contained the following notation: "7-26-76 per Murray Gennis [Caesars Palace casino manager] spoke to Morris Rothenberg [manager of Caesars' New York reservations office]. He will contact in New York thru other mustache accounts who all belong to same click." Other notations read: "Rothenberg says no chance of collection. Whereabout unknown. Mike DeRienzo cannot help. Morris says our error in giving credit to this man. Only good if Mike guarantees in advance."

What was intriguing about Russo's credit application was that it didn't contain an address or any other identification that would enable the casino to pursue its collection. Russo took Caesars for $45,000, which the casino wrote off.

In pursuing its investigation the division discovered that of 90 "mustache accounts," 39 had their losses written off. Other credit practices used by Caesars casino executives to circumvent credit procedures included their making "personal" loans to gamblers who had sustained losses up to their credit limit and permitting players to have several credit cards listed under aliases.

While going over the mustache accounts, investigators found a document signed by casino manager Gennis to Wald regarding the distribution of complimentary Super Bowl tickets. Included on the list for eight tickets was Stumpy Orman, Atlantic City's venerable racketeer; ten tickets to Jim Charga, a well-known drug trafficker; and eight tickets to Sam Klein, who was forced to resign from Bally Corporation by the Nevada Gaming Commission for his association with Jerry Catena. Rothenberg denied it was the same Sam Klein, saying the name was an alias, and that he collected Klein's outstanding markers by meeting him in restaurants and was always paid in cash.

Caesars' attorneys objected to Cole's introduction of mustache accounts because the "names of several people who are respected and prominent people in the state of New Jersey" were included in the transcript of the division's interview with Rothenberg. Lordi wanted to think about it a couple of days because the objections "give me some thought."

But a couple of days later there was something more important to ponder. The division announced that it had obtained a tape of a conversation between Malnik and FBI agents that had taken place in Howard Criden's apartment in Hallandale, Florida, during the Abscam investigation.

The division felt it had something as close to a "smoking gun" as it hoped to get. A Caesars spokesman called it "a cheap shot," a last-minute move to "overshadow" the real issues in the company's application for a permanent license. Up to now, the contention went, the division's case was nothing but innuendo based on allegations in government and media reports. The speculation in the media was that the tape could form the strongest evidence of Caesars' links to organized crime.

Caesars' attorneys vehemently objected to the admissibility of the tape, calling it "irrelevant" and "unduly prejudicial." Lordi immediately adjourned the hearings to hear William Glendon's arguments in closed session.

When the hearings reconvened, Lordi ruled the tape admissible but ordered that the names of all persons mentioned in it be deleted. In the process of making these deletions Lordi excised a paragraph that directly linked Malnik to Caesars Palace. During the actual conversation with Yassir's men, Malnik had used Caesars Palace as an example of what he could do to turn the Aladdin into a profitable operation: "What you have to do is what we did with Caesars Palace. We always, we never made any money because we always put it back into the joint. We always added two hundred rooms here, three hundred rooms there, till over at that joint we have two thousand rooms now."

Malnik used "we" six times in this brief passage, the "we" signifying his personal involvement with Meyer Lansky, whom he represented, and Clifford Perlman, the man giving the orders to Caesars' board. The purging of this paragraph from the transcript by Joseph Lordi turned the smoking gun into a cap pistol.

Not even the other members of the commission knew the contents of the Malnik statement deleted by Lordi. Members of the media, who were given transcripts of the tape, were unaware of the deletion. Even when Robert W. Greene's book on Abscam, *The Sting Man,* was published with the paragraph included, few reporters made the connection.

After 23 days of hearings, the record had grown to 800 exhibits and 5000 pages of testimony. Yet scores of potential witnesses hadn't been called to testify, including John Charles Piazza III, a convicted drug dealer, who had told the division and a U.S. Senate subcommittee of a major Mob sitdown at Malnik's Forge restaurant attended by Lansky, Malnik, and members of the Gambino and DeCavalcante families to discuss the obtaining of licenses and the skimming of profits if Florida legalized casinos.

Piazza said in an interview with division investigators that Malnik monopolized the conversation at that meeting. It was obvious "to me, he represented Meyer and Meyer's interest."

The group seemed certain that New Jersey voters would legalize gambling in Atlantic City. "I was led to believe they were already involved in Atlantic City, you know, that was completed already," Piazza said. "They weren't even worried about it."

Many refused to testify, including Billy Weinberger, ex-president of Caesars Palace, who had switched to Bally Park Place, which had since opened with a temporary license and was awaiting its hearing before the commission. Although the commission had subpoena powers in New Jersey, and could even grant immunity to compel a witness to testify, Weinberger's refusal was honored.

Again, as in Resorts' case, time was of the essence. The division had taken 17 months and spent $1.2 million of Caesars' money conducting its investigation, and now suddenly Caesars' temporary license was about to expire and 3000 employees would face unemployment unless the permanent license was granted.

On the final day of the hearings, Cole reminded the commission that "the scenario that is painted throughout is an eagerness to engage in business with persons of disreputable character." He charged that four directors of Caesars World were "unsuitable" for licensing. They were Clifford and Stuart Perlman, William McElnea, and Jay Leshaw. He said the four, who controlled 20 percent of Caesars stock, had shown their willingness to do business with Malnik, and that the Perlmans and Leshaw should be automatically disqualified because they had supplied "false and misleading information" to the commission.

"It is reprehensible for the division to stand up here and try to ruin three businessmen's lives by saying they lack candor," Glendon said, in his closing arguments. He asked the commission to reject Cole's "tunnel vision" and judge the company on the "entire spectrum of thousands" of transactions. The division's "new morality," he complained, was a product of Abscam and Watergate, and allowed "no margin for error, at least as to others." In retrospect, he admitted, the deals with Malnik were a mistake, but "a mistake isn't a crime," he said. "It doesn't show a fatal flaw of character." In exasperation, he said, "What does New Jersey really want? Does it want a sacrifice, an immolation?"

A week later the commission rendered its decision. Caesars Boardwalk Regency was granted a permanent license on condition that Clifford and Stuart Perlman were placed on immediate unpaid leave of absence from any position in the company. The Perlmans agreed to take a month's unpaid leave of absence, but Caesars World indicated that it might be a while before it made a final decision on its future in Atlantic City. The Perlmans appealed to the courts but the commission prevailed. McElnea resigned and sold his 450,000 shares of stock to the Perlmans.

Meanwhile, the Boardwalk Regency reported profits of $16.13 million on revenues of $226.85 million, which was twice the combined profits of the company's casinos in Las Vegas and Lake Tahoe for the previous year.

The squabble with the commission dragged on until December 1981 before Caesars World and the Perlmans came up with a solution the commission found partly satisfactory. Caesars World agreed to pay the Perlmans $99 million for their 4.8 million shares of stock, which amounted to $20 a share, a price that was 222 percent of the market value. The first installment of $30 million was to be paid immediately, with the balance of $69 million to be paid in six annual installments beginning in January 1983, bearing interest at 9 percent.

Clifford Perlman was to be retained as board chairman and chief executive office of Caesars Palace in Las Vegas, with annual pay of $350,000.

The gaming commission approved the stock transaction, but took the employment clause under advisement, which it eventually denied.

In April 1983 the Nevada Gaming Commission found the Perlmans suitable for a gaming license when they attempted to buy the Dunes from owner Morris Shenker, former attorney for Jimmy Hoffa and a longtime associate of organized crime figures in St. Louis, Kansas City, and Chicago.

The Dunes sale did not work out, but Clifford Perlman was jubilant about the commission's ruling. "My brother and I are extremely happy to be back in this community," he told the press. "I feel like we're back home again with friends and neighbors. I can't tell you how happy being with Nevada people again has made me."

18

Death of a Godfather

Ever since his appearance before the New Jersey State Commission of Investigation in August 1977, Angelo Bruno had been shuttling between grand juries and crime commissions in Pennsylvania and New Jersey, being grilled almost nonstop about organized crime. Although he fought subpoenas and grants of immunity in the courts, it was a losing battle.

In October 1979, exhausted and suffering from ulcers, diabetes, and high blood pressure, illnesses for which he had been hospitalized numerous times, Bruno ignored a subpoena to appear before the SCI and traveled for a rest to his homeland island, the island of Sicily, where the Mafia had been born and later exported to the United States.

Angelo Bruno Annaloro, who later dropped the Annaloro and assumed the maiden name of his paternal grandmother, Bruno, was only a year old when his father, a foundry worker, took the family to America, settling in South Philadelphia, where the father opened a small grocery at 4341 North Sixth Street. Angelo, who helped in the store, was 12 before he started school, which he pursued only a few years, dropping out of South Philadelphia High School to open his own store at Eighth and Annin Streets.

It was around this time that he was threatened by a "Black Hand" extortion ring which preyed on Italian immigrants. Angelo not only resisted but his testimony led to a ring member's conviction. That same year, 1928, he was arrested for reckless driving and destruction of city property, but was acquitted—the first of many evasions of justice.

In 1935 police found a 500-gallon still on the third floor of Angelo's grocery and caught his brother Vito running from the store. Angelo denied any knowledge of the bootlegging operation and was found not guilty. Two years later he was convicted of "disorderly conduct" and fined.

His sponsor in the Philadelphia Mafia family was Michele Maggio, the founder of the M. Maggio cheese enterprise, and a convicted murderer with a national reputation.

As a Mafia soldier, Angelo, who had been an obscure numbers runner, was now permitted to operate his own numbers book, which meant that he could put together his own team of writers and collectors on the street. Through organizational skill, he turned it into a lucrative enterprise. In 1940 police raided his book and collected 50,000 numbers slips as evidence. Angelo was charged with operating an illegal lottery, found guilty, and placed on probation. Three years later an arrest for the same offense was dismissed. In 1944 the charge was receiving stolen goods and violating the firearms act. Again he went free.

By now his various criminal interests were becoming major enterprises. Along with Pete Casella he joined forces with Marco Reginelli in Camden, the underboss of the Philadelphia family. They became known as the Greaser Gang and later as the Reginelli-Bruno-Casella Mob. Police estimated their profits at $50 million annually.

A reform Democratic administration in 1953, determined to break the link between ward politicians and corrupt police officials, appointed a new police commissioner, Thomas J. Gibbons, and gave him orders to crack down on organized crime. Gibbons's detectives compiled dossiers on 24 leading racketeers and Angelo Bruno headed the list. He and Casella were described as "chieftains of the South Philadelphia numbers mob."

Another police raid on Angelo's headquarters yielded 17,000 numbers slips. Seven top numbers bankers were convicted and jailed. Assistant District Attorney Samuel Dash—later to achieve fame as chief counsel of the Senate Watergate committee—asked that Bruno be given a jail sentence, but the judge fined him $500 and placed him on two years' probation.

When Reginelli died on May 25, 1956, Bruno became the family's underboss. Then in 1957, as recounted earlier, Joe Ida went into exile after being apprehended at the Apalachin conclave and Bruno became the boss after uncovering Antonio Pollina's treachery.

Gibbons was determined to "drive him [Bruno] out of business." In 1958 police raided the offices of Bruno's Penn Jersey Vending Company and carted off documents detailing $600,000 in financial transactions, but would soon find themselves carting everything back on a court order.

Big trouble came in 1963 with the testimony of Joseph Valachi on national television. A soldier in the Genovese family, Valachi became a government witness, the first initiated member of the Mafia so to testify. One of those named by Valachi was Angelo Bruno, who he said was one of the country's 26 family bosses. Valachi provided the FBI with enough details of Bruno's operation to interest Attorney General Robert F. Kennedy, who gave Bruno top priority in his drive against organized crime.

A federal investigation revealed that Bruno had extensive legitimate business holdings, with vast real estate interests in Pennsylvania, New Jersey, and Florida. Bruno's financial portfolio was said to include investments in gambling casinos in the Dominican Republic and London, a hotel in the Netherlands Antilles, travel junket clubs in New York and Philadelphia, a New Jersey trucking company, restaurants, motels, and firms dealing with catering, pest control, frozen food processing, trash collection, land development, home improvements, boxing, and vending machines.

Yet his lifestyle remained simple. He was a quiet family man, not one to flaunt his wealth and power. He continued to live in the same modest rowhouse, shunned nightclubs and expensive cars. His only weakness appeared to be a penchant for highly styled clothing. He wore heavy horn-rimmed glasses and preferred sporty caps to the more formal soft hats popular with Mafiosi.

With Kennedy hot on his trail, Bruno was indicted on charges of interstate extortion and conspiracy. Fearful of conviction, he fled with his wife, Sue, the former Assunta Maranca, to Italy, where their lifestyle improved considerably. They traveled to Naples and Rome, and rented an elegant villa on the Adriatic Sea.

He talked of retiring in his homeland but when his passport was invalidated in late 1963, he flew back to Boston and surrendered to authorities. He was released on $75,000 bail and later acquitted on all counts after a four-week trial. Federal prosecutors got a glimpse of his immunity from the law after their star witness, a loanshark victim who claimed to have been threatened in Bruno's presence, became the subject of an incapacitating prison "accident," and another important witness suddenly decided to recant.

In 1969 he was accused by a Philadelphia grand jury of paying $10,000 to a councilman to swing a local land deal, and in 1970 he was named in two federal indictments for conspiring with his wife in 1965 to evade income taxes and for participating in an international scheme to transport gamblers to London for a fee and a share of their losses. Nothing came of any of these charges.

His only other conviction was for a traffic violation in 1967. His only imprisonment came in 1970 when he served 32 months at Yardville for refusing to answer questions before the State Commission of Investigation after being granted immunity.

Now, in 1980, he returned from Sicily on the day the SCI was to issue an arrest warrant, and was once more embroiled in what had become his primary occupation in life: trying to stay out of jail by satisfying information seekers without really answering their questions.

By the middle of March it had gone from bad to worse. On Thursday, March 20, Bruno made another appearance before the SCI, this time for two hours behind closed doors. Although the session was described as routine, speculation in the press was that he had been questioned about possible Mob presence in Atlantic City.

A story in the *Camden Courier Post* quoted anonymous sources saying that Bruno and 16 of his associates were to be indicted by a federal grand jury on charges of racketeering, loansharking, and extortion. It was said to be the result of a five-year investigation into Bruno's affairs by a federal strike force. Earlier in the week, Giuseppe and Rosario Gambino had been arrested for conspiracy to import $60 million worth of heroin and for related charges. If nothing else, the arrests demonstrated that the Gambino family was taking over the narcotics trade in the Atlantic City area. This was further proof that Bruno was either incapable of keeping the Gambino family out of his territory, or had sanctioned their move. Either way, it was a sign of weakness that was certain to enrage members of his family.

On Friday evening Bruno had dinner with his attorney, Jacob Kossman, at Cous' Little Italy, a restaurant patronized by high-ranking members of Bruno's family—the owners had named a salad after loanshark boss Frank Sindone.

Bruno and Kossman were the same age—69—and had been friends for 40 years. On this Friday night at Cous' Little Italy, while they were having a leisurely dinner and a relaxed conversation, Raymond "Longjohn" Martorano came over to their table for a friendly chat. Besides being the front for Bruno in John's Wholesale, Martorano was the family's "speed king," having the exclusive distributorship of methamphetamine over their domain. Bruno, who was said to oppose the family's involvement in hard drugs, had apparently no objection to pills.

After Martorano left, Bruno and Kossman briefly discussed their next move in the pending grand jury indictment. Kossman didn't like it. He thought the ordeal of a trial could kill his friend. Even without a trial, his days seemed numbered. Kossman waved his hand in exasperation. "You should have taken my advice and stayed away from here for the rest of your life."

Bruno smiled. "And you should have taken my advice and bought real estate like I told you years ago."

Kossman laughed. "If I had listened to you, I'd have twenty-five million dollars now."

Bruno's parting remark as he shook hands with Kossman was about the Iranian crisis. "They keep calling the Americans hostages," he said, "but they're actually prisoners of war." This was the kind of situation a godfather understood.

It was eight o'clock when Kossman left his old friend at the restaurant and ran to his office. He wanted to watch "Wall Street Week" on television at eight-thirty. After Kossman had left, Bruno's part-time "donkey"—chauffeur and bodyguard, in Mob parlance—John Stanfa came over to the table, and a few minutes later Bruno released his regular donkey, Mario "Sonny" Riccobene, and left with Stanfa in his flashy maroon Chevrolet.

Bruno lived in a brick rowhouse at 934 Snyder Avenue, in South Philadelphia's Italian section. He had lived there with his wife Sue for most of their 48 years of married life. It was where they had raised their son and daughter.

On the way there Stanfa stopped at Broad and Snyder, and Bruno briefly got out to buy a newspaper. When they arrived at 934 Snyder Avenue, Stanfa pulled up into an empty parking space directly in front of the house instead of following the usual security procedure of driving around the block to make sure that everything looked normal and no strangers were lurking about. Sonny Riccobene often drove up on the sidewalk to drop Bruno right at his doorstep. Stanfa parked a good fifty feet away and in front of a truck.

Bruno was smoking, and Stanfa pushed the button to open the window on Bruno's side to vent the smoke. They talked for several minutes while Bruno finished his cigarette and tossed it out the window. When he turned back toward Stanfa, he was startled to see him hurriedly leaving the car. A split-second later, a man wearing a long green coat moved up from behind the car, poked the business end of a .12-gauge shotgun behind Bruno's right ear, and pulled the trigger. The heavy magnum-load shell tore Bruno's head apart and came out of his mouth and throat. His body jerked forward and blood gushed from his open mouth.

A few stray pellets grazed Stanfa's right hand and wrist before he could get out of the way. With the murderer and an accomplice running away, Stanfa reached into the car and pulled Bruno's body into a sitting position. The head tilted back and blood continued to stream from the mouth and run down the slack chin. There was no doubt that the godfather was dead. If Stanfa touched the mouth, he never admitted it to police, who would later theorize that Bruno's mouth had been propped open as the Sicilian sign of the squealer.

Stanfa ran into Bruno's house and a moment later, Sue came rushing from the house in her bathrobe. Neighbors, who were beginning to approach the car, stopped in respect as she flung open the car door and began screaming.

"She carried on something terrible," one of the neighbors later told police. "She was crying hysterically and screaming, 'It's not Angelo, it's not Angelo.' "

The corpse remained in the car for more than two hours while crime lab technicians, FBI agents, and homicide detectives searched for clues. When the police finally removed the body, a crowd of more than a thousand that had gathered behind police barricades began cheering. Someone shouted, "Don't disgrace the Italian race." There was another cheer and another push forward to get a closer look. Cars slowing down in front of the house created such a bottleneck that police had to direct traffic.

By then TV cameras and reporters were everywhere. Many picked up comments from Bruno's neighbors: "He was a terrific man, always the perfect gentleman. There was never enough he could do for the people in the neighborhood. Just a great next-door neighbor," said Don Coccia, expressing the view of the majority. But there were other views, as expressed by a neighbor with a more philosophical bent: "You live that way. You die that way. What's to be is to be."

The personal effects police found on Bruno's body consisted of a driver's license, a set of house keys, and $1.30 in change—the resources of a man so rich and so well known he had no need for money.

Stanfa was rushed to St. Agnes Hospital and placed under heavy police guard. When police tried to question him, he refused to talk, citing advice of his lawyer. Even Bruno's wife, Sue, refused to talk to police on advice of counsel.

Scenarios for the murder abounded: He was killed because of his recent testimony before the SCI; it was to silence him in the event he was indicted; Phil Testa, impatient with the aging Bruno's outdated policies, wanted more action in Atlantic City, particularly drugs; the Gambino family had formed an alliance with Bruno for dividing the spoils in Atlantic City, a move resented by Testa and Nicky Scarfo; the Genovese family had formed an alliance with Scarfo and Testa to take over unions and all rackets in Atlantic City; the growing casino industry created a feud among crime families on the East Coast for control of an estimated $500 million worth of service industries; the hit hadn't been cleared with the Mafia's commission and retribution would lead to the factions "going to the mats" in an old-fashioned gang war; it was an internal struggle within the Bruno family, pitting Testa, Scarfo, and Frank Narducci against Frank Sindone, Harry "The Hunchback" Riccobene, and Raymond Martorano, over the distribution of territories, money, and power; Bruno had fallen out of favor with New York Mafia bosses over Atlantic City and the hit was a commission contract; Bruno, depressed about his failing health and police harassment, had put a hit on himself.

The most important theory game was the one dealing with succession. The godfather was dead; long live the godfather. But who would it be? Before that would be decided, however, Bruno's murder would split the family into warring factions. Many would die for their treachery in retaliatory moves by the Bruno faction, and many others would die at the hands of Bruno's killers for "insurance" purposes, being taken out before they could retaliate. And other bodies, of course, would become rungs on the ladder to the top of the heap. It was the Darwinian survival of the fittest concept of evolution operating at its most basic level in the human jungle.

19

Exit the Slot King

On December 5, 1979, Billy Weinberger gave Joe Lordi and his commissioners a red-carpet tour of Bally's Park Place, and they came away singing its praises. "There's no question it is a colossal structure—an expensive colossal structure," Lordi said. "I'm quite impressed with what they have done with the Dennis Hotel and what they were able to do to the exterior of the building. If this is a patch and paint job, it's a very impressive patch and paint job."

What most impressed the commissioners was the massive escalator rising from the casino floor to an upper level of specialty restaurants and shops. Waterfalls flowed on both sides of the escalator and a fountain at the top highlighted several gargoyles retrieved from the towers of the Blenheim Hotel. The area was festooned with poinsettias, a reminder to the commissioners that Bally was planning on opening its doors between Christmas and New Year's.

All it had to do to receive its temporary license was for its board chairman and president, William T. O'Donnell, to step aside, severing himself from all operations of the Park Place casino as well as Bally Manufacturing until the Division of Gaming Enforcement completed its investigation. His 1.8 million shares of stock were to be placed in a voting trust, to be administered by Bally's corporate secretary. Bally's European representative, Alex Wilms, and his family were to place their stock in a similar voting trust, and his son Alfred was to resign his seat on the board.

So once again a corporation had to cleanse itself by removing its chief executive. O'Donnell's roots were in Chicago. In 1946 he had become sales manager of Lion, a manufacturer of slot machines. In those days, slots could be found in every poolroom, every corner grocery, drugstore, and candy store in town, not to mention social clubs and church basements.

But only in Nevada were slots legal. It was a federal crime to ship the contraptions over state lines, even to Nevada. Laws, however, have seldom stopped a lucrative enterprise from prospering. And so it was with slot machines.

When Frank Costello was the boss of the Mafia family founded by Lucky Luciano, which is known today as the Genovese family, he made a deal with Huey P. Long for the gambling rights of Louisiana. The company supplying the slot machines was the Lion Manufacturing Corporation of Chicago.

In 1946 New Jersey Mafia kingpin Jerry Catena, then a Genovese caporegime, formed the Runyon Sales Company to distribute Lion slot and pinball machines to counties and states where organized crime had a monopoly. The two "legitimate" businessmen fronting Runyon for Catena were Abe Green and Barnett Sugarman.

When O'Donnell joined Lion, its founder, Raymond Moloney, had told him that Runyon was owned by Catena and for him not to "stick your nose where it doesn't belong."

After Moloney died in 1958, Lion was administered by the American National Bank and Trust Company, the executor of the estate. One of the five directors appointed by the bank was O'Donnell. In 1962 the bank informed O'Donnell that Lion was available for purchase. Unable to swing the deal on his own, O'Donnell immediately turned to Runyon. At that moment Lion changed from being a supplier of illegal devices to organized crime to being a property of organized crime.

The initial record of ownership listed the following names and shares owned by each:

William T. O'Donnell...................................250
Sam W. Klein 333
Frank J. Prince 333
Emprise Corporation...................................334
Barnett Sugarman 250
Abe Green..250
Irving Kaye 250

Each of the original shareholders paid $100 per share, or a total of $200,000 for the 2000 shares of capitalization. But this was hardly enough to buy out Lion. That was accomplished by a loan of $1.2 million from Emprise. Following the formation of the new owner-ship, all shares were transferred to Emprise, as voting trustee, and used as security for a bank loan of $1 million, guaranteed by Emprise, to be used in completing the purchase.

Not visible on public records, but very much in the picture, was Jerry Catena. In a separate agreement with Green and Sugarman, he received a beneficial interest in one-third of their shares. Another invisible investor was Raymond Patriarca, the boss of the New England Mafia family, who in 1968 would be convicted of conspir-acy to murder a gambling rival.

But who were the new visible owners of Lion? And how did they relate to organized crime?

If anyone was the sparkplug behind the immediate success of the new company, it was Sam Klein. Originally from Cleveland, Klein was set up in the vending business in Cincinnati by Samuel W. Schraeder, who operated illegal gambling casinos in Kentucky and was considered a "junior partner" of Meyer Lansky. Klein was also involved in a Kentucky casino with Carl Glickman, a reputed Mob associate whom Klein considered his best friend.

Klein was alleged to have made a $65,000 loan to Catena. Klein was also a partner of Louis Jacobs in Kentucky Raceway in Florence, Kentucky, though his name never appeared as a part owner in state racing commission files.

Jacobs had parlayed a small popcorn and hot-dog stand into a giant family-owned business called Emprise. By 1970 Emprise had 162 subsidiaries and some 700 concession outlets in 39 states, many at baseball parks and football and basketball stadiums, horse and dog tracks, theaters and drive-ins, airports, bowling alleys, and even in-flight meals for airlines. It had vending machines in the New York subway system and restaurants on the thruways. It owned the Cincin-nati Royals and the Ice Capades, and had major investments in horse tracks, dog tracks, and jai alai frontons across the country. In the late 1960s it was already reporting a gross of nearly $100 million annu-ally, but many in law enforcement believed this to be a modest figure.

Jacobs' Horatio Alger success was reminiscent of the Perlmans with their little hot-dog stand in Miami which ended up with Caesars

World. Except that Emprise's links to organized crime were so visible that it became a target of both federal and local investigations.

For many years Jacobs acted as a private banker to various sports teams and race tracks, including $2.5 million to the Milwaukee Brewers, $2 million of which was inherited from the Seattle Pilots; $2 million to the Montreal Expos; smaller amounts to the old Philadelphia Athletics then owned by Connie Mack, and to three teams owned by Bill Veeck. With the loans came favorable long-term concession contracts for Emprise that followed the teams wherever they moved.

Similar arrangements on a far larger scale obtained at tracks, many of which figured in scandals. In Arizona alone, Emprise, under the subsidiary name of Sportservice, shared ownership in six dog tracks and one horse track, leaving only one horse track in the state not involved with Emprise.

Some of Emprise's modus operandi was revealed in a report from the New York State Bureau of Criminal Investigation, dated December 19, 1969: "[Sportservice and Emprise] have many admitted contacts and dealings with individuals who are hoodlums or alleged Mafia leaders. This is particularly true relative to their many concessions at stadiums, racetracks, ballparks, and so forth. . . ."

Jacobs often acted as a private banker to mobsters, especially when it was important for them to come up with large sums for legitimate investments. A classic example was the Hazel Park Racing Association of Detroit, a thoroughbred and harness racetrack that took in about $1 million a racing day in bets, making it one of the most lucrative tracks in the country.

Emprise shared ownership of the track with Anthony J. Zerilli and Michael S. Polizzi, two high-ranking members of the Detroit Mafia family—today they are the boss and underboss, respectively. Besides its own 13 percent investment in Hazel Park, Emprise provided all the money, at no interest, that Zerilli, Polizzi, and Giacomo "Jack" Tocco needed to buy their controlling interest in the track. Anthony Zerilli was president of the track until forced out by the Michigan Racing Commission; he then remained a major stockholder and director.

The scandal in Detroit was as nothing compared to that in Las Vegas after Howard Hughes bought the Frontier Hotel and Casino in 1968 and it came out that its ownership had been illegally concealed. The real owners were Tony Zerilli, Mike Polizzi, Peter Bellanca, Athony Giordano, Mafia boss of St. Louis—and Emprise. The charges were conspiracy and interstate transportation in aid of racketeering. Zerilli, Polizzi, and Giordano were sentenced to four years in prison; Bellanca drew a suspended five-year sentence.

Emprise was fined $10,000. After all, you can't send a corporation to prison. Both Louis Jacobs, who had died in 1968, and his son Max were named as unindicted co-conspirators.

During the trial it was shown that the mobsters had used "strongarm Chicago tactics" on Maurice Friedman, the Frontier's owner of record, to gain hidden control of the casino after they had been denied a license in March 1966. To make it appear that the Frontier was being bought legitimately by the nominees, Emprise made fictitious loans to them. As part of the scheme, Louis Jacobs and his son Max acquired shares in the casino by furnishing money to Max's father-in-law, Philip M. Troy, who bought shares in Vegas Frontier, Inc. Emprise and the Jacobses then allowed the nominees to represent and vote the secret shareholder interest they held in Troy's name.

Eighty percent of Bally's gross earnings came from foreign countries. The man picked by Klein and O'Donnell to operate Bally's international division was Alex Wilms. Operating out of Antwerp, Wilms became Bally's sole distributor for Europe, Africa, Southeast Asia, and the Middle East.

Thrice convicted for black-market offenses between 1945 and 1951, Wilms had formed his own company to distribute Lion slot machines in 1949. Twenty years later Bally purchased Wilms's company, since renamed Bally Continental, elected him a director of Bally Manufacturing, and placed him in charge of Bally Continental.

For two months in 1966 the FBI and CIA had conducted a joint investigation of two Corsican heroin traffickers, Marcel and Roland Francisci, who also had interests in gambling casinos. Caught in the web of that surveillance was Wilms, who in October was observed meeting with Charles "Charlie the Blade" Tourine in Washington, D.C., where they discussed their partnership in a casino in Lagos, Nigeria. That same month, Wilms met with Angelo Bruno in Philadelphia. Two weeks later Wilms and Bruno again met, this time at the London Hilton—Wilms was there to help Bruno obtain a casino interest in England.

In November Wilms represented the Francisci brothers at a meeting at the Dorchester Hotel in London, meeting with William Davis, who was representing Albert Dimes, an English mobster. Attending the meeting on behalf of New York Mafia figure Anthony Corallo was Herbert Itkin, an undercover agent for the FBI and CIA. Itkin's testimony would later result in the conviction of a score of people on charges of kickbacks and fraud involving the Teamsters pension fund.

In 1968 Wilms was told by O'Donnell to hire Dino Cellini—the same Cellini who with his brother, Eddie, had been so helpful in getting Resorts International started on the right foot in the Bahamas. Later, when Cellini sold Resorts International 188 Lion slot machines for its Paradise Island casino, his commission was $28,200 and it was paid to United Agencies, a Swiss company controlled by Wilms.

Like James Crosby before him, O'Donnell had nothing but praise for Dino Cellini. Cellini, he said, was "reputed to be one of the best casino men in the whole world." O'Donnell never asked the Bahamian or British governments why they had banned Cellini before he told Wilms to hire him. As far as he was concerned, Cellini was a straight shooter, and "I personally like Mr. Cellini."

After being expelled from the Bahamas, Cellini had gone to London, where Wilms, along with Glickman and Cyril Shack—two of the principal owners of Lion's British distributor—made him manager of their new casino, the Colony Club. The enterprise suffered a setback when the British government declared Cellini an undesirable person for his close association with Meyer Lansky and expelled him from England.

Having been thrown out of two countries, Cellini found himself on the run when the Justice Department indicted him and Lansky on charges of evading federal income taxes on money collected from gamblers at the Colony Club. With IRS agents in hot pursuit, Cellini fled to Rome because there was no extradition treaty for income tax violations between Italy and the U.S. To ease Cellini's burden, and at O'Donnell's direction, Wilms employed him as a Bally sales representative, with a $2000 per month draw against future commissions and an office in Rome, an arrangement that continued for four years. One of his assignments was to take O'Donnell's son, William, on a ten-day trip through Africa, at Bally's expense, to explore possible slot machine sales and casino purchases.

Meanwhile, Lion had decided to go public with its stock. First, however, there was the little problem of cleaning up its act. Catena's visibility was an embarrassment. To remedy that problem his shares were divided among O'Donnell, Green, and Kaye. Next to bow out was Frank Prince, an ex-convict and close friend of Louis Jacobs, who divided his shares in equal amounts between Klein and Emprise. Finally, it was Emprise's turn to exit, selling its stock back to the company. The sole remaining stockholders were Klein, O'Donnell, Green, and Kaye.

Then to sever all ties to Lion's checkered past, the company's name was changed in March 1968 to the present Bally Manufacturing Corporation. To give it a little class, a Cleveland judge, Adrian Fink, was put on the board, and the legal work necessary to secure SEC approval was turned over to Al Sommer, Jr., who would continue to hold his Bally stock after he became an SEC commissioner.

After completing its investigation, the SEC reported that Bally was free of gangster money and approved its stock offering. Suddenly Bally had the shiny new look of a winner.

Klein distributed shares of the new stock to trustees of the Teamsters pension fund. Trustees receiving free shares included Teamsters president Frank Fitzsimmons and Bill Presser, father of Jackie Presser, who is now president of the union. That same year, 1972, the Teamsters pension fund awarded Bally a $12 million loan with unusually generous terms: Bally would have 12 years to repay the loan and would pay interest only during the first four years. And the interest rate was 6.5 percent at a time when banks were charging their most reliable customers 10 percent.

Others alleged to have received free shares of Bally stocks included William Saxbe, who went from Attorney General of Ohio to U.S. Senator and finally to U.S. Attorney General. Saxbe said he paid for the stock. As for Klein's listing Saxbe as one of the persons who could testify to his good character when he filed for a gambling license in Nevada, Saxbe said he took the trouble to check Klein out and found him to be "clean as a hound's tooth."

In Europe, meanwhile, Alexander Wilms was branching out. Bally had plants manufacturing slot and pinball machines in Ireland and Germany. In 1971 Wilms toured Australia, Thailand, and Indonesia in an effort to expand Bally's Asian interests.

In a report to Klein and O'Donnell, Wilms suggested a practice of double bookkeeping to mask their business transactions, referring to "white bookkeeping" and "white money" for regular transactions and "black money," that is, money not subject to taxation, for paying bribes. In explaining how permits for slot machine operators could be obtained in Indonesia, Wilms reported he had told a local representative that Bally could talk only about white transactions. "I made him understand that if any bribery had to be done, it was to come from our partner, so that the Bally image would remain clean."

The partner he was referring to was Jack Rooklyn, Bally's Australian distributor. In March 1972 Bally, through Wilms, purchased all the assets of J. Rooklyn Amusements and Hong Kong Ltd., becoming the lessor of slot machines in Malaysia, Indonesia, Thailand, Macao, Hong Kong, and Singapore.

After an investigation of Bally in Australia, the Hon. A. R. Moffitt, a New South Wales jurist, found that Bally was offering bribes of up to $750 per machine. He reported, "The analysis I have made of the multiple connections of Bally with criminals or their associates in their operations all around the world makes it likely that crime and high-pressure methods have aided this march to financial domination of the industry."

Kickbacks and bribery had domestic application as well. It was illegal to ship "bingo"-type pinball machines—they paid off in coins to winners—into Kentucky. Bally's representative, Gilbert K. Brawner, thought he could do something about changing the law. What he needed, he told O'Donnell, was the services of Bally's Chicago lawyer to assist in the drafting of new legislation and a little cash to take care of the lawmakers.

In a letter to O'Donnell dated February 20, 1968, Brawner wrote: "Last night I gave the chairman of the committee, which this bill is in, $500. That is what he wanted. It seems as though word got out that we have given him some money. Now, they [other legislators] are trying to put me on for more money." O'Donnell responded by sending Brawner $4000.

In 1974 O'Donnell and Bally's distributor, Louis M. Boasberg, owner of New Orleans Novelty, were indicted on a variety of charges including conspiracy, interstate travel in aid of racketeering enterprises, and promotion of illegal gambling. At a trial in New Orleans, Boasberg pleaded guilty and O'Donnell was acquitted.

Bally's distributor in Nevada was Michael "Mickey" Wichinsky, a close associate of Abe Green and Lansky, and related to Catena through marriage—his nephew was married to Catena's daughter. It was Wichinsky who introduced Klein to Dino Cellini.

In the mid-1970s O'Donnell and Wichinsky went into business together, founding Westronics Inc., a company that manufactured electronic coin-operated horse-racing games that resembled slot machines. Westronics was able to place its machines in almost all the casinos in Las Vegas. In order to acquire his 18 percent interest in Westronics, O'Donnell had borrowed the money from Bally.

When Bally applied to the Nevada Gaming Commission for renewal of its probationary license in October 1977, it opened up some old battle wounds, for the control board had launched a two-year investigation of Bally, coming up with some unpleasant surprises for the gaming commission which had ordered Bally to cease doing business with Runyan and New Orleans Novelty.

It reported that Coin-Op, the company that had supposedly replaced Runyan in New Jersey, was controlled by Abe Green's son, Irving, and it shared with Runyan "adjacent" facilities in Springfield, New Jersey, shared the same warehouse, and Bally continued to receive purchase orders and checks from Runyon Sales. The only customer Coin-Op had was Runyon. To sum up matters, the board said that Irving Green had told O'Donnell in 1974 that Coin-Op was a "fictitious name for Runyon Sales."

As for New Orleans Novelty, Bally had continued doing business with Louis Boasberg through Playtime Sales which was a partnership of his five children. Playtime operated at the same address as New Orleans Novelty and used its stationery. Bally, the control board reported, had followed a "regular pattern of business dealings" with Boasberg that was "indistinguishable" from its prior transactions.

Alexander Wilms, who had been ordered by the gaming commission to resign as a Bally director, had divided his 8.3 percent beneficial stock interest in Bally among his wife, two sons, and two granddaughters, who executed the required proxies at the request of Bally's attorney. Bally Continental was renamed Wilms Distributing Company, but its principal business remained the sale of Bally machines. After Alexander Wilms had resigned as a Bally director, his son Alfred replaced him on the board. Alfred advised Nevada authorities that his father had no involvement whatsoever in the new company. Yet the control board discovered that when anything went wrong at Wilms Distributing, it was the father who interceded personally with O'Donnell on behalf of his "son's company" to get it straightened out.

Then in 1976 control board investigators took photographs of Klein playing golf with Catena in Florida—Green, Catena, and Klein all lived part of the year in the same exclusive Boca Raton development. Commission Chairman Peter Echeverria was shocked at the "horrible" disclosure that Klein had "openly and notoriously" associated with Catena in "seeming complete disregard" of the restrictions imposed by the state. The commission revoked Klein's license, ordered him to resign from his position as a vice-president of Bally, and ordered the company not to employ him in any capacity in the future. He was fined $50,000 and ordered to dispose of his Bally stock.

With Carl Glickman as the trustee, Klein set up the Michael Trust, for the benefit of his son, with assets of approximately $37 million. During its investigation of Glickman, the Federal Reserve Bank learned something unknown to Nevada and New Jersey gaming investigators. Klein and Glickman were partners with Jack B. Cooper in a company called Consortium Communications International. Cooper openly visited Lansky at his Collins Avenue apartment in Miami Beach, a privilege permitted to few of the old mobster's surrogates. In a sworn deposition taken during the bank's probe, Klein referred to Cooper as a "dear friend."

With Klein out of the picture, of the seven initial investors in the old Lion company only William O'Donnell remained on its board of directors in 1977 when Bally began angling for a spot on the Boardwalk.

But it wasn't long before Klein, in violation of the gaming commission's order, was back on Bally's payroll as a consultant at $50,000 a year and in Atlantic City looking for the right piece of real estate for Bally's proposed Boardwalk casino. In June 1977 Bally incorporated a New Jersey subsidiary and later one in Delaware, both named Bally's Park Place, with the parent holding 82.8 percent of the 22.6 million shares that would be traded over-the-counter by the end of 1979.

By the time Bally was ready to move into Atlantic City, it had succeeded in violating every order of Nevada's gaming commission, and, what is more, had gotten away with it. It was Nevada's primary supplier of slot machines and it also operated numerous mini slot casinos throughout the state.

In 14 years Bally's Mob links and unscrupulous business practices had transformed the old Lion company, then on the verge of bankruptcy, into a giant multinational corporation with annual revenues of nearly $400 million. Besides selling Bally slot and pinball machines all over the world, it was the only slot machine producer of any size in the United States and had an estimated 80 percent of the domestic market.

Diversification in the early 1970s saw Bally moving into video games with the introduction of Space Invaders, Pac-Man, and Ms.

Pac-Man, and operating more than a hundred family amusement centers in shopping malls under the Aladdin's Castle name. It acquired Six Flags theme parks, the Health and Tennis Corp. of America, which operates Holiday Spa Health Clubs, Jack LaLanne Fitness Centers, and Richard Simmons Anatomy Asylums, and in 1982 Scientific Games Inc., the country's largest supplier of lottery tickets, which spends millions each year promoting lottery initiatives in states across the country. Since lotteries are essentially Scientific Games's only business, the ballot has become its marketing strategy—to sway votes in favor of a lottery, it aims political campaigns to a specific need, such as public education. According to a Bally official, it is the fastest-growing new business in the country.

Bally came to Atlantic City with the usual ballyhoo. It bought the old Marlborough-Blenheim Hotel, and in no time the Blenheim's historic Moorish dome was blasted into dust and hordes of construction crews were feverishly working "fast-track" around-the-clock to erect what Bally publicists were boasting would be the most expensive and extravagant casino complex on the Boardwalk. Instead of building new hotel rooms, it paid $4 million for the old Dennis Hotel and spent another $7 million restoring 507 of its rooms to qualify for the 500-room minimum required by the commission. Rooms is not where it's at in Atlantic City.

And forget all that nonsense about a class operation. This was going to be strictly Las Vegas style, with "special" rooms equipped with round mattresses, mirrored ceilings, and group love tubs, familiar little touches to keep Las Vegas high-roller types in a pleasant frame of mind while away from the gambling tables. Waking up in the afternoon, after a hard night of gambling and drinking, many might well wonder which end of the country they were in.

Projected cost was $160 million. That was for a 50,100-square-foot casino, assorted restaurants and lounges, a 400-seat cabaret theater, and 30,000 square feet of convention space. The final cost, according to figures released by Bally, was in the $300 million-plus range.

Investigators from the Division of Gaming Enforcement traveled around the world in a probe that would take 2½ years to complete, cost $2.5 million, and end up revealing less than was available in any mid-size university library.

Whatever negative information the division would present to the Casino Control Commission, it was generally conceded that Bally would get its permanent license. Still, Bally wasn't sitting on its hands. It knew a few things about image polishing and public relations. It went out and hired people who could make a difference. They included baseball greats Willie Mays and Joe Rosen as public relations consultants; James Rochford, former superintendent of the Chicago Police Department, to supervise internal security; and Jim Powell, the investigator who had supervised Nevada's investigation into the company.

Bally outspent its prospective competitors in making charitable contributions to civic organizations that were in desperate straits, all with attending publicity.

To represent the company before the commission it hired Clive Cummis, a member of the firm of Arthur J. Sills, a former state attorney general. Picked as trustees to operate the casino in the event Bally was denied a license were William Dwyer, a Trenton newspaper columnist and frequent tennis partner of Governor Byrne, and press secretary to former Governor Hughes; George John Keto, a Washington lawyer who had been Byrne's roommate at Harvard Law School; Barry Evenchick, a lawyer and Byrne supporter who served on Byrne's staff when he was Essex County prosecutor in the 1960s. Each was paid an initial $15,000 simply to wait for the impossible to happen. Also coming on board was Kenneth McPherson, a friend of Byrne and major campaign fund-raiser.

Replacing O'Donnell as chairman and president of Bally was Robert E. Mullane, who had started out in 1963 as a vending machine salesman for American Automatic Vending Company, later known as AAV, moving over to Bally when AAV became the subject of a federal grand jury investigation in 1971. AAV pleaded "no contest" to charges of fixing prices of vending machine cigarettes and was fined. At the time of the investigation, Mullane was senior vice-president for operations.

At Bally, Mullane was sent to Europe to cut his corporate teeth under the guidance of Alex Wilms. Mullane served as managing director of Bally Continental in Belgium and returned to Chicago in 1978 in time to be groomed for his new post.

Bally's Park Place opened its doors to the public on December 30, 1979, with Billy Weinberger cutting the ceremonial ribbon. As anxious customers raced to the 97 table games and 1217 slot machines, Weinberger smiled. "Now we've finally got a store," he said.

Participating in the opening ceremony, Lordi said, "Man's ingenuity can do anything."

It would be another year before the division completed its investigation and the commission would begin its hearings on Bally's application for a permanent license.

In August 1980 the division issued a 111-page report that leveled its allegations against O'Donnell and Wilms, citing instances of bribery and associations with organized crime figures and convicted criminals. It recommended against permanent licenses for the casino-hotel, its parent company, and O'Donnell.

Bally attorney Clive Cummis lost little time in placing some distance between Bally and O'Donnell. "In each of the substantive issues they raise in their report, nowhere do they raise issues that point to the company," Cummis said. "It's our view that their issues really point to the qualifiers and that they're concluding if the qualifiers shouldn't be given licenses nor should the company. We disagree with that."

Cummis's thesis was that Bally was not liable for the behavior of its executives. "Sixty-five thousand shareholders and 11,000 employees of this company cannot be punished. These people are not wrongdoers. We believe O'Donnell will be found suitable, but if it's found that he's not, then it is not automatic that the company is not suitable."

Cummis agreed that company executives had made mistakes in the past but they were ones of judgment in a company "growing so quickly that some aspects were out of control. All of us suffer scars if we live long enough," Cummis reasoned. "You can be assured the mistakes of the past will not happen again."

The problem with Bally's "past" was that it was continuous. And who could separate the "mistakes" from the smart moves? As for Catena's rearing his ugly head, that was a problem that Joe Lordi knew a little something about, having had to explain his own links to the mobster only months earlier. For those in the media who wondered how Lordi would handle the Catena bugaboo, the question was answered simply. Lordi checked into the hospital with ulcers the first week of the hearings and spent the rest of the time recuperating at home, watching videotapes of the hearings, as he waited for his doctor to give him "a clean bill of health," which came the last week of the hearings, and which meant he had to abstain from passing judgment.

"Any suggestion that I am associated with or have been associated with, members of organized crime is totally untrue and personally abhorrent," O'Donnell said in a prepared statement. "I was very disappointed that the division should challenge my suitability for licensing. Why, I ask, would I risk my position with Bally, something built up over the majority of my lifetime, if I thought my character and integrity would be challenged?"

Why, indeed, would he, as he had to do in the end, surrender control of a $400 million business, as the Perlmans before him had done, if other more powerful voices were not calling the shots? Bally got its permanent license and O'Donnell sold his stock back to the company at a handsome profit, but the fact remained that he was out, finished, discarded after a lifetime's work of building a company that was never really his. There were seven initial investors, Seven Little Indians, and then there were none. Or were there?

20

Deaths in the Family

No one questioned that Antonio "Tony Bananas" Caponigro was a tough guy, even when they saw the word "mother" tattooed inside the heart on his burly right forearm.

Born in Chicago in 1911, his family moved to Newark in the early 1920s. Little Antonio was soon in trouble with the law and shooting it out with the cops when they came to arrest him. He served three years for being part of a gang that committed 31 armed robberies during a three-month period. Out of prison only a few months, he was arrested for shooting a policeman and sentenced to ten years in prison. In 1959 he was arrested for operating an illegal whiskey still that was tied to the city's water supply and sewage system.

When he was out of jail, he knew how to enjoy the good life. His lifestyle was altogether different from that of his boss, Angelo Bruno. He owned flashy Cadillacs and Mercedes, tweedy jackets and tailored slacks, and a luxurious estate in the affluent Short Hills section of Essex County.

Where Bruno was low-key, affable, and courtly, Caponigro was brash, hot-headed, and impulsive. On several occasions when FBI agents had come to arrest him, Caponigro, instead of shooting it out as in the old days, had tried to escape. One time he burst from his house, jumped in his car, nearly ran over an agent, and led the others in a wild chase before being caught. Another time, while his wife and other women barred the FBI from a family wedding, he escaped out the back door. And on still another occasion, he charged from the house, again jumped in his car, and rammed one of their vehicles.

Caponigro loved money and power and managed to accumulate a great deal of both in his lifetime. For years he exercised jurisdiction over rackets in an area extending from Trenton to Newark, including the lucrative Port Newark. Although technically a member of Bruno's family, he was pretty much his own man in the Newark area, with a crew numbering nearly 60 men. There were 18 gangland murders at Port Newark between 1971 and 1975 when he was shaking up the place.

Tony Bananas managed boxers who got in trouble with the boxing commission for accepting "loans" from him; he was in the restaurant, bar, and motel business; and he operated several social clubs in Newark that catered to high-stake poker players. He owned a lodge in Montana and was in businesses involving dry cleaning, swimming pools, recording, construction, and garbage collection.

At the age of 68, when most men are looking forward to retiring, he was still angling for more money and power. When gambling was legalized in Atlantic City, he became restive, resenting the prize Nicky Scarfo had inherited merely by being on the scene. There was big money to be made from spin-off rackets like prostitution, drugs, loansharking, unions, vending machines, and the thousands of ancillary businesses servicing the casino-hotels.

He let Bruno know that he wanted his piece of the action. Realizing that if rebuffed Caponigro might turn to the Genovese family, which was also involved in the North Jersey waterfront, Bruno, ever the compromiser, tried to reach an accommodation with his greedy capo instead of disposing of him with bullets. Bruno sought to placate him by giving him the honored position of consigliere that had long been vacant. A fatal mistake in judgment. In his attempt at appeasement, Bruno divided his family into warring factions that would cost him his life.

On Sunday, March 23, 1980, two days after Bruno's murder, police watched as Caponigro, Frank Sindone, Alfred Salerno, and several other senior members of the Bruno family met at John Simone's home in Yardley. The next day Simone was observed arguing with Phil Testa on a street in South Philadelphia. According to a police report, "Simone did all the talking, and Testa just stared at him. Simone was waving his arms."

A few days later, Simone and Sindone picked up John Stanfa, who had recovered from wounds sustained during Bruno's murder, and took him to Newark for a meeting with Salerno and Caponigro. In their investigation, police discovered that Stanfa had twice met with Caponigro the week before Bruno's murder, and had since given police three different versions of the circumstances surrounding the shooting. The morning after the murder, police discovered Sindone in Stanfa's hospital room, whispering something in Italian in Stanfa's ear.

When Stanfa suddenly disappeared, Philadelphia Assistant District Attorney Arthur Shuman told the press that Stanfa had "played a direct role in delivering Angelo Bruno to his killers. I have no doubt in my mind that he saw them [Bruno's killers] and very well knows them." Bruno's daughter, Jean Puppo, announced that she was told of a "Judas" among her father's friends.

On April 18, less than a month after Bruno's death, police found the nude bodies of Caponigro and of his brother-in-law and donkey, Alfred Salerno, in the South Bronx. They had been so brutally mutilated that it would take police ten days to complete the identification. Both had died in slow agony, their bodies tortured by repeated gunshot and stab wounds and heavy blows about the head and face.

"They suffered terribly before dying," said a police spokesman. "That was the aim of the executioners." And, no doubt, the aim was also to learn the names of all accomplices.

Salerno's nude body, bound hand and foot and stuffed in a mortician's body bag, with a canvas cover over it, was found in the street. Besides being beaten and stabbed, Salerno had been shot four times.

Caponigro's tortured body was found in a car trunk about a mile away. He had been shot 13 times, the bullets coming from five guns.

So there would be no mistake about the motive for the mutilations, the victims' money was torn and scattered about their bodies, with pieces of twenty-dollar bills jammed obscenely in their rectums, an ancient Sicilian sign that the victims had become too greedy.

There was a sudden exodus of disappearing family members. Frank Sindone, who had dreamed once of quitting the loanshark business and buying a little ranch in California where he would raise horses and grow grapes, took a vacation trip to San Jose, California, to look over the situation. According to police, he was the only caporegime who had yet to pay his respects to Phil Testa, who had assumed leadership of the family. By now even Testa had vanished, along with Frank Narducci.

Again police scenarios abounded. Caponigro had worked out a deal with Aniello Dellacroce, underboss of the Gambino family, who was also angling for leadership of the Gambino family after Carlo's death. Caponigro promised him a free hand in Atlantic City if he became boss. Being consiglieri, which made him the number three man, Caponigro believed he could take over if Bruno were killed because Bruno and Testa had split over Bruno's reluctance to traffic in drugs and to become more actively involved in Atlantic City.

It didn't work out that way. Caponigro had failed to realize that Testa was every inch as tough and mean and impulsive as he was, and a lot younger, with close ties to hungry young turks, and with far better New York connections.

As his underboss Testa picked Peter Casella, who had started out with Bruno in the days of Marco Reginelli. Casella, regarded as a drug expert, had served 15 years in the Atlanta federal penitentiary on a 1959 conviction for heroin trafficking. Casella's promotion indicated the direction the family was about to take toward drugs. While in prison Casella was said to have become closely allied with members of the Genovese family.

The new consiglieri was Frank Narducci, whose son, Frank Jr., was a business partner of Testa's son, Salvatore. Nicky Scarfo, who was then awaiting trial in the Falcone murder, was designated as the number four man, a giant step for the soldier Bruno had exiled to the desolation of a dead resort town in 1964.

On September 19 the body of John Simone was found near a landfill in a wooded area on Staten Island. He had been shot three times in the back of the head with a high-powered weapon. Although fully dressed, his shoes and socks were missing. A cousin of Bruno, Simone had been close to Bruno in social and business affairs.

Next to go was Frank Sindone, whose dreams of California ranching ended next to a dumpster behind a variety store in South Philadelphia. On October 29 his body was found stuffed inside two plastic trash bags. His hands were tied behind his back and the knees of his trousers were scuffed as if he had been kneeling, perhaps pleading for mercy before being shot three times in the head, one bullet fired directly into his ear.

That left only Stanfa, who had now become a prime suspect in the Bruno murder. In December police found him in the Washington suburb of Landover, Maryland, where he was operating a pizza parlor formerly owned by the Gambino family. Indicted for having lied to a grand jury about his trip to New York with Caponigro, Stanfa was tried, convicted, and sentenced to eight years in prison, all in the matter of a few months.

For the moment at least, the swift retaliation against Bruno's murderers, had left Testa as the undisputed head of the family.

For years, Big John McCullough had had it made in Atlantic City. He rode roughshod over people with long memories. He had no worries. His old pal Angelo Bruno was always there to run interference whenever he stamped too hard on the wrong toes.

McCullough was the hot-tempered boss of Roofers Local 30, a heavy-muscled outfit that launched an assault on the weak roofers' local in Atlantic City, annexing it after a series of forays that left warrants for assault and arson in its wake. With nine casinos on the drawing board, each anxious for an early completion date, labor trouble was the last thing their owners wanted. It was to be avoided at any cost. For McCullough that fact offered limitless possibilities for extortion.

McCullough's next stop was to gain control of the Building Trades Council, which was made up of all the construction unions in Atlantic City. The Council could offer both labor peace and its political influence in the city to obtain project approval from the planning, zoning, and parking authorities.

Yet Big John wasn't satisfied. Construction was a temporary situation. Once the casinos were built, what then? He was looking for something permanent, something with leverage, a niche of his own in this big-buck town. The casinos already on line were pulling in $600,000 a day, seven days a week, 365 days a year. The last thing they wanted was to be shut down by picket lines. And nobody could pull the plug on them faster than the unions. That was the real seat of power, and that was where Big John wanted to sit.

He lost little time in making his move against Local 54 of the Hotel and Restaurant Employees and Bartenders International Union, the one Nicky Scarfo controlled through Frank Gerace, its president. Scarfo took the problem to Testa who took it to Bruno, but McCullough kept the go-ahead sign. Scarfo could only fume in silence, for the time being.

McCullough started his own bartenders union, Local 491, and began raiding the membership of Local 54. Then he picked four Atlantic City patrolmen to help him organize a security union, Local 40B of the International Brotherhood of Law Enforcement and Security Officers. The idea was to gain control of the security guards in the casinos. Since a casino was required to have a full complement of licensed security guards during operating hours, a strike of security guards would close a casino immediately—at a cost of $600,000 a day. A union with the power to close a casino was in a position to extract not only enormous payoffs for labor peace but other concessions as well.

The options, McCullough knew, were limitless. He could get some of his people in the casinos' credit departments to make sure the right people were given credit. He could force the casinos to buy supplies and services from companies he controlled. He could have them hand out complimentary rooms, food, and drinks to anyone he chose. He could even put corrupt casino guards in positions to embezzle money or chips from the gaming tables or the casino count rooms. The way he saw it: control the guards, control the casinos. Big John would be sitting in the catbird seat.

What was really beautiful about it was that labor unions were not subject to the laws regulating casino agencies, but were regulated by the generally lax U.S. Labor Department. Even extortion payoffs, properly handled, were not in themselves illegal.

But McCullough was not alone in his quest. The moment casinos were legalized, just about every East Coast Mafia family began zeroing in on Atlantic City unions. Atlantic City became a tough union town. There were countless labor slowups, threatened walk-outs, nondeliveries of materials, and other tactics that sent construction costs skyrocketing. Union goons, representing various Mafia families, walked right in and took over union offices and meeting halls. Threats of broken legs and heads were heavy in the air.

With Angelo Bruno at his side, McCullough had had nothing to fear from any of them. But even with Bruno dead, McCullough continued with his forays on the membership of Local 54 and with the recruiting of security guards for Local 40B. The only thing he did differently now was to start carrying a gun.

Meanwhile, Scarfo was after Testa to do something about "eliminating the McCullough problem." The split in Local 54 was becoming costly. Besides, it was undermining Scarfo's control over other unions and it was lousy for his image. What he needed was a concrete example, something that would show everybody, once and for all, who was boss in that town.

At first Testa was opposed to taking direct action against McCullough, fearing that his death would lead to unnecessary union violence. Testa believed that an accord could be reached, but when McCullough summarily rejected four invitations for a meeting, Testa angrily turned the matter over to Scarfo.

Back in 1974 Willard Moran killed Richard Ottway in the Gateway Lounge because Moran's father, Willard Sr., had gotten into a fight with Ottway over a go-go dancer. Moran wasn't too happy about the few months he had to spend in jail, but he was proud of his deed. It established him in the right circles as a no-shit type of guy who could go the limit.

That was how he came to do odd jobs for Raymond "Longjohn" Martorano and Albert Daidone. When Pickwell Fine Foods refused to renew a contract to purchase cigarettes from John's Wholesale Distributors, Martorano asked Moran to pour chemicals on the meat counters of several Pickwell stores. Daidone supplied the chemicals.

Moran's regular job was distributing speed to street pushers for Daidone, who was supplied by Martorano. Daidone was then an organizer for Local 33, a Camden branch of Local 54, which was in the process of dissolution.

The first inkling Moran had that something special was going to be asked of him came when Daidone instructed him to rent a van that couldn't be traced back to him. Moran had a friend, Howard Dale Young, rent the van and drive it to the parking lot of Local 33 in Camden. Moran then walked into Daidone's office and handed him the keys.

Taking Daidone aside and lowering his voice, Moran said, "Al, what's going on? Are you going to hit [Ed] McBride [president of Local 33]?" Daidone said, "No, not Eddie. Raymond and the Little Guy, Nicky Scarfo, called it off."

Four days later, on the evening of December 15, 1980, Moran met with Daidone and Martorano at a local bar. "Raymond [Martorano] started the conversation about how things were going with Albert [Daidone]," Moran would later tell a courtroom. "He brought up my past history, my murder conviction and the things I was continuously doing for Albert—moving large amounts of speed. We talked about a lot of things. A lot of small talk. My going to Vietnam. Raymond said, 'When you kill somebody over here, it ain't like in Vietnam.' I said, 'When you kill somebody, you kill him.' "

They wanted to know if he had any "equipment" and he said he had two .22-caliber Ruger pistols that would fit the silencer he owned, and a Thompson machine gun. "I was looking to move up in the organization," he said. When they parted that evening, he was instructed to meet them at 5:00 P.M. the next day and to bring his equipment. He then "understood" there was to be a "tentative hit" the next night. "Al said, 'Junior, I'm your friend. I'm the one who opened the door for you. Don't forget it.' "

That evening Moran obtained "regular" .22-caliber long rifle ammunition to be used with the silencer. He didn't obtain "high velocity" ammunition because it travels faster and makes a louder noise with the silencer.

As prearranged, Moran met Daidone and Martorano the next day and the three men got into Martorano's sedan and drove across the Betsy Ross Bridge into northeast Philadelphia. "Raymond said, 'Don't talk in the car.' " They drove into a side street and parked behind the van he had provided.

"How many people are we going to kill?" Moran asked as they walked to the van.

"Do you remember the brushy-haired guy?" Martorano asked.

Two months ago they had gone to the Holiday Inn in Cherry Hill and Martorano had pointed out a gap-toothed guy with a Marine crewcut who carried on with a bunch of hard hats as if he owned the place. Daidone had told Moran to memorize the man's features.

"I remember him," Moran said.

"You're going to pose as a florist delivery man," Martorano said. "Get in the van and follow us."

Moran followed them to a flower shop and while Daidone was inside buying flowers, Moran told Martorano he would need a large package to conceal his gun because of the silencer. Martorano gave him two $20 bills and he went inside the flower shop and purchased a large box of poinsettias. Moran was then instructed to follow them to the home of John McCullough and not to go in until they were sure he was home.

"Deliver the flowers and leave if anybody else's there beside McCullough and his wife," Martorano said. "But if it's just John and his wife, take him any way you can."

At McCullough's house, Martorano parked up the street, and Moran drove around the block twice before seeing McCullough arrive. He quickly parked the van, picked up the small box of flowers Daidone had bought, and hurried up the walk.

"I knocked on the door. Mrs. McCullough answered the door. I said, 'Is this the McCullough residence? I've got some flowers for you and I've been driving around looking for your house.' "

"She said, 'Yes, it is.' "

"I gave her the flowers. I could see John standing there, talking on the phone. At this time I told her, 'I've got a much bigger flower. You'll have to make some room. I'll bring it back.' "

As Moran hurried down the driveway to his van, McCullough's wife got her purse and took out two dollars for a tip. Big John interrupted his conversation to whisper to his wife, "Give him three. It's Christmas."

"I went down to the van. I got the other flowers. I came back up and Mrs. McCullough opened the door part way. When she opened the door I had my hand on the gun like this [inside the box] and my other hand underneath the box. I sort of like pushed her out of the way and then I shot John. He was standing talking on the phone. I went like this," he said, extending his right arm and taking aim with his index finger. "I shot him one time in the head. He fell and I went over to him and I shot him like five or six times."

He fired all but one bullet, keeping it reserved in the chamber in case he encountered any trouble making his escape. As further protection he carried the other .22-caliber Ruger in his belt as a "backup weapon." Mrs. McCullough screamed and tried to run from the house, but Moran pulled her back. Out in the van, he flashed the headlights at Martorano's parked car, and they drove over to a parking lot at a nearby shopping center where they abandoned the van.

They drove away in Martorano's sedan, and Daidone whispered, "Are you sure he's dead?"

He said, "I hit him at least five or six times. He's dead."

Moran removed the silencer, dropped it in his pocket, and handed the Ruger to Daidone. Martorano stopped the car on the Betsy Ross Bridge, and Daidone threw the gun out the window.

"We were smiling because everything went smoothly and we made it back to New Jersey without getting stopped." Later that evening, Moran and a friend, Paul Reese, went to the Admiral Lounge in Camden to celebrate. "We took McCullough out," Moran told him. They ordered three drinks of whiskey and "Reese told the barmaid to throw that third one away. 'That's for someone who's no longer with us,' he said. I was happy. It meant I would be taken into the organization. I had reached that point.''

The next morning Moran met Daidone outside Local 33's meeting hall and ''Albert gave me a bag and said, 'This is five thousand dollars from Raymond. Raymond says buy yourself some suits.' Then we had a little conversation about my moving up in the drug business.''

A week later Moran asked Daidone why McCullough was murdered, and Daidone told him it was because McCullough was trying to organize a bartenders' union that would compete with Local 54.

On December 29, less than two weeks after the murder, Daidone was hired as a business agent for Local 54, becoming the only officer of Local 33 to be so absorbed following its dissolution. A few weeks later Daidone was promoted to vice-president.

In the investigation of the McCullough murder, the first to crack was Howard Dale Young, whom police had traced to the murder van. Young told them he had provided Moran with the two Ruger pistols. Moran was tried, convicted, and sentenced to the electric chair. That was when he agreed to testify against Martorano and Daidone in return for recommendations of leniency.

''We are talking about a hired killer,'' Assistant District Attorney Barbara Christie told the jury. ''You aren't going to like him. He is a killer and a bum, but he was their bum.''

Indicted in September 1982, Martorano, who had since the murder been sentenced to ten years in prison for drug trafficking, and Daidone managed to delay the trial nearly two years with eight postponements for health reasons. Daidone's attorney, Raymond Brown of Resorts commission hearing fame, was accused by Christie of receiving $350,000 in legal fees from Martorano's son.

''The fundamental issue is the ability of the defendant Daidone to proceed with counsel Brown,'' Christie told the court.

Brown called the accusations ''spurious, groundless, and irrelevant,'' but Christie argued that the payment raised ethical and legal issues surrounding Brown's role in the case. The defense had entered a standing motion for severance, seeking to have each defendant tried separately and indicating to the court that Brown represented Daidone independently of Martorano, who had his own attorney, F. Emmett Fitzpatrick. In a posttrial appeal Daidone could claim that his attorney's loyalty had been compromised by his co-defendant's secret payment.

Furthermore, the prosecution could now argue that Daidone and Martorano had a common defense, not a separate one, which meant that it would be more difficult for the defense to bar evidence relative to one defendant from implicating the other on grounds it was prejudicial. Disposition of the motion, in favor of the defendants, was made behind closed doors.

Barbara Christie presented the court with a document that listed 19 individuals, including Frank Gerace, Scarfo, Testa, and several others involved in organized crime, who "may have participated in planning and/or execution and/or cover-up of the alleged execution." The defense objected and Judge Paul Ribner ruled that it was "not sufficient" and expressly ordered Christie not to ask Moran any questions that would draw responses about organized crime or organized crime figures. She was precluded from trying the case as an organized crime conspiracy and was barred from presenting surveillance evidence of meetings between the defendants and other organized crime figures. The names of Scarfo and Local 54 President Frank Gerace, alleged unindicted co-conspirators, could not be mentioned.

It was a strange order, considering that the police had listed the crime as a gangland slaying. Christie was prevented from presenting recorded conversations taped prior to the murder and allegations of cover-up efforts after the murder, because, Ribner ruled, the evidence fell outside the time frame of the conspiracy.

At one point Christie asked Moran about a conversation he had with Daidone five days before the murder and he replied, "I said, 'Al, what's going on? Are you going to hit McBride?' And he said, 'No, not Eddie.' He said, 'Raymond and the Little Guy, Nicky Scarfo, called it off.' "

"Loudmouth, imbecile!" Brown screamed at Moran.

"We've been deliberately misled," roared Fitzpatrick. "It's prosecutorial misconduct."

"There's no way we can explain to the jury that this isn't Murder Incorporated," Brown said. "You've got a professional witness with a price on his head that he's trying to work off. He's being led by an animal trainer."

Judge Ribner, who consistently ruled in favor of defense motions limiting admission of key evidence against the defendants that wasn't integral to the actual murder, turned angrily on Christie. "I told you, you're not to bring up any reference to organized crime. I gave you a broad highway to travel and I told you not to go down any detours."

A few days later, Christie was in more trouble when she tried to show that Daidone and Martorano had tried to cover up the murder conspiracy when Moran was first arrested in 1981 by paying his legal fees and continuing paying Moran's wife the $800 a week he had been earning as a speed pusher.

Based on Ribner's ruling that testimony on events occurring after the murder had to be linked directly to the defendants, Brown's objection was sustained.

"Your honor, I don't believe this," Christie said, slapping her notes to the defense table and slumping to her chair in frustration.

Ribner was furious. "I don't believe that you're bringing in all of this nonsense that has nothing to do with the trial," he said, calling a recess. With the jury out of the courtroom, Ribner laced into her: "You are in contempt of court, Miss Christie. You are fined one thousand dollars and placed in the custody of the sheriff." Twenty minutes later Christie was taken to a holding cell by sheriff's officers and court was recessed. It was the second time Ribner had held her in contempt.

It was another victory for Raymond Brown, who referred to Christie as "sweetheart" in a voice dripping with sarcasm. In one exchange with her, Brown said, "You wear the superiority of an ass and a robot." The remark drew a loud gasp from the spectators and Ribner's response was, "Miss Christie, I don't want you to play to the press."

Asked by the press why he didn't hold the defense attorneys in contempt for hurling insults at Christie, Ribner replied, "They didn't call me a name." Christie, said the judge, directed comments at the bench.

Only days before he was to appear as a prosecution witness, Keith Pearson, a guard at Holmesburg prison, was found dead in the bedroom of his home. He had been shot in the head. A gun was found near his bed and the medical examiner ruled the death a suicide, but the FBI found it suspicious and launched an investigation. Pearson was to testify that he had been promised $10,000 by Martorano's son, George, for a false affidavit contending that Moran was trying to frame his father. Pearson was found dead only hours after he had gone to the FBI. Besides being a witness against

Martorano and Daidone in the McCullough murder, Pearson was also to have been a witness at an upcoming federal drug case involving Martorano's son, George, and Kevin Rankin, the attorney who allegedly had drafted the false statement. Both Rankin and George Martorano were later convicted on drug conspiracy charges.

But the defense efforts were all in vain. After being sequestered for 80 days, the jury deliberated less than three hours to reach a guilty verdict. And took less than half that time before reporting it was hopelessly deadlocked in its attempt to reach a verdict of either life in prison or the electric chair. Judge Ribner dismissed the jury, automatically invoking life sentences for both men.

Meanwhile, the bloodletting continued. On February 14, 1981, the body of Frank R. Stillitano, a Bruno family member operating out of Trenton, was found locked in the trunk of a car in a parking garage at Philadelphia International Airport. Dead 12 days, he had been shot in the leg and behind the left ear.

The black Volkswagen van stopped across the street from 2117 Porter Street, in South Philadelphia. It was a few minutes before three o'clock on the morning of March 15, 1981.

Inside the van, Rocco Marinucci was giving final instructions to Theodore "Teddy" DiPretoro. They had gone over the plan many times, but Marinucci was a cautious man. For years he had been the chauffeur and bodyguard of Peter Casella, the old-timer Testa had promoted to underboss. Marinucci owned a pizza parlor called Pop's, but it was his position with Casella that was important to him as a Mafia soldier—it could lead to a loftier promotion, particularly if his man became the boss.

"Okay, the coast's clear," Marinucci said. "Let's do it."

DiPretoro stepped out of the van and hurried to the front porch of a yellow house of mock-Spanish styling. He gently opened the storm door, placed a package against the front door, and closed the storm door. A moment later he was back in the van.

A short distance away a man sat in a black Ford LTD sedan that was equipped with a telephone. All that was visible from the street was the man's hat and the phone against his ear.

Inside the van the two men waited in silence. Both were experienced in murder. The year before, at the age of 19, DiPretoro had murdered Edward Bianculli because he had been too slow in repaying a debt. Marinucci, who at 30 was DiPretoro's mentor, had been a suspect in three murders in the past year alone.

A few minutes later, a man driving a black 1980 Chevrolet Caprice Classic double-parked in front of the house and walked up the porch steps to the front door. He reached in his pocket for his keys, but before he could place one in the lock, there was an explosion that sent shock waves that shattered windows blocks away. The bomb, detonated by remote control, was packed with finishing nails and shotgun pellets. It blew the horribly mangled body of Philip Testa through the front door, and parts of his body and of the door ended up in the kitchen, 30 feet away. Except for his shirt, all of his clothes were burned off his body. His trouser belt was found in the middle of Porter Street. A revolver loaded with dum-dum bullets and $14,000 in bills were found scattered in the debris. A search of the house would later uncover three rifles and $70,000 behind a false closed wall.

When Testa's son, Salvatore, arrived a half hour later, the scene was reminiscent of the night of Bruno's murder the year before. Police and curious neighbors were everywhere. Many of the more immediate neighbors had been literally blasted out of bed. Restrained by friends, Salvatore swore to avenge his father's death.

Detectives on the scene were already issuing theories. "It certainly doesn't look like a traditional organized crime hit," said the head of the organized crime squad. "Is it the Ides of March or a St. Patrick's Day message?" asked another lawman. Julius Caesar had been murdered on March 15, in 44 B.C. The date was also the eve of St. Patrick's Day. A popular theory in the next few weeks was that IRA terrorist friends of McCullough, whom he had supported, had avenged his murder. After all, everybody recognized that they knew how to make bombs.

Not a single neighbor admitted having seen anything. But most had kind words for their neighbor with the pockmarked, grim face, and the eyes that had cut through people like laser beams. "He was a gentleman. All this stuff about organized crime, I don't believe it," said one neighbor who refused to give her name. "It's a figment of someone's imagination. It could have been the FBI." Another woman screamed at the reporters, calling them animals, saying they should have been in the explosion, too. A teenager said, "Everybody liked him. He never bothered nobody. He did his own business and that was it."

A seventh-grader, with his grandfather, said he knew "some guys" who saw Testa "lying there, right where the blood is. It was neat." The grandfather said, "It's a big thing to order somebody killed. It's a big thing to blow up a neighborhood at night and kill the innocent, too." "They didn't kill nobody but Mr. Testa," the kid said. "There were two women who lived next door," the grandfather said. "What about them?" The kid shrugged. "They're real old," he said.

"They called him Chicken Man," a little old lady snickered. "Don't say that," a young man remonstrated. "He didn't like that. He would kill people for saying that." The police had given him the nickname. He once operated a chicken business and police found 8000 illegal numbers in plastic bags hidden in a pile of chicken feathers. No one dared use the nickname in his presence. One man who inadvertently used it was later beaten up by apparent strangers.

They gave him a Roaring Twenties, Chicago-style send-off. Everybody in the family showed up at the funeral home to pay their final respects to the dearly departed and briefly ensconced godfather. Everybody with the notable exception of Peter Casella, who was said to be somewhere in Florida for his health.

Four thousand "admirers" lined up outside for a chance to view the corpse in the bronze casket, whose features had been reconstructed by morticians with magical skills. "He looked just beautiful," a woman said.

Many were more interested in the live gangsters draped over chairs in the four parlors of the funeral home. "Hey, it's a fun event," said a bricklayer. "People get to see each other at these things." Besides gangsters, there were lawyers of gangsters and business associates of gangsters like Wilmington Teamsters boss Frank Sheeran.

A cordon of impeccably dressed, hard-faced young men weeded out reporters from mourners and opened doors of limousines that lined the curb. Across the street, the cameras were rolling from a third-floor window, compiling a rogues' gallery for the files of the FBI. All that was missing was klieg lights crisscrossing their beams into the heavens.

Following the hearse to Holy Cross Cemetery the next day were 14 flower cars, 8 silver limousines, and 44 other cars. Thousands of curiosity seekers lined the sidewalk. Unknown to many in the cortege, riding in one of the silver limousines was the next godfather, Nicodemo "Little Nicky" Scarfo, and his two bodyguards, his nephew,

Philip "Crazy Phil" Leonetti, and Lawrence "Yogi" Merlino, whose brother, Salvatore, would become Scarfo's underboss.

In a year's time, two godfathers and a half-dozen others had been brutally murdered, and the seat of power had shifted from Philadelphia, a city of 1.6 million population, to Atlantic City, with 40,000. Hidden somewhere in there was a message that few politicians and police cared to read. Meanwhile, the bloodletting would continue, at an accelerated pace.

21

The Golden Boy's Golden Nugget

Steve Wynn loves to recall the day he decided to bring the Golden Nugget to the Boardwalk. "Coming to Atlantic City took about as much perspicacity as biting into this cheesesteak [I'm eating]," he told *Fortune*. "I took one look at Resorts. It was June 16 [1978], a couple of weeks after it had opened, and I'll never forget standing on the steps [leading into the casino]. I saw more people betting more money than I'd ever seen in my life. It made Caesars Palace [in Las Vegas] on New Year's Eve look like it was closed for lunch."

At the suggestion of Resorts president Jack Davis, Wynn strolled down the other end of the Boardwalk to the Strand Motel and asked to speak to the owner, Manny Solomon. "I asked him how much he wanted for the place. I was standing in my sandals, wearing my Willie Nelson T-shirt, with my tie-string beach pants, and he looked at me like I was crazy." Twenty-five minutes later Wynn walked out, having agreed to pay $8.5 million in cash for what would become his casino site.

Fairy tales, magic, legerdemain, voodooism, miracles, supernatural financing, you name it and it took place on Manny Solomon's land. Phoenix rising in glittering style from its own ashes, the old Strand metamorphosed into the flashy Golden Nugget for a paltry $160 million. It was "fast tracking" all the way, a mere 16 months to erect a 22-story, 506-room hotel, a 40,805-square-foot casino, a 500-seat theater, a 500-car garage. Nothing described its mirrored walls, vaulted mirrored ceilings, stained-glass windows, marble columns, ornate gold leaf, gold-colored fixtures and slot machines better than its name: Golden Nugget.

Wynn had a perfectly logical explanation for his ostentatious creation. He wanted to create a fantasy world, an adult Disneyland, for his customers. "We perceived back in 1978 that the East Coast experience is basically a gray one. And if Atlantic City was ever gonna be exciting and successful it was gonna be because it offered the people in this part of the world a chance to break their ordinary course of disciplined daily life and get a big dose of color and excitement and distraction."

If anything the financing was even more of a fantasy world. By the summer of 1980 Wynn had raised $137 million with debentures sweetened with warrants to buy stock, followed by an equity offering. By selling 15 percent of the company's shares with a net worth of only $15 million, Wynn raised over $100 million. In only 30 months Golden Nugget assets grew from $64 million to $360 million. By 1984 the estimated value of his stewardship was about $650 million.

Steve Wynn likes to tell people that he owes everything to gambling: "I've never had a meal, a dollar for tuition, or a piece of clothing on my back that didn't come from gambling."

His fondest childhood memory is of a trip to Las Vegas with his father in 1952. Steven Alan Wynn was ten that summer and what he saw was burned into his brain forever. There were only a half-dozen hotel-casinos on the Las Vegas Strip then, and it was strictly Mob country. But "there was a magic in this place," Wynn would recall years later. "It was the heyday of Las Vegas, and it had all the aspects of the forbidden fruit: beautiful women, glamorous stars, untold money, and notorious people. I thought, 'What else could anyone want?' "

His father, Michael Wynn, a bingo operator from Maryland and a compulsive gambler, had made a deal to operate a bingo parlor on the second floor of the Silver Slipper casino, a venture doomed to failure. Whatever profits he made from the bingo parlor he squandered at the crap tables. "He used to go to bed with me and then sneak out at night and shoot dice at the Flamingo and the Sands."

It was the father's failure that shaped the boy's dream: "When you see a person crumble and lose his self-confidence, it's a very, very horrible experience. But one thing my father's gambling did was that it showed me at a very early age that if you wanted to make money in a casino, the answer was to own one.''

It took the father three weeks to go broke and the son 15 years before he could return to his magic carpet land, ready to fulfill his boyhood dream. In the interim, he went to the University of Pennsylvania, worked weekends at the 1100-seat bingo parlor at Wayson's Corner, Maryland, co-owned by his father, married his college sweetheart, whose father was also a compulsive gambler, and when his father died in 1963, during Steve's senior year, took over his share of the business, becoming general manager, thereby realizing the first part of his dream at 22.

Two years later he found his way back to Las Vegas. And there he met Maurice Friedman, an old bootlegger who was putting together the group that was to turn the Old Frontier Hotel into the New Frontier. Much of the money, as was later revealed in court, had come from Emprise and the Detroit Mafia family.

Using $10,000 of his own money and $20,000 from the bingo business, Wynn bought a 3 percent interest in the Frontier—or three points, as percentages were known in the days before Nevada permitted publicly traded corporations to be licensed. In late 1966 he moved his family to Las Vegas and became a slot machine supervisor and assistant credit manager at the Frontier. A year later Wynn found himself before the federal grand jury that was investigating the Detroit Mafia's hidden ownership of the hotel. He was 25 years old, in Las Vegas barely a year, and already suspected of playing hardball with the ''notorious people'' he had so admired as a boy.

No charges were pressed against Wynn, and, as luck would have it, he met E. Parry Thomas, the most powerful banker in Nevada, who was helping Howard Hughes invest the millions he squandered in Las Vegas. As president of the Bank of Las Vegas, no banker in Nevada history had made more loans to casino-hotels, some of which would be revealed to have Mafia links. And Thomas was proud of his contribution to the growth of Las Vegas. Being a Mormon, he neither drank nor gambled. All he did was make money for his bank and his friends.

At the time that he met Wynn in 1967, Thomas and 24 associates, including some fairly unsavory characters, had bought control of Continental Connector Corporation, a small specialty electronics firm in Woodside, New York, with assets of $5 million and sales of $10 million. They bought it for the simple reason that it was traded on the American Stock Exchange. Now they could go out and form a conglomerate like the big boys were doing in the 1960s.

Here was how Thomas worked it out. In 1963 Commerce Building Corp., a shell corporation set up by Thomas, bought the Dunes hotel from Jake Gottlieb, a Chicagoan whose entire business career had been sponsored by the Chicago Mafia and bankrolled by the Teamsters pension fund.

No money changed hands and three weeks later Commerce sold the Dunes to Leonard J. Campbell Enterprises, a partnership whose general manager, Leonard Campbell, was Gottlieb's brother-in-law. This was an "insulating device," said Thomas, to make sure Gottlieb finished the 22-story addition to the Dunes hotel.

The man who put Campbell Enterprises together was Charles "Kewpie" Rich, who got a $500,000 finder's fee for his efforts. Thomas took 4 percent of the partnership.

Kewpie Rich and his partner Sid Wyman had been identified in the Kefauver hearings as former St. Louis bookmakers who through bribes of employees had used Western Union offices as bookie drops. Both were fronts for St. Louis Mafia boss Tony Giordano and were moved about the Las Vegas casino scene like pawns on a chessboard, starting out at the Flamingo and moving on to the Riviera, with a brief stop at the Sands, and finally settling down at the Dunes for the duration. They came with empty pockets, lived the sweet life, and earned millions for their hidden sponsors.

The most notorious member of Thomas's Continental group was Morris Shenker, a St. Louis criminal lawyer and lifelong associate of Tony Giordano. For twenty years before coming to Las Vegas, Shenker had been characterized in the national press as the "mouthpiece for the Mob" and "a shadowy, devious character with arteries to the underworld." A secret report, filed in 1972 by a special task force of FBI and IRS agents, named Meyer Lansky and Morris Shenker as two of the most important financial figures in organized crime.

The same group that owned Campbell Enterprises and Continental Connector now formed a subsidiary called M&R Investment. Campbell Enterprises paid Gottlieb $2.8 million in cash and a note for $4.6 million for the Dunes. But through some fancy accounting the sale went on the books at $10.7 million. On January 1, 1967, Campbell Enterprises sold the Dunes to M&R Investment for $22.8 million and two years later Continental acquired the Dunes from M&R for $59 million in convertible preferred stock.

The question that intrigued the SEC was: Just who had taken over whom anyway? As part of the Thomas-Continental group, not only had Major Riddle, (Gottlieb's former partner), Rich, and Wyman retained their 68 percent controlling interest in M&R Investment, which continued as the Dunes' operating company, but they had become sizable stockholders and executives of Continental.

The Thomas group saw the transaction as something more than a means of vast instant and future profits for the parent company. In fact, when acquired by Continental, the Dunes owed Thomas's bank $14.1 million and another $1.8 million to American National Insurance Company, headed by two members of the Thomas group. As part of the purchase agreement, Continental agreed to repay both loans.

When the smoke cleared, the Thomas group had spent $4.8 million to acquire control of a publicly held company, which it used to acquire the Dunes and repay the hotel's debts of $15.9 million to firms run by group members, and in the process some old Mafia fronts, who remained firmly entrenched, were greatly enriched and elevated to positions of importance within the new parent company.

It had one SEC attorney scratching his head. "One big partnership selling something back and forth between themselves," he said, "except they kept marking up the price."

It was the kind of financial manipulations that had become a Thomas trademark since that day in 1955 when three Salt Lake City banking families had sent him to manage their Bank of Las Vegas.

That was three years after Steve Wynn's boyhood adventure in pioneering Las Vegas. When they finally met in 1967, Thomas took an immediate interest in Wynn and personally made sure that he recouped his $30,000 when the Frontier was sold. After all, Thomas was the man who had persuaded Hughes to buy the hotel for $23 million, a rather substantial price-tag in a depressed market.

A few years later, after Hughes had left Las Vegas with accusations that he had been defrauded out of millions of dollars, federal investigators concluded that Hughes's casinos had been heavily skimmed by employees and that he had paid highly inflated prices for his hotels and real estate purchases, many of which had been orchestrated by E. Parry Thomas.

Federal investigators wanted to know whether the money had been funneled into the hands of the underworld. Their first stop in Las Vegas was Thomas's new bank, the Valley Bank of Nevada. Thomas resented the intrusion into his affairs, characterizing the investigation as a rehashing of the thesis developed in the 1951 Kefauver hearings that gambling was the fountainhead of organized crime. "I've never met a hoodlum," Thomas asserted, "not knowingly, anyway."

Having taken a shine to Steve Wynn, E. Parry Thomas guided him toward what could be characterized as a bullpen assignment, sort of keeping him interested and available until the right spot could be found for him on Thomas's major league team.

And Wynn was opportunistic enough to recognize the knock of opportunity when he heard it. "Parry Thomas was the most significant banker in gaming's growth," Wynn would later tell *Fortune*. "His sponsorship was the equivalent of having Bernard Baruch hitting for you on Wall Street."

"I could see his brightness and quickness and ability as a young man," Thomas said. "The friendship grew into a very strong friendship. It might even be described as a father-son relationship."

The bullpen assignment was Best Brands, Inc., a liquor distributorship owned by Schenley Industries. In explaining his role in this transaction to the New Jersey Division of Gaming Enforcement, Thomas would say that at the time his bank had no liquor distributors as customers and so to gain such a customer, and because he thought it would be a good line of business for Wynn, he had contacted friends of his at Schenley and arranged for the sale of Best Brands to Wynn, which was financed by a $65,000 loan from his bank. With more loans from Thomas's bank totaling $600,000, Wynn built a warehouse and extended a rail spur to it.

Next came a real estate deal that took everyone by surprise. Thomas came up with a strip of land that Caesars Palace had leased from Hughes as an addition to its parking lot. On several occasions Caesars' president Billy Weinberger had tried to buy the land from Hughes, to no avail. Then one morning, Weinberger was awakened by a call from Clifford Perlman, who informed him that the land had been sold to Steve Wynn. Weinberger's understanding had been that Caesars was to have the right of first refusal. Also noteworthy was the fact that this was the first piece of property sold by Hughes in Las Vegas.

The price to Wynn was $1.1 million and Thomas advanced Wynn $1.2 million, the extra $100,000 to cover the interest while Wynn negotiated with Caesars for a deal. Caesars offered him a quick $250,000 profit but Wynn said he was thinking of building a small casino to pick up some of the in-between trade on the Strip. It didn't take Weinberger and Perlman long to realize that Wynn and Thomas had them pinned to the wall. Wynn's price was $2,250,000 and they paid it. In a few months' time, Wynn had made a cool million dollars on an investment that had cost him absolutely nothing. It was the kind of coup that got Wynn's name up in lights overnight in that town of superstars.

Why had Thomas been so generous? Being a banker, what was there in it for him? The answer, which wasn't all that subtle, still seemed to fool just about everybody. While the Wynn drama had been taking place off stage, Continental Connector had come a cropper in its attempt to merge with the Golden Nugget, a downtown casino with no hotel rooms but with vast real estate holdings and stock that was undervalued—a prime target for a takeover.

Continental's manipulations in acquiring the Dunes hotel had more than piqued the interest of the Securities and Exchange Commission. It decided it didn't like the arithmetic. So when the Thomas group took aim at the fabulously rich Golden Nugget in late 1968, the SEC stepped in and filed an injunction suit to block the move. It charged that false and misleading information had been issued in two proxy statements in Continental's acquisition of the Dunes. The Dunes had no adequate procedures for checking the control and collection of gambling markers (IOUs) and the casino's outside accountants had insufficient checks on the actual cash drops at gaming tables. In more precise language, its auditors were in no position to certify the accuracy of the count to stockholders. Casino operators, as of old, could still control the amount of revenue and profit they reported. Skimming was now a problem for stockholders, too.

Without admitting guilt, of course, Continental consented to the injunction in 1969 and abandoned its takeover of the Golden Nugget. And the American Stock Exchange suspended trading in Continental. Three months later a federal court in New York ordered an independent audit of M&R Investment. By January 20, 1972, the stock had drifted down to 9 ¾ in over-the-counter trading. That was when 11 of the 13 original M&R investors sold all or part of their Continental stock in a private deal for an average of $19.25. They had more than tripled their money. No wonder they liked doing business among themselves. However, there was one slight inconvenience. Wyman and five others were indicted on charges of skimming and income tax evasion.

Meanwhile, Steve Wynn had been busy. Starting when the 1969 SEC injunction had stopped Continental from taking over the Nugget, Wynn had begun borrowing money from Best Brands and Thomas's bank to buy Golden Nugget stock on the open market. By the time he sold Best Brands and his warehouse back to Schenley in 1972 he owed the company $360,000, which, as part of the sale agreement, was forgiven, and he still managed to come out with a profit of $51,000.

Wynn's only problem came in the form of a tax audit for the years 1968 through 1972 that found he had neglected to report $21,750 for 1971 and $14,985 for 1972, and had wrongly charged $11,695 in personal expenses to Best Brands. Minor infractions, hardly worth mentioning considering the rarefied executive suites Wynn was about to enter.

Between 1969 and the end of 1973, Wynn bought 912,600 shares of Golden Nugget stock for $1,244,745.15, most on the open market. Even with his million-dollar profit from the Hughes land sale to Caesars and the $360,000 he borrowed from Best Brands, he owed Thomas's new Valley Bank of Nevada $527,255 at the end of the year. Nonetheless, it was an impressive five-year achievement for a 26-year-old who had started with capital assets of $10,000 in a town that chews up hotshots and spits them out faster than a conventioneer can roll snake eyes.

The persuasive hand of E. Parry Thomas would help Wynn establish another record in Nevada. Wynn became the first person with outside gambling interests (his Maryland bingo parlor) to receive a gambling license in Las Vegas. In an interview given in 1973, Wynn said the state conducted a "ruthless investigation" into his background. "Everything I've ever been involved in I had to thoroughly explain. They completely audited my business back East. Three agents went back East and were there for a week." Gaming board member Shannon Bybee agreed that the Wynn investigation was "very thorough." All that for the price of $8000, which Wynn had to pay. As for the bingo operation, Bybee said the "clientele was mostly middle-aged women brought in by bus from the Baltimore and Washington area—not a threat to us, since they're not the type of clientele we're catering to."

Bybee later became a Golden Nugget executive.

With a block of stock he bought from Jerry Zarowitz, Wynn felt he controlled enough stock to be elected to the Nugget's board of directors. Buck Blaine, president of the Nugget, had some reservations until he received a visit from Thomas. Wynn was promptly elected to the board and named executive vice-president of the casino.

Almost immediately he found that the casino was in "pathetic shape" and that many employees were stealing money from it. Wynn visited Buck Blaine and said he had documented cases of stealing and gross inefficiency at the casino. Wynn then told the 63-year-old casino president that he would sue for mismanagement unless Blaine relinquished control of the company. Wynn described his encounter with Blaine: " 'We can do it easy or we can do it hard. What do you say?' Bucky, sitting in that office of his, just caved in. It was my situation as a businessman to rough up Bucky Blaine. I was real glad when he said he wanted to work something out."

Blaine was eased out and by August 1973 Wynn was in full control of the company. With a $14 million loan from the Valley Bank, Wynn built a 579-room hotel tower and garage, and made other improvements.

"Wynn was on his way," a profile writer noted, "though his cockiness, quick temper, and lightninglike dismissal of some employees made him unpopular in certain quarters of Las Vegas. He was certainly not looked upon as the shining light of the casino industry. Wynn was to achieve that stature in Atlantic City, where he rode the crest of the East Coast gambling wave to fame and fortune."

"Oh, yeah, lucky Las Vegas has been good to me," Steve Wynn told one interviewer. To hear him tell it, Horatio Alger plotted his life. "My father has been dead since I was a senior at the University of Pennsylvania. Parry [Thomas] has been like a father to me. He convinced me that this was a good place for a young man and that I should stay." Wynn briefly mentioned his investment in the Frontier, with no mention of the Detroit Mafia, and described Best Brands as a liquor company that specialized in distributing imported liquor and wine. "Imported wines was my business and my hobby and it still is. I wrote practically every wine list on the Strip." He frequently traveled to Maryland to supervise the family's bingo parlor and "I would invest in the stock market with Parry and we'd make some money and my bankroll kind of came up real slow."

As for Wynn's personal fortune, it illustrates the beauty of a gambler controlling a publicly traded company. By the end of 1973

Wynn had purchased 912,000 shares of Golden Nugget stock for $1,244,745. In 1980, with all the hoopla about his Atlantic City casino sending stock prices skyrocketing, he sold 60,000 shares for $1,823,690, half a million more than he had paid for his entire holdings. In March 1981 Wynn sold another 200,000 shares for approximately $6 million. In 12 years he had parlayed $10,000 into what has been estimated as $100 million, though only Wynn/Thomas knew the real bottom line.

But there were problems for the brash young man riding the golden crest of his dream. The Atlantic City Golden Nugget received a temporary permit for its casino on November 21, 1980, but only after Wynn agreed to take a leave of absence from the casino because a federal grand jury was investigating allegations of ''insider'' stock trading and drug sales by close friends who were employees of the Las Vegas casino.

The federal grand jury had subpoenaed corporate records for the years 1977 through 1979 and information about a 1973 nonqualified stock option plan and data about the company's acquisition of property in Atlantic City. The stock options that raised the most critical questions involved Wynn's brother-in-law, Michael Pascal, and E. Parry Thomas's son, Peter, a Golden Nugget director and executive vice-president of the Valley Bank.

The grand jury did not issue any indictments in its probe of insider stock trading at the Golden Nugget. But two close friends of Wynn's who had received stock options, Neil Azzinaro and Louis Cappiello, and another friend, Michael Jones, were indicted by the federal grand jury on charges that included a conspiracy to distribute cocaine between May 1977 and June 1980. They were believed to have sold drugs inside the Golden Nugget casino and to have used cocaine with Wynn and others.

The three men had been personally hired by Wynn, over the objection of Robert Maxey, the casino's executive vice-president. Maxey would later testify before the New Jersey Casino Control Commission that he thought it was wrong for Wynn to have hired Azzinaro and Cappiello—Jones, who was Azzinaro's roommate, had been hired by Wynn as a favor to Azzinaro. They had no casino experience and were, in Maxey's words, undisciplined and ''flamboyant'' characters.

But Wynn had told Maxey: ''I know these aren't your kind of guys but give them the same chance you would give anybody else.''

Azzinaro had been Wynn's hairdresser, and Cappiello, a constant companion of Azzinaro, was a professional "player," that is, sports bettor, and possibly also a bookmaker. When Azzinaro had problems with the Metropolitan Police Department, Wynn contacted Sheriff Ralph Lamb, who described Azzinaro as having a "big mouth" and warned he might get in trouble if he didn't straighten out. (The most powerful law enforcement officer in the state, Lamb would later be defeated for reelection because of a series of newspaper articles suggesting corruption in the sheriff's department during his 17 years in office, and then hired by Wynn as chief of security for the Las Vegas Golden Nugget.)

Despite their drawbacks and the fact that they had no casino experience, Wynn felt that his friends might be valuable because of what he perceived as their "customer marketing" talents. After attending gambling school, they worked as craps floormen. Ten months later, in December 1977, Wynn, over Maxey's objection, gave both Azzinaro and Cappiello stock options, an unprecedented move for floorpersons: stock options are normally reserved for high-level executives. They were given the right to purchase 5000 shares of Golden Nugget stock at $10 a share, with the requirement that they remain on the job until at least December 16, 1979, but the date was later "whited out" to December 16, 1978, without the authority of the company's stock options committee. Neither Wynn nor any other witness before the New Jersey Casino Control Commission could explain who had made the change.

Maxey said the three new employees "caused a lot of irritation among other employees. I felt they were taking advantage of Steve's friendship. It was borderline exploitation." When Maxey told Wynn that they were involved in drug use, Wynn said he would take it up with them. "He [Wynn] said he warned them that such conduct wouldn't be tolerated." Yet both men were soon promoted, with Azzinaro becoming casino coordinator, a position just under casino manager, and Cappiello rising to the rank of shift manager.

Late in 1979 Maxey and Azzinaro became involved in a test of will. When ordered to talk to Cappiello about his alleged abuse of a hostess in the casino, Azzinaro refused and later resigned. Six weeks later Cappiello also resigned. "I had been frustrated by their presence," Maxey told the commission. "I was glad they were gone." Not long after the hearings, Maxey was also gone, the victim of a "management shakeup."

*   *   *

Representing Wynn and Atlantic City's Golden Nugget before the gaming commission was Martin Greenberg, the state senator and former law partner of Governor Byrne. Greenberg became the Golden Nugget's lawyer one week after leaving the Legislature in 1980. After Wynn took his required leave of absence, Greenberg became president of the Nugget's Atlantic City operations. Besides having been on Lordi's staff in the Essex County prosecutor's office, Greenberg had also worked for New Jersey Attorney General John Degnan. And he had been chairman of the powerful Senate Judiciary Committee when it had routinely confirmed Lordi to head the gaming commission. While a senator, Greenberg had worked for the Amusement Technology Company of Asbury Park, which at the time had proposed contracts to supply 40 percent of the slot machines to be licensed in Atlantic City. He had also come under fire for his role in the Intercontinental Life Insurance Company, which was labeled one of the "six most offensive health insurers in the nation" by the House Select Committee on Aging.

"I have a lot of friends," Greenberg told the press, then quickly added that those friendships would be "virtually meaningless" during the licensing period.

The Division of Gaming Enforcement filed no objections to the company or any of its officers. The only areas of concern involved the stock options and Wynn's relationship with his three questionable Las Vegas employees.

The division had obtained statements from three women who alleged under oath that Wynn had used cocaine in their presence. One of the women, Kathy Thomas, who said she saw Wynn use cocaine at Azzinaro's home and on his corporate jet, later recanted her allegations in a separate statement. Anita Cosby, a former blackjack dealer at the Las Vegas Golden Nugget, and Shirley Ann Fair, an admitted prostitute, refused to testify during the hearings.

But Fair testified before the federal grand jury that she saw Wynn use cocaine at several Las Vegas parties during 1977 and at a New Year's Eve party that year. She gave the division the names of four persons who she said were at the New Year's Eve party, but three of the four named denied her statement. At a Thanksgiving dinner in Las Vegas in 1977, Fair said Wynn was present when cocaine was used. It was put inside the mouth of a roasted pig. Fair passed a lie detector test witnessed by a division investigator but Wynn supplied five affidavits from people who swore he was in Sun Valley, Idaho, on New Year's Eve in 1977.

In her statement, Anita Cosby said that drugs were sold on the casino floor and in the executive offices and that she once saw Azzinaro hand Wynn a matchbook containing a vial of cocaine. Wynn vehemently denied the allegation, adding that he had been deeply disturbed by the arrest of Cosby and the others on drug charges. It was "a source of deep embarrassment," he told the commission. When questioned about an incident involving a vial of marijuana found in his office, Wynn said it was left there by a group of musicians. "How did you know it was marijuana?" he was asked. "I know what it looks like," he said after pausing for a few seconds.

The New Jersey Casino Control Commission ruled that Wynn "has forthrightly and with candid demeanor denied Fair's accusations. . . . His appearance of candor and credibility is bolstered by the testimony of several witnesses . . . as to his good reputations for honesty, as well as by their opinions that he is an honest person." It dismissed Cosby's statement with the suggestion that she might have had a bias against Wynn for having been fired after her arrest on drug charges.

At their drug trafficking trial in Las Vegas, Jones was convicted and sentenced to four years in prison; Cappiello was found not guilty, and the charges against Azzinaro eventually were dropped. During the trial, the judge refused to allow anyone to mention the name of the Golden Nugget.

The decision to hire Azzinaro, Cappiello, and Jones could not itself reflect adversely on Wynn's character, the New Jersey Casino Control Commission ruled, but rumors concerning drug use at the Las Vegas Nugget could have been more closely investigated. "We would expect more aggressive action to be taken should similar situations arise in the future." As for the stock options, the commission found nothing that "negatively reflects" upon Wynn. In fact, Wynn had "demonstrated through clear and convincing evidence" that he should be licensed.

Wynn told the press he was pleased with the "surprising" turn of events but added that the licensing process had been "a difficult ordeal" for him. Asked if it had been worth it, he said, "Yes, for the company, but the answer has to be no for me personally." And asked if he would come to Atlantic City had he to do it all over again, Wynn said, "I'm just not sure."

The permanent license was granted November 13, 1981, and for the first six months that year the Golden Nugget reported $17.7 million in profits, which was more than the other seven casinos combined, and it continued to be one of the top-drawing casinos on the Boardwalk. Its pretax earnings for its first full year of operation were $40.3 million, or 20 percent of its revenues of $202.6 million, a 338 percent increase over the revenues of the previous year.

The Atlantic City Nugget became so rich that Wynn went out and hired Frank Sinatra, paying him $10 million plus, guaranteed over three years, along with generous stock options, to perform only for high-rollers, called preferred customers, at invitation-only affairs. Sinatra would become the hotel's "worldwide goodwill ambassador," appearing with Wynn in television commercials for the casino. Some of the perks included were the use of Wynn's $13 million Boeing 727, his helicopters, limousines, and one of the six lavish 22d-floor suites for high-rollers that had cost $4.5 million to build and decorate, plus free rooms in the hotel for his entire entourage.

"This has to be one of the greatest deals ever made," Wynn said. "What I wanted Sinatra to help us do rather than just packing the house—which he could do on a desert island anywhere—was to help us build the bond of affection between our employees and our customers. That's bottom-line marketing."

The marketing part was great. Sinatra's first appearance over a four-day engagement reportedly brought in $20 million in revenue. One high-roller alone lost $3.7 million at the baccarat tables. Gamblers were allowed to bet up to $500,000 at baccarat and up to $40,000 at craps.

The bond of affection between Sinatra and other employees was another matter. It wasn't long before Sinatra was displaying his venomous "Mr. Hyde" side. On December 1, 1983, accompanied by his wife, Barbara, and Dean Martin, Sinatra created chaos in the casino pit when he insisted that blackjack dealer Kyong Kim deal from a single deck of cards held in her hand rather than out of a dealing shoe holding six decks. When Kyong Kim tried to explain that what he was asking was illegal, Sinatra angrily shouted, "You don't want to play one deck, you go back to China." When she resisted, he threatened not to perform for the casino unless his demand was obeyed, warning her that the responsibility was on her head. The fear instilled by Sinatra cowed the dealer, the pit boss, the floor manager, and the shift manager into submission.

After an investigation by the gaming division, the four employees were suspended for various periods and the Golden Nugget was fined $25,000. Sinatra and Martin were absolved of any responsibility after they apologized, with pleas of innocence regarding the laws of New Jersey, and offered to pay the salaries of the four suspended employees.

Wynn rejected their offer, saying that the employees would remain suspended. As for Sinatra and Martin, Wynn said they were "just out to have a little fun. Sinatra and Martin were both unaware of the fact that the law was broken," Wynn said. "They told me that if they had known it was against the law, they wouldn't have done it."

Naturally. Who would ever believe otherwise? Surprisingly, gaming commissioner Joel Jacobson did after he read the employees' sworn statements. Three of the four employees had believed they would lose their jobs if they didn't "accommodate" Sinatra. Joyce Caparale, the floorperson who was supervising the blackjack table, said she didn't want to "ruffle [Sinatra's] feathers" because she had heard stories of how employees were fired when Sinatra didn't like them. Caparale recounted how Sinatra yelled at the pit boss and got "really irritated" at one point. "He just said he wanted a single deck and if he didn't get his way that he would not be putting on the show. When he started getting mad, and started to holler and waved off the pit boss like he was a little messenger boy and started to make statements that he was not going to perform if he didn't get his way, he scared the heck out of me."

The pit boss, Maxwell Spinks, said Sinatra was "loud" and "abusive" and seemed to be "pumping himself up into a very dictatorial attitude." Spinks said he didn't stop the game "because I felt all hell would break loose" and Sinatra would "probably hit the roof." The shift manager, Robert Barnum, said he felt Sinatra "was somebody special who had to be accommodated at any risk." The dealer, Kyong Kim, had other problems. Sinatra was "very mad at me," she said, for not dealing fast enough.

In reviewing the evidence, Commissioner Jacobson chastised the division for being too easy on the entertainers and not obtaining sworn statements from them as they had from the employees. He called Sinatra an "obnoxious bully" who "forced working men and women to commit infractions because of the fear of losing their jobs." Celebrities like Sinatra, he said, have the "occasional unfortunate combination of an uncluttered mind and a bloated ego."

Jacobson would not have the last word. The "obnoxious bully" remark had Sinatra seeing red again. After steaming about it for a while, Sinatra announced that he had canceled all future engagements at the Golden Nugget Casino in Atlantic City. In fact, he had canceled the state of New Jersey, crossed it off his list for good. Sinatra's attorney, Milton "Mickey" Rudin, said that his client wasn't going to sing in a state whose officials used him as a "punching bag." His $10 million contract, however, would remain in force and his 14 appearance dates at the Atlantic City Nugget would be shifted to his Las Vegas schedule. New Jersey would not have Frank Sinatra to kick around anymore.

Wynn's angry response was to blame the media for "turning a minor incident into international headlines" with devastating negative sensationalism. The publicity resulted in overwhelming "pain, humiliation, and embarrassment." As Wynn saw it, his staff had overreacted to the presence of "a forceful, assertive man trying to get what he wanted, believing strongly that he was well within the law in taking that position."

Wynn may have had a point there. Sinatra has demonstrated through the years that he is definitely "a forceful, assertive man" and strongly believes in getting his way.

For example, there was the episode at the Sands in 1967. It would later be described by witnesses as a nightmare. It began when Sinatra, who had verbally agreed to a month-long engagement at the Sands, then owned by Howard Hughes, turned up missing on Labor Day weekend. He returned a week later, accompanied by his child bride Mia Farrow, only to discover that his gambling credit had been cut off by Carl Cohen, the casino manager.

This so infuriated the singer, who was alleged to owe the casino nearly $500,000 in gambling credit, that he was quoted as declaring, "I built this hotel from a sand pile and before I'm through that is what it will be again."

Before indulging his volatile temper, Sinatra had repaired to Caesars Palace and managed to secure a performing contract at four o'clock in the morning. With his future assured, he had returned to the Sands and begun his demolition derby.

According to reports from employees given to reporters and police telling what they saw and heard about, Sinatra started out by setting fire to his room. Then, commandeering an electric baggage cart in the swimming pool area, he began knocking outdoor furniture into the pool. With that done, he sent a concrete ashtray careening through a plate-glass window, injuring a security guard. Screaming obscenities, he ran to the hotel's telephone room on the second floor and yanked out all the switchboard jacks. Back downstairs in the casino, with the flow of alcohol and language growing freer and louder, he began threatening employees, issuing his caveat: "I'm gonna break both your legs."

His final act came in the Garden Room restaurant. What happened next was described by a waiter: "Carl Cohen was sitting at a table. The next thing I knew Sinatra jumped up and threw a table right on Carl. Cohen then jumped up and punched Sinatra. Obviously, I can't give my name, but boy, did he have it coming." A security guard said: "Sinatra was yelling at Cohen because Carl had cut his credit off. The next thing I knew a table was flying in the air, and Cohen was pushing a table off his lap. He then hit Sinatra, and Frank started yelling at Cohen for punching him. It was terrible, somehow a chair, tossed by Sinatra, split a security guard's head." Said a floorman: "You would have had to see Sinatra Monday morning to believe it. He was yelling at the top of his voice, and everyone in the place was jittery. I came into the Garden Room right after the fight and Sinatra was still screaming about being punched. I don't have anything to say about it, but if I did, I would have gotten rid of Sinatra long ago." Said a bellman, "As far as I'm concerned Carl Cohen is a national hero. Why should Sinatra be allowed to act like a wild animal?"

After years of being at the mercy of Sinatra's temper, mild-mannered Carl Cohen had evened the score. With one punch, he had separated the singer from his two front caps and the Sands.

The next day Sinatra's New York dentist flew to Los Angeles to repair the damage to his teeth and bruised lips, promising that Sinatra's "great smile will be back in shape by tomorrow."

Acting as though nothing had happened, Sinatra issued a prepared statement: "I regret the termination of my long association with the Sands Hotel. I have admired and respected Howard Hughes for many years and regret that my decision to accept the offer of Caesars Palace comes so soon after his acquisition of the Sands. I have been impressed by the excellent unsurpassing facilities at Caesars in the management's efforts and policy to provide not only the best working accommodations for performers but also a wonderful atmosphere for the people who want to have fun and be entertained. I hope that my appearance will also attract other top entertainers, encouraging them to sign and appear here.'' That was interpreted as a veiled threat that Dean Martin, Sammy Davis, and Joey Bishop would soon follow him to Caesars.

"People who work in the hotels where Sinatra plays are always tense," the *Las Vegas Review Journal* said in an editorial. "They never know what his temperament will be like on any given day. Take for instance the day he ordered a pie and then promptly pushed it into the waiter's face who brought it to him."

For years Sinatra had treated the employees at the Sands in a most abrasive manner. That had been his joint and he had ruled the roost there. But now the old mobsters in the woodwork were gone and it was Howard Hughes's place, and his three-piece-suit executive types did not create the kind of swinging atmosphere that fitted into the Sinatra lifestyle.

Caesars was his kind of place—for a while. His gambling credit was allegedly nearly up to a million dollars when the explosion came, again during a Labor Day weekend. Around 5:00 A.M. on September 6, 1970, the cashier's cage called executive vice-president Sandford Waterman in his suite and informed him that Sinatra's hangers-on were cashing chips and that Sinatra was not only playing on credit but wanted the $8000-a-hand house limit doubled.

There were several versions of what happened next. Some had Waterman informing Sinatra that he could no longer play on credit. A violent argument ensued and Sinatra threw a handful of chips in Waterman's face, jumped out of his chair, and grabbed Waterman by the throat. Meanwhile, there was a wild scuffle between Sinatra's bodyguards and the casino's security guards. Then Waterman suddenly pulled a gun and Sinatra let go of his windpipe. "This gun shit went out twenty years ago," Sinatra yelled. "I'm leaving. Is anybody leaving with me?" Then someone accidentally closed a door on Sinatra's hand. Angrily, Sinatra reportedly warned, "The Mob will take care of you."

Waterman was arrested for assault with a deadly weapon but was released when District Attorney George Franklin found finger bruises on his neck. Franklin told the press that because of the Mob threat, his office was going to dig into Sinatra's background to see "who owned the nightclubs where he sang in his early days, who started him on his way, and his friendships with the underworld." As for Sheriff Ralph Lamb, he was "tired of [Sinatra] intimidating waiters, waitresses, starting fires, and throwing pies. He gets away with too much. He's through picking on little people in this town. Why the owners of the hotels put up with this is what I plan to find out." And, added the sheriff, "If Sinatra comes back to town . . . he's coming downtown to get a work card and if he gives me any trouble he's going to jail."

Sinatra flew to his Palm Springs home that day and a few weeks later announced that he had retired from the entertainment business. Two years later, "The Noblest Roman of Them All," as the billing proclaimed, was back in Caesars' fold. It was a triumphant return. All was forgiven. Sheriff Lamb's contrition was summarized in a five-column headline: LAMB DECLARES SINATRA SUPERSTAR. Sinatra, Lamb declared, had been his "personal friend for twenty years," and he was "very pleased Mr. Sinatra is coming back." District Attorney Franklin, who had been voted out of office, had nothing to say, but his successor, Roy Woofter, who had received a campaign contribution from Sinatra, supplied the singer with three volunteers from the district attorney's staff to beef up his regular security detail.

It was Caesars' policy to supplement its own security forces by 25 extra armed-to-the-teeth guards whenever Sinatra was in residence. Wherever he walked, they surrounded him, along with the D.A.'s men, and his own muscle detail—men with sunglasses, surly expressions, and the familiar bulge under the left arm. No one was allowed within 30 feet of the man unless he so ordained. When Sinatra sat at a table with friends in one of Caesars' bars or restaurants, behind each chair stood an armed guard with arms akimbo, giving everyone within range The Beady Stare.

Yet after three days, Sinatra left Caesars complaining of a "stomach problem." Then two one-week engagements in March 1974 were postponed because of a "persistent sinus condition." It wasn't until later that year that Sinatra finally completed an engagement in the Palace's Circus Maximus showroom. At last the "Noblest Roman" had rendered unto Caesars that which he had promised nearly four years earlier.

So now it was the Golden Nugget, and Steve Wynn's supportive stance was not enough to convince Sinatra to return to Atlantic City. It took a series of stinging cartoons in Garry Trudeau's Doonesbury comic strip to turn the trick. From June 10 through June 15, six Doonesbury installments satirized Sinatra's alleged links to organized crime. Two installments, depicting Sinatra receiving the Medal of

Freedom from President Reagan and an honorary degree from Stevens Institute of Technology, featured photographs of Sinatra with Mafia bosses. Another installment dealt with Sinatra's Golden Nugget incident.

Casino commissioner Joel Jacobson issued a statement critical of Trudeau's strip: "Mr. Trudeau has attributed words to Mr. Sinatra which he did not say. And he has depicted events involving Mr. Sinatra and Golden Nugget President Stephen Wynn which did not occur. . . . One post-midnight confrontation on a casino floor should result neither in the execution of a self-imposed exile nor the infliction of a permanent life-time scar."

Although Jacobson had met with Sinatra's attorney at least once since the publication of the Doonesbury cartoons, he said that his statement "was entirely my idea" and was not an apology to Sinatra.

After 317 days of self-imposed exile, Sinatra was suddenly coming back to New Jersey. "I cannot help but admire Commissioner Jacobson's forthrightness and want to thank him for having the courage to come forth and put things in their proper perspective," Sinatra said in a prepared release. "I agree with him it is time to place an unfortunate incident behind us and that it is time for me to return and perform in New Jersey."

"We kept persistently trying to find a way [to bring Sinatra back]," said a Golden Nugget spokesman. "Garry Trudeau created an opportunity for us."

Steve Wynn was happy to have Sinatra back. Still the Golden Nugget would have survived without him. The future seemed bright. There were plans on the drawing board for another Golden Nugget casino-hotel in Atlantic City, the cost projected at $250 million, later set aside. Millions were being spent to add a showroom to the Las Vegas Golden Nugget, with the idea that Sinatra would bring respectability to its downtown Glitter Gulch location.

So far Steve Wynn appeared to be a long-distance winner.

22
The Little Guy Is Mister Big

"We're Calabrese people," Nicodemo Scarfo had said to Joseph Salerno. "We're good people."

His father Philip Scarfo and his mother Catherine Piccolo were born in Calabria, Italy, and immigrated to this country in the 1920s, settling in Brooklyn. Nicodemo Domenic Scarfo was born there on March 8, 1929, but by the time he began school in 1935, the family had moved to South Philadelphia.

Although Philip Scarfo became a member of the Genovese family, bossed in those days by Lucky Luciano, his brothers-in-law—Joseph "Joe Buck," Michael "Mike Buck," and Nicolo "Nick Buck" Piccolo—were initiated into the Philadelphia family, a natural progression in that South Philadelphia neighborhood for high achievers with little education. Two cousins, Frank and Pasqualino Scarfo, were members of a New York outfit called the Sardeno group, which had its roots in Calabria, and dealt in narcotics.

After attending four high schools, Nicodemo graduated from Benjamin Franklin in 1947. In his yearbook he was described as one of two students who were "out to lick the world." A class poll voted him the "loudest," "most talkative," and the "best cutter" of classes. His studies prepared him for a career in airplane maintenance.

His parents and uncles had other plans for him. His first job was at Piccolo's 500 Club at 11th and Christian streets. The bar was a front for a gambling operation and Scarfo worked as a "runner."

His first arrest was in 1948, on a charge of atrocious assault and battery—a knifing—but the case was dismissed. Two years later, along with a cousin, Anthony Piccolo, he was arrested when police smashed through the back door of a numbers bank and charged with attempting to destroy some of the evidence. He was placed on a year's probation and fined $75.

At some point in the mid-1950s he was sponsored into the Philadelphia family by his uncle Nick Piccolo, who was a caporegime. Scarfo continued to work as a bartender and numbers runner until the night of May 25, 1963, when he fatally stabbed William Dugan in an argument over who should sit in a restaurant booth.

Sentenced to six months to two years for involuntary manslaughter, he was released after serving three months. This was when Angelo Bruno banished him to Atlantic City, then the family's Siberia. The city was in a state of terminal decline in those years and yet Scarfo managed to prosper, asserting himself as the man in charge of rackets in the area, which included bookmaking, loansharking, prostitution, and a small traffic in drugs.

He moved his family, including his parents and sister Nancy Leonetti, with her young son Philip, to Atlantic City. In time the family bought the two apartment houses at 26 and 28 North Georgia Avenue which were named Philip's Apartments after his father.

A bantam rooster of a man, Scarfo worked hard to present an impeccable public appearance. He wore his thick dark hair neatly combed straight back. He was fond of well-tailored dark suits, crisply pressed shirts, silk ties, and highly polished shoes of soft Italian leather. The only incongruous note to his cultivated image was a high-pitched voice that could be unleashed in a split-second by a volatile temper.

A turning point in Scarfo's life came when he was imprisoned at Yardville in 1971 for refusing to testify before the State Commission of Investigation and found himself in the heady company of Angelo Bruno and Jerry Catena.

He returned to Atlantic City in 1973, when excitement over the prospects of legalized gambling was beginning to heat up the resort town. When gambling finally was legalized in 1976, Scarfo was ready.

To benefit from the construction boom, he created Scarf, Inc., a concrete subcontractor, in Phil Leonetti's name, as a front to obtain a contractor license. Scarf, Inc., would eventually work on the construction of five of the first nine casinos. The companies that employed Scarf had to carry a large-scale ghost employee roster on their payrolls, but in return had no labor or delivery problems at any of their construction sites.

Scarfo's aim was to take over the Building Trades Council, but those efforts were thwarted by Big John McCullough. In those years McCullough, backed by Bruno, was too strong for Scarfo, a problem Scarfo would permanently solve nine months after Bruno's death. In the meantime he had beaten the Falcone murder rap and was the uncontested boss of Atlantic City. Three months later, Testa would be dead and Scarfo would have it all.

Convicted in federal court in June 1981 for possession of the derringer found in his home during a search for evidence in the Falcone murder case, Scarfo was sentenced to two years in prison. He was released on bail pending an appeal but ordered not to leave Atlantic City. That was not a problem, since he had no desire to wander too far from home while the bloodletting in Philadelphia continued to decimate the family. A steel mesh fence was erected in the driveway of his home, and he didn't go anywhere without Leonetti and one of the Merlinos at his side. When anyone knocked at his door, his wife or mother answered. His neighbors—whether out of respect or fear—kept him closely informed of the comings and goings on the block. No suspicious looking stranger could loiter at his end of North Georgia Avenue without his knowing about it.

During peaceful moments, Scarfo read books about his idol, Al Capone. (After Testa was killed, investigators searching his house found a video cassette of *The Godfather* and a copy of *The Last Mafioso*.) As one official put it, Scarfo longed for the days when cars had running boards and gangsters could stand on them and wield tommy guns.

For a man who claimed to be nothing more than a maintenance man working for his mother, Scarfo had expensive tastes. He was chauffeured around in a Cadillac, drank Cutty Sark, wore those well-tailored clothes, supported mistresses, and generally enjoyed the good life. Once or twice a week, he dined out with Leonetti, one or both of the Merlinos, and Nicholas "Nick the Blade" Virgilio, a twice-convicted murderer.

Scarfo's favorite restaurants and bars were Scannicchio's, Angeloni's, the Brajole Cafe, Club Ancoppa, the Lido Village, and the Easy Street Pub, all close to his home and all linked to him in a state police probe code-named "Operation Condor." Some nights Scarfo and his friends went to the boxing matches at one of the casino-hotels, Scarfo strolling down the aisle gangster-movie fashion, coat draped over his shoulders, enjoying the eyes riveted on him, arriving at ringside moments before the bell for the first round of the main event.

Was Scarfo there for the sport of it or did he have a piece of the action? That was the question asked by Irwin I. Kimmelman, the state's attorney general. He asked for an investigation because mobsters appeared to be too close to Atlantic City boxing promoters, who, in turn, were suspected of manipulating officials of the New Jersey Athletic Commission.

Atlantic City had replaced Las Vegas as the boxing capital of the world. The casinos used the bouts to lure gamblers into their gambling halls. Needless to say, nothing came of the investigation.

The gaming division investigated the Playboy casino when Scarfo, Leonetti, and Yogi Merlino were spotted ringside during the light heavyweight championship fight between Matthew Saad Muhammad and Dwight Braxton. They sat in $100 seats usually given free to high-rollers. Playboy officials denied they had "comped" them. "They've been known to frequent every joint in town," one complained. "So it's no big news and I don't think Playboy should be singled out in a sensationalistic story."

Although Scarfo gambled only occasionally, gaming division investigators reported that he and his friends received complimentary food, drinks, rooms, and boxing tickets, perquisites normally reserved for high-rollers.

None were blacklisted by the casino commission. Under the Casino Control Act, the state can bar people from casinos if they determine their presence is "inimical to the interest of the State of New Jersey or of licensed gaming," or if the person is a "career or professional offender" or an associate of such a person or anyone who has committed a crime of moral turpitude or a crime punishable by more than six months in jail. Or if the commission feels the person's presence would be "adverse to the public confidence and trust in the credibility, integrity and stability of casino operations."

Instead of barring organized crime figures, as was originally intended, the gaming commission concentrated on cheaters and others who committed offenses against the casinos.

Joining Scarfo and his bodyguards on some of their drinking and gambling excursions was Joseph "Chickie" Ciancaglini. A former official of Frank Sheeran's notorious Teamsters Local 107, Ciancaglini earned his stripes as a tough guy when he was wounded in the stomach during a gun battle in which a rebellious Teamsters official was killed. Two other Local 107 officials, who were about to expose the union's corruption, were found murdered in their offices.

Acquitted of the murder, Ciancaglini decided to become a professional. As chauffeur and bodyguard for Frank Sindone, he was precisely what the loanshark chief needed to persuade reluctant debtors. Sindone was so pleased with his new helper that he persuaded Bruno to initiate him into the family, a ritual the old boss had shunned for years.

When Sindone was found wrapped in trash bags, Ciancaglini knew it was time to switch camps. He was just the man Scarfo wanted to restructure the family's gambling operation in Pennsylvania and New Jersey. Whereas Bruno had permitted bookmakers and numbers bankers to operate independently of the family, Testa, and later Scarfo, wanted them to pay "protection" for the privilege, as they had in the days before Bruno. Assisting Ciancaglini was Pasquale "Pat the Cat" Spirito, a new member.

It took investigators 18 months to break the code Scarfo used to conceal the names and telephone numbers of over a hundred persons on a list found when they searched Scarfo's apartment in the Falcone case. Several were high-ranking members of the Genovese family. Scarfo the maintenance man knew the private telephone numbers of not only the most important members of the Philadelphia family but of top-ranked Mafiosi in an area stretching from Massachusetts to Nevada and New York to Miami. Police began to take a closer look. The theory behind his succession to power and survival was that he had struck a deal with the Genovese family allowing both to function in Atlantic City on a mutual basis.

Scarfo, who had once been generally dismissed as nothing but a two-bit punk and a success by default (all contenders eliminated), was now gradually being perceived as a master of Machiavellian strategy. The question uppermost in the minds of state and federal authorities was whether Scarfo was strong enough to prevent a major incursion into Atlantic City by other Mafia families. In other words, would Atlantic City, like Las Vegas, become an "open city"?

The New Jersey State Police reported that eight Mafia families were operating in New Jersey: Scarfo, Gambino, Genovese, Lucchese, Bonanno, Colombo, DeCavalcante, and Bufalino. More than two hundred bosses, caporegimes, soldiers, and associates were named, in what was described as the first major update of the Mob's scope of influence in the state.

A week after Testa's murder, Governor Brendan Byrne saw the murders in Philadelphia as an argument over Atlantic City. The state, he said, "has got to assume" that organized crime will continue its efforts to corrupt the casino industry. "If the citizens of New Jersey are looking for a governor who is going to relax the standards of integrity in the casinos," he added, "they would be making the biggest mistake in our political history.

As for the state police Mob update, it would remain in a state of flux as the bloodletting continued.

On March 18, three days after Testa was killed, the body of Anthony Bonaventura was found in a wooded area of the posh Philadelphia suburb of Gladwyne. He had been shot in the head and body and bound with sash cord. He was last seen alive when he rented a car on the night Testa died.

On May 26, 1981, the bullet-riddled body of Harry Peetros was found stuffed in the trunk of his gold Cadillac. Identified by police as one of the "elder statesmen" of the Greek Mob in Philadelphia, Peetros had been a close associate of Bruno in loansharking and gambling. Since Bruno's death, he had been in frequent contact with Harry Riccobene, believed to be the leader of one of the factions challenging the Scarfo group.

The next evening, two men entered a South Philadelphia restaurant. Both had their faces covered and both held .22 caliber pistols. They moved quickly to a large table occupied by eight people. "Don't nobody move," one of them shouted, firing two shots into the ceiling as an attention-getter. He waved his gun at Raymond "Longjohn" Martorano and growled "Get out of the way." Then his companion pumped five shots, four of them ripping into the face and head of Steve Booras, and the other into the head of Jannette Curro. In the span of thirty seconds, they had entered, fired seven shots, and left two dead in their wake.

An associate of Peetros and also a heavyweight in the Greek Mob, Booras's specialty had been the sale of methamphetamine on the Philadelphia waterfront. His supplier was Harry Riccobene, a competitor of Martorano, and since Bruno's death, the archenemy of Scarfo.

Curro, who barely knew Booras, was believed to be the victim of a stray bullet. Police would later theorize that Martorano had arranged the murder of Booras because of a dispute over a drug deal.

It had been five years since John Calabrese had hired Vincent Zabala to kill Tony Naccarota, owner of the Pike Beef and Beer Restaurant in Gloucester Township, days before Naccarota was to testify before a federal grand jury about Calabrese's criminal activities. Posing as an FBI agent, Zabala had picked up Naccarota and brought him to his home. "I took a few steps across the room and shot him," Zabala later told a jury. Then he buried him in a nearby junkyard owned by a friend. Calabrese then took over Naccarota's restaurant and listed it in his mother's name.

After Zabala became a government witness in a federal racketeering case involving Calabrese and six others, he revealed that Naccarota and two other suspected informers had been murdered and led police to the decomposed bodies of two of the three.

Calabrese was a money maker. Besides operating arson, robbery, and burglary rings, he distributed drugs and did some loansharking in Atlantic City through two jewelry stores, called "gold shops," catering to casino patrons in need of a quick cash transfusion. His mentor had been Frank Sindone, whose mistress Calabrese had taken over following Sindone's death.

Now it was Calabrese's turn to worry about whether others would think him capable of ratting on his business associates. He was invited to dine at Cous' Little Italy, and he brought his mother along for protection. In the whole folklore of Mafia bloodshed, nobody had ever been murdered in front of his mother. The dinner was pleasant and everybody parted amicably. Delighted with the way it had gone, Calabrese accepted another dinner invitation, this time without his mother.

The moment Calabrese stepped out of Cous' Little Italy on the night of October 6, 1981, he saw two men wearing ski masks coming toward him. Seconds later they opened fire and Calabrese died in the street.

They take their mobsters seriously in the City of Brotherly Love. In May 1981 the *Philadelphia Daily News* announced in bold headlines that Frank "Frankie Flowers" D'Alfonso was the new godfather. D'Alfonso, the paper reported, "a fairly dark horse in the race, has become Testa's successor. . . . And The Mob—which somehow blends courtly Old World manners with its everyday lawlessness and violence—is paying its respects. Members of the old Bruno family, high-ranking and low, are coming to D'Alfonso, at *his* place, as is the custom. So again, for the second time in little more than a year, it's, 'The king is dead, long live the king.' " And, the paper continued, "Perhaps the thought was that a negotiator like Frankie Flowers would be much more willing than other would-be bosses to let New York families share the casino-fed riches of Atlantic City, which is traditionally Philadelphia's territory."

Then the paper turned its attention to Scarfo: After Testa "was blown into eternity, Scarfo was quite literally strutting like the cock of the walk. Then, suddenly, after about three weeks, it ended. Scarfo not only stayed home in Atlantic City, he stayed home, period. . . . As Scarfo disappeared, trembling, from the picture, D'Alfonso came into it, calm and confident. And getting a lot of respect." Those said to be paying their respects were Raymond Martorano and Harry and Mario Riccobene.

However, instead of hiding out in Atlantic City, as Frankie Flowers would soon discover, Scarfo was busy carrying out the violent business of a godfather—from the safety of his home base.

Around eight o'clock on the evening of October 19, 1981, only 13 days after John Calabrese was caught without his mother on the doorsteps of Cous' Little Italy, disk jockey Jerry Blavat, a Mob groupie, dropped off D'Alfonso a block from the restaurant. Minutes later, D'Alfonso was found lying unconscious on the sidewalk only a few feet from the restaurant. He had been savagely beaten with a blunt instrument, possibly a crowbar or baseball bat. His skull was fractured, the bones under both eyes shattered, his jaw broken, his left kneecap smashed, two bones in his lower left leg broken, and a deep puncture wound, believed to be made by a crowbar, in his right thigh. It took sixty-four stitches to close his head wounds. No one reported seeing anything amiss, including D'Alfonso, who eventually recovered, but was never again touted as a possible contender.

What Frank Sindone had been to loansharking in Bruno's organization, Frank "Chickie" Narducci was to gambling. In a career that spanned thirty years, he had risen through the ranks to the number two spot under Testa. It had been a busy career, picking up some forty arrests along the way, mostly for gambling and loansharking. Convicted nine times, he served only one year in jail, and that for a probation violation.

But he had his darker moments. In 1959, during an argument with a man in a South Philadelphia bar over his use of profanity in a woman's presence, he picked up a revolver from behind the bar and fired a shot into the man's head. Charged with murder, he testified that he had "blacked out" and was acquitted. Other times it was his victims who suffered lapses of memory. Hauled into court and charged with beating up two delinquent debtors, the case was dismissed when the victims claimed Narducci's arrest was a case of "mistaken identity."

But when it came to gambling, Narducci was big time. In a 1976 raid on what the FBI called "the biggest organized crap game on the East Coast," 45 agents wielded sledgehammers to break down doors and arrest 60 gamblers. Narducci supervised the action from atop a stepladder, climbing down only to lend money to losers at loanshark rates.

In late 1981 Narducci was awaiting sentencing on a conviction of bribing two policemen, the IRS was suing him for $273,000 in back taxes, along with seven others, he was hit with a federal indictment charging loansharking, mail fraud, wire fraud, operating four illegal gambling operations, and unlawfully collecting debts.

On January 7, 1982, after the second day of jury selection, Narducci returned to his home in South Philadelphia. As he was getting out of his wife's Cadillac Seville, two men, armed with .38 caliber revolvers, stepped out of the darkness (the street light was broken) and emptied their guns into him, hitting him six times in the back, once in the face, once in the chest, and once in the left wrist. The tenth shot lodged in his clothing. He collapsed on his side, his blood spilling into the gutter.

Wallace Hay, executive director of the Pennsylvania Crime Commission, still wasn't sure who was in charge in his city. "The Mob has been a kaleidoscope of shifting sands," he told the press the next day. "With each death it seems to get less and less clear who's in charge. The thought struck me just a few days ago that we really don't know who is in charge. Usually, someone would assume control three to six months after someone gets knocked off. Is it going to be Scarfo, or will it maybe be Frankie Flowers? We don't know. Scarfo has always struck me as a little more career-oriented, if you will. Frankie Flowers doesn't seem as interested in getting as involved in all the things the job would take.''

Frankie Flowers had other things on his mind, like waiting for multiple cuts and bruises to heal, and hoping nobody would show up for a repeat performance.

Scarfo's enemies proved to be resourceful. Two days after Narducci was murdered, an ominous message was flashed on television screens in Atlantic City:

> Nicky and Phil,
> you're next.

The message left police scratching their heads, not to mention Nicodemo Scarfo and Phil Leonetti. Who, they wondered, had the technical capability to invade a cable television studio and escape undetected? The warning was televised 12 times. The studio where it originated was on the second floor of the Convention Center, only a few blocks from Scarfo's home. By the time police arrived on the scene, the message had been removed from the rotating drum from which it was broadcast. Police dismissed the incident as the work of a prankster.

Pietro Inzerillo, along with his parents, four brothers and two sisters, were Sicilians the Gambino family illegally smuggled into the country to work in their pizza parlors. In time all were deported back to Sicily except Pietro. "This one we missed," a federal official would later remark. Another they missed was Pietro's uncle, Antonio Inzerillo, the owner of Sal's Pizza in Delran, New Jersey, who was reported missing on October 19, 1981, and was never seen again.

Pietro himself was missing for a week before police found his body stuffed face down in the trunk of a new Mercury Cougar on January 15, 1982. His hands were handcuffed and he'd been shot several times in the head which was covered with a plastic bag. Before his uncle's disappearance, Pietro had worked at Sal's Pizza.

As a loanshark working for Frank Sindone, Vincent "Tippy" Panetta was convicted in 1976 for lending money at illegal interest rates. When police found Panetta's 60-year-old body it was on the floor of his bedroom in Cheltenham, Pennsylvania. Sprawled on the bed was the nearly nude 19-year-old body of his girlfriend, Michelle Podraza. Their hands were bound and both had been brutally beaten and died of strangulation.

Dominick "Mickey Diamond" DeVito's line was gambling and he had been pretty lucky at it until he gambled on the wrong faction in the continuing internecine slaughter.

Shot three times in the head, his body was found in a car trunk, his hands and feet tied together behind him, a la Scarfo "cowboy" fashion, and wrapped in plastic trash bags. His girlfriend said he had left home for a meeting at a pizza parlor, but had neglected to say with whom.

Beware the Ides of March. On the first anniversary of Testa's gruesome death, the body of Rocco Marinucci, the man who had made and detonated the bomb which killed him, was found in a South Philadelphia parking lot. He had been shot in the head, face, and chest numerous times and his hands were bound with clothesline. So there wouldn't be any confusion in police minds, three large firecrackers were found stuffed down his throat.

His accomplice, Theodore DiPretoro, lived in fear for three months before going to police for protection. In his zeal to impress the police with his sincerity, DiPretoro also confessed to having murdered Edward Bianculli, a neighborhood punk he disliked. Badly in need of credits for their side, Philadelphia police would claim that DiPretoro's conviction was the first solution of the murder of a Mafia boss in history.

On May 13, 1982, Frank Monte was struck by five bullets when he stepped out of his Cadillac outside a service station in South Philadelphia. Bullets entered his back, left eyebrow, both arms, and left hand. He was another one to die in the street like a dog.

An analysis of the murders by the Pennsylvania Crime Commission concluded that the average age of the victims was 58, that most deaths occurred during the hours of darkness, on a Thursday or Friday, the last half of the month, the favorite weapon being a handgun. Although several were missing, most of the bodies were left in the open as grisly messages between the warring factions.

Since no one could be sure to which faction the victims belonged, there was no way of telling who was winning.

June 8 was Harry Riccobene's turn. The Hunchback came a split-second from meeting his maker when he stepped out of a telephone booth near his home in southwest Philadelphia. When he saw the man moving quickly toward him in the darkness he ducked. The first shot grazed his forehead and he lunged at the assailant, grappling with him while bullets struck him in the chest, right elbow, and right armpit. But Riccobene stayed on his feet until the attacker ran away.

At the age of 71, the five-foot Riccobene had survived an attack from an armed assailant ten inches taller and at least forty years younger.

Riccobene's career and success in the Philadelphia family gave the lie to the myth that Angelo Bruno was opposed to family members dealing in drugs. Since 1949 Riccobene had been convicted five times on narcotics charges.

Salvatore Testa was another chip off the old block. Initiated into the family by his father, Philip "Chicken Man" Testa, former boss of the Philadelphia family, he was promoted to caporegime by Scarfo and given the serious responsibility that goes with that job when a family is at war. Also the dangers.

The attack on him came in broad daylight in South Philadelphia's bustling Italian market. Salvatore Testa was sitting on a stool outside a pizzeria eating clams when the driver of a black Ford LTD slowed down and his partner opened fire with a sawed-off shotgun, hitting Testa three times in the stomach, twice in the left arm, and three times in the legs.

When the driver spotted a police car in the rearview mirror, the shotgun and handgun went flying out the car's window. A dozen police cars were soon involved in the chase. The Ford raced through narrow, congested streets at speeds up to 70 miles an hour before crashing into a light pole.

Apprehended at the scene were Victor DeLuca and Joseph Pedulla, described by police as "low-level guys" in Riccobene's faction of the family. Both were later convicted of attempted murder. Listed in critical condition for weeks, Salvatore Testa recuperated from his wounds, and went back to work.

It would take nearly two years, but the attack on Salvatore would bring a solution to the murder of Frank Monte. It was the kind of break good policemen pray for but seldom get. The weak link was Joseph Pedulla. When he turned, he not only took five others down with him, but for the first time revealed that for a four-month period in 1982 Harry Riccobene had been the leader of a faction feuding with Scarfo. Indicted in March 1984 were Harry and Mario Riccobene, Victor DeLuca, Vincent Isabella, Joseph Casdia, and Pedulla.

A seven-page information filed with the indictment revealed that "in order to preserve the enterprise," the six men met "to discuss plans to murder Frank Monte, Salvatore Testa, Raymond Martorano, Salvatore Merlino, Nicodemo Scarfo, and other persons."

Harry Riccobene hated the nickname "Hunchback" almost as much as he hated his dwarfish size. Yet being small probably saved his life. It was nine-thirty in the evening and Riccobene was parked in front of a church in South Philadelphia, waiting for someone. He sat in the front seat of his tan Buick, stroking his full beard impatiently, his dark eyes nervously studying each pedestrian approaching his car.

The moment the jogger in the blue warmup suit came into sight, Harry kept his eye on him. When the jogger veered toward the Buick and drew a gun from his waistband, Harry was already on the floor, huddling under the dashboard. He stayed there while the jogger fired four shots into the car, dropped the gun, and disappeared into an alley.

Riccobene pulled himself off the floor and drove home. When detectives came to question him, he denied having any knowledge of a shooting. He was surprised to hear that there were four bullet holes in the window and door of the Buick parked in his driveway.

This second attack on Riccobene had come three weeks after the one on Salvatore Testa. And there would be other attempts on the life of Testa and members of Riccobene's family. Harry himself was temporarily taken out of circulation with a nine-year prison sentence in the racketeering case, but after serving a few months was back on the street while his case was pending appeal.

Murder, however, was about to take a short holiday. Following the attempted murder of Joseph Salerno's father on August 10, 1982, and the blatant parading about town of Scarfo, Merlino, Leonetti, and Virgilio in gray jogging outfits with blue stripes, similar to the one worn by the assailant, the FBI hauled Scarfo into court on charges that he had violated the conditions of his bail on the derringer conviction by associating with known criminals.

It was Scarfo's association with Virgilio, a twice-convicted murderer, that did it. His $50,000 bail was revoked and he was ordered to begin immediately serving the two-year sentence.

The next day Scarfo was shipped to the La Tuna federal penitentiary near El Paso, Texas. The day the cell door clanged shut behind him, and for the 17 months that it remained shut, the murder statistics rate in Philadelphia and southern New Jersey plummeted.

23

Hefner: Villain or Patsy?

The stretch limousine with the black windows pulled up in front of an office building in rural Lawrenceville, New Jersey. It had snowed during the night, and it was blinding cold out. Hugh M. Hefner looked out the window. This was the day he had been dreading. Inside that building, men he distrusted were waiting to pry into his life, to bring up old wounds that time had failed to heal, and new ones too.

It was January 14, 1982, and for two months now, ever since the gaming division had released its "statement of issues" on the suitability of Playboy-Elsinore Associates for a casino license, the media had been dredging up the past and selling it in boldface headlines. Hefner's gilded cocoon was beginning to collapse and there wasn't much he could do to stop it.

There was the old bugaboo about the New York State Liquor Authority and the $150,000 in bribes Hefner had agreed to pay in 1960 to obtain a liquor license for his Manhattan Playboy Club. The man acting as the conduit had been Ralph Berger, a Chicagoan with a police record. Payments were to be made in the amount of $50,000 to SLA commissioner Martin Epstein and $100,000 to L. Judson Morhouse, then Republican State Chairman and a close adviser to Governor Nelson Rockefeller. Initial bribes of $25,000 and $18,000 were given to Epstein and Morhouse, respectively, but before the balance could be paid, it was discovered that the case was under investigation by the Manhattan District Attorney's office.

Apprised of the investigation when Playboy's records were subpoenaed, Hefner hurried to the D.A.'s office to complain about a "blackmail" scheme. Later he would testify under immunity from prosecution before a grand jury. Epstein was not tried for reasons of health; Berger's conviction was later reversed on a technicality; Morhouse was convicted but his three-year prison sentence was immediately commuted by Rockefeller. Hefner and Playboy were never charged with any crime, and Playboy was granted its cabaret license by the outgoing Wagner administration. So, in the end, it had all worked out, except that the corpus delicti refused to remain buried.

At the time, Hefner had expressed his indignation: "I would not deny that pressures were brought to bear on us. I am certain they were on anyone getting a license in New York during the last several years. It is a shame that the biggest city in the country should have this sort of problem. We did not attempt to accomplish anything of an extra-legal nature."

Then there had been the recent problem in England. In October 1981, the Gaming Board for Great Britain had refused to renew licenses for two of Playboy's casinos in London, citing violations of credit regulations.

To defuse the situation, Playboy had quickly fired the company officials involved and announced plans to sell its British gaming operations, which included three London casinos, two casinos elsewhere in England, 80 betting shops, and a half interest in two other casinos. It was a surprising move considering that the British gambling operation had been the company's principal source of profitability—in 1980, profits from England had been $30.7 million, as opposed to $14.7 million from the worldwide sales of its numerous magazines.

Governor Byrne's new attorney general, James Zazzali, was not impressed by this costly gesture. He recommended that "no casino license be issued to this applicant" if evidence showed that any present Playboy official was involved in "criminal acts in connection with payments to New York public officials" in the 1960 bribery case, and if officials of the parent company in the United States knew about the alleged violations in London, or if it was found that they should have known but due to negligence hadn't been kept informed of activities there.

In the end, Playboy's license would appear to hinge entirely on the credibility of Hefner's testimony, or lack thereof.

Inside Hefner's limousine, 25-year-old Shannon Tweed was also looking out the window. Playmate of the Month in the November 1981 issue, Shannon had been Hefner's mistress for the last six months, having moved into his Playboy West Mansion in Los Angeles, a cloister Hefner seldom left. At 56 Hefner was still working hard at maintaining the hedonistic playboy lifestyle that had turned his magazine into a cult for a whole generation of white-collar swingers preoccupied with "sex and wealth."

A bodyguard opened the limousine door, and Hefner stepped out into the snow. At his side, the tall, blond Tweed towered over him. She wore black leather pants and her long blond hair fell in soft curls to her shoulders. Hefner had given some thought to her appearance at his side. "I hope and I don't think I flaunted it with her in a low-cut gown and me in a great suit," he later observed. "I am not a guy who smokes $30 cigars and talks down to people. I thought I was very respectful."

Awaiting Hefner inside the hearing room were G. Michael Brown, the director of the Division of Gaming Enforcement, and James F. Flanagan III, the division's deputy director and the attorney charged with presenting the state's case. Both Brown and Flanagan, who had spent two days taking Hefner's deposition about a year ago, agreed later that they had never questioned a company executive who appeared to know so little about the affairs of his own business. At one point during the deposition, when they were questioning him about a certain detail concerning the 1960 bribery case, Hefner had blurted out in frustration, "But you must understand, I was in love at that time."

After the hearings, Hefner would tell H. G. Bissinger of the *Philadelphia Inquirer,* "That's nuts, that's crazy, to go back twenty years about something. Everybody knows that we weren't corrupt, that we were approached, that everybody was paying, that we got a letter of commendation from the district attorney [for cooperation in later prosecutions]. What difference does it make? What are they talking about? Don't they know that everything, not only in New York, but in New Jersey, was corrupt? I'm sorry, I can't remember a lot of things twenty years ago. I can tell you who I was in love with, but I can't tell you every nuance of a liquor license in New York that didn't mean a thing. I've had pretty big events in my life, and this was not a big event."

Now seated in the witness chair, with his fist tucked under his chin, his head tilted slightly, Hefner listened with a small smile curling his lips as Flanagan said, "This is your life, Hugh Hefner."

It went badly for Hefner from the moment he opened his mouth. One of his first admissions was that he hadn't read the division's investigation report of Playboy and when asked if he had read the copy of his sworn deposition which had been given to him, he said he had "perused" it on the plane while flying from Los Angeles to New Jersey. Hefner bluntly admitted that he had come virtually unprepared to answer the panel's questions.

Hefner's stance on the bribery issue was that his company had been the target of a "shakedown" by corrupt public officials and the money was paid to "solve the problem."

"At Playboy, who was the final authority on whether money would be paid to Berger and Morhouse?" Flanagan asked.

"I don't know—I was consulted."

"Did you give the authorization?"

"I was aware of it."

"Did you authorize it?"

"I don't know."

"Could you have vetoed it?"

"I could have vetoed it."

"You did not, however."

"That's correct."

Speaking in a monotone that seldom changed during the hearings, Hefner went on to explain that he had refused to veto the payment even though he thought it was wrong. "There's a very gray area between extortion and bribery," he said. "In order to operate there, they expected something in return, in the first stages of what was ultimately a shakedown." After more questioning, he said, "It was obvious what we were really involved in was an extortion. We didn't approach anybody, and we weren't attempting to get anything we didn't have a right to. The officials considered us to be a victim and we cooperated with them fully. That's how the people responsible were brought to justice." On another occasion, he said, "I think we were a victim there, but I don't think we should have done it."

Through three days of questioning, Hefner insisted he couldn't remember the details of an event that had taken place "a generation ago." At one point he said, "Don't be upset when I don't remember precisely what you want me to remember. Because you have these other sources of information, as you appropriately should have. There is a continuing kind of implication and innuendo that my memory is conveniently spotty. This is not true. We are talking about something that happened twenty years ago.'' On several occasions, he pointed out that he wasn't a businessman, that he had never run the company, even from the beginning.

It is doubtful that Hefner was purposely being evasive. All the facts were already known by everybody, having been rehashed in the media on a daily basis, including in the *New York Times*. His behavior was more that of a man with a faulty memory cautiously treading his way, under oath, through the perilous minefield of exploding questions. The less said the fewer doors he would open for Flanagan to come barging in with more questions he didn't know the answers to.

"Do you remember testifying before the New York County Grand Jury?'' Flanagan asked.

"Yes.''

"And what were the topics that you testified to before that grand jury?''

"I have no idea.''

"Have you ever testified before another grand jury at any other time?''

"I don't think so, no.''

"Mr. Hefner, do you know whether or not you got immunity before the county grand jury in New York County?''

"I don't know.''

"Have you ever, to your knowledge, received immunity from any grand jury or prosecuting agency?''

"I don't know. I'm not aware of any. I don't know. It's possible in this case. I don't know.''

Commissioner Joel R. Jacobson was puzzled. "Couldn't a person with the courage and boldness you showed [in creating a new lifestyle in this country with your magazine] expose a couple of chiselers?'' he asked.

"Could have and should have,'' Hefner replied.

As for England, Hefner said, "I think some things were done in Great Britain that were inappropriate and improper, were things of which I didn't know of and didn't approve of.'' Pausing a moment, he said, "We were the ultimate losers.''

The man in charge of Playboy's British operation, Victor Lownes, who had been with the company 26 years, was dismissed after British authorities filed the charges. Lownes "misled us," Hefner testified, "and gave us no clear picture of the problems."

The charges were that the clubs had circumvented the prohibition against advancing credit by accepting checks from players made out to bogus accounts and holding them as credit markers.

"We were expected to take no hand in the operation of the gaming in England," Hefner said, going on to explain that Playboy had established an independent British subsidiary to operate its casinos, which meant that the parent organization in the United States was to keep hands off. "This was the request [of the British government], this was the requisite, and this eventually became the Catch-22." When Hefner fired the top management in London and sent executives from Chicago to take their place, British authorities filed additional charges that the gaming operations were improperly controlled by Americans. Thus the Catch-22 dilemma.

An accountant for British gaming authorities who testified as a division witness said during cross-examination that out of approximately 30,000 patrons who were allowed to cash checks at Playboy's London casinos, only about 50 had written checks against nonexistent accounts or been allowed to write them for more than was in their accounts. The scheme was more of a "convenience for players," he said. "There was a great deal of competition in London at that time to attract Mid-East players." He admitted that Playboy maintained a good record system and there was no indication the company attempted to hide the alleged violations.

This, in essence, was the case against Hefner, gone over a thousand times in a thousand different ways. It marked the first time Hefner had publicly testified about himself, his friends, his lifestyle, and the company that had made it all possible.

In his final argument, Flanagan had lashed out at the company's past. "Twenty years go by, and I suggest to you that a leopard does not change its spots." As for Hefner's defense that the bribery was an extortion attempt, Flanagan said, "They wanted it [liquor license] the easy way. That's the way Hefner wanted it. That's the way his cronies wanted it. That is the way they did it. What they did was bribery, it was not extortion. Actions speak louder than words."

Under the Casino Control Act, Flanagan pointed out, bribery automatically disqualified a person or firm from obtaining a casino license. (Actually, Hefner was never charged with bribery, and the casino act permits a finding of good behavior and character to wipe out earlier transgressions.)

In the British situation, Flanagan maintained that Hefner was equally culpable. "Playboy flaunted the provisions of the act to attract high rollers."

In rebuttal, Playboy's attorney pointed out that "there was no skimming, no cheating, no evidence of poor record-keeping, no corruption, and no tax evasion." Besides, under British law, officials of the parent company in Chicago were barred from exercising any control over its British subsidiary. "If Playboy didn't know," Flanagan replied, "they should have known, and could have known."

In conclusion, Flanagan said, "Unfortunately, Playboy's past does not inspire confidence in its ability to handle future law enforcement and administrative responsibilities."

The commission's verdict was closer than expected. Three commissioners found Hefner's testimony "reasonably consistent despite the passage of so many years. He has been candid," they said in their opinion, "and forthrightly acknowledged the events and the mistakes of twenty years ago." A "shadow" cast by the New York bribery incident "has given way to the light shed by a career of social commitment, honest business dealings, and an otherwise unblemished personal record of integrity."

Four votes, however, were needed for approval of the license, which made Playboy the first company to be rejected by falling one vote short. The two dissenting commissioners, one of whom had been a prosecutor in the Manhattan District Attorney's office at the time of the bribery case, found Hefner's testimony "to be untrue and insincere. His appearance was, quite simply, an attempt to mislead this commission." Hefner, in the words of one of them, "has not purged himself of a cavalier and manipulative attitude toward government processes."

In summing up for the media, Flanagan said, "The major reason they lost the license was Hefner's behavior and general demeanor on the witness stand. He definitely left the impression that he was above all this, that his conduct, whatever it was, would not hurt him."

Then in a more reflective mood, Flanagan noted that when off the witness stand, Hefner "was more cordial and, in fact, rather friendly. I can't figure it out. To have to go through your life like that, and have to talk about your life, and have some jerk like me asking off-the-wall questions—I don't really think he knew how to handle that. He was very much alone up there and maybe it was the first time in his life he had been alone.''

Unlike the decision to deny licenses to the Perlmans and O'Donnell for their association with organized crime figures, the decision on Hefner was the first, and no doubt the last, to be based on a moral judgment. They had brought him down off his high horse. ''It's rather easy to go against Playboy,'' Hefner would note. ''It's like voting against sin.''

The *Atlantic City Press* thought it was a good lesson. ''Trying to hold back information from the commission may be more damaging than any admissions the applicants may make,'' it said in an editorial. ''The commission is determined to ensure an honest casino industry and is correct in insisting on forthright and candid testimony about the past. Hefner came close. We believe he would have met [the] test for candor and qualified for a license if only he had been a little more open in discussing an unsavory incident of twenty years ago.''

In the *Philadelphia Inquirer* interview, Hefner said that the ''notion that I would be obliged to do some homework and bone up for the testimony did not occur to me. I guess I was naive. I didn't realize they wanted that kind of a dog-and-pony show. To me, on the face of it, what's happened here really doesn't hurt my reputation or Playboy's reputation as much as it hurts New Jersey's. It looks like the bad old days again. If you don't license the good guys, who are you left with?''

The answer, in this instance, was Playboy's partner, Elsinore, which slipped in almost unnoticed during the commotion and hoopla over Hefner. A Machiavellian strategist, plotting Elsinore's entrance into New Jersey gambling, couldn't have dreamed up a more diverting sleight-of-hand trick than the scenario that actually took place.

In his closing arguments to the commission, Flanagan had intimated more about Elsinore than he had articulated, saying that he was still ''troubled'' by unanswered questions about Teamsters' pension fund loans to Elsinore. Some of the loans had been made after the pension fund, the union, and various union officials had become the subject of extensive, negative publicity around the country. Other loans had been approved by officials later convicted on criminal charges relating to their handling of the fund. ''You get the feeling something is wrong,'' Flanagan said, but the division had found nothing concrete to show any wrongdoing, just ''smoke.'' Flanagan suggested that Elsinore "insulate or isolate themselves from the pension fund" by getting out of existing loan commitments.

Elsinore's attorney, David Satz, was furious. "There are very legitimate business reasons why we did business with them [Teamsters]," he said. "They [the division] just want to be out against us, and that's not fair." Flanagan's suggestions were "completely unacceptable." Elsinore, Satz said, didn't need instruction from the gaming division on how to conduct its business affairs.

When Flanagan had said, "This is your life, Hugh Hefner," he had meant that his life and his company were inseparable, and Hefner, as chairman and owner of 70 percent of the company's stock, was unlike the others before him who had been separated from their companies without creating any serious problem for the casinos involved. With Hefner, it was all or nothing. There was no way that he could be expected to divest himself of his 70 percent interest in Playboy Enterprises to save the casino's license.

This probability had already been anticipated. In Playboy's partnership agreement with Elsinore, it was stipulated that if Playboy was denied a license, it would sell its 45.7 percent interest in the $135 million, 500-room casino-hotel to Elsinore for the amount it had invested in the project or for its appraised value, whichever figure was lower, the amount to be paid over a seven-year period at 10 percent interest.

It wouldn't be long before Elsinore would be appealing to the gaming commission to force Playboy to live up to the agreement. But who was Elsinore?

24

The Pritzkers of Chicago

At the time of the gaming division's investigation of the Playboy-Elsinore license application, the owners of Elsinore, the Pritzker family of Chicago, had made a profound impression on G. Michael Brown, the division's director.

"They are money," he told me in an interview. "I mean just unbelievable money."

Asked if the division had found anything questionable in their background, he said, "Well, it's a family company, always has been a family company. I mean, when they didn't like what they had to file with [the SEC on] the Hyatt Hotels, they changed it from a public company to a private one. When Jay Pritzker was testifying on what he owned, it took him about twenty pages of testimony. We took a recess and he was on the phone for ten minutes and when he came back to continue his testimony he reported a railroad company in Montana he had bought during the break. We found nothing wrong with their past. They had inherited most of what they had from their father [A. N. Pritzker]. And we found for Jay Pritzker and his brother Robert without any problems."

A. N. "Abe" Pritzker was more than a father. He was the patriarch of a financial dynasty so vast and so well-hidden in a privately held corporate maze of holding companies, operating companies, and corporate shells that it is now near impossible for any outsider to measure the full extent of it. Their holdings are in basic industries, natural resources, and real estate.

The family's industrial empire, assembled under the Marmon Group, and run by Abe's son, Robert, was generating annual revenues of nearly $3 billion at the time he appeared before the gaming commission early in 1982. That same year, the Pritzkers paid $700 million for the Trans Union Corporation, which leases 60,000 tank and freight cars here and abroad and is a major financial services conglomerate.

Under the aegis of Abe's son, Jay, was a domestic chain of 74 Hyatt hotels, with annual revenues of $1.3 billion; an international chain of 45 Hyatt International hotels in 27 countries, with unknown revenues; the Elsinore Corporation with casinos in Las Vegas, Lake Tahoe, and Atlantic City; Braniff Airlines; and controlling stock interests in publicly traded companies such as *McCall's* magazine; Hammond organs; Levitz Furniture; the Masonite Corporation, the world's largest producer of hardboard; HMC Management Corporation, which operates sports arenas; and so many others that in 1974 the *New York Times* noted that the "Pritzker holdings . . . are too numerous for any one member of the family to recall at any given moment."

How was it possible for Abe Pritzker, an obscure lawyer in Chicago, to become one of the world's richest men? Was he a financial genius, or wildly lucky, or was it because he dared to associate with the kind of men who could make him rich, whatever their morals, ethics, or masters, in an era of flagrant gangsterism, political corruption, and labor racketeering? It is a question without any clear-cut answer, but an intriguing one nonetheless.

Abram Nicholas Pritzker was 86 when he appeared before the gaming commission. Using the initials A. N. was a pretension he had adopted rather late in life. In the old days he was known simply as Abe and his close friend and business associate Arthur Greene was known as Art. Back in the 1930s and 1940s, Abe and Art were the most mysterious financiers in Chicago.

The only information known about them was locked up in police intelligence files across this country and no organization in those days had greater access to these reports than the privately endowed Chicago Crime Commission, an organization that was held in high esteem by law enforcement agencies. The commission kept its finger on the city's pulse and wrote and received reports dealing with organized crime and political corruption.

"Arthur Greene of Room 889 Continental Illinois Bank Building heads the Domestic Finance Corporations of Indiana, New York,

Maryland, Delaware, California, and Illinois,'' the Chicago Crime Commission reported on June 17, 1944. "He is supposed to be the brains of all Chicago rackets. He is said to be the financial adviser to Jack "Greasy Thumb" Guzik and the entire Capone Syndicate. . . . He controls a half dozen business organizations through which he engages in his money making operations. He is able because of these numerous interlocking corporate entities to cover up much of his income for tax purposes.''

On November 21, 1958, the Los Angeles District Attorney's office reported the following allegations to the Chicago Crime Commission:

An official federal agency source that must remain confidential has supplied information to the effect that Arthur Greene has for many years been the investment agent for Meyer Lansky, Charles and Rocco Fischetti [cousins of Al Capone and high-ranking Chicago Mafiosi in their own rights], and Longie Zwillman in various enterprises around the country and abroad. Notable among these enterprises is the National Cuba Hotel Corporation. . . . The National Cuba Hotel Corporation also owns the National Casino and Hotel in Havana, Cuba. The gambling operation at the National is currently being conducted by Meyer Lansky. . . .

Stanford Clinton, Abram Pritzker, Jay A. Pritzker, Nicholas J. Pritzker, and Jack M. Pritzker are members of the law firm of Pritzker, Pritzker, and Clinton at 134 North La Salle Street, Chicago.

The law firm has represented such Capone mobsters as Joe Fusco and Elbert Crawford on liquor license matters in Chicago. . . . A search for corporations controlled by Pritzker and associates disclosed that since 1952 they have acquired, for cash, dominant interest in five companies having a net worth of $44,237,114 and an income from sales of $147,200,000. . . . The five companies are parent corporations that have recently swallowed numerous small but well-known and profitable companies.

A report from the files of the Los Angeles Police Department's Intelligence Division, dated January 2, 1954, alleged that "A. N. (Abe) Pritzker, a Chicago attorney with offices at 134 N. La Salle

Street, Chicago, which is the same address as that of Sidney Korshak's office, has been closely connected with members of the Capone Syndicate, Tony Accardo, and other underworld characters. It is believed by the undersigned that Pritzker may be active locally, that is in Los Angeles, as a front for eastern hoodlum money to be invested in the Los Angeles area. Pritzker was at the office of attorney Louis Hiller, 6399 Wilshire Blvd., L.A. Was there discussing the investment of money without any definite plan being indicated. Those present at the meeting included Hiller, Pritzker, and Louis Tom Dragna [a Mafioso and son of Tom Dragna, underboss of the Los Angeles family]. Hiller indicated that he had a million dollars available for investments.''

A 1958 Chicago Crime Commission memorandum reveals information received from Captain James Hamilton, then head of the Intelligence Division of the Los Angeles Police Department: ''We have previously received inquiries from [Hamilton] concerning Pritzker, and also the Nevada Tax Commission, since Pritzker has gained part ownership of certain gambling casino properties in Nevada. It will also be noted that Stanford Clinton is one of the members of the law firm of Pritzker, Pritzker, and Clinton. In this picture also appears Arthur Greene of Chicago. Arthur Greene is an individual concerning whom the Chicago Crime Commission has a file, and whom we suspected for some time of representing the Capone syndicate in certain financial operations. Arthur Greene and Abram Pritzker as well as the law firm of Pritzker, Pritzker, and Clinton were in certain financial joint ventures with Sam Genis (deceased 1955) in California. As previously indicated, Sam Genis has been tied up with Alex Louis Greenberg [notorious Capone mob investor, later murdered] for many years, and is understood to represent the mob.''

Another Chicagoan who was involved in some of Pritzker's financial dealings was Sidney Korshak, a man whose name has appeared in countless police intelligence reports in the past forty years. In 1978, in a report from the Organized Crime Control Commission, California Attorney General Evelle J. Younger described Korshak as ''an active labor lawyer, an attorney for Chicago organized crime figures and the key link between organized crime and big business.''

By 1942, according to an IRS intelligence report, Korshak was ''often delegated to represent the Chicago gang, usually in some secret capacity.''

In 1944, in trial testimony, movie union boss Willie Bioff described how Capone mobster Charley "Cherry Nose" Gioe had introduced Sidney Korshak to him in a Chicago hotel room in 1939.

"Sidney is our man, and I want you to do what he tells you," Gioe had told Bioff. "He is not just another lawyer but knows our gang and figures our best interest. Pay attention to him, and remember, any message he may deliver to you is a message from us." A few years later, Gioe's body would be found in a car trunk.

In the mid-1940s Sidney and his brother Marshall opened a law office at 134 North LaSalle Street, the same building as the Pritzkers, an address rendered notorious in law enforcement reports because of the number of top hoodlums who had offices there.

Through the years, Sidney Korshak has been the subject of mounting interest to law enforcement agencies. For example, an FBI report, dated September 13, 1963, delved into various aspects of his career:

"In 1958, during the course of an interview with Sidney R. Korshak in Chicago, Korshak advised that he was a friend of Gus Alex but only due to the fact that his wife, Bernice, is a close friend of Alex's wife, Marianne." But investigators would soon be referring to Korshak as "Gussy's man," meaning that Alex was Korshak's direct link to the Mob.

A protégé of Jake "Greasy Thumb" Guzik, Gus Alex succeeded Guzik as the Capone Mob's boss in the Loop and First Ward. Described in a police report as a "ruthless, vicious killer," Alex was a prime suspect in at least six murders—two gave deathbed statements naming Alex as their slayer, and three received death threats from Alex shortly before their murder. His police record, dating back to 1930, listed more than 25 arrests for violent crimes. Investigators believed that any message the bosses wanted delivered to Korshak came through Alex and vice versa.

"In 1960 information was received from a confidential source that Sidney Korshak exerted a great deal of control over the health and welfare resources of the Teamsters Union," the FBI report continued. That same source called Korshak "one of the most powerful individuals in the country" because of the important national and international corporations he represented. And he also represented numerous movie stars and was closely associated with some of the most powerful men in the movie industry. In the words of former *Los Angeles Times* Hollywood columnist Joyce Haber, "Sidney Korshak is probably the most important man socially out here. If you're not invited to his Christmas party, it's a disaster.''

In its 1981 report, New Jersey's gaming division noted: ''During the entire period of the 1930s, the major practice of Pritzker and Pritzker involved real estate acquisitions and reorganizations, resulting from foreclosures and mortgage defaults. The firm itself expanded in number and employed, among others, Stanford Clinton.''

Stanford Clinton and Korshak were close friends and business allies. If anything, Clinton was more daring in his representation of Mob members, including the boss himself, Anthony ''Big Tuna'' Accardo. According to the 1963 FBI report, Korshak also represented Accardo. ''In May 1959 information was received that Sidney Korshak had drawn up the original contract between Premium Beer Sales, Inc., and Tony Accardo, wherein Accardo was hired as a salesman at a stipulated salary of $65,000 per year.''

For years the Pritzkers have steadfastly denied that the law firm ever represented hoodlums. In 1978 both Abe and Jay got an opportunity to answer that question under oath during an SEC investigation of questionable Hyatt business transactions.

When the SEC asked if the Pritzker law firm had ''ever represented Al Capone, Anthony Accardo, one of his successors, or other such hoodlums,'' Jay Pritzker said ''No,'' and his attorney angrily objected to the line of questioning, charging that it was ''really a shocking abuse of authority to ask people because they come from Chicago or anyplace else, whether they know'' such people.

At the same hearing, Abe Pritzker denied knowing Meyer Lansky, but he admitted having known Korshak ''very well'' over the past forty years, pointing out, however, that neither Hyatt nor any other of the family's businesses had ever retained him as counsel.

Yet, back in 1970, when asked a similar question by the same agency, Korshak had played it cagey. ''It is possible that Hyatt Hotels talked to me about their making an acquisition in Nevada.''

Abe Pritzker also denied ever having known Los Angeles Mafioso Louis Tom Dragna.

As for Stanford Clinton, his law partner, Abe Pritzker had an answer for the New Jersey gaming division. ''When [in the early 1960s] I started hearing about the type of clients he had, which included some infamous hoodlums,'' he said, ''I asked him to move out of our office. We gave him a free ride pretty good.'' But, of course, he had never met any of those clients ''with one exception which I'll tell you about, and whether you consider him a hoodlum or not, it's a matter of definition, and that's Mr. Hoffa.''

The "free ride," as it turned out, was reciprocal. Stanford Clinton, with Korshak's backing, became the general counsel for the Teamsters Central States Pension Fund in 1959, the same year the Pritzkers received their first loan from the fund—$2 million for the Burlingame (California) Hyatt House, followed by another pension fund loan of $4 million in 1960, this one in the form of a Hyatt debenture sale, which raised a question of its legality under the fund's bylaws, in the minds of some trustees.

The Teamsters fund was then under the control of the Dorfmans. A Chicago tough guy, Paul "Red" Dorfman had come up through the ranks of the Capone mob as the man who convinced Mafia bosses in Chicago, Detroit, St. Louis, and Kansas City to back Jimmy Hoffa's bid for the presidency of the Teamsters Union.

As a reward for their support, Hoffa gave Paul Dorfman's son, Allen, who was then a college physical education teacher, the exclusive rights to handle all the Teamsters Central States Health and Welfare insurance. The next step was for Hoffa to allow Allen to help him distribute loans from the pension fund. By 1967, the year Hoffa went to prison, Allen Dorfman had attained almost single-handed control over the pension fund, which was taking in $14 million a month and had assets of $400 million.

In 1972 Allen was sentenced to two years in prison for taking a $55,000 cash kickback in arranging a $1.5 million pension fund loan, for which he served ten months. Out of prison two years, he was again indicted for conspiring with Mafia members of the Chicago family to defraud the pension fund by arranging a $1.4 million loan to a company they controlled and for siphoning off its assets until the company had gone bankrupt.

The prosecution's chief witness was Daniel Seifert, who had been a partner in the bankrupt company. Early on the morning of September 27, 1974, Seifert arrived at the company's office with his wife and two-year-old son. Waiting for him were two ski-masked gunmen, who first pistol-whipped him in front of his wife and son, and then when he tried to run away, killed him with a shotgun blast that ripped away the back of his head. Nothing came of the murder investigation, and without Seifert's testimony, all were acquitted in the fraud case.

*　　　*　　　*

Not only had Clinton introduced the Pritzkers to Jimmy Hoffa and the Dorfmans, but he has since admitted that he got "a piece" of the Burlingame Hyatt for his efforts.

The September 17, 1963, FBI report contained this notation: "In 1961, information was received by the Los Angeles Office that J. A. Pritzker was an officer and owner of the Hyatt House chain of motels, and that this company was arranging a pension fund loan from the Teamsters Union. Listed among the associates of Pritzker was Sidney Korshak."

During the SEC deposition, Abe Pritzker was asked if Clinton was involved with the Teamsters pension fund. "Hell yes, he was," he replied. "He was general counsel for the whole fund and for Hoffa. That's how I happened to meet Hoffa. He introduced me to him, but he never was in our office, either. None of his [Clinton's] clients were ever in our office."

By the time Clinton began representing Tony Accardo, the mobster was as famous in Chicago as Al Capone. In fact, Accardo had started his climb to Mob power as a bodyguard for Capone. His police record dated back to 1922, and listed more than 27 arrests: carrying concealed weapons, gambling, extortion, kidnapping, murder. His only conviction, later overturned on appeal, was an income tax evasion case.

Jay Pritzker was questioned by the New Jersey gaming commission about Clinton's representation of Accardo. "Well," he said:

Mr. Clinton's undertaking the representation of Mr. Accardo raised some very difficult philosophical questions, I thought. Such as how we believe our democratic society should be operated. You had here a case where Mr. Accardo was generally regarded as a leader of the Mafia, maybe a murderer, I don't know. That was his general community reputation. On the other hand, apparently, there had not been an ability to indict him on any of the serious crimes of which he had been accused in the newspapers [sic], and, therefore, he was indicted, as I recall, it was an indictment, on some small item in connection with some automobile, three- or four-thousand-dollar automobile.

It sort of raised the same problem that had been raised in the legal community over the indictment of Al Capone. Certainly well known as having been [a] highly undesirable character on an income tax count, so you had a difficult issue here, and I lost no respect for Stan Clinton for being willing to undertake this kind of an unpopular case, because if you don't protect those kinds of liberties, I'm afraid we're all in danger.

On the other hand, from our standpoint, much as I may have respected him for the courage to do this, from our standpoint, it was very damaging. We were involved in the business community, not the legal community. We weren't trying cases. We weren't accepting all kinds of clients, and it was damaging to us to have our names associated with this sort of thing, and, therefore, that sort of became the issue over which we felt that Stan should practice law, which he's absolutely entitled to do, but not in conjunction with us, and that was a difficult thing to do. Remember, you're now talking about a person who you've been associated with for thirty years, for whom you have a great deal of respect and affection and who's been loyal, but his vision of what he ought to do and our vision of what we wanted to do digressed and, therefore, we separated.

It wasn't long after the Pritzkers had ousted Clinton that they sought his help once again in arranging for another loan from the Teamsters pension fund, this time $2.45 million for the San Jose (California) Hyatt House. It was one of two pension fund loans made in 1966 on the same hotel.

When the Pritzkers applied for another $2 million loan for the San Jose Hyatt House, Allen Dorfman, taking his lead from the Chicago Mob, had the trustees reject the Hyatt application. As a result, Abe Pritzker wrote two "Dear Al" letters to Dorfman: the first in November 1968, the second in January 1969. "I will be grateful if you could put this loan through," the first letter read in part.

Testifying about this before the gaming commission, he was asked if he thought Dorfman could get his loan application approved. "Yes," Abe Pritzker replied, "I thought he could—without a bribe."

At another point in his testimony about the Dorfman letters, Abe Pritzker said, "Naturally, if I was paying him money under the table, I wouldn't bother writing this letter."

"First of all, nobody is suggesting that you paid money under the table," the deputy attorney general replied.

"No, but it's sort of in the back of your mind," Abe shot back.

Yet Pritzker admitted he wasn't exactly sure what Dorfman's position was with the pension fund. "I've always been suspicious about him," he said.

Asked if he wasn't bothered about the ethics of borrowing from the scandal-ridden pension fund, he said, "I wasn't bribing anybody . . . why would I worry about that."

Between 1959 and 1975, the Pritzkers received Teamsters loans totaling $54.4 million. When questioned about the loans by the New Jersey gaming commission, Jay Pritzker responded: "You are making a legitimate borrowing at a legitimate rate of interest, and you are going to pay it back. What difference does the lender's reputation really make, other than the risk of unfair accusations? Morally, I see nothing wrong with it."

Aside from the unsavory reputation of the people involved with the Teamsters fund, the casino act prohibited casinos from receiving Teamsters money. At the time of the hearings, the Pritzkers' unpaid balance at the pension fund was $49 million, and most of this money had gone to finance their casinos in Nevada.

The Pritzkers' first venture into Nevada gambling was in 1972, when Elsinore, a wholly owned subsidiary of Hyatt, was incorporated in Nevada to purchase and hold all of the outstanding stock of the Four Queens, a typical sawdust grind joint in Las Vegas's downtown Glitter Gulch section.

Then Nathan Jacobson, who with Jay Sarno had given the underworld Caesars Palace, had gone north after selling out to Lum's, Inc., to try his luck again, this time with a disaster called King's Castle in Incline Village on the north shore of Lake Tahoe.

Again financed by the Teamsters pension fund, Jacobson's free ride at Tahoe lasted from 1969 to 1972 when he became insolvent and filed for reorganization under Chapter 11 of the Federal Bankruptcy Act. It was time for Jacobson to move on again and time for his Chicago backers to find a replacement.

Then Melville "Sonny" Marx, a Hyatt director, got together with Teamster Asset Manager Alvin Baron, who was substituting for Dorfman while he was serving a prison term for defrauding the pension fund, to discuss the possibility of Hyatt taking over King's Castle. "Mr. Marx subsequently brought this opportunity to the attention of Jay Pritzker, who indicated his interest, subject to the condition that the Pension Fund, as part of the sale transaction, would make a substantial debenture loan to Hyatt," the New Jersey gaming division noted in its report.

The result was a deal so favorable to the Pritzkers that it set off alarm signals at both the SEC and the Labor Department.

It involved two loans from the Teamsters pension fund. First a purchase loan of $19.5 million carried at a 6 percent interest rate, four points below the market rate of 10 percent. As a result, the Pritzkers received a discount of approximately $8 million. And for having taken King's Castle off the Teamsters' hands, at no cost to the Pritzkers, the pension fund purchased $30 million in Elsinore debentures, carrying an 8.5 percent interest rate, and secured by the Four Queens.

The Labor Department, finding the $30 million loan "undersecured," and the rate of return to the pension plan "not commensurate with the risk of loss to the plan," filed a civil suit against the pension fund. Not mentioned was Hyatt's success at that time in preventing the Teamsters Union from organizing front-desk clerks at a number of its hotels.

The SEC investigation focused on alleged conflicts of interest and inadequate disclosure to Hyatt stockholders, and also scrutinized arrangements under which the Pritzkers built hotel complexes and then leased them to Hyatt, which they controlled, assuring themselves of a guaranteed profit while the risks were borne by the public company. In studying the loans and leases between the Teamsters and the Pritzkers and Hyatt, the SEC found that when many of the leases were negotiated, members of the Pritzkers family simultaneously represented the family and Hyatt. In the period from 1974 to 1978 alone, the SEC suit claimed, the Pritzkers received at least $4 million a year more in lease payments than they paid in debt service.

The Pritzkers staunchly defended the arrangement. Jay Pritzker's view was summed up in the gaming division's report: "He emphasized that he would not have purchased the King's Castle without the incentive provided by the debenture and stated that, in his view, the criticism of the Labor Department was unfounded, since the overall effect of the transaction was to transform a derelict facility into an attractive and viable hotel, to the mutual benefit of the pension fund, Hyatt, and the Lake Tahoe community."

In his defense of the debenture sale before the SEC, Alvin Baron of the Teamsters gave his opinion that the Four Queens was worth considerably more than $30 million. But a few months later Baron found himself in a Detroit federal courtroom answering to criminal charges that he and Peter di Tullio, President of Hyatt International, and others had "defrauded the pension fund" by converting a $7 million loan "to their own use and benefit and to the use and benefit of others."

The $7 million had been used to finance a personal hotel venture arranged by Peter di Tullio. The deal, di Tullio told the SEC in a deposition, had started in 1974 when he acquired the Claridge Hotel in Atlantic City. It was a complex transaction, involving two other Hyatt International officials, who put up no cash for the venture. This was before gambling was legalized in Atlantic City and the plan was to convert the old hotel to condominiums and a medical clinic to be operated by the Hyatt Corporation.

Jay Pritzker told the SEC that Hyatt had agreed to manage the building, but denied knowing anything about how the venture had been financed. In 1975, only a year later, like so many other seemingly self-serving projects financed by the Teamsters pension fund, it quietly slipped into bankruptcy.

When asked during the SEC deposition if he knew Lansky, di Tullio acknowledged he had known him in the 1950s when he was the treasurer of the Hollywood Beach Hotel in Hollywood, Florida, and Lanksy was a member of the hotel's cabana club and golf club.

All in the Detroit criminal case were acquitted and in early December 1978 the SEC completed its two-year investigation with a lengthy report, finding that Hyatt had failed to make adequate and timely disclosure of material facts concerning certain transactions between Hyatt and the Pritzker family, and concerning the acquisition of the King's Castle from the pension fund, and the sale of the Four Queens debenture to the same fund.

Hyatt agreed to a consent decree which constituted neither an admission nor a denial of any of the allegations. But early the next year, the Pritzkers acquired the outstanding equity of the Hyatt Corporation, converting it into a "private" company, and then spun off Elsinore, transforming it from a subsidiary of Hyatt into a "public" company, following a public sale of 1.2 million shares of its common stock.

Back in 1965 the IRS had initiated an intelligence investigation of the activities of Meyer Lansky and his couriers in the Bahamas. It was code-named Operation Tradewinds. Gradually, as the investigation gained momentum, it began to include other individuals, finally zeroing in on the customers of the Castle Bank and Trust Company

Ltd., which was owned, in part, by an organized crime figure, and the Mercantile Bank and Trust Ltd. Both banks, located in Nassau, were involved in vast offshore holdings of secret American accounts. This new phase of Tradewinds was code-named Project Haven.

One night an attractive IRS operative succeeded in luring a Castle Bank official from his Florida apartment while her accomplice went in and photographed the contents of his briefcase, which included a list of the bank's customers.

It was a "black bag" job and it would die an ignoble death at the hands of IRS Commissioner Donald Alexander, who not only halted the investigation but demanded to know the names of the informants involved. A few years later, the *Los Angeles Times* would reveal that Alexander's former law firm in Cincinnati had, in a debt collection case, represented a company managed by Castle Bank.

However, before Alexander could successfully kill it, Project Haven was to blow a little more smoke in the face of the Pritzkers. A November 1974 IRS memo, which became an exhibit in a congressional probe of Project Haven, alleged that a "multimillionaire family of Chicago" that owned a "chain" was generating "an annual cash flow in the hundreds of millions of dollars, but paid little or no taxes in recent years." The IRS's Audit Division, the memo said, was "contemplating the nonrecognition of the legitimacy" of the Chicago family's trusts, which would result in a tax deficiency of $11 million. And "the Intelligence Division is contemplating fraud charges on the same issue." The family in question was later identified in court papers as the Pritzkers.

The case ended in civil court with charges against some Pritzkers for alleged tax deficiencies.

Besides the Pritzker family, the bank's customers included Stanford Clinton, Peter di Tullio, and other family associates. But long before the "black bag" job, the IRS was suspicious of the Pritzkers. A September 1972 IRS document, filed in a Miami probate case in 1980, revealed this notation: "An informant with access to the records of Castle Trust has stated that the Pritzker family of Chicago, through their Hyatt Corporation, received their initial backing from organized crime." The informant was a former vice-president and director of Castle Bank, and it was his estate that was being probated. The IRS allegation was included with a list of "known racketeers and gamblers" doing business with Castle Bank.

The man who seemed to exert the most power at both the Castle and Mercantile banks was Paul L. E. Helliwell, a Miami lawyer. For example, when Mercantile got into financial straits in 1972, Helliwell forced the transfer of a number of the bank's accounts and loan portfolios to Castle over the strenuous objection of the bank's president. When he asked why they had been "rammed . . . down my throat," Helliwell replied that the transfers were made at the behest of Burton Kanter, who had expressed the fear that if the trusts were not transferred, "he'll [Kanter] end up with his face down in the Chicago River."

Kanter denied making such a remark, and said he could not recall being involved in the transfer of the trusts.

Burton Kanter, described as a key figure in Castle Bank, was a member of the Chicago law firm of Levenfeld, Kanter, Baskes, and Lippitz, tax law specialists whose clients included the Pritzkers and both Hyatt corporations. Kanter also was a director of Hyatt International.

Before Alexander could kill Project Haven, Kanter and three associates were indicted on tax conspiracy charges. Although Kanter was acquitted, his partner, Roger Baskes, was convicted. And three years later, Calvin Eisenberg, another Kanter law partner, was convicted on Castle-related charges.

In its report to the New Jersey Casino Control Commission, the gaming division said: "When questioned by the division, Jay Pritzker acknowledged some apprehension about continuing to use the services of Burton Kanter as a tax advisor. Mr. Pritzker explained, however, that in his experience Mr. Kanter had always acted properly, and had demonstrated himself to be extremely capable. He also stated that he had had discussions with unspecified individuals associated with the Internal Revenue Service at the time of these occurrences, and that these individuals saw no reason not to continue to retain Mr. Kanter, following his acquittal. The Pritzker family and trusts have, at various times, also been involved in several personal business ventures with Mr. Kanter. Mr. Kanter presently serves as a director of Hyatt International as well."

In June 1984 Bunny Wanda was the last of the Playboy bunnies working in Atlantic City. Finally, after losing out in the courts and shopping around for a buyer, Hugh Hefner had been forced by an impatient attorney general to sell his 45.7 percent interest in the casino-hotel to his partner, Elsinore, as called for in their agreement.

The price was $53 million, which was precisely Hefner's investment, plus 10 percent interest, to be paid over the next six years. As part of the management agreement, Hefner was to receive a fee of approximately $5 million, an amount equal to 1 percent of the company's gross revenues for the time Hefner was a partner.

Bunny Wanda didn't like being a symbol. She cried when they paraded her out in front of the media for a public shaving of her fluffy tail and ears. Prior to her shearing, Elsinore work crews had spent weeks removing the bunny logo from every nook and cranny of the hotel and casino. The Playboy sign was lowered and up went the new one—rising from the seashore, so to speak—proclaiming the gamblers' new mythical continent: Atlantis.

In an editorial on June 8, 1984, the *Atlantic City Press* again felt the need to reassure the local citizenry of the wisdom of their gaming authorities: "But the ritual [the shearing of Bunny Wanda] concocted by the public relations experts underscored a transition far more significant than the breakup of a Hefner hutch. The removal of Playboy from Atlantic City's gaming scene reaffirms the determination of the state of New Jersey, through the Casino Control Commission, to keep the gaming industry free of criminal taint.''

25

Bribes, Kickbacks, Hookers, and Other Licensable Practices

Although unsavory characters were mostly absent from the gaming division's reports in the licensing of Harrah's Marina, the Sands, and the Claridge, there were enough unsavory practices to keep investigators busy. And during the hearings many of these practices came under scrutiny.

Harrah's Marina Hotel Casino

Bill Harrah was a sharp operator, and his casinos at Reno and Lake Tahoe were two of Nevada's biggest money-makers. His decision to try his luck in Atlantic City came only months before his death in 1978. Had he lived, it is doubtful that he would have sold a 99 percent interest in his company to Holiday Inns, Inc., the Memphis-based hotel chain that for years was controlled by conservative Southern Baptists staunchly opposed to gambling. In fact, when the company finally decided to buy out Harrah's for $300 million, its president, L. M. Clymer, resigned because he was morally against gambling.

Harrah's Marina was the first casino to be built outside the Boardwalk casino strip. Located at the foot of the Brigantine Bridge, about a mile from the Boardwalk, the 506-room hotel complex overlooks Absecon Inlet, and the northern wall of the casino is all glass, which probably made it the first casino in the world to permit natural light to invade the perpetual night ambience preferred by gamblers.

After its investigation, the gaming division reported that Bill Harrah had personally approved the practice of providing prostitutes to high-rollers and had even tried, unsuccessfully, to write off some of those expenses as tax deductions. His policy was discontinued in 1975 but only after the Nevada Gaming Control Board had demanded it be stopped.

At Holiday Inns, according to the division's report, "sensitive" payments, the company's euphemism for bribes, to various government officials in Mexico, France, Belgium, the Far East, and the Persian Gulf had totaled $703,227 between 1969 and 1980.

Although the company had investigated the matter in 1976, the division questioned the "sincerity" of the company's attempts to uncover such payments and its ability to report the facts accurately. For example, bribes had continued to be paid after the investigations and the alleged adoption of a policy severely restricting such activity. Additionally, the company made incomplete reports of the bribes to the IRS and the SEC, and the bribes had violated laws in several foreign countries. And from 1976 to 1979, the company continued paying bribes in Mexico even after its chief legal counsel and its outside auditors indicated that "these payments in whole or in part were either improper or illegal."

On the opening day of the Casino Control Commission's hearings, Holiday Inns' counsel, Howard Goldberg, promised the commission that he would "put in perspective" the allegations raised about the company's qualifications. He reminded the commissioners that Holiday Inns was in Atlantic City because Governor Byrne and Senator Steven Perskie had traveled to Memphis to invite the company's directors to build a casino in Atlantic City. It was after the governor's presentation in 1978 that Holiday Inns had changed its long-standing policy against investing in gambling and had formulated plans to accept the governor's invitation. Pleased with its decision, Holiday Inns had since bought 40 percent of the Riverboat casino in Las Vegas, giving the company an entry into the country's four major legal gambling markets.

Harrah's Board Chairman Mead Dixon told the commission that the "sensitive" payments would "have caused me great concern had I known about them when the merger discussions began taking place, but I would have wanted to go through with the merger." And, he pointed out, "sensitive" payments were a common practice. "Some of our greatest corporations were caught up in practices that wouldn't stand up in the light of day." As far as Holiday Inns' reputation was concerned, he added, "They had a good reputation before the report and will have a good one after it, too."

Rallying to Holiday Inns' defense was Lloyd Cutler, who had been Jimmy Carter's chief counsel during his presidency. The "sensitive" payments, he conceded, were probably illegal under foreign laws, but the bribing of foreign bureaucrats was so widespread that the laws were rarely enforced.

Granted "expert witness" status by the commission, Cutler testified that his Washington law firm was asked by Holiday Inns to study the legality of the "sensitive" payments and it was his conclusion that such "grease" money was specifically exempted from the Corrupt Foreign Practices Act, which outlawed most foreign bribery, as long as the payments were used to spur low-level officials into performing their normal duties. It was no more, he said, than the money journalists paid to telegraph operators to make sure their stories were transmitted.

Yet Holiday Inns' SEC expert, Rodney Dayan, testified that the company had withheld the information from the SEC because it would have been "embarrassing, agonizing, and humiliating" for Holiday Inns. "The company didn't want its reputation tarnished," he said. "It didn't want these facts made public unless they had to be."

No witness could say who had eventually received the bribes. Yet all assumed that they went to low-level officials. Still the low-level officials were high enough to lower taxes in Beirut, provide a building permit in Paris, grant increased room rates in Acapulco, settle a Social Security payment dispute, and settle a strike in Acapulco by paying off the union leaders.

When division attorney James Flanagan asked Dayan why company officials never tried to discuss the payments with the persons who ultimately received them, Dayan said, "You really don't go traipsing around the capitals of foreign countries and asking who took bribes. You wouldn't be received all that well."

Jose Torres testified that he had reluctantly approved several "under the table" payments when he was in charge of the company's Mexican operations. "It is something that I didn't like doing at all, but it was like someone putting a gun to your head—either you cooperated or you suffered the consequences.'' Dayan had called it "extortion.''

It all sounded quite familiar, for these were phrases not unknown to Hugh Hefner and Playboy executives. The difference was that this time the bribery had taken place in somebody else's country.

In his closing remarks, division attorney Flanagan referred to ''an aura of stinkiness'' around Holiday Inns, calling the company "a corporate ostrich that has buried its head'' in the foreign soil where it made payoffs. It "even buried its head [during the hearings] in Lawrenceville'' because it failed to provide witnesses who had any firsthand knowledge about the bribery.

"The Mexican lawyers who made the payoffs didn't come here to testify,'' he told the commissioners. "And neither did the controllers who released the money. All they gave us were historians who read reports and concluded from those reports that low-level government officials got the money. But we really don't know how high up that money went. We aren't talking about paying for draperies for the Holiday Inn in Bordentown. The company should have tried to find out what they were applying for in Mexico. Again, that is the problem here, we just don't know. The whole thing stinks.''

Flanagan praised Mead Dixon for expressing remorse over the practice of providing prostitutes to high-rollers. Holiday Inns, however, had failed to show the same kind of regret. In fact, from what he had learned in the division's two years of investigation, the company had failed to convince him that it had discontinued its bribery practices.

In the end, however, Flanagan stopped short of asking the commission to deny a casino license to Harrah's Marina. Which was just as well with the commission. It seemed more interested in Howard Goldberg's interpretation: "The company's treatment of a very difficult area reflects well on its character and integrity.''

The commission voted unanimously to grant a full license. "We have concluded none of the areas of concern identified by the division negatively impacts on the qualifications of Marina Associates, Harrah's, or Holiday Inns,'' said Acting Commission Chairman Martin Danziger.

Holiday Inns President Michael Rose said, "We are pleased that the Casino Control Commission recognized our management's fine reputation for honesty, integrity, and business ability and our company's financial strength.''

The same month it was granted its license, Holiday Inns reported record-breaking earnings in the three-month period that had ended October 2, 1981. Michael Rose conceded that increased earnings were largely a result of gambling earnings.

The Sands

For a while it seemed that an applicant for a permanent license would finally squeak through with the full blessings of the gaming division. The Brighton, built by Greate Bay Casino Corporation, on the site of its former namesake, was the first all-new casino-hotel to open in Atlantic City.

Costing $69 million, the 19-story complex, with 506 rooms and a small 32,200-square-foot casino, was in money trouble almost from the moment it opened its doors in August 1980.

The principal stockholders of Greate Bay, a publicly traded company, were Eugene V. Gatti and Arthur J. Kania, both of Ocean City, which made the Brighton also the first casino-hotel built by local businessmen.

And Gatti and Kania were the first license applicants to be praised by the gaming division: "There are some issues that we investigated . . . but they satisfied us that there was nothing in the conduct of any of the people involved in the company to warrant any problems," G. Michael Brown said. "In the future, we hope that this is the rule and not the exception."

Yet by the end of October, the owners were denying bankruptcy rumors, but it wasn't long before they would announce that the Brighton had been sold to the PPI Corporation, a newly formed company jointly owned by the Inns of Americas, Inc., a Dallas-based hotel chain, and two financiers, Burton and Richard Koffman, of Binghamton, New York.

The Inns of America, privately owned by the Pratt brothers, Jack, Edward, and William, operated franchised Holiday Inns in the United States and Latin America. It had just bought the Sands in Las Vegas from the Summa Corporation, and to capitalize on the Las Vegas reputation, the Brighton was renamed the Sands of Atlantic City.

"We intend to develop the Sands of Atlantic City into a major East Coast property," Jack Pratt said, and he announced that a whole cadre of top Caesars World executives, including its chief operating officer, Stephen F. Hyde, had moved over to the Sands.

Nine months after the merger, the division issued a 128-page report on the Pratts and Koffmans that burst its own bubble of enthusiasm for a trouble-free future. It raised a whole series of questions for the Pratts and Koffmans to answer before the commission.

Among the problems cited was the gambling casino at the Condado Holiday Inn in Puerto Rico, the franchise of which was owned jointly by the Koffmans and the Pratts. Since 1975, the report noted, the casino's operation had been "deficient and irregular in several areas," including internal controls, recordkeeping, and credit given to "junket" patrons, or high rollers, whose visits were paid for by the casino. The Condado's New York junket office kept no financial ledgers on its activities.

Puerto Rican authorities had twice fined the Condado for violating its prohibition on advertising, and was "currently reviewing three other" violations. Additionally, the government was "seeking to revoke the gaming license of the Condado's casino manager for violations of gaming regulations."

As for the dozen or so Holiday Inns the Pratts operated in Mexico, the division "ascertained that for a number of years sensitive, facilitating, or expediting payments to regulatory and governmental officials in Mexico have not been an uncommon occurrence."

Further into the report came the names of Morris Shenker, Allen Dorfman, Jimmy Hoffa, the Teamsters pension fund, and Alvin Malnik, a dramatis personae by now quite familiar to the division.

Since 1966 the Koffmans and their companies had made 15 loans to Shenker totaling $15.6 million. But in 1965, before this business relation had started, Burton Koffman had asked Shenker to arrange a $6.5 million Teamsters pension fund loan for American Motor Inns, for which Burton Koffman received a $100,000 finder's fee from American Motor Inns and an option to purchase 100,000 shares of its stock for $3.50 a share, a deal that was to earn Koffman $1,022,000.

If at first the Sands' chances for a license looked bleak, they improved considerably on the first day of the hearings when Nicholas Casiello, attorney for the Sands, announced that further division investigations had resolved some of the troublesome issues cited in the report. No evidence had been developed that the Koffmans and Pratts had made "sensitive, facilitating, or expediting payments in

Mexico." The news from Puerto Rico was equally uplifting. "That investigation is now complete," Casiello said, "and the Condado Holiday Inn has been absolved of any wrongdoing." In addition, Casiello said that an action to revoke the gaming license of the casino manager had been unsuccessful.

In his testimony before the commission, Jack Pratt said that negative media reports coming out of Atlantic City had nearly kept him from investing in the Sands. "I can't recall reading anything positive for eighteen months," he said. "If the press stayed off its back, the industry would prove itself to be a very viable one [in Atlantic City]."

In response to questions about the Condado casino, Pratt said he wasn't aware of the violations since items like that were generally taken care of by lower-level officials. He admitted to having held discussions with Shenker to learn about the industry in Las Vegas. However, a decision was made not to deal with Shenker, he said, because of his "street reputation" and the impact it could have on attempts to get licensed in Nevada. But Shenker, he said, was "a likable individual."

When it was his turn, Burton Koffman testified that the trustees of the Teamsters pension fund had been under the impression that they were the ones who deserved the finder's fee and stock option from American Motor Inns. Koffman had been called to a meeting of the trustees, chaired by Dorfman.

It was like "an inquisition," Koffman recalled. "I was never threatened but I was intimidated. Here I was in this room with sixteen burly men and all I wanted to do was to get out of there with a profit. I had read the newspaper articles" about what happened to people who opposed the Teamsters, he said. "I made more than a million dollars and decided it wasn't worth the effort to fight this." So he gave up $112,500, or half of the difference between his profit and what the trustees received from their own, but less lucrative, stock options.

Prior to his appearance before the commission, Burton Koffman had talked with the division about his dealings with Shenker. "I feel he has been a hundred percent honest with us," he said. "He never asked me to do one iota under the table. He has never offered me any [payoff], intimated or done anything but conduct his business in a businesslike manner, except he's a slow pay."

At the end of his testimony, the division announced it had no witnesses and wouldn't oppose the license during closing arguments. All it asked was that the commission attach special conditions on the license prohibiting the Koffmans from any further business dealings with Shenker and the Teamsters. In his testimony, Burton Koffman had said he wouldn't object to such requirements.

The commission was more generous. It voted unanimously to grant the license without any special conditions, leaving the door wide open for Shenker and the Teamsters pension fund.

The Claridge

As a baseball player Del E. Webb wasn't good enough to make the major leagues, but as a contractor in Phoenix, Arizona, he became rich enough to buy a half-interest in the New York Yankees.

That was long ago. It was also long ago that Bugsy Siegel picked Webb to build his fabulous Flamingo Hotel. Not long after Siegel was murdered in 1947, Webb provided an insight into their relationship.

"He was a remarkable character," Webb told friends. "Tough, cold, and terrifying when he wanted to be—but at other times a very easy fellow to be around. He told me one night, when I was waiting for my money"—Webb waited in Siegel's office every night to be paid a portion of the day's receipts—"that he had personally killed twelve men, but then he must have noted my face, or something, because he laughed and said that I had nothing to worry about. 'There's no chance that you'll get killed,' he said. 'We only kill each other.' "

At the time of Siegel's death, Webb owned a 10 percent interest in the Flamingo, along with Meyer Lansky and the Mafia bosses Lansky represented. Webb also built the Sahara in Las Vegas and ended up owning it. By the time he died in 1974, his casino holdings included the Mint in downtown Las Vegas, the Sahara Reno, the Sahara Tahoe, and the Nevada Club in Laughlin, Nevada.

After Webb's death, Robert H. Johnson, who had been at Webb's side some forty years, assumed control of the company. Then in late 1979 the Webb company entered into an equal partnership agreement with Claridge Associates, a group of Connecticut investors headed by F. Francis "Hi Ho" D'Addario. Claridge Associates had bought the old Claridge Hotel on the Boardwalk and had run out of money after they started renovating and modernizing the 300-room hotel. The project included the construction of a tower with 200 new guest rooms, a 30,000-square-foot casino, and a 500-car garage. The final cost would be reported as $150 million.

At the time of the partnership agreement, the Del Webb Corporation and vice-president James Comer were awaiting trial in federal court in Las Vegas on charges of conspiracy to commit mail fraud, wire fraud, and transportation of money and property obtained by fraud. The allegations were that $1 million had been diverted through kickbacks from construction loans from three Teamsters pension funds during the building of a high-rise addition to the Aladdin during 1975 and 1976—a time when the Detroit and St. Louis Mafia families were in control of the Aladdin.

While serving as general contractor, the indictment said, Webb and Comer assisted in the alleged "division and misappropriation of funds" kicked back by suppliers and subcontractors, by concealing such payments under the guise of fees, finder's fees, and commissions. The Aladdin corporation assisted in the scheme by submitting fraudulent billings and pay requests to the pension fund. The indictment charged that the hotel's general counsel, Sorkis Webbe of St. Louis, received $150,000 and that the total misappropriation was nearly $1 million.

Not what the gaming division would call an auspicious entrance into Atlantic City gambling. For one thing, James Comer was in charge of construction at the Claridge and would retain that position for nearly a year after being indicted.

After its usual two-year investigation, the division issued a 170-page report that for the first time opposed the granting of a temporary license: "To permit this company to operate a casino in New Jersey, even on a temporary basis, while on trial for criminal conspiracy, would seriously undermine the public's confidence in the regulatory process."

And there was more. For eleven years, Webb casinos in Nevada had paid prostitutes to act as "escorts" for favored players. During an SEC investigation in 1977, Webb claimed it had paid out $178,294 for this service between 1969 and 1976, but an outside accounting firm hired to check the records concluded the figure was $416,881. Although the company claimed it had discontinued the service in 1977, the division charged it had continued unabated until the division began its investigation in February 1980.

"All the women used in this arrangement were prostitutes," the report said. "The women would either be introduced to the player or sent to his room by a Webb employee. At some later point, the girl would return to the employee who initially contacted her and that employee would fill out a miscellaneous paid-out slip at the casino cage. Sometimes, the player or woman would be required to sign as receiving the money. In most cases, the words 'air fare' or 'transportation' were usually written on the form for justification of the payment. Cash was then obtained from the casino cage."

Later, the system was changed and cash was kept in a safe deposit box in the casino cage area. Money from the sale of hotel furniture, meat renderings, and other similar sources were deposited in the box, which the division said employees referred to as the "hooker box," and paid out to the "escorts." None of the money was reported on the company's books.

Between 1969 and 1973, the report went on, the Webb company received $42,000 in illegal "rebates" from the Schlitz Brewing Company as payment for Webb casinos and hotels serving Schlitz beer. The secret arrangement involved the falsification of corporate records. The scheme was the subject of inquiries by the SEC and the U.S. Attorney's office in Milwaukee. Schlitz was indicted for accepting false invoices from Del Webb and at least fifteen other national corporations and pleaded nolo contendere to misdemeanor charges. It was fined $11,000 and paid $750,000 in civil penalties. Del Webb was not prosecuted.

For years, through its subsidiary, the Sahara-Nevada Corporation, the Webb company had routinely made political contributions without worrying about limits or disclosure. But when Nevada passed a law in 1977 that required all contributions in excess of $500 to be reported, the company, through its numerous subsidiaries, circumvented the law in 1978 by contributing $112,000 to state and local candidates in amounts under $500.

In addition, the division noted, political contributions came from an "off-the-books" bank account, contrary to official corporate policies. The account had remained open until February 1981 and was closed only after company executives became aware of the division's investigation. Also, in violation of its own policies, it made cash contributions from the cage of the Mint casino to the campaign of former Nevada Governor Mike O'Callaghan. The Mint's general manager "would put a marker in the Mint cage, take the cash out and give it to a representative of the O'Callaghan campaign." The Mint's general manager would then receive a personal check from Webb made out to cash to cover the amount of the marker, which he would deposit in the cage and destroy the marker. Between $16,000 and $18,000 was contributed to O'Callaghan's campaign this way.

In 1979 a group of 15 New Jersey gamblers, most of them using aliases, defrauded the Sahara Vegas and the Sahara Reno out of $810,000. The group obtained credit after only partly filling out credit applications, using false names, addresses, and telephone numbers. The casino never tried to verify any of the information provided. After signing markers, they were given chips, which they cashed, and walked out with the money.

To compound the problem, the gaming division discovered that just a year earlier, 17 Kansas City gamblers had pulled an identical scam which had cost the Sahara Vegas $178,000. Even after both scams, internal control violations persisted at Webb casinos. The division found violations of credit procedures in July 1980, 17 months after the New Jersey scam. Of 108 credit slips examined, 87 were not completely filled out by the customer, 86 lacked bank or financial credit information, 76 didn't indicate an effort was made to check central credit, and all of them lacked the required number of signatures needed to approve credit. When so-called strangers can walk away with a million tax-free dollars, it begins to look more like a skim than a scam.

Finally, for a dozen years, ending in 1980, "employees bilked the company of hundreds of thousands of dollars" by taking rebates from food suppliers. The amount stolen was estimated at $1.5 million and was because of an "unprofessional and incompetent financial organization."

The way it looked before the hearings, even if Webb and Comer were acquitted in the Aladdin case, the company would have a problem demonstrating the "pattern of corporate responsibility" that the casino law required of a licensee.

Webb's answer was to clean house by switching executives around its 67 subsidiaries. The dozen or so singled out by the gaming division in its report quietly vanished from the scene. Even Robert F. Johnson, after 45 years with the company, decided to retire and was replaced in July 1981 by Robert K. Swanson, formerly with Greyhound Corporation and General Mills, a man totally unblemished by events the division considered obstacles to the company's license.

To avoid being denied a temporary license in July 1981, when the Aladdin trial was still pending, Webb formed Claridge Management Corporation to take over its 50 percent interest, and an "institutional trustee" was named to handle financial transactions between the new company and Webb.

"With this plan, Del E. Webb will be completely isolated from the operation," Joseph Lordi told the press through a commission spokesman. This decision would mark Lordi's last official act as commission chairman. Under pressure since the Abscam scandal, and suffering from ulcers, he retired a year short of completing his five-year term.

Interviewed by the *Press*, Lordi said he was "very optimistic about the future of Atlantic City. I think this city is going to progress and progress and progress in the years to come. We've made tremendous strides already. Unfortunately, other aspects of the city haven't progressed at the same pace as casino gaming, but given a little support, I don't see why all of the things that were promised to the people of Atlantic City and the state of New Jersey wouldn't be achieved."

Six months later, Webb and Comer were acquitted in Las Vegas and the gaming commission allowed the company to reacquire its interest in the Claridge, despite the opposition of the division which warned that allowing a "suspect" company to return to Atlantic City posed "an unacceptable risk to casino gaming operations in New Jersey."

But Claridge attorney Nicholas Ribis predicted "dire financial trouble" without Webb's management help and an immediate infusion of some $10 million in new Webb funds. "Without them [Webb management], forget about us," D'Addario pleaded with the commission. He said that he and his partners had invested $40 million in the complex and Webb an additional $120 million and the investment was in jeopardy.

When the hearings for a permanent license opened in May 1982, new Webb Chairman Robert Swanson was optimistic. "I'm hopeful the commission will feel there really is a new Del Webb and we will receive our license," he said. "We have tried to eliminate the problems, and would have done so even without a division report, since we were going to turn Del Webb into an ethical company."

Robert F. Johnson, on whose back the blame for years of corporate corruption was placed, was not entirely out of the picture. Although he had resigned as the company's chairman, president, and director, he remained as president and director of the Webb foundation, the company's largest stockholder.

That didn't stop the current executives from ganging up on Johnson during the hearings. Several would testify that they held Johnson "responsible for the failures of the company."

As the first witness, Swanson spoke eloquently about the high standards of honesty and integrity he set from his very first day on the job. He had made "major management changes at all levels" in the last 18 months.

Ribis said the company has admitted to almost all the gaming division's allegations, but "since January 1981," Ribis said, "Mr. Swanson has created a new corporation, with new corporate planning, with new corporate ethics."

"The mere substitution of personalities does not serve to wash away all the problems this company has had," Flanagan reminded the commissioners. Despite its acquittal in Las Vegas, he added, the indictments raised questions about the company's "ethics and integrity."

To counter this charge, Webb hired former U.S. Attorney General Elliot Richardson. Richardson said he had reviewed documents from the federal case to see "whether the record as a whole raises any substantial question as to the honesty, integrity or good faith" of the company and found "no justifiable basis" to question its integrity.

Richardson, who gained national attention during the Nixon era for refusing to fire special Watergate Prosecutor Archibald Cox, assured the commission that his testimony was not for sale. "Mr. Ribis didn't know until last night what my opinion was going to be," he said. As far as the Aladdin case was concerned, Richardson acknowledged that it was true that some of Webb's co-defendants had taken kickbacks but there was no evidence that Webb or its employees did anything "improper," much less illegal.

It was also true that Comer and other Webb executives had known about the kickbacks and had done nothing about it. Even after Comer had been informed that some of the subcontractors who had complained to him about the kickbacks had finally gone to the FBI, he decided, after consultation with a Webb attorney, that his first responsibility was to complete the project. He testified that he was aware of the FBI and grand jury investigations in progress during the construction, but since Webb had done nothing wrong, he decided they had no obligation to become involved in the investigations.

"I didn't see enough to tie the Webb people with these activities to make them aware completely of what was going on," Richardson said. "There were flaws and defects in the behavior of some of the company's people," but there "is no evidence to support charges of duplicity." His advice was that the commission should "wash it out of the case" and judge Webb on its qualifications in other respects.

But, asked Flanagan, wasn't it every citizen's obligation to inform the authorities of a suspected crime?

"As a former prosecutor, I think that if every citizen exercised his obligation to tell the authorities about every suspected wrongdoing, we would be living in a very different society," Richardson replied. As for Comer and others turning a deaf ear to the reports of kickbacks that subcontractors were being forced to pay, Richardson said he wasn't "sure this would meet the grounds of conspiracy, whether Webb employees knew or guessed or inferred these actions. I think the bits and pieces taken out of this transcript really had hurt them [Webb Company]. Does this add up to enough to lead you to think the company is prone to behave dishonorably? I don't think it does. It's too thin, too fragmented and ambiguous."

On that note the company rested its case. The next day Webb announced that it had agreed to buy out D'Addario's group. A week later Robert Johnson was granted a separate hearing before the commission. As far as he was concerned, he had done nothing wrong. His only mistake was in trusting his top executives, many of whom had since left the company. If licensed, he promised to follow the lead of the company's board of directors in voting the foundation's stock.

When it came time for summation, the division suddenly relented and withdrew all its objections to licensing Webb. Its only opposition was to Johnson, who had agreed to resign from the foundation if his license was denied by the commission.

Without surprising anyone, especially the gaming division, the commission voted unanimously to grant a regular operating license to the Claridge.

In discussing Johnson's qualifications, the commission noted that the gaming division "conceded there was no proof" that Johnson "initiated" any of the "improprieties," but contended he must "share responsibility'' for failing to uncover and stop them. The commission found Johnson's explanations of his tenure as chairman ''credible,'' adding, ''We do not find any action or inaction on his part of such a nature as to render him unqualified.''

The Claridge was the eighth casino to be licensed in Atlantic City. Still waiting in the wings was the Tropicana, the last in the first wave of casino development in Atlantic City. A hotel-casino with a history as lurid as any in Las Vegas, its welcome into the fold, as with all the others, was never really in serious contention.

26

Putting On the Glitz

Governor Byrne wanted the old Ambassador Hotel demolished. He didn't want dinosaurs mucking up the Boardwalk. His new gambling haven deserved nothing but the best. The hotel, he said, "epitomized the deterioration of Atlantic City."

On November 9, 1979, the day the first bricks were knocked down, the governor was there to applaud the action. "I think that what is happening today is symbolic of the excellence that Mayor Lazarow and Senator Perskie—and I think I had a small part in it—have insisted upon in the redevelopment of Atlantic City. We didn't want to see Atlantic City redeveloped in a shabby way."

At his side was M. William Isbell, president of Ramada Inns, who was planning on erecting a splendid edifice on the ashes of what was once the "Monarch of the Boardwalk." Isbell was wearing a cowboy hat, a reminder that the hotel chain's corporate headquarters were in Phoenix, Arizona. And he was in a jovial mood. "On more than one occasion Governor Byrne has expressed an unusual amount of concern about these bricks," he joked.

Byrne pointed to the top floor of the building where workers were removing the brickwork. "That's the part I like. I'm not hung up on steel," he explained later. "I wouldn't recognize the steel work if it were new or old. I just think the hotel was a monstrosity."

Isbell could joke, but he couldn't have been too happy about Byrne's insistence on new construction. Ramada had paid $20 million for the Ambassador, which was a lot more than it had cost seventy years ago, and the cost for a new hotel of 528 rooms with a 48,000-square-foot casino was estimated at $139 million. The proposed renovation plan, priced at $80 million, would have converted the existing Ambassador into a 546-room hotel complex with a 60,000 square-foot casino, a 1200-seat dinner theater, a 1000-seat ballroom as well as roof-top tennis courts, a jogging track, and shops along the entire Boardwalk frontage of the property. And it would have allowed Ramada to open the facility within one year, while an entirely new facility would take over two years to build. But Byrne had called the proposal a "paint and patch job."

Joe Lordi had gone along with Byrne but he made a point of praising Ramada for its expertise in constructing and operating convention hotels in the United States and abroad. "Ramada," he said, "is the type of applicant most likely to make casino gaming successful in New Jersey." Yet the commission had to be very careful to ensure that it lived up to the spirit of the Casino Control Act to restore the city to being the Playground of the World. "Convention, vacation, and other potential visitors are more likely to psychologically be attracted to a newly constructed Atlantic City than a reconstructed Atlantic City."

Having been forced to capitulate, Isbell was now happy with the new project, calling it "symbolic of the casino industry's efforts to modernize and revitalize Atlantic City." However, when the commission had first rejected his renovation plans, Isbell had threatened to appeal the decision in the courts. "We are greatly distressed that the commission would apply to Ramada a whole new set of rules than it applied against previously approved casino developers." The commission, he pointed out, "has approved other plans to renovate existing structures which were far less ambitious or costly, architecturally less desirable, offering fewer luxury features and less convention capacity than that contained in Ramada's proposal."

In fact, on the same day the commission rejected Ramada's plans, it approved the Ritz's renovation proposal, described by one commissioner as a unique design: "It looks like the Wizard of Oz, but that's what you need in an adult fantasy land." Lordi was also impressed by the Ritz plan: "The existing structure disappears into a new, totally different, and integrated architectural visual experience." The Ritz decision would later come to haunt Lordi when Abscam was exposed and Senator Williams's taped remark that he and his attorney had sold Lordi and MacDonald a "bill of goods" came to light.

Interpreting Isbell's criticism as referring to Resorts, Byrne had hastened to explain that his position had changed from a year ago when he had pressed to have Resorts open by Memorial Day because "there was a great advantage of having Resorts open last summer," he explained. "Now we are applying standards based on what we learned with Resorts." Yet, while the state had not "compromised" on Resorts, a few things could have been done better. "Probably some of the windows in Resorts stick but they won't stick in future hotels. The accommodations could have been a little better. For example, I think the doors in Resorts could have been a little more elaborate—and the bathrooms." And then the governor reminded everybody that "Atlantic City is not—and we do not intend it to be—a casino city. It is a resort city."

While the governor worried about decor, Isbell had more serious problems on his mind. Out in Las Vegas earlier that November, the Nevada Gaming Commission had forced Tropicana owners Deil Gustafson and Mitzi Stauffer Briggs to surrender their gaming licenses. At that moment Ramada had announced that it was purchasing the Tropicana.

From its very beginning in 1957, the Tropicana had been a "Mob" joint. Always a poor money maker, the hotel was on the verge of bankruptcy in 1971 when it was sold to Gustafson, who described himself as a "Minneapolis entrepreneur." By 1974 the Tropicana was having a serious cash-flow problem caused by organized scams involving junkets of Detroit Mafia figures who gambled on credit that was never repaid. Ordered by the gaming commission to inject additional capital or face a shutdown, Gustafson sold a majority interest to buyers who a year later sold 51 percent of their stock to Mitzi Stauffer Briggs of San Francisco, a niece of the late John Stauffer, chief executive of Stauffer Chemical Company.

Next joining the scene was a group of investors called Associates of the Tropicana. The group's key figure was Joseph "Caesar" Agosto, who had arrived in Las Vegas in January 1975 and had been immediately appointed administrative manager of the hotel's *Folies Bergère* show, which the Tropicana had sold to a new company and leased back. Besides occupying a plush suite in the hotel's executive quarters, Agosto lived in a palatial home on the Tropicana golf course. He had achieved this lofty position in a matter of weeks without investing anything in the hotel or the show.

Five months later Agosto was propelled into the public limelight when an order to deport him as an illegal alien was upheld by the Board of Immigration Appeals. The Immigration and Naturalization Service (INS) claimed that Agosto's real name was Vincenzo Pianetti and that he faced a ten-year prison term in Sicily on a conviction in absentia for fraud and forgery. Pianetti, the INS claimed, had illegally entered the United States from Canada in 1951 using the name Agosto.

Agosto was released on a $10,000 bond pending an appeal. The gaming commission investigated Agosto for any links to possible hidden financial interest in the Tropicana and found none. Meanwhile, Agosto's mysterious influence at the Tropicana grew until he was literally in charge of the hotel's entire operation.

The mystery was solved when Agosto was featured in an FBI taped six-hour Kansas City Sunday conference held on November 26, 1978, that turned out to be an advance course in the intricacies of Las Vegas skimming—equally applicable to Atlantic City. Besides Agosto, it involved Nick Civella, Kansas City Mafia boss, his brother, Carl, the family's underboss, Carl "Tuffy" DeLuna, a caporegime and the family's most feared killer, as well as Carl Thomas, owner of the Slots-O-Fun and Bingo Palace in Las Vegas.

The transcribed tape ran over 600 pages and covered everything from murder to sex. Because of the length and complexity of the tape transcript, and the need for brevity and clarity, ellipses are not used to indicate omissions in the quotes that follow.

At the beginning of their conversation we learn that Nick Civella had decided to end a moratorium on skimming he had imposed at the Tropicana because he suspected that some of his functionaries were secretly keeping cash for themselves instead of passing it along to Agosto. The idea for the moratorium had been to expose the "leakage": if the house's win didn't increase by the amount Agosto had been authorizing the employees to steal, he would know they were continuing to snatch cash on their own. But after six weeks the moratorium had proved inconclusive and Nick wanted to call it off. The problem now was how to control the situation when they started stealing again.

The functionaries, headed by casino manager Don Shepard and his assistant, Billy Clinton Caldwell, had been recruited by Carl Thomas, who acted as the family's technical adviser on the skim. To control them, Agosto had the keys to the vault changed and had not given Shepard a duplicate as he had in the past.

"He should never had the key to begin with," Agosto said.

DeLUNA: Yeah, Nick [Civella] has to be familiarized with all this shit. Shepard had the key to the cage only due to Joe's [Agosto's] magnanimity, you might say. There was never no talk of no key to no cage when Carl [Thomas] put his crew in the joint to do this work, you know, and they had Junior stealing and other guys stealing with the jackets and best way they could steal here, there, wherever. So, he comes with this key shit. Now, they've got statutes on the keys.

AGOSTO: The guidelines by the Gaming Control Board say the key to the safe, you know, gotta be changed every so often, under the supervision of the Auditing Division. You see, the cage doesn't come under the casino manager. It comes under the cage manager and he's directly responsible to auditing.

NICK: Then nobody has access to it.

AGOSTO: Nobody has access to it. You see, that's the regulations so any time that he ask me to go in the audit department to subvert the system in order, so I can facilitate, so I can give him access to—I don't mind giving him access to, you know, the cage. But in certain cages they don't let the casino man even go behind the cage, inside the cage, they are to stay on this side of the cage. And I've recently ruled for him, you know, to let him go inside the cage and do whatever he wants to do, which is contrary to good principle regulations.

DeLUNA: Don [Shepard] was trying to more or less sneak in there at three or four o'clock—

AGOSTO: No, I'm talking about his counting-room key, you follow me? I still allow him to go in the cage and do whatever the hell he wants to do in the cage.

DeLUNA: Where is it he puts the fill slip? Count room or—

AGOSTO: In the counting room, in the boxes. You see he wants the key to the boxes. Nobody has the goddamn key to the boxes. When the time came to change the key I didn't give him a duplicate.

NICK: And you don't want him to have one and your position is you would rather—you are better off, or essentially we are all better off without him having one.

AGOSTO: By him having the key draws a lot of suspicion on the counting room.

NICK: And temptation.

In his explanation of the regulations that require new keys to be made at certain intervals, Agosto mentioned that it was against regulations to hire an outside locksmith. Nick is quick to see the opportunity.

NICK: Well, well, the in-house locksmith works for the hotel. That alone circumvents the system. So there could be a lot of scamming going on just with him. Is that correct?

AGOSTO: Well, yeah, if the locksmith is his man—

NICK: Which is what you say you have?

AGOSTO: Well, I have access to the key upstairs. Upstairs I'm in control of everything.

NICK: That's different than the counting room? I've lost you.

AGOSTO: In the administrative office we have access to anything.

NICK: How does the money get upstairs?

AGOSTO: The money don't get upstairs. I go downstairs and get it.

NICK: You go to the counting room.

AGOSTO: Yeah, I go down there to get it and then I explain to him [DeLuna] the mechanics I use.

NICK: Yeah, well, I'm really not, you know, concerned with what the mechanics are.

DELUNA: Well, his other concern is you tried to just drag it out of him just now and I don't know why he [Agosto] don't tell you bluntly like he told me. Giving this guy [Shepard] the key back, the duplicate key, gives him the ability if he so chooses to steal from us and we would never know it.

NICK: Yeah, it's temptation. Right, it's the danger.

AGOSTO: The danger is we have no control.

NICK: Yeah, all right—no, except we had the same danger with you, except we assume that you're with us closer and we don't have the problem with you.

AGOSTO: Yeah. Yeah, yeah.

NICK: Correct?

AGOSTO: I understand.

NICK: But you have the same temptation?

AGOSTO: Yes, but—

NICK: All we have from you is what you tell us, too.

DeLUNA: Yeah, but Don could put in fill slips.

AGOSTO: But I cannot put in fill slips. I got to put checks on it, which is my job and is very hard to do it.

DeLUNA: He's [Agosto's] stealing the money downstairs. Actual cold money. Then he puts a check in from the *Folies Bergère* to cover it. Then when the figures get upstairs to the administration office, he changes the figures and takes the check out.

NICK: Suppose you can't function for three, four days. What happens?

AGOSTO: The check will go through. That's the way I did it this month.

NICK: But doesn't it expose the system?

AGOSTO: Oh, definitely. My system is for an emergency situation.

This involved a long discussion of the new skimming methods being devised by Carl Thomas.

AGOSTO: I want to help him with all the assistance I can give him.

NICK: Without creating a lot of suspicion.

DeLUNA: The shot he's got going for him, the lady [Mitzi Stauffer Briggs] ain't there steady every day. Jack's [Jack Urich, a California oil man and business partner of Gustafson] not there full time. Gus [Gustafson] is not there all the time. But the lady got on a fucking period here a little while back where she was bitching and bitching and bitching about PC [percentages]. She'd harp on this game, she'd harp on that game. Well, if you remember, Joe out and out had a cold turkey talk with Jack Urich and Gustafson that we're going to have to take care of friends of ours. We're going to steal for them, too. That's been many months ago he told them that. Well, last night I asked him, I said, Joe, when the lady was on the rampage about the PC, I said do you think it could have entered the mind of Gus and Jack that, hey, what the fuck, maybe Joe was fucking us, you know, individually, not together. Gus asked him the other

day, said when we going to start taking stuff. You know why
Nick he wants to ask that question. Tell him what you did in the
last two months out of the business, in the black.

AGOSTO: We, we, our firm made its first half-million profit
[this month].

NICK: How many dollars per machine?

AGOSTO: About three hundred dollars a machine.

NICK: Well, good, you're now getting wise. See, that's being
done the proper way. You'll be minting money in there pretty
soon. Just bring some of it this way.

AGOSTO: I done it to the best of my ability, you know, with
the tools I have to work with.

NICK: I wasn't complaining. You don't have to take it personal. You could have taken that as a compliment.

Although Agosto's reply was garbled, it was obvious that he was
upset.

NICK: All right, let me put it different. Continue to bring
some, how's that? Sound better?

AGOSTO: That's better. That's better.

NICK: You're like my case worker used to be in jail. I had to
be very careful of the words. I walked into his office one time
and I said, "Good morning, Mr. H. I need a favor." He said,
"I don't do favors." I said, "Excuse me." I walked right out,
closed the door, and came right back in. I said, "I want to start
all over again. I need your help, Mr. H." He said, "That's better," and he gave me what I wanted, too.

When Carl Thomas joined them at noon, the conversation again
turned to skimming. During his twenty years of banging around Las
Vegas, Carl Thomas had worked in most of the big casinos and had
learned all the tricks of the skimming game. Told that the moratorium
on skimming at the Tropicana had been lifted, Thomas quickly laid
out his proposed scenario.

THOMAS: There's been some changes made for Shepard and
Caldwell to get the money. They must get back in the cage
before the count team comes or put the fill slip in or grab the
cash. They must have the security chief. They don't care about

Moran running corporate security, but they need the security chief that's on the outside door, won't let anybody back there, watch their backs. See, by changing those locks on those boxes and changing the time of the count team, there's no way you can move. The count team goes at eleven o'clock and when he wants to go back there at three or four, they're still there.

AGOSTO: The count team can always be changed, there's no problem.

Although Agosto talked fast and tried to put the blame for changing the locks on the comptroller, Thomas wanted everybody to know the importance of his men having duplicate keys.

THOMAS: We had to give him [Shepard] a key because it's the best system, they gotta get back there in the fucking bank. When you go back in the counting room, you go in the back and there's a mirror, see, and you hide from the glass, plus you're blocking the camera off—

AGOSTO: You cover the plunger, see. I have control of the camera. There's no problem with the camera.

DELUNA: Is it in your office?

AGOSTO: Yeah, I can shut the camera off.

NICK: How many keys are there for the lock?

THOMAS: There's two locks on the box. One key's supposed to stay in the cage, one key stays with the comptroller upstairs. When the count team comes in the morning, they come get this key and they get the key over here. Now what I've done for the last—I don't know how many umpteen years—when they take those keys, you have a key made that you keep in the palm of your hand and you go back that night. See, the cashier's with us. You follow me? You grab the cashier's keys, go in the vault, open the boxes, and snatch the money. I can remember one night in Circus Circus we had an obligation to meet. When I was young and had some balls, I guess. There were two guys from the state outside [the vault] and I was in there on my fucking back, snatching that money and they weren't as far from me as that refrigerator. Putting money in my pockets. I think if you do things out in the open, you stare the guy right in the face, the guy won't think you're doing nothing.

NICK: Sometimes the most obvious is the best way.

THOMAS: Yeah, well, what they've been doing in the past, which is very dangerous, is the fucking fill slip. You make a fill slip for $10,000, or any amount, but you've got to get the fill slip in one of the drop boxes [that are under each gaming table and later taken to the vault where the money is removed and counted]. The problem is that the Tropicana hasn't had that much cash in the past to snatch.

Fill slips are used by the casino manager and his assistants to get chips from the cashier's cage for tables that need them. The slips are in triplicate, stating the amount, and are signed by the cashier and the casino person receiving them. One copy stays in the cage. The boxman at the table receiving the chips initials the two remaining copies, puts the chips in the rack, and drops his copy into the drop box. The third copy stays in the pit until the end of the shift. When the drop box is opened by the count team, the slips in the box have to agree with the ones in the cage and pit.

THOMAS: So [when you're stealing] they would put the fill slip in the cage and instead of taking $10,000 in chips to the table, they take it in cash. That's why we need the cashier. Now this time instead of going over to a boxman at a table that's playing, they go to this game where the boxman has closed the game up. You get his initials and drop the slip in the box. Later that night when one of the three cashiers goes to lunch, Caldwell goes around this other cashier, talks to him, looks at a credit card, they do it all day long. Shepard goes to his cashier, gets the $10,000 and puts it in his pocket.

NICK: That's when they steal it?

THOMAS: Yeah, but it's very dangerous cause their names on them slips. Most amateurs get nailed cause they're making phony fill slips. You can look at a fill record and see where it'll jump up at you. Ten thousand this game. Then you go look at the credit cards. Well, who was playing that kind of game. Besides, some nights you just can't get the fill slip into the box, there's too many people watching, too busy, too much action. There's four dealers on the table and they're pretty sharp guys. They see the slip going in the box. Hey, Shepard's taking the joint off.

AGOSTO: Suppose I have a guy in the count team. Rocco,

he's in accounting, holds the slip in his hand and when he goes in with the count team, he opens the box and throws the slip inside.

THOMAS: That's a possibility, but your man's got to be a dumper. Every count team has a dumper, a caller, and counters. He's got to be the guy that opens the boxes and sticks the slip in as he dumps it. Got to do it with one move. The best way, once the drop [winnings] starts going up, is to go in [the vault] and just grab the cash and there's no record of anything, but he [Shepard] has got to get the keys [to the boxes], unless he goes some other way. Now the way I'd like to go—I could do it in my own joint, 'cause my joint's small and everybody belongs to me. But you can't do it in the Trop. See the best way to go in the Trop is the slots. It's always the best. Up until the scam in Argent [Stardust and Fremont casinos], everybody was making some money. And then the heat comes down and they put a new regulation on it, but you can still beat it if you got the comptroller.

AGOSTO: I have the comptroller.

THOMAS: No, what I mean by have, Joe, I don't mean you gotta have him to come in [unintelligible], see, you can feed the computers the wrong weight on the scales. You can snatch some money off, then you've got the guy in slots that's a hundred percent he'll do business with you. What we did at Argent, and I think we can set it up again, is set up a separate bank and a separate count for the slots. A little room with its own vault, everything separate from the tables. With that scale, I think we can beat it. I got the designs already on paper, space wise.

AGOSTO: If we can close them out on the weight—let's say I can control—

THOMAS: You have the guy counting slots your guy, and you can take Clyde and put him in auditing.

AGOSTO: Right, Rocco.

THOMAS: Yeah, whoever Rocco is, Rocco'll be your guy with Vince. Vince'll show you how to do it, but see, the problem in the past [the Tropicana] didn't have no bankroll. You can convert to cash. You skim off forty thousand a week in coins and grab forty thousand in C-notes and nobody knows that. My concept of this place is these guys hit the slots one month and the drop boxes the next. Never set a pattern. Then, Nick, if we could add a racing sports book, it would give us another tool for grabbing money.

NICK: The scales can be adjusted?

THOMAS: Well, no, the scales won't be adjusted, but the guy that reads the scales is your guy. I bought one of them [scales] myself, it cost me fifteen thousand, but my guy reads it.

NICK: Where do you draw the line? I mean where do you stop trusting people? How many people are involved?

THOMAS: Okay, at Circus Circus, the Riviera, at the Fremont, they had people and we had a ball. We had Frank and Caldwell, we had two cashiers and I got my comptroller, plus my security man's fronting it. McBride's outside the door, the cashier gives Frank the key, they go in and grab the money. The comptroller upstairs is not actually involved but we take care of him. Okay, same thing the Stardust does. There's not that many guys involved, but they gotta be key guys. Nick, the guy that's on the outside, the security guard, he don't know what's going on. He just knows they're back there. You pay this guy off anywhere from five hundred to a thousand a month, he's your guy. He knows something is going on but he don't know what or what magnitude or anything. These guys want to make a living, too, Nick.

NICK: Yeah, but they're weak spots somewhere down the line. They'll say, "Yeah, I let them in. I wasn't sure they were fucking around." But we have to have them.

THOMAS: Right. Because as the joints get bigger, they get tougher and tougher. Of course, you're putting yourself in these guys' hands, too. Now, I guarantee these two guys [Shepard and Caldwell]. They go back there, open the boxes and snatch the cash. I've used that system as long as I can remember. There's no record. They take the money and go off, they count it down, boom, boom, boom, boom. Now the bad part about that system, if they say they're grabbing two thousand a day, they could be grabbing twenty-four hundred.

NICK: Yeah, how do you know?

THOMAS: Nick, I only know it 'cause the guy's been with me fifteen years and always done what I told him. I just can't believe this guy will do that to me. I'd bet my life on Shepard. But you've got to realize what if they get nailed. Nick, you know what these guys are giving up? They'll never work again.

So you're asking these guys to jeopardize their livelihood. But, Nick, as much as I love you, as close as we are, you know better than anybody that every time I come here to see you, I jeopardize everything I have.

NICK: Absolutely.

THOMAS: I come out of friendship. Same way with these guys. They're taking this money because they're our guys. You've got to give them some leeway. If Shepard's taking an extra buck, shit, that's part of life. That's part of running this kind of business.

NICK: Now Joe's after a system to lessen the suspicion upstairs, downstairs, all the way around.

AGOSTO: Let me tell you, I'm not concerned about Gus and Mitzi and Urich. Because, if worse comes to worst, you know, we can work out something to satisfy them. You understand what I'm saying. I am very concerned with the hired hands, the people with the gaming board.

THOMAS: I know. You've got to beat the bookkeeper. You know, Nick, some nights me, Frank, Shepard, and my bookkeeper have sat around in my kitchen thinking for six hours of ways to beat these joints 'cause I like to take money out of them.

AGOSTO: How did it work at the Stardust? Maybe we can duplicate that system. If it worked there, why won't it work at the Tropicana?

THOMAS: Shepard at the Hacienda, with my cousin. I put one of my cashiers there. I had Caldwell at the Fremont.

NICK: All right, did you have a key to the box?

THOMAS: Yeah. The thing is, in those joints we had our own people. And if they weren't in, they would turn their heads.

AGOSTO: I told Carl myself that I'm not a thief on the ground level. I'm the thief on the fourth floor.

NICK: Get out of comparing to a thief, you just don't have—

AGOSTO: No, no, I don't know nothing about downstairs. No, because I never worked downstairs. So I cannot come up with a system downstairs.

NICK: Okay, you've got something upstairs that will take care of what we want to do.

THOMAS: He had an idea last night that was absolutely brilliant. If he ever gets this going it would take all the pressure off everybody out there.

NICK What was it?

THOMAS: With the show and with the Swiss bank accounts, everything. That is if we could get the Lido Show [at the Stardust] and the Folies show. And if we could get the money out of Switzerland.

AGOSTO: Now, if we were going to get the Stardust, I think we have devised a system up here where we could get money without going all through this shenanigan on the ground floor. Let's say we had the commitment of a million dollars a year, or a million and a half, or whatever it is. We can steal that here without us going downstairs.

NICK: Is there a limit on the commitment?

AGOSTO: Well, you've got to be within reason. The Stardust could generate a million dollars a year, without any sweat, and the Tropicana a half million. I'll say those type of figures—

NICK: [laughs under his breath].

AGOSTO: What? I'm serious, really, those are the type of figures that we could steal from up here.

NICK: The way you're making it sound is like you think that's a lot of money.

Later, after Carl Thomas had left for the airport, Nick said to Agosto, "You've got to have larceny in order to know how to figure it out."

AGOSTO: Right, but we got ours done.

NICK: They're always looking to lock up the loopholes.

AGOSTO: Sure.

NICK: And we're always looking to find ways to open them up.

AGOSTO: New loopholes.

NICK: That's the way it's got to be.

When the conversation turned to the connections Agosto had with state politicians and the district attorney, Nick said, "Boy, don't lose this guy, you know. Also don't abuse him, don't misuse him, don't [use him] for every little deal. In other words, save him for important matters." Then the Mafia boss added his own assessment of Las Vegas: "I believe that in time everyone out there, the fishes out there get corrupted. They can't help it. You know, they live right in the midst of it.''

Civella's courier was Carl Caruso, who had two nicknames: ''The Singer'' and ''Enrico,'' and operated junkets to the Dunes. During the time the FBI had him under surveillance, Caruso carried $280,000 in seven $40,000 ''sandwiches,'' the code word he used for the packages he received from Agosto, which he delivered to Carl DeLuna and Charles Moretina in Kansas City. Caruso received $1000 for his services, Nick Civella took his cut, and in compliance with an agreement he had with Chicago Mafia boss Joey Aiuppa, he had two underlings deliver $17,500 to Aiuppa in Chicago.

When the FBI arrested Caruso on February 14, 1979, at the Kansas City International Airport, they got a little surprise. Besides the $40,000 ''sandwich'' he was expected to be carrying, there was a second ''sandwich'' containing $80,000 in markers. Simultaneous raids were conducted in Kansas City and Las Vegas on the homes and cars of the Civella gang members and the Tropicana.

It would be two years before a federal grand jury in Kansas City handed down a 17-count indictment against 11 defendants, charging them with conspiring to use interstate facilities to ''unlawfully promote, manage, establish, and carry on the gaming operations of the Tropicana Hotel and Country Club.'' The suspects also allegedly transported money ''stolen and taken by fraud from the Tropicana'' to Kansas City and on to Chicago. The 11 named were Nick and Carl Civella, Carl DeLuna, Carl Caruso, Charles Moretina, Anthony Chiavola, Sr., Peter Tamburello, Carl Thomas, Joseph Agosto, Donald Shepard, and Billy Caldwell.

On the same day, November 5, 1981, a federal grand jury in St. Paul, Minnesota, returned a 32-count indictment against Agosto, Deil Gustafson, and four others for their part in a $4 million check-floating scheme that illegally infused millions of dollars into the Tropicana. Two Minnesota banks owned by Gustafson almost failed because they had honored worthless checks from the Tropicana.

Two years later Agosto and Gustafson were convicted and sentenced to 20 and 10 years, respectively. Both men then agreed to become government witnesses in the Kansas City trial. The way Agosto saw it, he didn't want to become ''another statistic like Allen Dorfman,'' who had been murdered in Chicago after being convicted in a Teamsters bribery case.

PUTTING ON THE GLITZ / 313

No charges were filed against Agosto for having defrauded the
Mineral Bank of Nevada of several million dollars in a similar
check-kiting scheme that had led to that bank's failure.

In the spring of 1983, only weeks before the Kansas City trial,
Nick Civella died of cancer. Agosto, the government's star witness,
didn't fare much better, dying of a heart attack only days after the
jury convicted Carl DeLuna, Carl Civella, Charles Moretina, Anthony Chiavola, Sr., and Carl Thomas. Peter Tamburello was acquitted; Carl Caruso was found guilty by stipulation; Shepard and Caldwell
pleaded guilty.

But now, in November 1979, the Tropicana was about to get a new
lease on life from Ramada—and so was Deil Gustafson.

Ramada's purchase was what is known in Nevada as the revolving-
door policy. It is when the old bad guys are supposed to sneak out the
back way as the new good guys come in the front door, thereby
creating a change in management without causing the slightest interruption in the casino's play.

In the Tropicana's case, however, most of the old bad guys stayed
right in place. In its investigation of Ramada's operation in Las
Vegas, the New Jersey gaming division reported that although Ramada was aware of allegations that the previous owners "may have
been fronts for organized crime and allegedly condoned a massive
skimming operation," a letter of intent on the sale indicated that
Ramada had originally approved giving Gustafson "the power to veto
any material changes in casino operations proposed by Ramada."
While image problems had kept that provision out of the final agreement, "there is evidence which suggests that Ramada may have
agreed to carry out such an arrangement through a verbal 'side
agreement' with Mr. Gustafson."

The reason Ramada considered such an arrangement was because
the sale price was to be determined by an "earnout formula" from
the Tropicana's earnings during the second and third years of operation under Ramada's management. The more profitable it was, the
more Gustafson would receive. Gustafson had refused to sell unless
he could exercise control over the new management.

Division Director G. Michael Brown disapproved of the deal.
"When you're dealing with someone being forced out by the Nevada
Gaming Control Board, you negotiate a fixed price," he said, "and
don't let the outgoing owners maintain any control over you."

In September 1979 the company's general counsel had provided Ramada President M. William Isbell with an analysis of Agosto's skimming operation, in which he stated, "It appears that the scheme survived for a significant length of time due to Agosto employing 'insiders' in certain key areas of the casino; i.e., cage and credit, security and the management of the games. Furthermore, because there were so many participants in the 'skim,' Agosto relied on the rest of the store to condone his activities."

However, said the division, "the issues and recommendations contained therein were never discussed by the full board." Yet 18 months after Ramada had taken over operation of the Tropicana, the division would complain that "approximately 75 individuals holding key positions within the Tropicana hotel/casino were employed by Ramada as holdovers from the previous management, including five individuals in the accounting department and 20 employees in job positions of cage, shift manager, cage manager, casino cashier and count room. Some of these individuals, such as Gamdolph V. Asciutto (Floorman—Dice) have questionable backgrounds. Consequently, the board lacked knowledge of significant facts concerning the Tropicana, thus effectively reducing its ability to provide meaningful direction and control to management."

As for management, "There was never a systematic attempt made by Ramada to identify holdover employees in key positions and take appropriate action within a reasonable period," the division concluded.

A year after it began operations, Ramada found itself with a real need of an asset protection plan to help it identify and eliminate sources of "drains" and "leaks" in casino revenues. It retained the firm of Philip R. Manuel Resources Group Ltd. to conduct a survey of management controls and accountability systems at the Tropicana. Although the report was kept confidential, the division said that it could be "summarized as being highly critical of the Tropicana operations, particularly in the areas of junkets, credit, and collections. However, its major criticism addresses the extensive percentage of holdover Tropicana managerial and supervisory casino employees allowed to remain after the Gustafson era.

"The report concludes, 'Based upon the results of this survey, the conclusion is inescapable that the Tropicana's casino management and supervision can be characterized as corrupt, weak, inattentive, and inefficient.' Its recommendation to Ramada management is that a complete 'overhaul' be conducted of casino management and supervisory personnel at the Tropicana.''

On August 19, 1981, Ramada announced the resignation of its chairman and chief executive, M. William Isbell, the 47-year-old son of the company's founder. No reason was given for Isbell's resignation.

Although based in Phoenix, Ramada's roots were in Chicago. Back in the 1930s its founder, Marion W. Isbell, Sr., owned several restaurants and coffee shops at a time when the Chicago Restaurant Association was dominated by the Capone Mob. Formed in 1914 to defeat legitimate unionization, the association was destined to become the victim of its own greed.

In those days the Mob used unions as one more tool in the pursuit of its ''protection'' racket. A threatened strike was settled with a payoff, not with increased benefits for workers. As long as the payoffs were kept within reason, the association was more than willing to go along.

To help maintain the proper balance, the association retained the services of Abraham Teitelbaum as its labor relations counsel at $125,000 a year, a king's ransom in Depression days. A former attorney for Capone, Teitelbaum had often stated, ''Alphonse Capone was one of the most honorable men I ever met.''

As his labor relations expert, Teitelbaum hired Louis Romano, president of Local 278, Chicago Bartenders and Beverage Dispensers Union, who was described in police reports as a psychopathic killer.

With Teitelbaum and Romano, the Mob's strategy had now come full circle: the Mob controlled the unions, and its attorney handled all of the restaurant association's ''labor relations.'' In effect, the money flowed in from both ends at once.

The arrangement was kept simple. Association members paid initiation fees and dues for a limited number of employees, who were not consulted and rarely knew they had become members of a union. The arrangement usually continued for years. Dues were collected on members who had changed jobs, left the state or county, or even died. It made no difference to either party in the deal.

Association members contributed to a ''voluntary fund''—aside from their regular membership dues—for use when labor troubles arose, which happened with unerring regularity. Mediator Teitelbaum somehow always managed to arrange ''settlements'' at a cost that kept the voluntary fund flowing from the restaurateurs to the gang-

sters. It was a classic "sweetheart" arrangement, for the restaurateurs were still coming out ahead by paying below-scale wages, the
lowest in most instances in the country. There was something in it for
everybody but the workers.

By the time the McClellan committee (Senate Select Committee
on Improper Activities in the Labor or Management Field) focused its
attention on the Chicago Restaurant Association in 1958, violence
had become part of the arrangement.

Testimony before the committee disclosed that 40 restaurants
[nonmembers of the association] had been destroyed by arson in the
18 months preceding its hearings in July 1958. Before the Mob's
collusive invasion of the industry, there had been about one or two
cases a year. A total of 39 unsolved murders were linked to the
criminals under investigation. Another bombing and arson epidemic
flared up in 1963 and by the end of 1965 the score totaled 124.

In its Second Interim Report, dated October 23, 1959, the McClellan committee said, "Evidence adduced at Committee hearings estab-
lishes conclusively that it [Chicago Restaurant Association] has
functioned in recent years principally to defeat and destroy legitimate
unionization and has callously and calculatedly used men with underworld connections to make collusive arrangements with dishonest
union officials. There is additional undisputed testimony that gangsters and hoodlums were employed to handle the association's labor
relations . . ."

The committee found that Teitelbaum and some others hired by the
association as labor consultants were nothing more than Mob fronts
who funneled money which was in effect extorted from a "voluntary
contribution fund" to organized crime figures and corrupt union
officials in exchange for labor peace, nonunionization, and protection
from arson. And in some cases, the nonprotection from arson of
nonassociation members.

Marion Isbell became a member of the restaurant association in
1938 and served as its president between 1942 and 1945, thereafter
becoming a member of its board of directors. During their years of
working together, Isbell and Teitelbaum developed a close personal
relationship that lasted until Teitelbaum's death in 1980. In the
interim, Teitelbaum had served several prison terms for tax evasion
and other crimes.

According to the New Jersey gaming division, Marion Isbell "mini-
mized" his relationship with Teitelbaum during his first interviews

with division investigators, "denying friendship with Teitelbaum and maintaining that Teitelbaum was more of a nuisance than anything else."

The division's report stated that all Isbell could recall was that Teitelbaum had once appeared in Phoenix, "apparently destitute and requested a personal loan. He could not recall the specific date and indicated that he loaned Teitelbaum approximately $5000 which was never repaid, in order to 'get rid of him.' . . . He testified that he was not aware of the findings of the McClellan Committee or that Teitelbaum had invoked the Fifth Amendment."

It defies credulity that Isbell was unaware of the committee's findings when it was front-page news for weeks in Chicago, with many of the stories carrying Isbell's name as the man who had signed the contracts with Teitelbaum.

In 1953 Teitelbaum had fallen into disfavor with Accardo and had subsequently lost his magical arbitration touch. It was a story that continued for years to make headlines in Chicago. On orders from Accardo, two Mob thugs, Paul "Needlenose" Labriola and James Weinberg, had threatened to push Teitelbaum out of his office window. Also labor racketeers, they had organized the Cook County Licensed Beverage Dealers Association to shake down owners of liquor establishments. They wanted to make their association a rival organization to the Chicago Restaurant Association. A few months later, in typical Chicago fashion, they were garroted and their bodies stuffed in a car trunk. The whole sordid story was repeated dozens of times during the McClellan hearings.

After obtaining various documents that indicated additional contacts with Teitelbaum, the gaming division reinterviewed Isbell under oath. With his memory refreshed, Isbell conceded that in 1969 Teitelbaum had settled a nine-month-old strike at a Phoenix Ramada Inn in two days and had been paid $7500 for his services. Later that year, Isbell wrote a letter of reference for Teitelbaum, praising him for settling the strike and for his fine work with the Chicago Restaurant Association, closing with: "I personally recommend Mr. Teitelbaum as a man of great ability and integrity."

In 1973 Isbell drafted a letter to all Ramada Inn operators requesting favorable rates for Teitelbaum's son. The next year, when Teitelbaum was serving a 2–20 year sentence for grand theft and violation of state corporate securities laws, Isbell wrote a character letter to the California Parole Authority which stressed Teitelbaum's personal honesty and integrity. In 1979 Teitelbaum was interested in acquiring a Ramada Inn franchise in Guatemala City, and Isbell drafted a memo to the Franchise Division with instructions to follow up on the inquiry and a letter to the manager of the Ramada Inn in Antigua, asking for courtesy to Teitelbaum and his associates.

Marion Isbell's first hotel acquisition was the Flamingo in Flagstaff, Arizona, built in 1954. The name "Ramada Inn" was first used in April 1959 when signs were erected at three locations and Isbell began selling franchises. By the time the company went public in 1962, the Ramada Inn chain already had 25 motor hotels in Arizona, New Mexico, California, Louisiana, and Oklahoma, as well as 15 licensed franchises.

Expansion was rapid in the 1960s and investors came and went quickly in those early years. They were just names, none of any apparent importance, except perhaps Jerrold Wexler, board chairman and president of the Jupiter Corporation, which owned 7.5 percent of the Ramada chain in the early 1960s. Because Wexler's Jupiter Corporation (now Jupiter Industries, Inc.) was financed by Teamsters pension fund loans, there had been published allegations that Jupiter was Mob-connected, but the gaming division found that "the statement that 'the Ramada Inn Chain was in part built by Jupiter' has been unverifiable. The Division has not identified any Ramada Inn built by Jupiter or with funds provided by it. The Division has interviewed Jerrold Wexler, Marion Isbell, and M. William Isbell [Marion's son] regarding Jupiter's association with Ramada Inns and each of them deny the published allegations."

With the Teamsters and Mob issues resolved, the division turned its attention to the chain's meteoric growth. In eight years it had gone from 3 motels to 200 motor hotels and into the luxury resort hotel field. It had spawned a dozen or so subsidiaries that specialized in construction, interior designs, mortgage banking, hotel equipment and supplies, franchise services, computerized reservations, restaurants, and the acquisition of a medical complex in Oakland, California, consisting of a general hospital, medical offices, extended-care facility, and six convalescent centers.

Two years later, when Marion's son, M. William Isbell, became president in 1970, the Ramada chain had grown to 311 motor hotels and had started its international operations through a new division called Ramada World Wide, Inc. The next year three more general hospitals were acquired. By the time Ramada came to the Tropicana's rescue it was operating 644 hotels and motels in 18 countries. A remarkable achievement for an uneducated orphan boy whose start in the business world was as a dishwasher at the age of 16.

It was an astonishing success story, a Horatio Alger epic, and yet, besides its horrendous miscalculations in Las Vegas, there were a few more problems that didn't sit too well with the New Jersey gaming division.

There was the $250,000 "finder's fee" paid to James G. Ryan, a convicted felon, for acting as Ramada's advance man in the purchase of the old Ambassador and Deauville hotels in Atlantic City. At the time of his association with Ramada and its president, William Isbell, Ryan was free on bail pending an appeal of a federal conviction on a 12-count indictment for mail fraud and was awaiting trial on charges of conspiracy to deal in counterfeit U.S. Treasury bills and perjury.

Because they had a "general awareness" of Ryan's background, the "$250,000 finder's fee was paid to him by the sellers . . . out of the proceeds of the sale," the division reported. "This method of payment was effectuated at Ramada's request after it agreed to pay a corresponding $250,000 increase in the total purchase price. Ramada caused payment to be made in this fashion in an attempt to disassociate itself from Mr. Ryan and minimize or conceal its true involvement with him."

When it purchased the property, Ramada assumed a mortgage held by a group of investors who included John "Johnnie Gray" Wademan, a convicted loanshark and associate of Ruggiero "Richie the Boot" Boiardo and other members of the Genovese Mafia family. For a $5000 investment Wademan had bought an 8.3 percent interest in a $4.8 million mortgage that was to earn him quarterly payments of $26,114 over the life of the mortgage.

"The Johnny Wademan hidden interest is a classic example of what we are trying to prevent," Mickey Brown said. But it was a "situation that occurred without the knowledge of the present owners."

There was also the charge that Ramada had received $158,000 in illegal rebates from Seagrams, but after an SEC inquiry the arrangement had been discontinued, and by now the division was getting somewhat inured to sleazy business practices.

Still the division's report angered the Isbells. William Isbell, who had been completely separated from the company, said the investigators were wrong in their charges against him and his father, Marion, who had not only resigned his honorary position as board chairman but had placed his stock holdings in a trust.

The elder Isbell was more caustic in his comments, calling the report a "hatchet job" that made untrue statements about him and his son. "For over seventy years, I lived with a clear record," he said, "and now in the last few years of my life, they are trying to make me a crook."

By the time the gaming commission was ready to open its hearings on a permanent license in October 1982, there was no one left in the Ramada organization who could be associated with past indiscretions. All that remained to talk about was the company's financial stability.

Its Boardwalk casino, initially projected to cost $130 million, had cost overruns that boosted the price to a record $330 million before its opening date and was expected to reach $400 million before it was completed a year or so down the line, making it the world's most expensive gambling resort. This for a hotel with 521 guest rooms and an average-size casino. You could bury the whole place in a single wing of the MGM Grand in Las Vegas, which has a casino larger than two football fields and 2800 rooms within its nearly 3 million square feet—and yet cost $126 million.

The question uppermost in the division's thinking was one that nobody really expected to be answered: Had the Tropicana been ripped off by corrupt unions, politicians, and construction companies? Like most of the Boardwalk hotels, the Tropicana was built on a schedule known as "fast track" construction: working crews around the clock, with architects sketching plans only hours before they are implemented. Even if the division was sincere in its desires to get at the answers, the paperwork would take years to unravel. One thing was for sure: lots of people had made lots of money, and in the end it would all be written off for tax deductions.

Spurred by the high cost overruns, the FBI began what it characterized as a "comprehensive probe into the construction industry in Atlantic City, specifically as it relates to the casinos . . . with possible organized crime involvement in casino construction," as well as widespread bribery involving a number of construction firms.

U.S. Attorney W. Hunt Dumont said, "There have been millions of dollars in cost overruns on these projects. We have been attempting to determine how such overruns could have come about." Dumont said that casino developers are virtually "dictated" what contractors to use for various aspects of the projects. At the same time, he pointed out, developers were routinely "squeezed" to pay commercial bribes to avoid costly delays. "Since a casino may lose $600,000 a day in gambling revenues for every day it is delayed from opening, a lengthy delay could mean the difference between success and bankruptcy for a company. It's easier to pay off than face difficulties on the job site. It's the price of getting up on time."

Fast track or not, the Tropicana lost its gamble for a July 1981 opening. A partly completed hotel would open in late November and it would be another year before it would get its permanent license.

The completion of the Tropicana marked the end of the casino building boom in Atlantic City. Nine new glitzy gambling complexes had come on line and the last of the old hotels had fallen victim to the wrecker's ball. City officials called this era the "first plateau" and predicted that the second boom in casino construction was just around the corner. Meanwhile, the citizens the officials had been elected to represent still had to learn to live with this one.

27

The Mayor and the Mobsters

Standing on a table, Michael J. Matthews waited patiently while the band played and his happy supporters shouted their way through a medley of election victory songs: "For He's a Jolly Good Fellow" and "Happy Days Are Here Again."

It was June 15, 1982, a historic moment. After seventy years of bureaucratic bungling and rampant corruption under a commission form of government that had been tailor-made for the likes of Nucky Johnson and Hap Farley, but had floundered miserably since their departure from the scene, the disgruntled citizens of Atlantic City were finally going to have a popularly elected mayor and a nine-member city council.

If ever a city needed a change, it was this one. But it had been long in coming and divisive in its rebirth. Many residents still longed for the good old days of Nucky and Hap, when bossism, corruption notwithstanding, at least got things done. Under the iron-fist discipline of their political machines, the weaknesses of the commission government had gone unnoticed.

Without a boss to keep them in line since Hap Farley had bowed out in 1971, the five commissioners had acted like jealous despots fighting to protect their personal fiefdoms. They had submitted a separate budget, competed for political power and prestige, and haggled and horse-traded among themselves for any advantage that would perpetuate them in office. It was government by deal-making at its most basic level. When unable to arrive at gratifying compromises, they had waged costly legal battles, at the city's expense.

As one former commissioner put it, "There was no leader. You needed three people out of five for anything. It lent itself to trade-offs. You support me one time and I'll support you the next. If you question my budget, I'll question yours."

The compromises and constraints made effective government impossible. It was government by one-upmanship. It also made for abuse of power and corruption. No one better demonstrated these weaknesses than the five commissioners elected in May 1980: Joseph Lazarow, who acted as mayor, Joseph Pasquale, Edmund Colanzi, Willie B. Clayton, and Michael Matthews.

Even before taking office, they had decided to seek a 60 percent pay raise that would have made them among the highest-paid public officials in the state. "I feel the salaries are fair, considering the responsibilities we have," Lazarow argued at the time. "We work plenty of hours. There are many sleepless nights. And we take a lot of gaff and guff from people." The increase would have boosted his pay to $49,000, but the salary hikes were reduced to 27 percent by a petition drive—the only weapon the voters had to protect themselves from their elected representatives.

The commissioners retaliated by buying themselves new luxury cars—at the city's expense—for both official and personal use. "We want to show people we drive around that it's a classy city, not a dump," explained Pasquale, who had taken leave as the city's deputy police chief. This was the same Pasquale whose name in 1970 had surfaced on an FBI tape-recording of a telephone conversation between Gyp DeCarlo and Frank Ruggieri—Pasquale, then a police sergeant, was identified as a bookmaker and gofer for Ruggieri and Farley. The references, as they pertained to Pasquale, were eventually discarded by his superiors as unsubstantiated chatter.

Commissioner Colanzi added fuel to the fire of public protest when he used his car, a 1980 Chrysler New Yorker, for a vacation trip to Disney World in Florida. When a Police Department employee refused to fill Colanzi's car with gasoline, Colanzi sponsored an "obedience" resolution that required city employees to obey all five commissioners, regardless of their individual departmental jurisdiction.

Clayton, a career policeman, became public safety director and took over supervision of the police department. His first action was to appoint Albert Peyton, a hot-tempered patrolman with an arrest record, as his deputy director. Before public outcry had a chance to subside, he proposed giving Peyton a new luxury car. He then promoted 20 patrolmen, including Peyton, to sergeant, despite impartial reports that the department was top-heavy, and then tried to promote himself to deputy policy chief.

For a while Clayton stood at the center of a public firestorm that was not quelled by his suggestion during a radio interview that prostitution be legalized or decriminalized. At Clayton's urging, Mayor Lazarow appointed a civilian task force to review police operations. Among cronies and city employees named to the panel was Lazarow's wife and Clayton's wife, brother, and sister-in-law.

While his fellow commissioners were battling the public and the media, Michael Matthews had cleverly slipped into the role of maverick by opposing most of their harebrained schemes. Over the next two years, he became the voice of reason in City Hall—a characterization not entirely accurate.

An accountant by profession, Matthews' first important political office was as a member of the Atlantic County Board of Freeholders in 1971. A month after his election, he announced he would oppose Joseph McGahn in the state senate race. Unlike his opponent, he promised not to tie himself to special interest groups. He supported the upcoming gambling referendum, calling for a casino industry "very similar to a Las Vegas style." Las Vegas, he said, "has eliminated almost all of the criminal element in that town by an effective means of policing free enterprise." As for organized crime, "Legalized gambling would eliminate much of organized crime in the state. It would be competition for the gambling syndicate, effective competition."

Preliminary tallies had him winning the senate race by 166 votes, but the final count gave McGahn 51 more votes. Matthews threatened a lawsuit seeking a recount, saying "It's not my style to give up," a phrase that would become his motto as his political skirmishes grew more bitter in the next few years.

There were those who questioned his motives. They knew of his hatred for the McGahns. It was this hatred that had led him to being called before a grand jury in the spring of 1973. In a conversation tape recorded by an undercover agent, Matthews had tried to enlist the agent's help in planting narcotics in McGahn's car as a means of sabotaging his campaign.

When the grand jury probe became public in the final weeks of the campaign, Matthews lashed out angrily at the McGahns: "The proof is certain that Pat McGahn and his stooges have connived and schemed and plotted this whole dirty stinking mess." Matthews later abandoned his lawsuit, and the grand jury was quietly disbanded without taking any action against him.

Barely out of that mess, he announced he would challenge William Hughes for the congressional seat of the second district, which meant he would be taking on the top guns of the Democratic party: Senator McGahn, Assemblymen Steven Perskie, and Charles Worthington, all Hughes supporters. It was no contest. And it led to more bitter recriminations.

Only days after the loss, Matthews declared he was planning to "pull out of politics—at least temporarily and maybe permanently. It leads to this," he said. "I guess I don't have the money to compete and the thing is that apparently I don't know my political place, because I won't accept being dictated to, nor do I believe in patronage, nor will I be intimidated, and as long as I keep those kinds of principles, the big money I'll never see. And elections are still being bought. Maybe I'm before my time, or after my time, but it certainly isn't my time."

But it was his time in 1977 when he was elected to the assembly on a campaign theme of honest government. He triumphantly told his supporters on the night of his victory: "I want to clean up the position of politician in New Jersey. I will try to remove any smell of conflict of interest. I'm very intent on disallowing any legislator from deriving one cent based on his political influence."

For voters who had lived a lifetime in a morass of political chicanery, these were uplifting words. "I feel that politicians have given politics a bad name," Matthews said at his first press conference. "I know morally what I want to do. Now I have to convert that into legislation." His campaign expenses had totaled only $10,000, he said, and 70 percent of it had come out of his pocket and most of the rest from bank loans. "I have no obligation or commitment to anyone except the people who elected me."

Already in 1977 Matthews was worried that the awaited casino bonanza would not be fairly distributed. "The city has a tendency to fleece everybody," he said. "They just take advantage of people. I hope it doesn't happen [with casinos]. I hope they have more class." And he was worried about minorities. "A lot of people are going to want a piece of the action," he said. "The minorities in Atlantic City right now, for all intents and purposes, are going to be excluded. Should they be, because they don't have the financial resources to build a palace?''

He was reelected to the assembly in 1979 but not without the familiar cry that his political enemies were plotting against him when he was cited and fined by the Election Law Enforcement Commission for failing to report contributions collected at a fund-raising dinner. When newspaper reports revealed that he had received $1000 in credit from Resorts International on three occasions, he shot back that the ''inference stinks. Yeah, I borrowed money. I also borrow money from banks, I borrow money from Sears, from Sunoco, so what. I won't let anyone question my integrity.''

With his integrity intact, he announced that several union leaders had asked him to consider moving into Atlantic City and running for the city commission in 1980 and later for mayor if the effort to change the commission system should succeed.

His most enthusiastic supporter was Frank Gerace, president of Local 54 of the Hotel and Restaurant Employees and Bartenders International Union, which had already been identified by the State Commission of Investigation as being under the thumb of Nicky Scarfo. It would be four years before the degree of Gerace's and Scarfo's enthusiasm would become known.

Matthews moved into Atlantic City in November 1979, registered to vote, and five months later threw his hat into the city commission race. When informed that his registration failed to meet the two-year residency requirement, Matthews charged, ''It's a cheap political trick. Somebody must be running scared.''

He would get his ''lawyers lined up,'' he said, and when he lost in the lower court, he attacked the judge, and the appellate court when he lost there. ''It's apparent that these big money interests expect monetary gains if I'm not elected. I'm suspicious there is a coward who won't come forward.'' Twelve days before the election, the state supreme court ruled in his favor. His election margin was the smallest of the five commissioners.

''I can work well with anybody,'' Matthews said on election night. ''I'm committed to harmony.''

There were many who would dispute that claim as he became embroiled in numerous clashes with his fellow commissioners which he defended as efforts to ''stop these guys from running rampant.''

''There's always a fear of the unknown, and I think some of my fellow commissioners are paranoid with my presence, but I do not tell lies to my fellow commissioners," he said. "I get the feeling they think there's ulterior motives behind everything I say or do."

His motives were no more ulterior than those of the politicians he served with. They all wanted to be mayor. When it came time to run for the office under the new system in the spring of 1982, Pasquale and Colanzi, unable to muster sufficient support for themselves, reluctantly aligned themselves behind Matthews.

His opponent in the mayoral election was James Usry, a black community leader who was an assistant superintendent of schools and a former member of the Harlem Globetrotters. In a televised debate, Matthews had charged that Usry "compromised his position" by accepting $3500 in campaign contributions from Pat McGahn, Resorts' attorney and political functionary. Backing Matthews was the McGahns' archrival, Senator Steven Perskie: Perskie's law firm contributed $2500 to Matthews' campaign, and Perskie and his allies helped to run Matthews' race.

Perskie was worried about the voters getting "a bunch of clods in there." Among the 46 candidates for city council were some "who by their manner, style, and lack of substance could destroy the city government," Perskie warned. Such a fate could spell perpetual political doom for the city. "I don't know if there is such a thing as a last chance. But if there is, this is it for the city."

Gathered in the ballroom of the International Motel on the night of the election, Matthews' supporters shouted "Go! Go! Go!" as Senator Perskie wrote the returns on a large tally board. When the last ward was in and Perskie had scribbled in the total vote, the crowd let loose with a mighty roar.

At that moment Matthews came into the ballroom and the crowd started singing its medley of victory songs. Afflicted by a bad back, Matthews walked haltingly, his face drawn and beaded with perspiration, his eyes dulled by painkillers. As the band played "McNamara's Band," friends gently lifted Matthews onto a table so he could address the happy troops.

He waited for the noise to subside, a taut smile on his handsome face. At 48, with his hair stylishly long, Matthews still cut a dashing figure in his three-piece suit.

"Will you still love me in September?" Matthews called out, drawing an appreciative roar from the predominantly white crowd. "I love you all very much," he said. "You all worked so damn hard.

To pull out that kind of vote and still have a squeaker is unbelievable.'' His victory margin was 359 votes.

"There were some things during the campaign that were not very
nice,'' Matthews conceded. "I'm looking forward to talking with Jim
[Usry] and working with Jim in the transition. I want to be a mayor
for all the people.''

The things that "were not very nice'' had been downright divisive, polarizing voters along racial lines. At Usry's storefront headquarters some 15 blocks away, there was no band, no dancing, no
ice-cube-clicking toasts to the future.

"The battle is not lost,'' Usry told his supporters. "The victory
will be won. I am still your candidate. There is no concession
because we have not lost.''

There was "hanky-panky'' in the absentee ballots, Usry's campaign manager, Bernard Fulton, told the crowd. The official vote
count by his campaign people showed that Usry had won the election
by 23 votes. The District Attorney's office was impounding 643
absentee ballots. "There is a cloud over this election, and we have to
follow it to the nth degree,'' Fulton said.

Two weeks later, on a sunny, breezy July 1, Michael Matthews
and five councilmen were sworn in on the steps of City Hall. The
inaugural ceremony was billed as one of a "gala'' series of events.
But the new government of Atlantic City was off to a less than festive
start.

While Matthews was promising "unity'' and "no division along
racial, religious, or political lines,'' four black councilmen, who had
boycotted the ceremony, were holding their own swearing-in ritual
inside City Hall at what was described as the "alternative'' ceremony. The keynote speaker was James Usry.

The night before the inaugural Usry had charged that roughly 500
voting irregularities had been discovered, including the voting of
nonresidents. "When Mr. Matthews is sworn in tomorrow, he is the
mayor,'' Usry said. "However, being mayor tomorrow does not
mean that he will be mayor two months from now . . . The election
was a robbery. The fight's not over yet.''

The rhetoric had grown heated. "I would rather drink muddy water
and sleep in a hollow log than get sworn in with the mayor,'' one of
the rebellious councilmen declared.

"I don't really give a rat's tail whether they get sworn in with me or not," Matthews had replied. "I think they're being foolish. Some people don't realize the election is over."

But it was not over. Alleging massive voter fraud, Usry took Matthews to court. After 17 weeks of testimony the case was dismissed, but the mayor was left with an $80,000 legal bill and a divided City Hall. That bill would become the subject of further litigation when Matthews tried to force the council to pay it on the grounds that it was the city's responsibility to finance any successful legal defense of the mayor's office.

Battle lines were drawn when Matthews announced plans to make appointments to government posts without consent of the council. Again Matthews was back in court, this time asking for emergency power to run the city. In time the forum for political action would shift from the city council to the courts. It took six months to adopt the administrative code needed to establish the new departments and set guidelines for the new government.

When the court gave him authority to make certain appointments Matthews packed the new planning board with his friends, naming as director Thomas Russo, his campaign's finance manager. Many old faces rejected by the voters gained high positions, with Colanzi becoming transportation director and Pasquale police chief. The same old characters were doing business at the same old stand.

His appointments prompted more litigation; this time the court ruled in favor of the council, giving it the power to make appointments to the various boards and authorities. Matthews' appeal was unsuccessful. In the end, only the planning board remained under the mayor's jurisdiction.

Then when Governor Thomas Kean, Brendan Byrne's successor, appointed members to the new Convention Hall Authority without consulting Matthews, he attacked the governor over what he called his "unilateral" appointments. The dispute became so bitter that Kean joined with Usry in a recall petition to oust Matthews from office in a special election.

The reasons for the recall were rather vague. The petition charged him with failing to keep campaign promises and with packing City Hall with supporters, failings that have been rather standard form among politicians. The recall petition was followed a year later by another with even more signatures.

The attorney Matthews chose to fight the recall movements was his close friend Edwin Jacobs, Jr., who had gained notoriety as a Mob lawyer, having represented Philip Leonetti first in the 1977 murder of Pepe Leva and then in the 1979 murder of cement contractor Vincent Falcone. The second recall petition was filed on December 3, 1983, three days before the FBI stepped into the picture to deliver the coup de grace.

On the evening of December 6, 1983, FBI Special Agents James B. Darcy, Jr., and James McGuigan waited in the parking lot of the Knife and Fork Restaurant in Atlantic City. At approximately ten o'clock, Michael Matthews came out of the restaurant, and Darcy approached him as Matthews entered his car. Darcy would later reconstruct the scene in court.

"Good evening," Darcy said, showing his badge to Matthews. "I'm with the FBI. I'd like to talk to you."

"Certainly," Matthews replied. "Why don't you jump in?"

Darcy quickly explained that Matthews had been the subject of an FBI Atlantic City corruption investigation and that the man Matthews knew as James Biacco was actually James Bannister, an undercover agent with the Drug Enforcement Agency (DEA). When Matthews became agitated, Darcy said, "Relax, you're not under arrest. But don't say anything that can be used against you." Then Darcy told him the FBI had three tapes and were willing to let him listen to them. "There isn't anything you have to do. It's of your own free will. We just want you to listen."

Matthews shrugged. "It doesn't hurt to listen," he said, and offered to drive Darcy to his apartment. Darcy agreed and McGuigan followed them to the mayor's bachelor apartment. At the apartment Matthews listened intently as the first two tapes were played. The first concerned a meeting on April 13, 1983, between Matthews and Bannister, posing as James Biacco, and involved a contract between the city and Flag Chemical. The second covered the mayor's accepting a $3000 payoff.

When Darcy went to play the third tape, Matthews said, "I don't want to hear anymore. That's my voice. I believe you got everything on tape."

The person who had introduced Matthews to "Biacco" was Frank Lentino, a former Teamsters official who was an organizer for Frank Gerace's Local 54. Lentino's "primary responsibility," according to an FBI memorandum, "is to directly supervise the leadership of a number of labor unions [including Local 54 and Teamsters Locals 107 and 158] for the Scarfo organization.''

Back in 1980, while working undercover for the Drug Enforcement Agency, Bannister, using the alias of Biacco, had purchased $5000 in drugs from Lentino, to establish his relationship with Lentino, whom investigators wanted to use as a guide to lead them to Scarfo and Atlantic City rackets.

A year later Biacco again appeared on the scene, posing as a sales representative of Flag Chemical, a dummy FBI company supposedly selling janitorial supplies. Biacco and the 72-year-old Lentino became friendly. In the course of their socializing, ''Lentino repeatedly stated to [Biacco] that the Scarfo organization was able to completely control and dominate Matthews' office—so long as their demands were not too unreasonable,'' the FBI memorandum said.

In 1981 Leonetti and Scarfo, through Local 54, had secretly contributed $150,000 to Matthews' campaign in return for promises that he would ''use his influence, upon being elected mayor, to assist the Scarfo organization.'' Scarfo's money helped put Matthews in office, a Mob payoff not reflected in Matthews' campaign records.

''Lentino has disclosed, in intimate details, the hierarchy and the operation of the Scarfo organization and identified its members, associates, and their criminal activities,'' the FBI memo said. Lentino told Biacco he took his orders from Leonetti. To get Biacco accepted by the Scarfo Mob, Lentino had lied to ''Leonetti and others'' by telling them that ''he [Lentino] had been criminally involved with [Biacco] for 10 years.''

And to gain Biacco's respect, Lentino had boasted about his complicity in conspiracies to distribute heroin, methamphetamine, and cocaine, to commit arson, to sell counterfeit gold coins, to extort money in return for labor peace, to operate a brothel, to threaten a union official by holding a gun to his head, to suborn perjury, to destroy documents, and to commit perjury and obstruct justice in the Vincent Falcone murder case in which Scarfo, Leonetti, and Lawrence Merlino were acquitted.

Now in Matthews' apartment, Darcy said, ''It looks real bad. I'm not a lawyer but I think we have a good case against you. We just want you to look at it. I don't want you to tell us about it. Anything you say can be used against you.''

The two agents and Matthews drove to FBI headquarters in Linwood. On the way over Matthews was quiet as Darcy ticked off the litany of crimes the mayor was believed to have committed during the government's 22-month undercover investigation. What he did not mention was a conversation between Matthews and Biacco at the Peking Duck House, an Atlantic City restaurant, on November 18, 1983.

During lunch that day, Matthews had conspired with Biacco to sell a marshy 21-acre parcel of city-owned land, known as the H-Track, near Harrah's Marina casino hotel in the city's inlet section, to a group of investors called Piedmont which Biacco claimed to represent. Excerpts from that taped conversation follow:

BIACCO: Did Frank [Lentino] ever straighten out those lot things with you?

MATTHEWS: Well, what I did was—I was speaking with Phil [Leonetti] on Sunday. I said, "Phil," I said, "send somebody up that knows." I said, "I've got in my office a whole color-coded map that shows who owns what. And if you send somebody up that knows what the hell they're talking about to see what you want." . . . Like I told him [Leonetti], I need somebody to show me. . . . And I know Resorts is interested in buying it, and a few others. So, that's the only time I have rulings on property, is when we have to put it up for auction bid. . . .

BIACCO: Did Phil and Frank tell you what your end was going to be in this thing? See, when this thing was brought to me by these people, they gave me fifty thousand dollars out front, okay, to get the thing firmed up commitmentwise, okay. I can do with it whatever I want to. Plus, when the deal was finalized, I get five points. Well, I told Frank I would divvy up the point, and we'd divvy up the money out front, so that everybody gets assured here. So I don't know, you know, it's been taking so long.

MATTHEWS: Yeah.

BIACCO: I just, you know, we're on the verge of losing something. I mean, you're talking a point. Regardless of what they plan, it's going to be a minimum of two hundred thousand dollars, to each of us involved. You know, down the line, but still we got to get some action on this thing. . . . I said, "Frank, listen, I'll give you ten thousand plus a point. Phil will get a point and ten thousand for the [Scarfo] organization. And then we'll give Mike [Matthews] a point and ten thousand.'' Okay? As soon as we get this thing lined up, we can do it.

. . .

BIACCO: The thing is, what would be the first step? You would have to see what the land is?

MATTHEWS: No, the first step is that . . . I'd want to know what they want to use it for. I can very discreetly get appraisal prices. And say, okay, this is minimum bid. And then throw it out to council and I'll put a resolution from me. That I want to bid this land. That we just want to bid it. And then we have, probably, an auction bid with the check. Just say for the sake of an argument, the land is worth five hundred thousand dollars. So we ask for each bid to be presented with a certified check for five thousand, or something like this. And then you have an auction bid. Some of these guys, like Resorts, really doesn't need it.

BIACCO: Well, they just would like to try to buy as much as they can.

MATTHEWS: Sure, but if we hit them by surprise, they don't know it's coming off. Put a little ad in the paper, something like this.

BIACCO: Say we're successful in getting the land, then we have to go to the planning board first?

MATTHEWS: Well, if you want something after that, yeah, the planning board's mine. That's mine. No problem with the planning board. Whatever you want with the planning board. In fact, what I need to know, is there anybody in Atlantic City that doesn't work for the city that we can all trust. I got a full-time appointment to make on that [board]. We got another alternate, another full-time, I need somebody I can trust. A guy just died last week. And one guy said he wants to put his grandson on that. He wants his grandson. The thing is, it's not my control, it's his control. It's Mike Marshall, who's done me some favors in the past, but he's getting a little dangerous.

BIACCO: Yeah, you need somebody that you can definitely control.

MATTHEWS: And the thing is, and I got myself and Tom Russo, you know, that's definite. And I've got a couple others. I mean, I control all of them, but it's nice to have that trust.

'Cause the chairman, he'll listen to me too. Two black people are in there just for show and tell, you know.

. . .

MATTHEWS: Make sure you have all the insight, before anyone else bids on it. And then we can figure out some strategy. . . .

BIACCO: I'll tell you what I was going to do today, okay? I was going to offer you out of the fifty [thousand dollars], there is an extra ten because there's four people involved, I was going to offer you the extra ten. Just so we can get some movement on this thing, fast.

MATTHEWS: I'm going to talk to my guy down there with, you know, a little more intelligence, so I can tell him what I want.

BIACCO: See, tell you something too. I really don't like to step on anybody's toes or screw anybody in the deal either, that's the thing. That's why when I originally was offered this thing I discussed it with everybody and I said, now because this is how we're going to have it, it's going to be divided up this way. So, you know, I don't know what Frank had told you what your end was going to be or anything like that. But—

MATTHEWS: Well, he didn't say much, because we were always in my office. But Phil [Leonetti] indicated the first time he mentioned it to me that we could all do well.

. . .

BIACCO: Like I told you, I got fifty thousand out in front to get this accomplished. Now I can give you ten out in front. You can have that now. The extra ten I didn't want Frank to know about it.

MATTHEWS: Okay, what I'll do is talk to Tom on the side after we talk Monday. I'll talk to Tom. I'll say, "Look, Tom, you know there's something in it for you in order for you to straighten it out right now, this is what we want done." . . . I'll take care of him.

It was a long lunch and not all the conversation was shop talk. Separated from his wife, Matthews' thoughts would often turn to his swinging-single lifestyle. Excerpts follow:

MATTHEWS: I just got a letter from a guy from Antigua. . . . I met him once at a cocktail party. And I was sitting at the pool, no one knew I went there. I hear this, "Mayor Matthews." He said, "I told someone last night I think we have the mayor of Atlantic City with us." And he says, "The assistant vice-president and I run this whole operation for my company. I took the liberty to go in and check the records." Well, I was signing my right name. He says, "Do you have a suite?" And I said, "Well, no, I asked for the best room, and this is all they gave me, what I have." He says, "Well, we don't have many suites, we don't advertise them, for the high-rollers." 'Cause they have a little casino there. He said, "I'll move you into a suite for no extra charge." I said, "Fine, when can I move in?" Then he called his principals and took me out to dinner and he says they're comping the whole thing. I said, "Jesus Christ." Well, see, I went to check out and the woman says it's fourteen hundred dollars. So I paid it. Okay, well, you know, maybe something happened. He calls me up the next day and he says, "a terrible mistake. There's an envelope for you at the desk." I went down there and got all my money back. No one knows that story. . . . I mean they treated me so royally down there. I was in the casino and one guy's giving me bottles of Jack Daniel's and French water, you know, to take back to room. I said, "Fuck that. I don't want to drink in the room." "Well, just in case, take it back to the room." And if they saw me at the bar or something, they'd pick up everything. And then I had the comp and ate out dinner at all the restaurants every night.

BIACCO: You went down with your girlfriend?

MATTHEWS: Yeah.

BIACCO: I guess there really isn't any way you can travel without your girlfriend or wife.

MATTHEWS: Oh, Christ. I went down there with some girl. Boy, was she built. And I would say I think she was from Germany. Speaking of travel, I picked a girl up last year. I picked a Polish girl. I had to stay away from her too much because she didn't have her green papers yet. I mean, it's illegal. I didn't find this out until—I mean she was working as a waitress in a restaurant. Absolutely gorgeous. And built. She can't speak very much English. . . . At first I thought she was Italian. So I called her up one night and we got together. So then . . . I said call me and I'll get you a better job. So I got her a job at Playboy. Then she calls me up and broke the news.

She says, "I don't have my green papers." And I said, "What the hell does that mean?" Then I found out what it meant. She shouldn't be here. Now she got a lawyer working on it. I took her to New York. It was my birthday, got a limousine, and took her up. Bob Guccione [owner of *Penthouse* magazine] invites me over to his place. So I'm in his mansion up there. It was Bob and his girlfriend, Kathy. I said, "I'll take this girl." A private dinner, he had, and all the people waiting on us. Then he brought out some homemade ice cream with a candle in it and gave me a little present, and gave her a present. You know, really nice.

BIACCO: That's nice. Yeah.

MATTHEWS: The next night we went out with some ex-congressman from up in New York. I had this goddamn suite in the Carlisle. Gorgeous suite. Expensive. Two-fifty a day. But what the hell. So, I went, I figure I got the limousine free, I ate the dinner for free. I went to see *Chorus Line,* which was comped to me. So all I had to do was pay for the goddamn room, you know, and some food. For the whole weekend there it cost me a few hundred bucks, but that'd be like a two-thousand-dollar weekend.

At FBI headquarters Matthews was questioned by Assistant U.S. Attorneys Peter Bennett and Stuart Peim, and three FBI agents, including Darcy. Bennett informed Matthews that his appearance was voluntary and that he was free to leave at any time. Asked if he had been drinking or was on medication, Matthews replied he had had one drink at the restaurant and was not on medication.

According to an FBI memorandum detailing the events of the next 36 hours, "Matthews stated that he desired to discuss the case in detail."

Bennett "explained in detail the violations of Federal criminal statutes that Matthews has participated in relating to his receiving payoffs from the undercover agent in the amounts of $1000, $3000 and $10,000. He was advised that each violation subjected him to a 20-year sentence if convicted. Bennett advised Matthews that if he fully cooperated with the government to include, but not limited to, testimony against other subjects in this investigation the government would consider allowing Matthews to plead guilty to one 20-year count." The government retained the option of seeking a lenient sentence.

Full cooperation meant that Matthews would have to divulge everything he knew about the criminal activities in which he had participated and be willing to take polygraph tests to verify his truthfulness.

When Matthews appeared receptive to the idea, he was taken into another room to talk to "a former public official convicted for violations similar to those discussed above." Matthews "expressed appreciation for the opportunity." The two men talked privately for about an hour and afterward the mayor said he was ready to cooperate fully with the government, even to wearing a concealed recording device while meeting with the Mob members involved, to testify against them in court, and to enter the federal witness protection program.

With Matthews in a cooperative mood, they talked until dawn. During that conversation, the mayor, according to the FBI memorandum, orally "confessed in total to his involvement in each of the crimes" of bribery and extortion alleged against him, and provided the following information:

• He had received $14,000 in payoffs from Biacco for purchasing supplies from Flag Chemical and for promising to help expedite the purchase of city-owned land.
• Before he was even a formally declared candidate for mayor, Matthews had met with Frank Gerace, Albert Daidone, and Frank Lentino, all officers of Local 54, and "made it clear . . . that he needed approximately $125,000 to win" the upcoming mayoral election. On December 16, 1981, at a meeting at Giovanni's Ristorante in Folsom, Lentino gave Matthews the $125,000. An additional $25,000 was contributed on May 25, 1982, to finance Matthews' runoff election— Matthews' brother, Robert, acting as courier, accepted the cash payment directly from Scarfo and Leonetti at a meeting in the Lido Restaurant. "Ken Shapiro was introduced to Matthews as a contact between Matthews and Gerace, Daidone, and Lentino. Daidone was responsible for the introduction. Matthews stated he understood that Gerace, Lentino, and Daidone were speaking to him as representatives of the organized crime family headed by Nicky Scarfo."
• With that kind of money involved, Matthews and Shapiro became fast friends. "Matthews has met with Ken Shapiro almost every

weekend since his election. Matthews understood that these meetings were as a result of the financial support from the Scarfo group furnished through Shapiro and were to discuss matters of interest to the Scarfo organization.''

• It was at Shapiro's condominium in Margate that Matthews met with Leonetti and Arthur Pelullo to discuss Biacco's H-Tract land deal. ''Matthews stated that Leonetti advised him that he would make money on the deal in return for placing the city-owned property up for sale.'' Matthews, Leonetti, and Lentino were to divide $668,000 if the deal was consummated.

• Three days after the Peking Duck House lunch, ''Matthews stated that he met with Biacco [who gave him] $10,000. Matthews understood the money was for expediting the sale of the city-owned property, and that he would receive an additional $10,000 and one point interest'' valued at $200,000. And in return for assisting Flag Chemical sell its janitorial supplies to the city, he received $4000 in payoffs.

• He used his accounting business to launder payoffs and he used hidden business interests in Florida to disguise his ownership in some projects.

• He met with Leonetti on numerous occasions and once he sought Leonetti's help after being threatened by a businessman. Leonetti had quickly mediated the dispute.

• But Matthews was terrified of Leonetti. He was convinced that Leonetti was involved in at least four unsolved Mob murders: Giuseppe ''Pepe'' Leva, Judge Edwin Helfant, Vincent Falcone, and Louis DeMarco. ''I want to fully cooperate,'' Matthews was quoted as saying to Darcy. ''These guys are a bunch of animals. I want to help get them off the streets.''

At five o'clock that morning, before FBI agents drove Matthews to his apartment, Bennett warned him to stay away from Mob lawyers. ''I told Mr. Matthews that one of those good friends to whom he had looked for advice was Ed Jacobs. I pointed out to Mr. Matthews that Ed Jacobs represented Mr. Philip Leonetti in connection with a number of proceedings. 'You've got to understand we'll make a judgment,' I told him. 'If you go to Mr. Jacobs and solicit his advice with respect to our proposed offer of taking a plea from you and getting your cooperation, you're going to be telling him about Philip Leonetti, because you've had dealings with Philip Leonetti in connection with this case. You will create in Mr. Jacobs a conflict. Mr. Jacobs may feel duty-bound, one, to tell you he can't represent you, also duty-bound to Philip Leonetti.' ''

After they arrived at his apartment, the agents waited while Matthews went to the top shelf of a closet and retrieved an envelope containing $7000 of the money he had received from Biacco and handed it to the agents. That evening he returned to the FBI office and gave them an additional $1000.

At that time it looked like the FBI's gamble to use Matthews to ensnare Leonetti and others had paid off. But within a matter of hours he changed his mind. The deal was off. He was innocent of any wrongdoing and he would see them in court. In searching for an answer, the FBI said that Leonetti had discovered that Matthews had met with them. Darcy would later testify that Matthews had contacted him and said, "I'm scared to death of these guys, not so much for myself as for my family."

The next day the FBI raided Matthews' City Hall office and seized boxes of documents. Planning Director Thomas Russo, who had been Matthews' campaign treasurer, was hustled out of a crowded banquet hall at Bally's Park Place and carted off to City Hall where he turned over the contents of a locked cabinet containing details of Matthews' campaign finance records. No explanation was given to the public, which led to wild speculation in the press. Matthews was nowhere to be found.

Some councilmen were outraged, but Council President Henry Tyner was willing to give the mayor the benefit of the doubt: "I can understand him wanting to go away and get himself together and to plan his defense. My gut reaction is that I would not have gone, but let's not condemn the man because he went away."

Tyner was sitting on top of his own little powder keg. Only two weeks before a story in the *Press* had proclaimed:

MYSTERY PLAN TO GIVE CASINO $100 "BARGAIN"

ATLANTIC CITY—City officials cannot explain the origin of a proposed ordinance that would enable Caesars New Jersey, Inc., to pay $100 for a city-owned parcel [Shinn Terrace] valued at more than $700,000.

All of the city councilmen contacted Tuesday denied authorship of the measure, which would cement Caesars' plan to acquire the prime piece of casino-zoned property at minimal expense and proceed with its multimillion-dollar expansion project. . . .

As council president, Henry Tyner has ultimate control over City Council's weekly agenda. He said, however, that he was unaware of the existence of the . . . ordinance until he arrived at City Hall on Tuesday. "I was surprised today when I saw it on the agenda," he said. . . . Despite the confusion over the ordinance, Tyner said he did not disagree with its intent. He said he will not push it because of the opposition of other councilmen. "I'm not going to get into a bloodbath over it," he said.

At first Caesars insisted the parcel was worth no more than $50,000, but ended up paying $500,000 for what they almost got for $100.

The state police began an investigation and discovered that not only had Tyner authorized the preparation of the phantom ordinance, but he had been distributing business cards that identified him as a sales representative for Silvi Concrete, a major subcontractor working on Caesars' $70 million expansion site. Questioned by the press, Tyner explained that the business cards had been printed prematurely in an apparent attempt to "lure" him into accepting the job. He admitted to pursuing the job to draw "extra income," and that negotiations had produced a preliminary "typed agreement," but that "nothing had been firmed up." He conceded that his actions could create "the illusion of a conflict," but maintained that it had nothing to do with his authorization of the ordinance.

Some time later Tyner was cleared of criminal wrongdoing after he passed a state-administered polygraph test, which ended a grand jury investigation into the episode. He would later "firm up" his job with Silvi Concrete and begin drawing that needed "extra income."

Gradually, as the drama began unfolding, more information about James Bannister's role as undercover agent Jim Biacco was leaked to the press. In the summer of 1980, while posing as a wheeler-dealer land developer with financial backing from a French company interested in building a casino in the city, Biacco had been at meetings attended by Lentino, Robert LoCicero, president of Toro Construction Company, and Vincent LaManna, Jr., a municipal judge in four Cape May County towns.

During meetings at the Cafe Brajole in Atlantic City, Lentino and

LaManna promised Biacco labor peace if he channeled construction contracts to firms approved by Scarfo. In one of the meetings, Lentino told Biacco that Scarfo, through LoCicero, would pay him a $50,000 kickback for the first concrete contract awarded to any of the Scarfo-approved firms, preferably Toro Construction. LaManna promised to structure the money made from the deal in a manner to beat federal taxes. It was at one of these meetings that Lentino agreed to supply Biacco with illegal drugs.

When Tom Russo was interrogated by the FBI at City Hall, Matthews' former campaign treasurer had disclosed that in late November Matthews had handed him an envelope containing $2000 in hundred-dollar bills, saying it was from a man named Jim Biacco. Russo said he deposited it into the account of "The Friends of Matthews Campaign Fund," which had been set up to defray the costs of Matthews' ongoing court battle against the recall petitions. What he neglected to tell the agents was that the deposit was made on December 8, the day Matthews decided to renege on his promise to cooperate with the government.

The only communication from Matthews was a letter to his secretary that said: "To whom it may concern: I will be taking a short vacation. While I'm gone, Ms. Kitty Johnson will be in charge with all my powers."

In its probe of corruption in Atlantic City, the federal grand jury was looking into the possibility that the Scarfo Mob was attempting to infiltrate the casino industry by sneaking in "through the back door" —that is, using financial leverage to gain influence over Matthews and other city officials.

"They wanted to be in a position where anyone interested in a corrupt deal would have to go through them, and they would have to give their 'blessing' before the deal could be approved," a federal source explained.

Matthews' involvement with the Scarfo Mob went much deeper than his deals with Biacco. One example was Seatex Associates, Inc., an umbrella company with seven associations that had acquired vast landholdings in Atlantic City. The principals in Seatex were Barry Shapiro, brother of Matthews' close friend Ken Shapiro, and Elliot Goldberg.

One of Seatex's associations owned a 60 percent interest in Columbus Plaza Associates, which was planning to build the city's largest parking structure on a city-block-sized site it owned, a project Matthews had enthusiastically lobbied.

From April through late July 1982 Seatex was the subject of a state police investigation. Surveillance at its Atlantic City address revealed that it was a hangout for organized crime figures. Visiting the Shapiros at Seatex during those four months, before and after the June 1982 mayoral election, were Scarfo, Leonetti, LoCicero, Lentino, and Matthews. Other visitors coming on a regular basis included three soldiers from the Lucchese family and one from the DeCavalcante family, all with extensive police records. Matthews' frequent visits to his good friend Ken Shapiro were not without political benefit. Shapiro collected $65,000 from contractors and business people, including at least $35,000 in cash that was used by Matthews "for has own personal benefit." In July 1983 the parking garage proposal received unanimous approval from the zoning board for its variances.

Another Shapiro company Yacenda Associates was also favored by Matthews when it obtained the right to buy, without competitive bidding, the Old Garwood Mills site, a city-owned four-acre tract in the Northern Inlet section zoned for future casino development. At the time it received its approval to purchase the land, its declared intentions were to build 125 moderately priced housing units. Matthews would later claim that he was unaware of Shapiro's financial involvement in Yacenda.

Then there was Arthur Pelullo, owner of General Ambassador Limousine Corporation. One day in February 1983 Matthews had had an idea. Turning to Russo, he said, "Wouldn't it be neat if we took a limo to Florida. We could play cards all the way down." Matthews explained, "I knew Artie had a limo business and I asked him, 'What would it cost?' " And so Matthews, Russo, Councilman James Sykes, and mayoral aide Thomas Manning enjoyed a leisurely ride to Florida.

A few months later Pelullo's Ambassador Limousine Corporation became one of only two firms awarded the right to use space in the city airport terminal. The other firm, Casino Limousine Service, agreed to pay the city 37.5 percent of the gross income earned from using the space, more than twice the amount—15.5 percent—paid by Ambassador.

Matthews said his Florida vacation had nothing to do with Ambassador getting the airport space. They had paid for the service. At that time he had known Pelullo all of one month. "He was a friend of mine," he said. "He knew about my dilemma [about raising funds for my legal costs], and he was interested in doing business in Atlantic City, very interested in Atlantic City in general.''

Not to be outdone by the Feds, the state police launched its own investigation into what it called "irregularities" by the mayor, councilmen, and other city officials—past and present—in several transfers of city-owned land to casinos. "They're doing their thing, and we're doing ours," was the way one state official put it.

On December 19, ten days after he had left town, Matthews appeared at the federal courthouse in Camden. One newspaper reported that "it was an uncomfortable situation for the mayor, who spent much of the afternoon avoiding eye contact with Leonetti," while their respective attorneys were meeting with prosecutors and the federal judge in charge of the grand jury. Around five o'clock, Matthews left the building with an unidentified man and returned a half hour later—the unidentified man had been observed most of the afternoon speaking with Leonetti. When asked by reporters where they had gone, Matthews said they left to check their cars in the parking lot. Another newspaper reported that Matthews and Leonetti had arrived at the courthouse in the same car.

The mayor appeared as breezy and flippant as ever. Asked if he would resign, he replied, "Where did you get that? I'm not planning to resign at all." As he had insisted all along, he said, "I've never walked away from a good fight yet. They've got a tiger by the tail.''

Asked if he had received a letter from the Justice Department telling him he was a target of their investigation, he said, "I don't know. I haven't checked the mail." As for his absence, he had spent the ten days in Florida, a golfing vacation. Asked if he was concerned with his safety, he laughed, "Only by getting hit by a golf ball." His golf game had been terrible, he complained. "My God, I three-putted so many greens. You don't know how slow they were."

At City Hall the next day, when asked what he would say to the people of Atlantic City concerning the FBI investigation and his disappearance, he said, "I'm glad to be back. Merry Christmas and Happy New Year." Pressed for a more responsible answer, he snapped back, "Who do I owe an explanation?"

Although he refused to talk about the investigation, he acknowledged having met Scarfo "a couple of times," adding, "I didn't know anything about organized crime. Organized crime is something I read about in the newspaper."

It was more real for U.S. Attorney W. Hunt Dumont. "The state has done a good job keeping organized crime out of casino management," he said, "but organized crime is insidious. It has found other ways to infiltrate the city—through the hotel unions, the Teamsters and construction unions, and in ancillary industries."

The new director of the gaming division, Thomas R. O'Brien, believed that the Mob was "significantly involved in ancillary services" such as laundries, junket organizations, liquor and food suppliers, and vending-machine companies. "Once a Mob-oriented group, through a front, is able to do business with a casino, they can work a system of extortion and kickbacks."

In January, Matthews' six-year stint in the Assembly ended. He conceded that his critics were right. It was "too big a job to be both the mayor of Atlantic City and a member of the Legislature," he said. "Near the end, there's no question in my mind that I got too tied up with Atlantic City and its problems. I'd have to say that I probably did that at the expense of the rest of the county."

Two months later he was dethroned by a two-to-one vote in a mayoral recall election. His response was that he was staying put. "I will spend the rest of my damn life, if I have to, fighting the damn judiciary," he said. "I am sick with the whole judiciary system." He charged that Judge Philip Gruccio, who had refused to grant an injunction barring James Usry from taking office, had been influenced by Governor Kean and state Republican leaders in exchange for advancement in the judiciary. "His [reward] will come in November," he said of Gruccio. "He will be elevated."

As for Usry taking over the mayoral suite, Matthews would "take care of him. Even though he is bigger, I can probably take him." He refused to acknowledge Usry's overwhelming victory at the polls. "I'm going to court tomorrow. They're still short [of petition signatures]. The recall is illegal. People will be indicted, will go to jail, for false swearing."

The next morning dawned on another bizarre and chaotic day in Atlantic City. While attorneys for Usry and Matthews were in court arguing whether the recall election was legal, hundreds of Usry supporters were demonstrating at City Hall. Police Chief Pasquale warned the court that the crowd could turn violent if Usry was not promptly inaugurated.

On that day, the casino commission announcement that gamblers were dropping $5 million a day in Atlantic City went virtually unnoticed. Equally unnoticed by gamblers and casino workers was the turmoil at City Hall. The spectacle at City Hall was of no importance to them.

"In the opinion of many people here, last week's events vividly demonstrated the overriding fact of life in Atlantic City," Fen Montaigne wrote in the *Philadelphia Inquirer*. "The casino industry is king, and the stumblings of the city government in the last six years have made very little difference to the gambling halls."

A month later, the federal grand jury returned indictments against Matthews and Lentino, charging conspiracy to commit extortion "under color of official right," attempted extortion, and two counts of extortion. Matthews also was charged with violating the Travel Act by traveling in interstate commerce to accept $65,000 in bribes from Kenneth Shapiro.

According to the 27-page indictment, "It was part of the conspiracy that Michael J. Matthews would receive payoffs, approximately $150,000, from associates of the Scarfo Organization in return for his agreement to corruptly influence the governmental processes of Atlantic City for the benefit and profit of the Scarfo Organization and its associates by: 1) Extorting money for himself and the Scarfo Organization from various businesses seeking to do business with or in Atlantic City, and, 2) Corruptly utilizing the power and influence of the Mayor's Office to assist projects and businesses identified by associates of the Scarfo Organization."

The indictment listed specific meetings between Matthews and "members of the Scarfo Organization" at which the terms of the agreement were sealed. Shapiro, who was named an "agent of the Scarfo Organization" in the indictment, was given immunity in return for his testimony before the grand jury. Leonetti was named as an unindicted co-conspirator. Asked why he was not charged in the indictment, U.S. Attorney Dumont said, "You will hear more from us on this matter. This is truly a continuing investigation."

Reached in his Lauderhill, Florida, hotel room, where he was vacationing, Matthews said he would return to Atlantic City "whenever I run out of clean clothes."

At the arraignment on April 12, while Matthews waited outside the courtroom, reporters asked how he felt about the upcoming hearing. Matthews, neatly attired in a slate gray pinstriped suit, shrugged and replied, "In the words of Doris Day thirty years ago, *que sera, sera* [what will be, will be]."

Later that day, the mayor of Atlantic City was escorted from the courtroom in handcuffs and leg chains. But the confident smile was still there for the cameramen. While members of his family scrambled to raise the $300,000 bail, he spent four days in jail.

The *Press* predicted a rather unrealistic possibility in the event that the mayor was convicted. "Critics of the 1976 casino gaming referendum warned that corruption and organized crime infiltration of government would be a by-product of casino gambling. Even those people, though, must be stunned by the magnitude of the indictment. The repercussions could be so strong that the Legislature might even start to think about ending the casino experiment."

In May 1984 Matthews was hit with a second indictment. He was charged with accepting $10,000 from realtor Lou Zaris in exchange for approval of plans to build a new McDonald's restaurant, including zoning variance for a 65-foot sign. And that he received another $1000 from Zaris for the owner of the Merrill Lynch building, who sought variances for rooftop signs.

Then in July Matthews' defense team was dealt a crucial blow when U.S. District Judge Harold Ackerman ruled that Matthews' confession could be used against him in his upcoming trial. In a related ruling, Lentino failed in his effort to strike from the indictment all mention of the Scarfo Mob, with Ackerman ruling that the allegations "are not irrelevant to the crimes charged."

During legal arguments over the admissibility of taped conversations, the government claimed that two conversations linked Matthews and Scarfo to the acquisition of a brothel. Matthews, sitting at the defense table, laughed and shook his head in disbelief.

Five weeks into his trial, Matthews stood up and pleaded guilty to one count of extortion. Saying that "greed got the better of me," he admitted taking a $10,000 payoff from the undercover agent." But he denied he had ever conspired with any members of organized crime. "I want to take this opportunity to apologize to your honor," he said, "and the citizens of Atlantic City and of course to all my family and friends."

Later, outside the courtroom, Matthews told reporters he had made the decision because of the stress the trial had placed on his family. "A wise man once told me that sometimes the best way to win a tug of war is to let go of the rope."

On December 31, 1984, one week before his 51st birthday, Matthews stood before Judge Ackerman and awaited his sentence. For once the smile and good humor he had maintained throughout the ordeal was missing. He appeared pale but composed.

"As I listened on November 27 to the plea of guilty which you entered," Judge Ackerman said, "I think I heard from an individual who I might describe as dapper, debonair . . . and it sounded like a press release, not a plea of guilty. For the most part it was a lot of hot air. It was delivered with a paucity of contrition.

"Fifty years ago, an individual was elected mayor of a particular city. He was a short, dumpy individual with a squeaky voice. His hair was never styled. I don't remember ever seeing a picture of Fiorello La Guardia with a suit that fit him. But he was absolutely incorruptible. He spent his life working for the city of New York. He spent every waking hour trying to help the people. Fiorello La Guardia left a legacy that has never been equaled. He served the people and his name is respected to this day.

"When I think about La Guardia, I think about you—because you served the people shamefully. The people of Atlantic City thought they were electing a mayor, not a crook, because that's what you turned out to be, a crook."

Judge Ackerman had a lot more to say but the important words came after his statement: 15 years in prison and a $10,000 fine. Not only that, but the judge refused to recommend that the U.S. Bureau of Prisons assign Matthews to a level-one minimum security institution. "You don't rate it," he said.

Moments later Matthews was whisked out of the courtroom in handcuffs. Three weeks later the former mayor of Atlantic City was on a prison bus headed for the Federal Correctional Institution in Seagoville, Texas, a trip, he complained, that took an "ungodly" 15 days.

Next to enter a guilty plea was Frank Lentino. "I regret my participation in the crime," he told the court. "I'm extremely sorry for the mental anxiety I caused my sick son and the pain I caused my lovely wife," he said, wiping tears from his eyes.

"You made a very good deal with the government because you really rate more time," Judge Ackerman told him. "Because you're a real pro. To some people, you are the salt of the earth. To other people in the know, you are far less. All of the good deeds on one side, all this evil on the other side." Then the judge gave him ten years in prison and a $10,000 fine.

A few months later, and in the same courtroom, Matthews' planning director, Thomas Russo, was acquitted of extortion and conspiracy charges.

An editorial in the *Press,* taking inventory of 1984, concluded that "all things considered, 1984 wasn't a bad year for Atlantic City—and 1985 should be better."

28

Murder Takes a Little Holiday

The murder holiday had lasted for about 9 of the 17 months that Scarfo served at La Tuna federal prison. The first important one to go was Pasquale ''Pat the Cat'' Spirito. He was shot in the head while driving his car in South Philadelphia. The two assassins were passengers in his car, who fled on foot.

On November 10, 1983, the body of Salvatore ''Toto'' Sollena, wrapped in green trash bags, was found in the trunk of his Cadillac. His hands were tied behind his back, and he had been shot in the head several times. Nine days later the body of his brother, Matteo, was found in the trunk of his wife's Ford LTD, his death also due to multiple gunshot wounds in the head.

The Sollenas had been smuggled into the country by the Gambino family and had operated pizza parlors in South Jersey as fronts for their drug activities. They worked directly under Rosario, Giuseppe, Mario, Erasmo, and Antonio Gambino, all Sicilian aliens living in the Cape May area who dealt directly with drug laboratories in Palermo and Milan and controlled the flow of heroin into Philadelphia and south Jersey, including Atlantic City. Police theorized that the Sollenas had run afoul of the Scarfo Mob in their dealings and their deaths had been a business matter between the Scarfo Mob and the Gambinos and had nothing to do with the gang war still going on within the various factions of the Philadelphia family.

Salvatore ''Sammy'' Tamburrino was inside his parents' variety store in South Philadelphia when two men walked in and fired four shots, hitting him in the head, the chest, and in each leg. Tamburrino had been the manager of a video-game parlor owned by Mario Riccobene.

Robert Riccobene, half-brother of Harry "The Hunchback" Riccobene, was walking with his mother on the night of December 6, 1983, when a man in a jogging suit killed him with a blast of buckshot in the back of the head as he was trying to scramble over a fence. His screaming mother was hit over the head with the shotgun that killed her son.

Three days later, the Riccobenes retaliated with another attempt on the life of Salvatore Testa. Accompanied by three bodyguards, Testa was driving in a warehouse area of South Philadelphia when his car was blocked by a second car carrying four men. There was a furious exchange of gunfire until police arrived, but no one was killed. After questioning, Testa and his men were released. The men in the other car had escaped.

Enrico "Ricky" Riccobene, son of Mario and a nephew of "Harry the Hunchback," was 27 when he died four days after the attack on Salvatore Testa. His body was found inside a walk-in safe in the rear of the jewelry store he operated in South Philadelphia. There was a bullet wound in his left temple and police found a .38-caliber automatic in his left hand. His death was listed as a suicide. In police logic, he had killed himself because of his fear of the Scarfo Mob. Yet that morning he had arrived at the store in the company of four bodyguards. Harry Riccobene's attorney, Charles Peruto, Jr., said, "I'd bet a million dollars of my own money that he didn't kill himself."

Around the time of his death, police had stopped a white Cadillac near the jewelry store and questioned its four occupants: Salvatore Testa, Philip Leonetti, Lawrence Merlino, and someone identified as Favio Iannarella. Testa and Merlino produced identification and were allowed to drive off. Leonetti and Iannarella, who had no identification, were taken in for questioning and later released.

A few minutes before 8:00 A.M., January 20, 1984, Nicodemo Scarfo, wearing a red windbreaker and tan cotton pants, walked out the gate of the La Tuna prison and was met by his son, Nicodemo, Jr., his attorney, Robert Simone, his nephew, "Crazy Phil" Leonetti, and Lawrence Merlino. Ignoring a contingent of reporters, he was whisked away in a limousine to the Marriott hotel in El Paso where

Salvatore Merlino and Salvatore Testa, along with a group of about thirty associates, waited to celebrate his release with a party.

The festivities at the Marriott were monitored by FBI agents and Texas Rangers. They saw Testa, attired in a three-piece suit and ten-gallon hat, kiss Scarfo on the cheek. Later Testa carried Scarfo's bags and rode with him to the airport in the limousine. The group occupied almost all of the plane's first-class section. Shades of Al Capone.

When the party arrived at Philadelphia International Airport that evening, Scarfo, now attired in a dapper, dark blue suit, appeared annoyed by the welcoming glare of television lights and the barrage of media inquiries. Brushing aside questions concerning his destination and future plans, he and his retinue settled into white Cadillac limousines and drove off into the night.

It was pretty rich going for a man who had not filed a federal income tax return since 1975. His story was that he performed maintenance work at his mother's apartment house and lived on handouts from her. To avoid showing any source of income, he bought nothing in his own name. How he paid for his fancy clothes, late-model Cadillac, and high style of living was not explained.

After returning home Scarfo opted for a change, taking a page out of Angelo Bruno's book of hoodlum economics. He formed his own business in Philadelphia, N & S Enterprise, to manage, market, and promote concerts for entertainers. The mailing address was the office of his attorney, Robert Simone. And he became a commissioned salesman for Gennaro Shirtmakers in Philadelphia. "He'll be selling shirts and acting as a go-between for entertainers and management," Simone said.

There were dire predictions that the Mob war would heat up now that Scarfo was back in action. But on North Georgia Street everything was calm. A developer who was rehabilitating a house two doors from Scarfo's apartment building was quoted in the *Press* saying it was the city's safest block. "During the whole construction period we didn't lose a piece of wood. I can only attribute that to [the law enforcement agents] being on the block."

Not all was rosy for the Scarfo Mob. For one thing, Scarfo was named as an unindicted co-conspirator in the Matthews-Lentino trial. And there were serious problems in the ranks. Nick Virgilio had been sentenced to three years in prison for making terroristic threats, and Virgilio's son, Michael, had been indicted in the shooting of two people in a bar and was currently a fugitive. Frank Gerace and Robert LoCicero were awaiting retrial for union fund embezzlement; Edward "Rick" Casale was awaiting trial in federal court on mail fraud and filing false tax returns, and in state court for extortion and conspiracy; Joseph Altimari, the Mob's local vice boss, had been sentenced to five years for promoting prostitution; attorney Robert Simone was awaiting trial on charges of evading nearly a million dollars in federal income taxes, money Simone claimed he had lost gambling in Atlantic City casinos (he was acquitted after he told a jury he was a compulsive gambler and owed the money to loansharks); and even Scarfo's son, Nick, Jr., had been arrested for consuming alcoholic beverages while under the age of 21.

But worst of all was the problem with the Merlinos. Both Lawrence and Salvatore were in serious trouble. Lawrence was awaiting trial in Philadelphia on a charge of disorderly conduct and making terroristic threats to a policeman, and in Atlantic City he was awaiting trial for drunken driving.

Salvatore, Scarfo's underboss, was in even deeper trouble. Arrested in Margate for drunken driving, he had tried to bribe the arresting officer, an effort that began at the time of the arrest and continued throughout the booking and interrogation period. It was so brazenly overt that he was videotaped in the act.

With the videotape and the testimony of the officers, Merlino was convicted and faced a possible ten-year maximum sentence until Superior Court Judge Steven Perskie became embroiled in the Matthews' controversy.

During four taped conversations Frank Lentino had told undercover agent Jim Biacco that he had personally delivered undisclosed amounts of cash to Perskie for his legislative campaigns which Perskie had failed to report to election officials as required by law.

The disclosure was made by District Attorney Joseph Fusco on the day Perskie was to begin Merlino's presentencing hearing. Fusco said the Lentino conversation had been recorded between December 1981 and March 1982, when Perskie was a state senator, but he refused to say how much cash was involved. Fusco had received transcripts of the conversations after his office had "reached out" to other law enforcement agencies seeking information that would show Merlino was involved in organized crime and should receive the ten-year sentence.

Perskie termed Lentino's remarks "outrageous lies" and promptly disqualified himself from the case before transcripts of the tapes could be introduced by the state as evidence against Merlino.

Merlino's attorney, Carl Poplar, who was also Matthews' attorney, objected to Perskie disqualifying himself unless he granted his client a new trial. Perskie, he said, "was in a unique position to judge the credibility of the witness [Lentino]."

Lentino, who was in serious trouble with the Scarfo Mob for having blabbed to Biacco, seized the opportunity to recant. He submitted a sworn retraction asserting, "I have never made any cash contributions either directly or indirectly to Steven P. Perskie. I did not deliver any cash contributions to Perskie from others and I have no knowledge of any cash contributions to Judge Perskie."

Perhaps with the upcoming trial in mind, Lentino took the opportunity in his affidavit to add: "Many of the statements that I made to agent James Bannister were not true but were made in order to make special agent Bannister believe that I was an important individual."

"I am pleased that the public may now be assured that there was never a shred of truth in these allegations," Perskie said in a prepared statement. His attorney said Perskie saw no need to take a polygraph test now that Lentino had come forward and disavowed his earlier statements.

The Division of Criminal Justice closed the case after Perskie was interviewed. "The investigation and the report I reviewed did not in any way indicate there was a case against Judge Perskie," said the division's director, but "we will reopen it in a second if we get more information."

At the time, prosecutor Bennett refused to comment on the effect this would have on the Matthews-Lentino case. How would a jury separate "puffing" from fact? Was it what a hoodlum said, or was it about whom it was said that made the difference?

It wasn't long before the matter came up in court. In September Leonetti was indicted on extortion conspiracy charges involving Matthews and Bennett asked the court to disqualify Leonetti's attorney, Robert Simone, who was himself an unindicted co-conspirator in the case.

Bennett told the court that Simone had been the necessary link between the organization and Scarfo while he was at La Tuna. In a letter to Simone entered into the court record, Bennett charged that Simone had been present at meetings of Matthews, Leonetti, and others, when "Leonetti asked Matthews to utilize his influence as mayor to assist" Biacco in acquiring the H-Track. And he had been present at the Mars restaurant meeting of Matthews, Leonetti, and Merlino.

As for Salvatore Merlino, assistant prosecutor Jeffrey Blitz told the court, "We had intended to produce testimony to prove that the defendant is involved in organized crime activity and the substantial likelihood that he is a member, and a ranking member, of the Cosa Nostra family operating in the Philadelphia-South Jersey area and headed by Nicodemo Scarfo."

The testimony was especially important, Blitz said, because Judge Perskie, in an earlier ruling, had found that factors in the case favoring a lesser sentence outweighed those favoring a more severe one. With that in mind, Blitz had opened negotiations with Carl Poplar, Merlino's attorney, because he felt that "the certainty of incarceration was more important than the length of incarceration." So instead of the ten years he would have received if the organized crime link had been established, Merlino plea-bargained it down to four years.

Before passing judgment, Judge Philip Gruccio delivered a little sermon. "This is the type of crime that strikes at the very essence of the law. The law to be effective must be obeyed by everyone. The nature of this offense is a very serious one and the gravity and seriousness of this crime must be considered." Then noting that Merlino had no prior criminal record, was a family man, and was gainfully employed, the judge ruled, "I accept the four-year sentence as appropriate."

Merlino promptly appealed, which meant he would remain "gainfully" employed for at least another year.

Another controversial name that surfaced during the undercover operation was that of Police Chief Joseph Pasquale, who had prospered to the point where he had actually contemplated running for mayor against Matthews. Until, that is, Scarfo had stepped in to back Matthews and arranged for Pasquale to be appointed police chief by Matthews following his election. According to Lentino, Pasquale's appointment was part of the package deal accepted by Matthews when he received the $150,000 from Scarfo.

Instead of the Mob war heating up, as predicted, things remained relatively calm. With Harry and Mario Riccobene in prison and Robert and Enrico dead, the feud was pretty much dead itself. There was nobody left to challenge Scarfo's leadership. Except, perhaps, for the people in his own faction.

While Scarfo had been cooling his heels in Texas, Salvatore Testa had made headlines not only locally but in the national press. Any mention of him always included references to his father, Philip "Chicken Man" Testa. Salvatore, because of scars from gunshot wounds on his left arm, had gained the nickname "Chicken Wing." There was much police speculation that the son would soon inherit the father's Philadelphia kingdom.

Yet, with all his notoriety, when the Division of Gaming Enforcement had sought to place him on the exclusion list in May 1984, the casino commission voted four-to-one against blacklisting him, noting that he had no criminal convictions and his only connection to organized crime was through his father. The division argued that Testa was a "highly visible" figure at various casinos and had even received "comps" totaling about $4000 from at least one unnamed casino. Commission vice-chairman Joel Jacobson, who had gained national attention for his remark that Sinatra was an "obnoxious bully," expressed the commission's consensus when he said that the division's case was built largely on "hearsay evidence from faceless informers."

Some of that "hearsay evidence" had appeared in a front page, full-length feature in the *Wall Street Journal* on April 19, 1984, with the headline: "A 28-Year-Old Is Said to Be Heir to Top Job in Philadelphia Mafia," and accompanied by a flattering artist sketch of Testa.

In the story, Testa was described as the "fastest-rising star in Philadelphia's organized crime family. At an age when many people are just starting to climb a career ladder, Mr. Testa is said by law-enforcement agencies to be on the brink of controlling this city's Mafia—a job usually held by men twice his age."

If that wasn't bitter enough medicine for Scarfo to swallow, the next paragraph must have sent him into one of his celebrated screaming rages: "Partly because of his youth, partly because of his exploits and largely because of his uncanny ability to survive gunshots, Salvatore Testa is certainly the Mob's most celebrated figure these days. A handsome, stocky 6-footer, he has appeared numerous times on the front pages of local papers. . . . And to local lawmen, Chicken Man's son symbolizes a new, swaggering breed of mobster that has become dominant in recent years. . . . Salvatore Testa is almost never seen in public here without several husky friends, who surround him when he frequents this city's stylish nightclubs. . . . Mr. Testa has consolidated his power, bringing many friends into the Mob. He has also inherited many of his father's allies.''

The story alluded to his wealth, saying he had inherited property valued at $800,000 from his father and that he had made ''an additional $1.1 million last year from the sale of his Atlantic City nightclub, bought through a third party by developer Donald Trump.''

The rain had started about an hour before the anonymous telephone call was received at the Gloucester Township Police Department. It was Friday, September 14, 1984, and the time recorded by the dispatcher was 10:23 P.M. There was a body on the shoulder of Garwood Road near Hickstown Road.

Police hurried to the scene and found Salvatore Testa, his body wrapped in a blanket, his hands and feet tied ''cowboy-style'' behind his back, and a single, small-caliber bullet hole behind each ear. He was dressed in white jogging shorts, a Temple University T-shirt, and white running shoes. He was clean-shaven, his hands were manicured, and $200 was found in the pockets of his jogging shorts.

It was an almost letter-perfect reenactment of the Falcone murder. It was as bold an admission of the crime as one could make without leaving a calling card.

In the next few days police would discover that on the night of the murder, Scarfo, Leonetti, and Lawrence Merlino were seen at the bar of Daniel's Restaurant in Somers Point, drinking toasts in a rare public appearance. But that was all police had. ''We have no eyewitnesses, no one who saw the body or the car, no recovered weapons, nobody even to attest to what his last hours were,'' said a police official. He called most of the theories published on the case ''pure conjecture.''

Five days later the body of Michael Micali was discovered along Hickstown Road, less than a mile from the spot where Testa was found. He was 22 years old and believed to be a low-level drug dealer and a recent recruit of Testa's. There were obvious similarities in the two murders. Like Testa, Micali was killed by two small-caliber gunshots to the head—one penetrating the right temple, the other through the right eye, both at close range. There was not much blood, indicating, as in Testa's case, that he had been killed elsewhere and dumped at that location. About $200 in cash was neatly folded and placed between his head and left arm. Although he was not bound and wrapped in a blanket, blankets were found nearby. Police alluded to "symbolism," that the arrangement of the body conveyed a "message," but refused to elaborate. Micali was said to have sworn allegiance to Testa's "faction" after Testa was killed, vowing never to work in the Scarfo organization. This raised new questions about another factional war and how many more bodies would be found before peace would once again reign in the late Docile Don's family.

One of the great social events of 1984 occurred during the Perskie controversy. Skinny D'Amato died.

"Paul E. 'Skinny' D'Amato, 75, the colorful former nightclub owner credited with 'single-handedly making Atlantic City swing' for three decades, died Tuesday morning," said the lead paragraph in the *Press* on June 6.

"While known primarily as the host of a nightclub where major stars like Frank Sinatra, Sammy Davis, Jr., and Nat King Cole performed, associates say D'Amato also established a reputation as an unusually generous and kind man.

" 'He was known as Mr. Atlantic City. That recognition couldn't have been more deserved,' said Atlantic County Sheriff Mario Floriani, who was a close friend of D'Amato since the 1940s."

People lined up around the block to pay their respects. And all had their eyes peeled, for "rumors drifted among the crowd that perhaps there would be visits by some of the stars who were friends with D'Amato." Even the weather was sad, turning "a dusty gray and the wind picking up" as the viewing continued into the night.

In the end, the only star who came was Sinatra, and he barely made it, arriving at the back door of the church, accompanied by bodyguards, as the other pallbearers were going out the front door with Skinny in his silver casket. A legend was being put to rest and with it much of the sub rosa history of Atlantic City.

It was a hot summer night and the streets of South Philadelphia teemed with people out to get a breath of fresh air. On a street corner near the Italian Market, Frank "Frankie Flowers" D'Alfonso stopped to light a cigarette. A black Cadillac rolled up to the curb and two men stepped out while the driver remained behind the wheel with the motor running.

Moments later five shots rang out and D'Alfonso slumped forward, dead before he hit the pavement, with bullets in his brain, chest, shoulder, and arm.

It had been four years since D'Alfonso had been found unconscious in front of Cous' Little Italy restaurant with shattered bones that took many months to heal. He had continued operating as a bookmaker and had faced charges only once, in 1982, when he was sentenced to a year's probation for conducting a bookmaking operation that police claimed netted him $20,000 a day. He was 55 and police theorized that his murder "appears to be a cleanup act of older people" in the Mob.

But only days before he was slain, it was disclosed that he was the subject of a widening FBI probe into the Mob's control of boxing in Atlantic City.

On July 23, 1985, the day of D'Alfonso's murder, Lieutenant Colonel Justin Dintino, deputy superintendent of the New Jersey State Police and a member of the President's Commission on Organized Crime, had presented the commission with a report from the New Jersey State Commission of Investigation alleging that the Scarfo crime family was deeply involved in promoting and managing boxing.

"What you have here is a Who's Who in organized crime in New Jersey," said Dintino, noting that the report indicated the Mob's presence in most aspects of prizefighting, including ownership of boxers, fight promotions, and management.

The New Jersey commission identified members of New York Mafia families involved in boxing and produced surveillance photographs taken of New Jersey State Athletic Commissioner Jersey Joe Walcott and Deputy Commissioner Robert Lee attending a fight at Resorts International in the company of Frank "Blinky" Palermo, described in the report as a "veteran soldier in Scarfo's gang."

In the early months of 1985, the Casino Control Commission, after being upheld by the U.S. Supreme Court, was finally able to force Frank Gerace to resign from the presidency of Local 54 of the Hotel and Restaurant Workers and Bartenders International Union. Also ousted were Frank Materio and Karlos LaSane.

But Gerace was soon back on Local 54's payroll as a $48,000-a-year consultant and trustee in charge of the union's severance fund and the health and welfare fund. The local was netting $2 million a year in dues from its 18,500 members and about $18 million from the casinos for health and benefit plans.

Besides their unhappiness with Gerace's new position, casino investigators were suggesting that the local's new president, Roy Silbert, who was elected without opposition, was a puppet handpicked by Gerace, who was still calling the shots he received from Scarfo.

Silbert denied the charge, calling it "absurd," and going on to say that "there is nothing I can do to change the public's opinion or what the media prints. I really don't care what the public or law enforcers think. My only concern is my membership's opinion."

What worried casino regulators was that the money for pensions and benefit plans was paid directly to unions, giving the trustees complete control over the funds. "Follow the money and you'll find the real issues," one investigator said.

It was not long before Gerace was back in the news. The U.S. Department of Labor filed a civil suit against the trustees of Local 54, charging that they had paid "excessive and unreasonable sums of money" for the union's dental plan.

Scarf, Inc., continued doing landoffice business in Atlantic City. In July 1985 it was revealed that on September 13, 1984, it had received a $483,600 contract on a private housing project financed by the state and the Atlantic County Improvement Authority.

Five days after the loan was approved by the New Jersey Housing and Mortgage Finance Agency, Crazy Phil Leonetti, who was fronting the company for his uncle, was indicted in the Matthews extortion case.

For eight weeks in the spring of 1985, Lawrence Merlino, who with his brother Salvatore owned Nat Nat Inc., which specialized in concrete reinforcement, was observed overseeing the concrete reinforcement for Resorts International's proposed $400 million 44-story hotel tower.

News reports revealed that Nat Nat was working through a minority contracting firm, M & M Steel, Inc., of Philadelphia.

Gaming division director Thomas O'Brien said they were "looking at the contracts, and so far we haven't found anything out of the ordinary."

Resorts International's corporate counsel, John Donnelly, said that the company would rely on the findings of the gaming commission. "If they have decided that Mr. Merlino is an undesirable person who should not be doing business, then most certainly that company will be removed from the site immediately."

In July 1985, Lawrence Merlino, who through the years had been implicated in seven murders, was again in trouble. He and Joseph

Ligambi were charged with disposing of the bullet-riddled body of Salvatore Sollena which had been found hog-tied in the trunk of his Cadillac on November 10, 1983.

At the time of his death, Sollena was awaiting trial on federal charges of laundering drug money in Europe to avoid U.S. taxes and was being investigated for his part in a $100 million international heroin ring.

In its investigation of Sollena's murder, police had two theories. The first was that Sollena and his brother, Matteo, also murdered, had run afoul of the Scarfo Mob in their drug dealings in Atlantic City. The second involved Mary Barbella, the sister of Gina, Leonetti's girlfriend, who was also indicted for allegedly testifying falsely to the grand jury that she had met Sollena only twice, had never had drinks with him, and had only engaged in brief, casual conversation. Sollena, who operated a pizzeria in Atlantic City, frequented Angeloni's II and was allegedly a close acquaintance of Mary Barbella, a waitress there.

As for Merlino, it was just another day in court. He posted $2000 and was released on bail.

July 1985 was a tough month on Scarfo's associates. His close friend, Phillip "Disney" McFillin, in whose home Vincent Falcone was allegedly murdered, was indicted for making terroristic threats against a policeman after he was arrested for serving alcohol to minors during a graduation party for his son.

But there was also some good news in July when Leonetti's extortion trial was again postponed, this time until spring of 1986, because his attorney, Gustave Newman, was representing one of the 21 defendants in the complex racketeering case involving Paul Castellano, boss of the Gambino family.

29

A Gambling House Is Not a Home (Builder)

"You know, I'm really not that bad," Matthews had said after his recall defeat. "They'll find out I was a damn good mayor."

A few months later it was still funny business as usual at City Hall, with councilmen trying to raise their salaries and Mayor Usry firing pro-Matthews municipal workers and hiring his own patronage hacks. This from a mayor who had pledged during the recall campaign that there would be no wholesale firings at City Hall, adding that each worker would be reviewed regarding his "competency, efficiency, and loyalty, possibly in that order."

The council continued as a deeply divided body, as much at odds with itself and Usry as it had been with Matthews. For one thing, some sixty workers fired by Usry were supporters of the five councilmen opposing Usry. In retaliation, the councilmen proposed a salary ordinance that would cut more than 140 positions requested by the mayor, including two of his top aides. The councilmen called it their hardest pitch yet in the ongoing game of "political hardball." Usry's supporters in the council called it an "idiot program" and "a bunch of backroom smoke-filled dirt."

Two months into Usry's mayoralty, a blue ribbon task force likened the city's government to "an $80 million company that went 'el wacko.' " From a management standpoint, the city was starting from "ground zero."

At a time when the crime rate was skyrocketing, it found "apathy" within Chief Pasquale's police department. "Nobody seems to give a damn,'' a member of the task force said. ''There doesn't seem to be any accountability or degree of authority or responsibility. Somewhere in the structure there has to be.''

The one thing that became clear with Usry's election was that the city's 20,000 black residents had finally gained control of the political machinery. There was apprehension among some whites. Like others before him, Usry had promised to close the rifts between blacks and whites. ''Atlantic City,'' he said in his inaugural address, ''can and will finally start on its long-awaited rise from the ashes. Like the mythological phoenix, this city will be renewed.''

And, of course, there was controversy. For $5000 a contributor could buy a one-year membership in the mayor's ''Inner Circle Club,'' but that, the mayor insisted, would never buy favors from the administration.

At a $350,000 fund-raiser at a casino-hotel, the more a supporter pledged the closer he got to sit to the mayor and governor. The $5000 contributor bought entry into a ''VIP reception,'' with Governor Kean and Mayor Usry and a ''priority table at dinner'' for eight. The invitation promised: ''Special arrangements will be made to have the municipal, county, and/or state officials of your choice join your table (if available).'' For $2100 a contributor could attend the VIP reception but no special arrangements to rub elbows with power brokers; $300 bought dinner and entry into a cocktail party that followed the VIP reception. Heading the affair was Robert Paschon, the attorney who had spearheaded Usry's recall fight against Matthews in the courts.

''People can read into it what they want,'' Usry said. ''When you go down to sit in a place, you sit in a reserved seat, you sit in general admission, or you sit in a box seat. The fact that you sit in a box seat does not make you anything but closer to the boxer or the ballplayer or the basketball player.''

How close Usry was to Paschon would create another controversy. Usry awarded Paschon an $850,000 city contract but later was forced to withdraw it when he realized he lacked the needed five votes for approval in the city council. Paschon's law firm would have replaced four law firms working for the city as well as the employees in the solicitor's office. Based on a specified number of hours the firm would bill the city per year, the contract allowed the firm to continue billing if more work was needed after the $850,000 was exceeded.

Although Usry protested that he had not pushed for a favorable vote, the *Press* reported that "at least three councilmen were approached, and were threatened that friends or relatives on the city payroll would be fired or that opponents in the [upcoming] May council elections would be backed by Usry's supporters."

Those involved in the lobbying effort were identified as "Atlantic City Housing Authority Executive Director W. Oscar Harris, Jr., a key Usry [financial supporter and] adviser; Usry chief of staff Karen Ennous; and Edward DiNicolantanio, a city businessman and Usry supporter."

The contract was withdrawn and Usry angrily denied he ever intended to give Paschon an $850,000 legal services contract, adding that he had rebuked Harris for lobbying for it.

It wasn't long before Harris was in far more serious trouble, but this time the mayor was keeping a low profile. The first problem to come to light concerned Robert LoCicero, Scarfo's favorite concrete contractor, who, along with Donald Martinelli, had been convicted of perjury in a Local 54 embezzlement case.

Both were spared a three-year federal prison term when Harris wrote a letter to U.S. District Judge John Gerry, offering project work that could be performed as community service. So on July 6, 1984, Judge Gerry set aside the prison term and ordered them to serve a thousand hours at the Housing Authority.

This was not exactly what the Justice Department had in mind when it decided to prosecute the case. Consequently, an investigation was launched, and a quid pro quo uncovered. A document had been altered to hide a personal financial benefit Harris was to receive in exchange for his letter of recommendation to the judge.

LoCicero and Harris had been involved in a proposed $1.7 million land transaction and when Harris had pulled out of the deal, LoCicero had filed a lawsuit to recover a $25,000 deposit. The FBI learned that on the day Harris wrote to the judge, he received a letter from LoCicero. A key sentence at the end of this letter had been whited out but a physical examination revealed that LoCicero had promised to drop his lawsuit in return for Harris's letter to the judge.

It wasn't the first or last time that Harris would use his public office to reap private gains. The *Press* had accused him of using loopholes in the state conflict-of-interest law and the casino-ethics code to build "his personal empire . . . [while] it appears his agency, empowered to solve the resort's most crucial social problems, has fallen into financial trouble."

Included in Harris's ''personal empire'' were the following: Ebony Construction, Inc., was building a $900,000 warehouse for the Golden Nugget; Geordans Concerts, Inc., was booking entertainers at casinos, including Resorts International, which was developing a second casino and other projects on the Housing Authority's 56-acre Uptown Urban Renewal Tract—Harris owned stock in Resorts and sold a house to a Resorts subsidiary; Atlantic Linen Service, Inc., was created to service casinos; Harris was part owner, with Usry's wife, of a liquor store called Cheers, the first on the Boardwalk. Harris's personal business partner had taken over Ocean Manor Apartments, the most valuable residence on the Boardwalk, with Harris' help, and this partner had done more than $25 million in business with the housing authority. Harris had created a gaming magazine called *Winner,* to be distributed at the casinos, and he had financial interests in a boxer, in a bus company bringing gamblers to resort casinos, and in horse racing.

Harris was so close to Usry that he headed the mayor's transition team and the patronage line between the city and the Housing Authority was so thin that it was for all practical purposes invisible. Leaders in Usry's campaign were rewarded by the authority: one was awarded a contract for a coin-operated laundry without bidding; another received a $16,000 contract to help the authority understand its computer system; another received a $3000 contract to evaluate the authority's security system; Usry's campaign manager was given a $25,000 contract to process housing subsidy applications for the authority; a large contributor was paid $62,500 to perform a study for the authority; another contributor sold the authority a photocopier without bidding, with Harris later admitting he had altered the invoice by $1 to avoid the public bidding ceiling; Usry and his wife, Laverne, owned Sunset Laundries, a company that operated the coin laundry in the Jeffries Towers housing project which came under Harris's Housing Authority—Usry denied he was in violation of the 1979 city ethics law that prohibited an Atlantic City official or employee from benefiting ''directly or indirectly'' from municipal contracts because ''I'm not doing business with the city.''

In December 1984 the names of Usry and Harris surfaced in Judge Ackerman's courtroom during Matthews' trial. In his wide-ranging conversations with undercover agent James Bannister, alias James Biacco, Frank Lentino described payments made to Usry, through Harris, during the 1982 mayoral election between Matthews and

Usry, in an effort to cover both sides of the political fence. The following excerpts were recorded on February 23, 1983:

> LENTINO: I want to tell you something, ah, we're all right with the colored guy [Usry]. . . . There was another investment made, it's much smaller, but there was a commitment he did, too.''
>
> BIACCO: So you can't lose either way . . .
>
> LENTINO: There's a guy, Oscar Harris, who is the big sponsor of his opposition. And he's the head of the—ah, we, the Teamsters have him under contract, my organization—he's head of the housing project there. The financial contributions were made to him. With, you know, a promise that, ah, to work together.
>
> BIACCO: If the other guy wins, yeah.
>
> LENTINO: That's right.

Although Lentino said they backed both candidates, in a conversation dated May 23, 1983, Lentino expressed a preference: "We helped them [Usry and Harris], too. And we had the commitment from him. So we can't lose either way. Though I'd prefer Mike [Matthews].''

"I don't even know the man [Lentino]" Usry told the press. "I will attack the allegations when I see the allegations. First, I'll have to see those documents. I'll get them in due time. I'm on vacation now.''

Harris's salary of $76,566, the highest pay for the authority's executive director in Atlantic City history, consumed more than 10 percent of the agency's salary budget. The *Press* described him as ''a high-priced public official who walks the tightrope between personal profit and conflict of interest with both bravado and artistry.''

"I think I'm an expert when it comes to conflict of interest as it relates to me,'' Harris told an interviewer. "I know a conflict when I see one, be it me or anyone else. I've given it a lot of examination. They [his critics] just don't like to see niggers in charge of anything. That's a quote. The problem is, you white folks don't like to see black folks in charge of nothing and making a success out of it. . . . White folks have a problem with black folks who are successful. Always have and always will.''

The Housing Authority's board of directors is appointed by the mayor, city council, and governor. The board, in turn, hires the executive director. Authorities usually have aggressive boards, but in Atlantic City, where housing was the most precious social commodity, the board, cowed by Harris's flamboyant personality, had long ago abdicated its responsibilities to him. This made Harris the city's most powerful nonelected executive, with the power to condemn property, approve housing and other development projects, and grant zoning variances in urban redevelopment zones strategically located throughout the resorts, powers Harris called "one-stop shopping."

When it was announced that a federal grand jury was going to look into whether the LoCicero letter involved possible obstruction of justice, the authority's board decided to ask Harris to take a paid leave of absence until the matter was cleared up. Harris' immediate reaction was to threaten the white board members with costly civil rights suit, charging they were racists. The board reversed its stand and Harris remained in control.

"I've been examined and reexamined," Harris said of the grand jury probe. "I would invite everyone to take a close examination of me. I'm just a poor black boy from the ghetto trying to manipulate my environment." In fact, Harris was the son of a prominent Atlantic City physician.

As for LoCicero, who had certainly played his part in the obstruction of justice scheme, Judge Gerry ordered the U.S. Probation Department to find another agency to supervise him and Martinelli in their performance of public work, preferably one serving "the elderly and poor in Atlantic City."

With this scandal still simmering on the back burner, Usry was back in the headlines. This time his eager officials were using city time, personnel, and materials to persuade municipal workers to purchase tickets to a private picnic to raise funds for the mayor. Calling themselves "Jim's Men," they had employees buying the $6 tickets in pairs and blocks because, as some would later anonymously complain, they feared losing their jobs or, if protected by Civil Service, feared transfers or other negative changes in their working conditions. "There was definitely an intimidation factor," said one employee. "There was no doubt he expected you to buy the tickets." Included in the solicitation were businessmen and professionals doing work with the city. The officials selling the tickets were described as "muscling" employees and asking for payments in cash.

Usry's response to the heavy criticism was to suspend a couple of his key officials for five days. He blamed their action on "poor judgment." His reason for not firing them was described as a gesture of compassion to their families.

Next to come to light was the tax break given to Jack Blumenfeld. A $5000 member of Usry's Inner Circle Club, Blumenfeld hired Robert Paschon to help steer his Greenhouse project through the mayor's office. All Blumenfeld wanted was a 40-year, $19 million tax writeoff for his planned 960-unit apartment and retail building at Michigan and Atlantic avenues. Councilman James Whelan, who opposed the tax break, said that moments after Paschon talked to the mayor, Usry sent a brief supportive memo to the council which approved it, leaving Whelan and other councilmen with no bargaining position.

State Senator William Gormley was shocked. "That's the future of Atlantic City, the next forty years," he said. "What you're doing is taking that property tax burden and placing it on the backs of the other property owners." Hit by a storm of criticism, Usry said he would reexamine his "philosophy on tax incentives."

When resort voters rejected a proposed $6000 pay raise to councilmen, the councilmen voted themselves a $4000 raise. Councilman Harold Mosee boasted that the council could pass salary hikes for itself as often as the voters turned in petitions rejecting them. A few weeks later it was announced that the council had received seven new 1985 automobiles.

The mayor and city council were continuing their antics and mindless feuds, and the city was falling apart, while the casinos were grossing nearly $6 million a day. The people who had danced in the streets the night gambling was legalized were now bemoaning their fate as property taxes, water, sewer, and utility bills tripled and quadrupled, street crimes, prostitution, and drug abuse sextupled, and the quality of life continued to worsen.

Thousands were forced not only out of their homes but out of town. Thousands more were living like gypsies, two steps ahead of land speculators, as they shuttled from one festering slum to another, until finally for many there was no place left but the street. The army of street people was growing at an alarming rate.

In the brutal winter of 1984, when the city's Welfare Department continued to refuse temporary lodging and aid to the homeless, David Sciarra, a deputy state public advocate, filed a lawsuit against the city, the first of its kind in the state, charging violation of state constitution and public assistance laws by "refusing to provide emergency shelter, immediate assistance, and general assistance payments to homeless persons."

The Welfare Department denied emergency shelter and assistance to people without a permanent local residence. It was a Catch-22: a person with a permanent residence would hardly be homeless. Almost a year after a judge had ordered emergency housing for the homeless, little had changed. Sciarra charged that "confusion over responsibility" stood in the way of resolving the problem.

The Women's Chamber of Commerce pounced on the advocate. "How many transients must we handle in any given time period?" they wanted to know. The group was concerned that the advocate's action would turn Atlantic City into "a mecca for vagrants, thus jeopardizing the health, safety, and well-being of the residents of our city. In addition, the tourism industry, on which all our economic well-being depends, will certainly be adversely affected by the stream of undesirables that will be drawn to Atlantic City." The group was "extremely distressed" that the city was being told it "should be responsible for every undesirable that comes into our area looking for a handout."

According to the suit, at least 20,000 homeless people lived in the state and there were only 700 beds statewide to accommodate them. "Nowhere is this statewide tragedy more evident than in Atlantic City," the suit stated. "Throughout Atlantic City, homeless men and women wander about the casinos and under the Boardwalk, search for food in trash containers, huddle in doorways to keep warm in the winter, or sleep in public places and abandoned buildings."

And nowhere was the contrast between rich and poor more dramatically juxtaposed than on the Boardwalk. While homeless men and women huddled helplessly under the Boardwalk, twenty stories above them other men and women, high-rollers by definition, drank champagne and feasted on caviar, clams, oysters, shrimp, lobster, pheasant, orange duck, steak tartare, the choicest cuts of beef, and dozens of other gourmet offerings, served by waiters in sparkling white uniforms, and entertained by celebrities who were paid a king's ransom just to rub elbows with them for a few precious moments.

Unemployment among the city's largely poor Hispanic and black population remained at a dismal 20 percent. Of the 36,000 new jobs created by the casinos, only 6000 had gone to city residents, and real unemployment declined by only 1200 because most of those hired were switching careers, from teacher, nurse, secretary, to dealer, cocktail waitress, and other higher-paying casino jobs. Of the Hispanics and blacks hired at casinos, most assumed their historic role of performing menial tasks.

"What you've got here is a jungle and you need a benevolent despot to sort it out," said Casino Commissioner Joel Jacobson. "Trouble is, nobody around here could ever agree on the despot."

And after seven years of bickering in Trenton nobody had yet agreed on how to cut up the reinvestment bonanza which mandated that after a casino's gross earnings exceeded its construction costs it would set aside 2 percent of its gross winnings for the "public interest" in Atlantic City. The political game in Trenton was the interpretation of "public interest."

The idea suggested by the gambling proponents during the campaign to legalize casinos was that the reinvestment fund would be used to provide low-cost housing, but as soon as the law was enacted no one in Trenton seemed quite sure how the money should be used.

The promise was that the economic boom generated by the casinos would be used for the city's revitalization, an urban renaissance; and nowhere was that need greater than in housing. Like an invading army, speculators had cut a terrible swath through the city, leaving in their wake demolished or burned-out houses, with drug dealers, pimps, prostitutes, muggers, vandals, street gangs, and assorted predators on every corner. In the first four years alone, 3540 housing units were destroyed to make way for casino-hotels and parking lots, or as bargaining pieces in the speculation game. To replace them were plans for 1907 high-priced condominiums with ocean views.

The poor people were the pawns in the land speculation game. The wheeling and dealing, as speculators maneuvered for a financial killing, drove land values through the ceiling. The people occupying the buildings being bartered back and forth among speculators were, more often than not, left in buildings without heat, water, gas, electricity, or the most basic conveniences, in buildings already condemned by the city, many to be finally evacuated by the arsonist's torch—speculators want vacant land, not old buildings.

Slumlords flatly refused to repair properties. Usry declared "open warfare" against them but was helpless when it came to using traditional measures such as condemnation, which would only put more people out on the street. "We have a situation here where landlords are openly telling their people that they're not going to upgrade their properties," Usry said. "They're telling them that they're going to sell."

Even when the city finally condemned a building, the tenants fought eviction. Low-income housing was described as tougher to find than a seat at a $5 blackjack table. Rats, cockroaches, raw sewage leaking through ceilings, flooding basements, plaster walls crumbling, buildings precipitously close to collapsing, broken windows, walls destroyed by fire, clogged sewage lines, garbage and human waste piled alongside buildings: these features didn't come cheap. Rents ran about $300 a month, plus another $150 for utilities, whether available or not.

That was nothing compared to the $50 a night the city was paying for rundown motel rooms on the Black Horse Pike. Under state law, the city is obligated to find shelter for people displaced when a city inspector condemns a dilapidated building. So the city went out and paid $1400 a month for single rooms, without kitchens, for families with two and three children.

The biggest wheeler-dealer speculator was Resorts International, the city's largest private property owner, which also made it the biggest slumlord. During his testimony before the gaming commission, Resorts board chairman James Crosby had assured the commissioners: "We didn't come here just to operate a casino. We were interested in helping develop the entire community."

Encouraged by his remarks, he was asked what Resorts intended to do with the 80 properties, many of them dilapidated homes and apartments, it had bought in the South Inlet. Well, Crosby explained, he had this idea about building churches. As a boy he had grown up in a town that had all its churches on the same street, and he recalled how nice it was on Sundays to hear all the bells ringing. That same week, the city's Health Department cited Resorts for 121 code violations in an apartment house it owned in the South Inlet. The tenants, poor Hispanic families, had no heat, faulty plumbing, poor electrical wiring, and leaking sewage lines.

Although tax assessment for homeowners jumped 500 and 600 percent between 1978 and 1980, the city was subsidizing speculators. A typical example was Resorts' 30 purchases along South Congress Avenue. It paid $3.56 million for properties that were assessed at only $230,000. While small homeowners were paying $3000 and $4000 in new property taxes for their humble domains, the city collected $9360 in taxes for Resorts' lots. If assessment had reflected market value, Resorts would have paid the city $145,000 on that one block.

"This kind of inequity could be found in block after block in the Inlet," reporter George Anastasia wrote after making a study of the city's housing. "For three years the city literally subsidized speculators in the area, while poor residents were driven from their homes, and middle-class residents were taxed out of theirs."

Statistics showed that land prices in some parts of Atlantic City had risen 3200 percent between 1976 and 1980. In 1983, the going rate in the business district of $33.98 per square foot was higher than land costs in downtown Manhattan.

Between 1977 and 1982, 20 percent of the city's housing stock was demolished and the housing that remained standing was allowed to deteriorate until almost 25 percent of the total housing units were substandard.

By the summer of 1985, it finally dawned on city officials that speculators were slowing down the city's promised development because they were keeping land prices too high. In a speech before the Exchange Club, Mayor Usry lashed out at the casinos, the city's largest land owners. He accused them of neglecting their civic responsibility to make Atlantic City a better place to work and live.

He singled out Resorts International, which, he said, owned 26 percent of all of the casino-zoned land in Atlantic City and 18 percent of the total land mass. It also owned half of the city's large, developable tracts, and it was engaged in land speculation for big profits.

"It's obscene to make that much money without giving something back to the community," said the mayor. "We won't see changes one block off the Boardwalk until these industrial giants learn to share." As far as Usry was concerned, the city would no longer grant tax deferrals to casinos who claimed to have cash-flow problems, only for them to turn around and make other investments. "These people try and get away with anything," Usry said, adding that they had a great deal of audacity.

Of particular concern to the mayor was the plight of Atlantic City High School. In March 1985, the Middle States Association had threatened to revoke the school's accreditation if the 62-year-old facility was not replaced. The only practical site for a new school was Great Island, which was owned by Resorts International.

The city wanted 35 of the 90 acres Resorts had bought in 1977 for amounts varying from $6300 to $25,000 an acre. According to Resorts officials, it was now worth $1 million per acre. But Resorts was willing to swap the 35 acres for city-owned properties, including the Garden Pier and casino-zoned land in the marina area. Resorts was already building a 1250-room hotel-casino with a 120,000-square-foot casino in the marina on land that was part of the 56-acre Uptown Urban Renewal Tract it had purchased from the Housing Authority for $5.6 million, to be paid over a period of years as it found use for the land. Except for building its second casino its only use of the land so far was to lease 8 acres to Showboat, Inc., for 99 years, at $6.4 million a year.

City officials were not in a land-swapping mood. The mayor was described as "adamant against giving up more city land." Another official said, "They asked for the whole world."

There were vague threats of condemnation and eminent domain, and Senator William Gormley introduced a bill that would give the Casino Control Commission the power to force a casino to divest property if the commission believed the casino was using the land to speculate. It could limit casino-land ownership to three sites suitable for casino development—a casino licensee was prohibited from owning more than three gambling halls.

"Casino gambling wasn't passed for the purpose of serving as a land speculation tool," Gormley said. The senator wanted the state Judiciary Committee to look into the agreement between Resorts and the Housing Authority, saying that the 56-acre Uptown Urban Renewal Tract had been sold to Resorts for the purpose of developing new housing but nothing had been built in eight years. The agreement, he believed, violated HUD anti-speculation regulation. Gormley was particularly intrigued by the deletion of the anti-speculation clauses in the HUD section of the agreement. "Can they [the Housing Authority] supersede HUD regulations?" he asked. "I think the intent and spirit of the whole redevelopment program was not to foster speculation." If a violation were found, Gormley believed, the Housing Authority could be entitled to the amount of rent charged to Showboat above the $100,000-per-acre price Resorts was paying for the land.

The answer would not soon be forthcoming. The HUD office in Camden was disbanded a few years ago and William Downey, the Housing Authority's executive director when the agreement was signed was now an executive with Showboat.

Cora Boggs, president of the Atlantic City Congress of Community Organizations, blamed Resorts for starting the speculation that crippled the city. "None has displayed the cold-hearted avarice of Resorts International in its efforts to buy and control the city," she said. "From the beginning, Resorts has thrown money around like drunken sailors. It's all a well-thought-out scheme. Resorts came to town with an open purse, creating almost mob hysteria."

In December 1983 Governor Thomas Kean proposed to reduce the casinos' 2 percent reinvestment requirement to 1.5 percent, with half the money to be used to buy bonds of a new development authority, and the balance to be invested directly by casinos in projects approved by the authority—a minimum of 15 percent of the funds to be used for affordable housing.

The casino industry's response was to demand that the requirement be reduced to 1 percent, arguing that it would generate the same amount of money as the existing 2 percent if the casinos were not allowed the five-year delay permitted in the act. Any amount over 1 percent "would be excessive and would threaten the future health and growth of the gaming industry in New Jersey," the industry's report concluded.

Then-Senator Steven Perskie opposed Governor Kean's proposal, suggesting that a new commission composed of city, county, and state representatives be appointed to administer the reinvestment fund. "It would get away from the idea that we need a superagency, another bureaucracy," he said. "In retrospect, it never should have been left to the Casino Control Commission." Under Perskie's plan, the County Improvement Authority or Oscar Harris's Redevelopment Authority would build the housing. The casinos would supply the funds to purchase bonds issued by either authority.

Harris liked that idea a lot. "We're responsible for 25 percent of the city's current housing stock, both subsidized and nonsubsidized," he said, "and we've been in this business since 1939." Resorts International couldn't have been happier. "This makes a lot more sense than additional taxes with no bearing on profitability," a spokesman said, "and more sense than the current formula that requires investment whether a casino is profitable or not."

Governor Kean countered with a revised proposal. He would cut the reinvestment percentage to 1.25 percent, with 20 percent of the money to be spent for low- to middle-income housing for people who were Atlantic City residents when the bill was enacted. Casinos which didn't invest would have to pay a 3 percent tax. According to the governor's calculations, the measure would raise $1 billion in twenty years, of which $880 million would go directly to Atlantic City.

The $1 billion figure was somewhat exaggerated. Based on projected annual revenues of $2 billion, the 1.25 percent would amount to $500 million in 20 years. But it was only a proposal, one slipping quickly downward, and even if passed in its present state, it would mean $5 million a year for housing, which would buy about 80 low-income units. The industry was still lobbying for 1 percent, and—logic being what it is in power politics—it wasn't all that farfetched to assume that further squabbling would not only reduce the numbers in favor of the industry but target the funds for far different goals.

A few months later, the state assembly amended Kean's proposal by taking $285 million away from Atlantic City and giving it to north Jersey. The governor was appalled. "It was," he said, "the worst of all possible alternatives."

"We are not going to have a bunch of glittering casinos looking out on poverty behind them," Kean said, no doubt remembering what it was like to gaze out of a window in one of those glittering towers and see nothing but water on one side and a blighted landscape everywhere else. He pledged to fight for the restoration of the funds. He blamed casino lobbyists for gutting portions of the bill that was designed to create "the kind of Atlantic City that was predicted and promised at the time the original casino referendum was passed." With the amended bill, "we could not do the American City [redevelopment] Plan. Changes casinos, through their lobbyists, wrote into the bill will not produce the kind of revenue to do the housing for the people of Atlantic City."

But did anyone really care about *those* people? Certainly not Resorts. From the beginning, as far as it was concerned, "affordable housing" was a pipe dream. "We read the law to mean that this is an investment, not a gift to the city," a Resorts spokesman said. "We are entitled to make a fair rate of return on our investment, commensurate with where we might invest elsewhere." The only feasible solution, he said, was to build profit-bearing middle-income housing on land donated by the city. And even that proposal would sound philanthropic in time to come.

Crosby's church bells notwithstanding, the bottom line was the determining factor when Resorts got into the housing business, spending $13 million on 200 units in Egg Harbor Township, another development in Galloway Township, and other projects for Lake Lenape. Nothing there for the blacks of the North Inlet, the Hispanics of the South Inlet, or even the Irish and Italian of the once proud but rapidly deteriorating Chelsea area, or certainly for the homeless under the Boardwalk.

Cora Boggs, not only cared about *those* people, but understood the game being played in Trenton: "I think the plan is to move all the poor and moderate-income people out of Atlantic City. That's no secret. The corporate tentacles reach far." As she saw it, the "power brokers" and the "money people" wanted to stop the development of affordable housing in the resort and that was what the interminable battle over reinvestment was all about. "They're still trying to make this city what they wanted it to be all along," she said. "It's not just the casino industry. It's far reaching, and a lot of people you don't even see are involved. I think Atlantic City is up for grabs." The failure to provide the funding for affordable housing would result in "a wall" of new "luxury apartments all along the waterfront" while "they push the poor people back." Preferably into the "beautiful sea" on the other side of the island.

Even Mayor Usry had definite ideas about the poor. "I don't want low-income housing in Atlantic City," he told members of the Atlantic Builders Association, "and that's because I don't want low-income people in Atlantic City."

But Jack Wood, director of affirmative action for the gaming commission, was beginning to worry about the dwindling supply of dishwashers, stewards, housekeepers, and other menial laboring jobs. "The casino industry should be standing on its soapbox pressing the issue of housing and transportation because their future depends on it," he warned. "We don't have a bottomless supply of labor candidates. It we don't hurry up . . . we're going to have some real problems." Half of the 36,000 casino workers earned less than $15,000, which meant they couldn't afford the rents in Atlantic City and neighboring communities. What the resort needed, it would seem, was a fast and inexpensive means of transportation that would enable the industry to tap outside labor markets—perhaps, like the ghettoes of Camden and Philadelphia, hustle in the darkies on a daily basis.

By the end of 1984 the reinvestment fund, now worth almost a hundred million dollars, was still the subject of legislative squabbling. The casinos' powerful lobby was keeping the pot boiling and the money safely in hand. The reason the assembly was restricting local control over casino reinvestment funds, said Senator Gormley, was because they believed the city government was "incompetent."

Finally in December 1984, six years after the first casino came on line, the state adopted a casino reinvestment bill. It requires casinos to invest 1.25 percent of their revenues in community renewal projects or to deposit the money into a fund overseen by a new nine-member Casino Reinvestment Development Authority to be appointed by the governor. It will raise an estimated $700 million for Atlantic City and $900 million for the rest of the state over the next 25 years.

Senator Gormley was happy. "I think we're going to have a situation where the city will now move forward," he said.

The question, however, was when. It would take time, lots of time, and much opportunity for publicity-seeking debaters. The *Press* was already worried about the quality of appointments the governor would make to the reinvestment authority: "If Kean appoints the wrong people, the bright hopes of the moment will fade away—and Atlantic City once again will feel cheated. . . . He shouldn't attempt to pay political debts with appointments to the $18,000-a-year jobs; the quickest way to wreck the program would be to let partisan politics influence the authority's decisions."

Anyone expecting a miracle would have a long wait. First the board would have to be filled, the members interviewed by the judiciary committee, and then voted upon by the full senate. Then a staff would have to be selected, offices found, regulations written, with public hearings. Once the authority was in place—which could take a year or more—the real job would begin: conducting a study to determine housing needs. When it knew what had to be done, the authority had to select a contractor, have plans drawn, prepare a bond offering, and complete the sale before the contractor could start work. When that would happen was anybody's guess.

First they would have to get the money from the casinos. And the way things were going, it wasn't going to be easy. The gaming commission was inundated by requests from casinos seeking millions of dollars in credit against their reinvestment obligations.

Resorts International wanted $50 million in reinvestment credit for improvements to its hotel that included a new indoor parking garage, health spa, ballroom, bar, deli, meeting and gaming rooms, expanding its Superstar Theatre, as well as remodeling its high-roller suites; $1.5 million for a sewer line, and $1.9 million in charitable contributions. Another $15 million in credits for housing projects outside Atlantic City. One million dollars in bonds purchased from Harris's Housing Authority had been collecting interest since 1981 without creating or rehabilitating a single housing unit—while Harris was trying to persuade Resorts to rent rooms for its guests at a luxury building Harris was personally thinking of buying.

The city's public advocate thought that Resorts' request "shows a contempt for the people of Atlantic City." Resorts spokesman Philip Wechsler thought that all the advocate wanted casinos to build in Atlantic City was low-income housing which was really "building dormitories for the permanently poor." To emphasize his point, Wechsler said, "We have provided four thousand jobs. How many jobs has the public advocate generated for Atlantic City?"

The granting of the full $65 million in credit by the commission would wipe out Resorts' reinvestment obligation for the next 20 years.

Harrah's, Golden Nugget, and Hilton (which had started construction on a casino-hotel) wanted $34 million in credit for road improvements they planned around their hotels. Golden Nugget also wanted credit for installing a new sewer line and runway realignment at Bader Field, as well as $653,065 in contributions to charities, many to organizations in other states. Caesars wanted credit for the $349,477 it paid for its share of the Pacific Avenue sewer line, $9.4 million it spent acquiring the site of the Traymore Hotel, plus $1.5 million for purchasing and then leasing the Lombardy Motel and the old Warner Theater (now a Boardwalk fast-food joint), and $625,000 for a granite statue of Caesar Augustus. Bally wanted $4 million in credit for a project still on the drawing board. Atlantis wanted to write off its parking lot, and the Tropicana, which was not required to make any reinvestment payments because it would be a while before its revenues exceeded its building costs, submitted a list of contributions anyway, in anticipation of any future changes in the law.

Included in the various lists were gifts of Cabbage Patch dolls, T-shirts to softball teams, dinner tickets, turkeys and sweet potatoes, contributions to St. Jude's Children Hospital in Memphis, the Young Men's Philanthropic League in New York City, the Variety Club in Philadelphia, sawdust to the Philadelphia zoo, and ads in program books—all deductions they had used to reduce their income tax. And in some cases there was more than charity involved. For example, some of the turkeys and sweet potatoes were given to councilmen to hand out to loyal voters, a little side dish of political gravy.

"It sounds more like a bazaar on the Boardwalk than a reinvestment program," said casino commissioner Carl Zeitz.

So what had happened to the "ripple effect" the casino boom was to have had on the local economy? According to Chamber of Commerce projections, of the 2100 businesses operating in 1976, "only 210 will be left by 1985." Was this some new form of local "supply side" economics? Steven Perskie, one of the drafters of the casino act, took it all in stride, blandly explaining that legalizing casino gambling was "a means to an end, not an end in itself."

30

Trumping Up the Boardwalk

Donald Trump was ecstatic. Governor Kean and Mayor Usry were praising him for having invested in the future of Atlantic City. It was May 22, 1984, and a large crowd had gathered to help him launch Harrah's Trump Plaza, the flashy hotel-casino that Trump had proudly described as full of "brass, glass, and class." Now he was telling the crowd that his hotel was the finest building in Atlantic City and perhaps the finest in the country.

The "perhaps" was not an insignificant concession. Later, at a press conference, he would describe it as "the tallest, most spectacular, best-looking casino in town." When the hotel had neared completion, Trump had described his creation to a magazine writer this way: "I think it's going to be an incredible building. I think it's going to be the largest and one of the most spectacular hotels anywhere in the world. It's magnificent. It's three blocks long. It's a megastructure. It's incredible. It's the largest casino in the world. It just dominates."

Actually, the hotel had 614 rooms, seven restaurants, a health club, a 750-seat showroom, and a 60,000-square-foot casino floor with 123 gaming tables and 1734 slot machines, all of this crammed into a narrow 2.6-acre tract.

Superlatives and hyperbole came easily to this 37-year-old wunderkind who built a billion-dollar real estate empire in less than a decade. That's not to say, however, that he's a billionaire. Others were involved, including banks and insurance companies. Although the Trump organization was a private family company, Donald's expertise was leverage. He came up with the ideas and others put up most of the cold cash.

"I was looking to make a nice statement in Atlantic City," he said. "I felt the facility was going to be so good. It's a funny thing about a facility, you never know until you open it. You don't know if you're using the right bronze, the right marble. This building really seems to have what it takes. I don't say that modestly or immodestly."

Brass, beveled mirrors, and Tivoli lights were everywhere, accented by vivid reds, deep burgundies, and walls painted in shades of lavender that changed at each level: Trump called it New York Art Deco. (It wasn't all that long ago that Trump himself was wearing mauve suits with matching shoes.) Even the slot machines were in brass cabinets that sat on brass stands. Fixtures in the restaurants and lounges were brass and there was even a brass dance floor. As for the building's architecture, it has been described as looking "like nothing less than two '58 Edsel grilles placed together to form an inverted 'T,' [which] should catch the weekend gambler's eye, even among the other garish monstrosities in Atlantic City."

"Atlantic City is somewhat of an enigma to a lot of people," Trump told the opening-day audience. "A lot of people—in a certain strata in New York, let's say—don't really know or understand Atlantic City. They say, 'Why would you do that? Why would you go to Atlantic City?' I looked at Atlantic City a long time ago, probably in the middle of the first wave [of construction]. . . . I remember walking on the Boardwalk [in 1980]. . . . You couldn't walk more than twenty feet it was so cold. It was a time very much depressed." Trump shrugged and the reporters were reminded of other stories about him that had created the impression that a savior had come to Atlantic City that day.

Seven weeks before the opening, at a press conference held at Trump Tower, that citadel of glitz on Fifth Avenue, James Usry had told the press, only hours before Michael Matthews was indicted for extortion and bribery, "I stand before you as a newly elected mayor of the city of Atlantic City, the city which will be the recipient of the largess which comes to us as the result of these two [Harrah's and Trump] fine organizations coming to our town. . . . Their coming to Atlantic City is not just bringing brick and mortar . . . they've brought heart and soul to Atlantic City, and they've brought dedication and commitment to the community. . . . I'm very pleased that the opening in May will be the initial second coming, the second wave, the second catalyst group to help revitalize the city of Atlantic City.''

Asked at that time if his firm had specific plans for assisting the community, Trump said, ''We do have some very specific plans, we're dealing with the mayor, and we look forward to announcing those plans. We're going to be very involved with Atlantic City and the community as a whole. . . . And I must also add that I feel Atlantic City and the community is very lucky to have Mayor Usry as its new leader. We feel very strongly about that.''

At the press conference in Atlantic City on opening day, there were, as always, questions about Trump's spectacular land deals in Manhattan, about the dazzle and pizzazz his name added to a real estate project, and the possibility that his name might bring respectability to Atlantic City in particular, and the gambling world in general.

''Sometimes I'm surprised by it all,'' he said, referring to his media appeal. ''It's not something I personally enjoy. It's just something that happens. People say, 'Do you have a public relations firm?' And the answer is no.''

Seated at his side was his close friend Roy Cohn, the enfant terrible who had helped Senator Joseph McCarthy's orchestration of the anti-Communist hysteria that had swept the country with so much paranoia in the 1950s. Cohn had fallen upon hard times in the 1960s and early 1970s when he spent more time in court as a defendant in criminal actions than as a trial lawyer defending clients.

Once when asked to explain his friendship with Cohn, Trump said, ''All I can tell you is he's been vicious to others in his protection of me.''

Now, at the press conference, Cohn was quick to take up the public relations cudgel. ''I'm telling you, the governor, the mayor [were there at the annual dinner of the Brooklyn Democratic Organization held at the Sheraton Centre in Manhattan], but the ratio of people coming over and taking pictures of Donald . . . was twenty to one over all the political figures. There seems to be an aura of excitement that surrounds everything he does, and he has a very dynamic personality. The perception of mystery is that he's a young man, a young, good-looking guy with a good-looking wife—the ideal American family, a fine set of parents to whom he's very close. He's just surrounded by a complete aura of success in every field of life, personal and business.''

Even with Cohn's glib explanation, in interview after interview Donald Trump has appeared baffled by his own aura. Referring to an article in the business section of the *New York Sunday Times,* Trump told *Gentlemen's Quarterly* that it ''was big. Let's see . . . it was half a front page, and a whole back page and some more. It was crazy. They tell me it was the longest story ever done on a person as a profile. They did a larger story on IBM. That was literally the largest, but it couldn't have been much longer. It was wild.''

There are times when words like ''crazy'' and ''wild'' seem to be the only ones capable of explaining how he feels about his newfound fame, or the popularity of his creations. Visitors from all over the world come to New York and all they want to see, he says, is Trump Tower: ''It's crazy.'' And ''It's crazy, people are coming to me now because I have credibility.''

Shannon Bybee, the former Nevada gaming official brought into the Golden Nugget organization, thought that Trump and Bybee's boss, Steve Wynn, were much alike. Wynn's persona, like Trump's, was a ''very effective marketing tool,'' he said. ''They are both articulate, aggressive, creative, exciting people, people who create excitement.''

Daniel Lee, a gaming industry analyst with Drexel Burnham Lambert, Inc., carried it a step further. ''He [Trump] is his own best PR guy. The guy has class. If you look at how he builds, it is high-quality stuff—and it is glitzy. It doesn't matter if it's a condo in New York or a casino, he has taste.''

The banner hanging over the hotel entrance at the opening ceremonies proclaimed: ''New York Comes to Atlantic City.'' ''That wasn't my slogan,'' Trump explained. ''I thought it was nice.''

Superlatives and hyperbole have their limitation. Once one has decided that something is the best in the world, there's nowhere to go, at least on this planet. Both in Las Vegas and Atlantic City, ''the world'' is the only superlative that adequately describes the local phenomenon to its owners. Every new hotel-casino is ballyhooed as the ''world's largest resort hotel,'' its restaurants the ''world's finest,'' its jackpots the ''world's biggest,'' and so on, all of it proclaimed in neon.

In commenting on Trump's penchant for exaggeration, architect Philip Johnson said, ''Oh, he lies a great deal, but it's sheer exuberance, exaggeration. It's never about anything important. He's straight as an arrow in his business dealings.''

Trump's exuberant exaggerations include the announced heights of his buildings. He has added ten or more stories to the Grand Hyatt by marking the first floor of guest rooms as the 14th floor; Trump Tower is 56 stories, not the 68 he claimed; and Harrah's Trump Plaza is 32 stories, not the 39 that were supposed to make it the highest building on the Boardwalk. Even at 39 stories, it would have been topped by the 42-story Ocean Club condominium. Asked about these discrepancies by the *Wall Street Journal*, Trump said, ''I pride myself on telling the truth. But obviously there's a promotional element [involved] whether I want to realize it or not.''

Reminded at the opening-day press conference that the Ocean Club was taller, he said, ''Are we shorter? I thought we were taller. Well, we'll have to add a few floors.'' When caught in an outright lie, Trump has downplayed it by saying it's just part of the sell in real estate, sort of ''comes with the territory.''

His role model was his father, Fred Trump, a driven man who owned his first house before reaching voting age. Starting out as a carpenter, Fred Trump was soon building low-cost apartments in Brooklyn, Queens, and Staten Island. Today the Trump organization owns anywhere from 20,000 to 40,000 rental units, depending on which story one reads.

Donald lived and breathed real estate, along with the finer points of being competitive, from the time he learned to crawl. ''My father was one tough son of a gun,'' Donald has recalled. ''You had to be asserting yourself all the time with these old guys.'' The family minister was Norman Vincent Peale, the guru of positive thinking. Today Dr. Peale is not sure how much credit he can take for Donald's attitude. ''Maybe all my preaching about faith the size of a mustard seed helping to move mountains bolstered his character.''

No fancy prep school for Donald. His father told one writer that ''I tried to bring Donald down to earth many times.'' Finally, he shipped him off to New York Military Academy. ''They straightened him out,'' his father recalled, ''but he always had a nose for quality and we could never get it out of him.''

''When I graduated, I was, like, the top-ranking guy in terms of the military,'' Donald told a writer. Almost every profile ever written about him states that he graduated first in his class at the University of Pennsylvania's Wharton School of Finance. Yet the commencement program for 1968 doesn't list him as graduating with honors of any kind. When confronted with this revelation, Trump's response was that he had never made that claim to anyone. Nor was he responsible when the television show "Lifestyles of the Rich and Famous" reported that his Greenwich, Connecticut, waterfront home was a "$10 million estate." Admitting that he paid more like $3 million, he said, "I didn't tell them that."

In 1975, at the age of 28, Donald Trump was ready to try his wings in Manhattan real estate. His father had strong ties to the Brooklyn Democratic machine that launched the political careers of New York Governor Hugh Carey and New York City Mayor Abe Beame, both of whom happened to be in power when Donald decided to cross the East River. (Today the ties are with Governor Mario Cuomo and Mayor Edward Koch.)

Not only had the Trump family contributed generously to their campaigns ($135,000 to Carey's alone), but Donald hired as a special advocate Louise M. Sunshine, chairman of Carey's campaign finance committee, who became instrumental in getting the city and state to build the New York convention center on the site of the defunct Penn Central railroad. For his efforts in putting together the convention center deal, Trump received a $500,000 commission plus $88,000 in expenses.

Trump took a $500,000 option on the old Commodore Hotel, adjacent to Grand Central Station, and owned by Penn Central. With the land option in hand, Trump worked out a fifty-fifty partnership deal with Hyatt: Trump would build a hotel on the leased land and Hyatt would manage it. He then rounded up pledges for $70 million in mortgage money from the Equitable Life Assurance Society which he and Sunshine took to Mayor Beame at City Hall. "One of the conditions was that I would obtain a tax abatement," Trump told the *New York Times*. "I told the city, I will build you this incredible, gorgeous, gleaming hotel. I will put people to work in the construction trades and save hotel jobs, and the Grand Central area, which was pretty depressing at the time, will come around. So the city made a deal."

The deal, the first of its kind ever granted to a commercial property, exempted the hotel from paying city taxes for the next 40 years—a bonus estimated to be worth $50 million. When the dust finally settled, Trump ended up the co-owner of the 1407-room chrome-and-glass Grand Hyatt Hotel without having invested any of his own money.

Trump Tower was an even more lucrative deal. Sunshine introduced Trump to David Evins, a powerful Carey supporter and major stockholder in Genesco, which then owned Bonwit Teller, a department store on Fifth Avenue near the exclusive Tiffany & Company. It was in conversation with Evins that Trump first learned that the Bonwit lease might be available. Equitable owned the land under Bonwit and Tiffany owned the air rights over it. Although Genesco had rejected other offers, it found Trump's acceptable. Trump lined up the necessary credit from the Chase Manhattan Bank and went into a fifty-fifty partnership with Equitable to build his tower.

The upper half of Trump Tower consisted of 263 condominiums and, although they were priced at $600,000 to $10 million each, Trump had no trouble selling them. "So we have about a $277 million sellout," Trump announced before even any of the tenants could move in, "just for the upper half of the building. And then we own the lower half for nothing." The $277 million paid off all mortgages, with a handsome profit to boot, and rent from the 13 floors of office space was $50 a square foot and $150 to $450 a square foot for the six levels of retail space in the shopping atrium. "It's a crazy deal," said Trump. "It's better than working."

The annual rents for some of the retail outlets run as high as a million dollars. "It's the greatest group of stores ever assembled under one roof," Trump boasted. "Well, it's probably the most expensive set of stores, certainly. And the greatest. And they're the most important stores." As one writer noted, "Trump's declarations have a habit of sliding up or down in magnitude. If he thinks he can get away with it, the statements become broader and more encompassing. When he has overstepped himself, he retrenches."

Donald summed up Trump Tower this way: "The finest apartments in the top building in the best location in the hottest city in the world." This manner of talking is called Trump-speak. The tower is for the "world's best people," which included Johnny Carson, David Merrick, Sophia Loren, Steven Spielberg, oil-rich Arabs, and Donald Trump himself, who with his wife and three children occupies a $10 million penthouse apartment. "It's strange," said Trump of his tenants. "It's an unbelievable situation. There are some people that won't be here more than a week a year. It's crazy."

Another property, Trump Plaza on Third Avenue, also houses the world's best people, including several heads of large corporations, Phyllis George, Martina Navratilova, Dick Clark, Chuck Barris, Norman Fell, and Regis Philbin. Trump owns 90 percent of this one, a cooperative building partnership. If this deal is like his others, most likely he has already recouped his investment and will continue to recoup it for many years to come. "Let's face it," Trump said of Trump Plaza, "it's on Third Avenue. But we're getting disproportionately high prices because of the name. Everyone who couldn't afford Trump Tower is there."

In assessing his superior salesmanship, Trump said it required three elements: "One is imagination. The other is being able to capitalize on your imagination and make it reality. I like to think I have both. The third element is the ability to let people know what you've done. What good is it if no one knows about it? You've gotta be a promoter." Asked who else had all these qualities, he conceded that a "lot of people have one element or another, but very few have it all." As for his catering to the rich, he said, "It costs nearly as much to build low-income housing as it does luxury housing." In other words, you also can sell fantasies to poor people, but not at $1000 a square foot.

Another "crazy" deal was the Barbizon-Plaza Hotel and an adjacent apartment building. Trump purchased the property for about $13 million and two months later took out a mortgage on it for $65 million. Today the value of that parcel on Central Park South is estimated at $125 million. "Donald," said one developer, "has the uncanny ability to smell blood in the water."

It was inevitable that Trump would make enemies along the way. "He's incredibly arrogant, the epitome of egotism," said one broker. "He comes into a meeting and takes over like he's king."

In October 1983 it was reported that Trump paid $10 million for the New Jersey Generals, one of 18 teams in the fledgling United States Football League. What he actually paid was closer to $1 million, but he received publicity easily worth $10 million. And in 1985 received another avalanche of publicity when the Generals signed Doug Flutie, Heisman Trophy winner from Boston College, to a reputed five-year, $7 million contract. The USFL voiced no objection when it discovered that a casino operator now owned one of its teams. "It is our understanding that Mr. Trump is a partner in the building development and that Harrah's will run the casino," said a USFL spokesman. "And from that standpoint we have no problem."

Harrah's Trump Plaza became Atlantic City's tenth casino. The joint agreement with Holiday Inns, which owned Harrah's, once again demonstrated Donald Trump's skill at negotiation.

Trump's total commitment was $22 million when Holiday Inns came into the picture. For a half interest, it not only reimbursed Trump for the $22 million he had already invested, but paid him an additional $50 million in cash plus financing in amounts estimated to be from $170 to $250 million. The total cost of the hotel-casino was reportedly $220 million, which means that Trump came away with a handsome profit plus 50 percent of the new hotel-casino without risking any of his own money. As an extra bonus, Holiday Inns agreed to manage the property without charge and guaranteed Trump no financial losses in the first five years.

However, within six months of the grand opening in Atlantic City, Holiday Inns and Trump had a falling out. Harrah's name was removed from the casino and it became known as Trump Plaza.

The split was played down in the press. "This will eliminate any potential confusion in the public's mind because we have two Atlantic City properties in such close proximity," said Philip Satre, president of Harrah's Marina. But Holiday Inns had no intention of selling its half-interest to Trump.

One of the obvious problems was that Harrah's name was associated with low-budget gamblers, with the concentration on its slot operation. Trump had built 85 luxury suites for high-rollers, but instead of booking big-name entertainers that would attract them, they brought in country-and-western stars like Eddie Arnold.

Even with its expertise in attracting low-rolling slot players, Harrah's had failed to meet expectations at Trump Plaza. Because of serious problems in its accounting system, a large percentage of the slots were closed for most of the first month of operation, costing the facility millions in lost revenue.

Trump was said to be furious. Everything seemed to go wrong in the first few months. It started with a false fire alarm on opening day that forced the evacuation of the entire hotel and casino, with several patrons reporting injuries. Two months later a real fire on the 31st floor forced the evacuation of guests on three floors—one guest was found lying in a tub full of water with his wrists slit. The fire appeared to have been set deliberately.

There were security problems. One man was robbed of $1800 while riding an elevator, and another who picked up a hooker in the casino's bar and brought her to his room was fleeced out of $25,000 in cash. Then an outbreak of salmonella food poisoning closed two of the hotel's restaurants after a dozen people became ill. But the major problem was the casino's bottom line. Earnings for the seven months of operations in 1984 were $125.6 million, with a profit of $16.4 million before deductions for federal income taxes. For a man who liked being number one, Trump Plaza had placed seventh out of ten in the revenue sweepstakes.

Besides, Trump had initially argued persuasively to have his name on the building, and now with Harrah's name being erased from the marquee, Trump said, "I'm very honored to have my name on the greatest hotel facility anywhere in the world."

As for the future of the partnership agreement, Trump said, "I hope that Trump Plaza will be managed as well as it was built. I'm used to being number one, and until it is number one or close to it, I can never be satisfied."

Back in March 1982 Donald Trump had breezed through his license hearing. The gaming commissioners had never seen a genuine, high-powered 37-year-old mogul who was so squeaky clean that the gaming division could find nothing to complain about in its report. Given that luxury, the commission moved swiftly to license everyone concerned. It was the first casino to open with a full gaming license rather than the temporary operating permit given the preceding nine casinos.

Donald Trump was clean, but still there was his relationship with Dan Sullivan, a convicted criminal and Teamsters official, who owned part of the land on which the hotel stood.

In an interview with the *New York Times,* Trump had said that he had sent 14 people to Atlantic City to buy 15 parcels of land—"If the seller was Italian, we sent an Italian," he explained. In looking over the mortgages the division had run across Dan Sullivan, Ken Shapiro, and Elliot Goldberg. It was the same Ken Shapiro who had helped funnel some of Scarfo's payoff money to Michael Matthews, and

Elliot Goldberg had been a partner of Shapiro in Seatex Associates, described by the state police as a hangout for organized crime figures.

Sullivan's arrest record included impersonating a police officer, larceny, grand larceny, felonious assault, and possession of a dangerous weapon. His prison record included 10 days for larceny, and 60 days for grand larceny later downgraded to attempted petty larceny. Born in New York City on December 9, 1938, Daniel J. Sullivan worked as a truck driver before gaining various executive positions with the Teamsters. He claimed to have been a member of 37 locals.

There was also the question of Sullivan's possible role in the mysterious disappearance of a Teamsters lawyer. "On December 6, 1966, Sullivan met with Abraham Bauman, an attorney representing a [dissident] union faction of [Teamsters] Local 812," the gaming division stated in its report to the commission. "As a result of an election held in that local, David Levinger retained control of the union by defeating Jimmy Gallo. Bauman disappeared after speaking with Sullivan on the foregoing date, and neither he nor his body were ever located."

According to newspaper stories quoted in the division's report, "Sullivan refused to disclose the nature of his discussion with Bauman to Brooklyn detectives investigating the matter. During the course of the August 20, 1981, interview with division representatives, Sullivan related that he had met with Bauman on December 6, 1966, to discuss the differences between David Levinger and Jimmy Gallo."

A *New York Times* article dated August 13, 1975, and entitled "The Hoffa Puzzle: Pieces Still Don't Fit," identified Sullivan as an associate of Jimmy Hoffa.

In April 1980 Sullivan, Ken Shapiro, and the Goldberg brothers (Elliott, Sheldon, Erwin, Martin) formed SSG Enterprises and assumed $2.8 million in mortgages to take control of the land under the proposed Trump casino site just one week before they signed their 99-year lease with Donald Trump. Sullivan had a 50 percent interest, with 25 percent each to Shapiro and the Goldbergs.

> According to Sullivan [the division reported], in approximately April 1980, Howard Goldberg, Esquire [no relation to Elliot Goldberg], who was representing Trump in Atlantic City, contacted his partner in SSG, Ken Shapiro, and explained that Trump was interested in the Boardwalk, Columbia Place, Mississippi Avenue, and Pacific Avenue property. Magnum, Plaza,

SSG, and Trump were represented during and participated in the negotiations regarding the leasing of the foregoing property.

. . . During a substantial reconstruction of the Grand Hyatt Hotel, previously known as the Commodore Hotel, Sullivan represented a number of subcontractors, including Circle Industries Corporation, which were employed at the construction site. As said construction was nearing completion, Sullivan became aware of disagreements between the Grand Hyatt management and the Hotel and Restaurant Employees Joint Board of the City of New York.

According to Sullivan, during the lease negotiations relevant to the proposed Atlantic City casino-hotel site, Trump mentioned that he had noticed Sullivan at the Grand Hyatt facility, and Trump and Sullivan discussed the labor difficulties with the foregoing union. Sullivan continued that Trump suggested to him during that conversation that he contact Fred Alexander, the general manager of the Grand Hyatt Hotel, to discuss the labor matter. After meeting with Sullivan, Alexander referred him to Daniel Lombardi, president of Hyatt Hotels. Lombardi in turn retained Sullivan to represent the Grand Hyatt Hotel with regard to the labor problems involving the Hotel and Restaurant Employees Joint Board of the City of New York. . . . Sullivan successfully negotiated a labor contract with the union on behalf of the Grand Hyatt. Currently, Philip Lombardi, chief of the labor section of Hyatt Hotels located in Chicago, Illinois, is Sullivan's immediate supervisor pertinent to his labor representation of Hyatt Hotels. [In April 1985 the President's Commission on Organized Crime charged that the Mafia controlled the International Brotherhood of Teamsters, the Laborers International Union, the Hotel and Restaurant Employees and Bartenders International Union, and the International Longshoremen's Association.]

With regard to the foregoing matter, Trump explained that during the Atlantic City lease negotiations he realized Sullivan's abilities in the labor negotiation area and recommended Sullivan to the Grand Hyatt Hotel management. Further, Trump stated that Sullivan had shown him various documentation from governmental agencies which related that Sullivan had represented those agencies in labor negotiations.

An article in the *Bucks County Courier Times* on July 24, 1980, quoted Sullivan as stating that Trump is "an old friend from New York," and that "it's nice being friends with a millionaire." Questioned about the story by the division, Sullivan denied knowing Trump prior to the lease negotiation.

According to the division's report, when Sullivan began negotiating to purchase Circle Industries, "Trump arranged appointments between Sullivan and bankers, including Conrad Stevenson of Chase Manhattan Bank who is listed as a voucher by Trump and who is Trump's personal banker, with regard to obtaining financing for the proposed corporate purchase. The Chase Manhattan Bank offered a $3.5 million line of credit to Sullivan and a co-investor. The bank and the purchasers requested that Trump guarantee the loan." Trump declined. That was going too far. That's what other people were expected to do for Trump, not vice versa.

"As is evident from the foregoing discussion, the division has investigated the background of Sullivan and the relationship between Sullivan and Trump. The division generally questioned Trump regarding his relationship with Sullivan. In response thereto, Trump informed the Division that he had been in contact with a law enforcement agency in New York regarding Sullivan and that he had obtained no derogatory information. Further, Trump advised the division that he would not have any future personal, social, or business dealings with Sullivan other than in the context of their Atlantic City lessor-lessee relationship. During the course of the division's investigation, it has ascertained that the matters related herein do not impact in a negative manner upon the credentials of Trump."

Tall and trim-looking in a dark suit, with his sandy hair modishly styled, Donald Trump had made a brief but impressive appearance before the commission. Sullivan, Shapiro, and the Goldbergs were not called to testify before the commission—Shapiro and the Goldbergs were not even questioned by the division. No one seemed interested in SSG's timely acquisition of the Boardwalk property or in exploring the possibility that Shapiro might be fronting for Scarfo. In the federal indictment of Mayor Michael Matthews, Shapiro was named "an agent of the Scarfo organization," and on the day of his appearance before the grand jury Shapiro was accompanied by Sullivan, who was not called to testify.

During his testimony before the commission, which lasted less than an hour, Trump was asked how his facility would impact on Atlantic City and his answer was classic Trump: "Well, I think Atlantic City really is a place that has a potentially—it could be really a fabulous city and a fabulous place. Up until now, most people, if you go outside of this room, and people that are not familiar with Atlantic City, but I am trying to give an honest statement of Atlantic City, and I don't want to talk out of turn, people do not think of Atlantic City as being the kind of a place which I think it can be. I think Atlantic City needs some quality. It needs some pizzazz. It needs some—something that's going to bring people and right now it really has certain elements but it doesn't have the right combination of elements. We feel our facility will be the finest in Atlantic City. It will be a quality facility. It will employ thousands of people, hopefully, happily, and we just think with this facility it's going—of course it's one piece in a very complicated puzzle—but we think that with this facility it's going to be a big step for Atlantic City."

Asked if he knew a "man named Daniel Sullivan," Trump replied, "He is one of the landlords on one of the parcels."

"At what point did you come to know that he was involved in this project?"

"I met him probably at one of the closings or during the negotiations, let's say, and then ultimately at the closings for Holiday Inns' parcel. He had the middle parcel. He and a group of people that I guess are associated with him had a piece in the middle and obviously without that piece or without any of the pieces it wouldn't have worked."

That was the first and last time Sullivan's name was mentioned. Asked to what extent he, Trump, was personally involved in the negotiations, he said, "Well, I like to personally get myself involved in really any negotiation. When the day comes that I can't on a magnitude of this, then I think I'm going to have to close up shop."

As for the lessors, Trump said, "Now, you know, people are human beings. These people are owners of a piece of land and they are not bad people from what I see. I have no—I don't think there's anything wrong with these people. I have met with these people on a number of occasions. Most of them have been in Atlantic City for many, many years and I think they are well thought of. . . ."

"Mr. Trump, let me set forth the worst possible scenario I think I can think of. One of these landlords turns out to be somebody that is part of the Mob and he decides he's going to shake you down for whatever reason. What would you do then?"

"Well, I think I would immediately report it to whoever there would be to report it to. I don't know that it would have any—what would the difference of that be as opposed to being a landlord or not being a landlord. Again that's really the key. That can happen whether somebody is a landlord or whether they are not a landlord. And if it did I would report it to the authorities."

"You would agree then it would be the responsibility of this commission to take corrective action?"

"Yes, Yes. Absolutely."

With that hypothetical problem solved, Trump was excused and the hearings concluded. The division, which had followed a hard-line policy when it came to licensing applicants involved with people of questionable repute, voiced no objection to Sullivan and Shapiro, taking the position that as landowners they did not have to meet the licensing requirements. It seemed to be an inconsistent position. In its report on Golden Nugget, for example, it had forced the company to cut its relationship with McDonnell Douglas Finance Corporation, from which it had borrowed $4 million, because the aircraft manufacturer had paid bribes overseas.

All that seemed to matter was that Trump be approved in record time and that his cleanliness be trumpeted for all to rejoice in. After the parade of scoundrels who had preceded Trump into Atlantic City, the division and commission were overjoyed with his shiny image. Even the slightest attempt to tarnish it would have been counterproductive. The commission, however, insisted that all the landowners be licensed and Trump solved that problem by buying out SSG for $8 million.

Some eighteen months later, Sullivan again cropped up in the news. As the casino's director of security Trump had hired Edward F. Wunsch, police chief in Lower Southampton Township, who was denied a casino license because he lied in an attempt to cover up Sullivan's involvement on his behalf in securing the job from Trump.

But none of these problems diminished Donald Trump's triumph before the members of the gaming commission. He had demanded their blessings before deigning to bestow his own on Atlantic City. He showed them how a sharp New York entrepreneur played the game: heads I win, tails you lose. That's how it's done when one is on the greatest winning streak in the "world."

Others had more serious problems. Hilton was to make history in Atlantic City. Almost immediately it started its investigation, the gaming division found some unpleasantries. For one thing Heinz "Henri' Lewin, executive vice-president in charge of the company's casino-hotel division, had enjoyed unsavory relationships. The list included Jay Sarno, old Cleveland mobster Moe Dalitz, Morris Lansburgh Allen Dorfman, Sidney Korshak, and Rudy Tham.

In 1979 Lewin had been indicted by a federal grand jury for unlawfully providing complimentary rooms and entertainment for Tham at the Las Vegas Hilton. Tham, a Teamsters boss in San Francisco, was identified by the California Organized Crime Control Commission as "the almost constant companion of Aladena 'Jimmy the Weasel' Fratianno," a Mafia killer and then acting boss of the Los Angeles family. Tham also had been provided with suites at the San Francisco Hilton that were used by Fratianno for assignation purposes.

Harry Claiborne, the federal judge at Lewin's trial, had accepted Lewin's explanation that the complimentary services were provided to Tham not because of his union role, but because of his status as a casino customer—ignoring the fact that there was no casino at the San Francisco Hilton. Lewin denied that Tham was involved in labor negotiations for Hilton, although his relationship with Tham had been helpful during labor negotiations in San Francisco and Oakland.

After Claiborne dismissed the charges, Lewin invited the judge to his son's wedding, asking Hilton to pick up the tab. Lewin also arranged a hotel room for Claiborne in Hawaii, but assured the division there was nothing improper in these courtesies. (In 1984 Judge Claiborne was convicted for filing false federal tax returns and received a two-year prison term.)

Of greater concern to the division was the 13 years Sidney Korshak had been on Hilton's payroll as a "consultant" with an annual retainer of $50,000, plus out-of-pocket expenses. In the past ten years alone, Hilton had paid Korshak approximately $700,000, plus another $365,000 to his brother, Marshall, a Chicago attorney.

Hilton's senior vice-president and general counsel, E. Timothy Applegate, said he had been "shocked and surprised" by a series of articles in the *New York Times* in 1976 that dealt with Korshak's connections to organized crime. It "gave me some concern," he said, but he "felt helpless" because he was unable to verify the allegations. Besides, the Nevada gaming commission "did not consider it necessary to discharge Mr. Korshak."

Under questioning, Applegate characterized Korshak's $50,000 fee as "an outstanding bargain" for Hilton. Asked if he could explain why Hilton got such a bargain, he replied, "No, I can't."

Noting that much of the work done through Korshak's law firm apparently was performed by two other attorneys, Commissioner Carl Zeitz wanted to know whether Korshak "ever did a lick of legal work for the company" and Applegate responded, "I don't know." Yet while he couldn't pinpoint specific legal work performed by Korshak, Applegate was insistent that Korshak wasn't retained in order to keep labor peace.

Which was surprising, considering that is what Korshak has been doing for everybody else in the last fifty years. A 1967 Los Angeles police report described Korshak as "*the* fixer in the labor-management field. His activities in his chosen field date back to the 1930s during the Capone era. Subject has many well-placed friends in the labor movement and is recognized by union officials—large and small—as a representative of the 'group' that has the 'connections' and makes the decisions for the 'mobsters' or 'racketeers' who prey upon the labor unions."

Sidney Korshak had been settling labor disputes in Las Vegas since the mid-1940s when Bugsy Siegel first built the Flamingo Hotel, which is now owned by Hilton. It would be astonishing, indeed, if Hilton had never availed itself of his mysterious negotiating powers. When it became apparent that gaming officials would not look favorably upon Korshak's continued employment, he was severed from Hilton, and Applegate was given the unenviable assignment of writing the termination letter.

"I appreciate very much your understanding the action we feel we're forced to take in dissolving the long-standing relationship between you and Hilton Hotels Corporation," Applegate wrote on March 10, 1984. "As I stated in our telephone conversation on Wednesday, we very much regret this situation. We feel, however, that we cannot risk jeopardizing in any way the huge investment we have committed in Atlantic City." But he added: "My own inquiries and reading of the public press have never revealed to me any reason to consider terminating our relationship." However, he observed, gaming officials "appear to believe that you have questionable associations and have made an issue of your retention by Hilton." He ended his letter with: "You can rest assured that you continue to be held in high esteem and affection by those of us at Hilton who have had the privilege of having you as a friend and advisor."

Hilton's board chairman, Barron Hilton, took the responsibility for having hired Korshak. As far as he was concerned, reports of Korshak's criminal associations were not enough to fire him, since Korshak had never been convicted of any crime. And Korshak had performed valuable services for the company.

Commission chairman Walter N. Read told Hilton that "it is not necessary in New Jersey for a person to be indicted or convicted to find their presence is inimical in this industry."

Later, under intense questioning by division director Thomas O'Brien and commission members, Hilton said, "I wish to hell we would have never hired him, because I can see it's a very distinct problem here in the minds of you gentlemen about this fellow's integrity. I'm sorry we ever had this problem occur."

Testifying again a few months later, Barron Hilton had come to realize that the problem was more than "in the minds" of the commission members. By then he knew that his application was in serious trouble. "I want to say that I certainly appreciate the concern that this commission has that any applicant [for a license] be free of any type of association [with] an individual such as Mr. Korshak, and I can say that today we would not be involved in any fashion with Mr. Korshak, and as you are aware, we . . . discontinued our relationship with the individual and I have to agree with you that it should have been done before, rather than now."

Hilton's contrition came too late. As commissioner Joel Jacobson would later phrase it, "The corporation apparently didn't get religion until it was pounding on the pearly gates of licensure."

Although the division didn't oppose the license, it was denied by the commission, which had been operating with only four members since the resignation of Don M. Thomas. Barron Hilton issued a statement to the effect that he was "shocked and stunned," and promised that the company would take its appeal to the courts.

Chairman Read and commissioner E. Kenneth Burdge voted to

grant the license on condition that some of the executives be forced to resign, but Hilton needed a majority vote to be licensed. Jacobson and Carl Zeitz decided the issue against Hilton. Zeitz said he couldn't find "that the wrongdoing in this case was limited to certain persons."

(Zeitz pointed to other charges besides Korshak. In 1975 the Las Vegas Hilton had cashed $100,000 in checks for Sorkis Webbe, "which we know were kickback payments on the Aladdin hotel-casino construction financed by the Teamsters." Webbe was later convicted and sentenced to prison for concealing the kickbacks on his tax returns and federal prosecutors charged that the checks were "laundered" at the Hilton. And there was the matter of Henry Lewin and the "comps" to Teamsters boss Rudy Tham.)

Two weeks after the commission's rejection, Barron Hilton received a letter from an angry Sidney Korshak. The letter, dated November 29, 1984, contradicted Hilton's testimony that he had never asked Korshak to intercede with Las Vegas unions to prevent a strike:

Dear Sir:

I find it extremely difficult to address you in any other fashion.

I read with interest your disparaging remarks about me to the New Jersey Gaming Commission. When did you discover that I was unworthy of being an attorney or that I was associated with characters that shocked your most decent sensibilities?

I have in my possession a number of letters from your staff extolling my virtues as an attorney and telling me how happy the hotels were with my representation of your corporation. Those letters were also sent to your office for your personal perusal.

I am sending them to you again today.

Was I in a sorry plight with you when I met you in New York and worked out a deal with Charlie Bluhdorn of Gulf & Western, giving you their airport hotel and the Arlington hotel to manage without you investing one penny, despite your offer to pay Gulf & Western some $10 million for a one-half investment in these hotels? If you recall, you will remember calling me in Las Vegas at six one morning while you were with [MGM

owner] Kirk Kerkorian and [MGM executive] Frank Rothman
for me to ask the [Las Vegas] unions involved not to strike you,
namely Dick Thomas of the Teamsters and Bob Fox of the
Engineers? As you well know, there was no fee involved.

   You have caused me irreparable harm, and as long as I live I
will never forget that. When did I become a shady character? I
imagine when you were having difficulty getting a license in
Atlantic City.

Very truly yours,
Sidney R. Korshak

Less than a month after it denied Hilton a gaming license, the
Casino Control Commission agreed to reopen its hearing into Hilton's
qualifications for a license. The key vote to permit the rehearing was
delivered by Carl Zeitz. Joel Jacobson, whose vote would not be
needed if Zeitz reversed his earlier stance on the license, saw no
reason to change his mind or to send the commission into "sudden
death overtime." It was also hoped that Valerie Armstrong, who had
been appointed to fill the vacant fifth seat on the commission, would
be sworn in by the time the new hearings began.

   "It clearly now appears the applicant has additional material which
is both material and necessary to this case," said Commission Chairman Read. "Fundamental fairness" warrants new hearings, he said.
"Who is to be hurt? Indeed, who can complain if we allow a
rehearing?"

   After the commission's vote, Barron Hilton said that "recent days
have seemed like a bad dream for Hilton directors, executives, and
employees. Our reputation is our most important asset. [The company takes] this second opportunity with full seriousness and a commitment to completely and fully tell the story of Hilton. We are
confident this new look at Hilton, and our record, will substantiate
our position in the eyes of the commission."

   A few days later, Steve Wynn, who had abandoned plans to build
a second Golden Nugget that would serve only the wealthiest of
gamblers, made a bid to buy control of the Hilton Hotels Corporation.

   In a letter to Barron Hilton, Golden Nugget offered to buy up to
6.78 million shares, or 27.4 percent of Hilton stock, for $72 per
share, or a total of $488.3 million. They said that the company

"would consider providing similar values in a negotiated transaction to all of the shareholders of Hilton," which meant that the transaction could be worth as much as $1.8 billion. Golden Nugget, said one of its spokesman, "stopped short of saying that we're planning a take-over [because] that's the reality."

The block of 6.78 million shares was owned by the estate of the late Conrad Hilton, and when Golden Nugget suspected that Hilton was making moves to thwart its takeover attempts, it filed a lawsuit against Hilton charging securities law violations. According to Steve Wynn, the proxy statement sent to Hilton shareholders "is materially false and misleading." The suit asked the court to enjoin further solicitation of proxies by Hilton and to invalidate proxies previously granted. But a federal judge denied Golden Nugget's requested injunction.

The Golden Nugget filed its lawsuit on April 19, 1985, one day after it learned that Barron Hilton was considering an offer to sell its Atlantic City casino-hotel to Donald Trump. In a statement from a Golden Nugget executive, Hilton was "putting its tail between its legs and running away from New Jersey" without vindicating its name.

A week later Golden Nugget offered Hilton $344 million for its Atlantic City property—the package consisted of $260 million in 8 percent notes and $84 million in undeveloped Atlantic City property. Hilton countered that the notes would be discounted to "far below" their face value and the property's value was "a matter of conjecture" —Wynn had paid $25.5 million for the property last year.

The next day Hilton announced that it had accepted an offer of $325 million from Donald Trump. Hilton had spent about $308 million on its nearly finished hotel-casino.

After touring his new property which overlooks Absecon Inlet and the Frank S. Farley Marina State Park, Trump declared that it was an "absolutely fabulous facility overall." But he planned to make a "few modifications." He would follow Hilton's original plans to expand the casino from 60,000 to 70,000 square feet and enlarge the hotel from 614 rooms to 2000 rooms. In a meeting with his new employees, he vowed to make it the "finest casino-hotel in the country."

All that remained was for Donald Trump to find a suitable name. At first he thought he would call it Trump Palace, but after a week of thinking it over, he decided to call it Trump Castle. "Mr. Trump," said a company spokesman, "felt that Castle was the most appropriate name for such a beautiful, vast and majestic facility. The name 'Trump Castle' gives us a distinct identity yet benefits from the strength of the success of Trump's name on the Boardwalk."

At the formal ribbon-cutting ceremonies on July 16, 1985, a month after the Castle's grand opening, Governor Thomas Kean said, "Anything that the Trump organization has ever been involved in means excitement and means success." As for Atlantic City, Trump's investments signified that it was going to be rebuilt "into one of the world's great cities." The governor called Trump's Castle an "architectural wonder."

With the press in full attendance, Trump took a swipe at Harrah's, his partner in Trump Plaza. "There's never been a smoother, more successful opening of a casino in Atlantic City," he boasted. Without mentioning Trump Plaza by name, he reminded everyone that "we don't manage the other facility."

Besides being Trump's partner on the Boardwalk, Harrah's Marina was the Castle's only neighbor in the inlet. In fact, it was right across the street, which placed Trump in direct competition with his Boardwalk partner. The feud that had been brewing for a year finally ended up in the courts.

In a suit filed in federal court, Harrah's accused Trump of lying about his casino plans and breaching the partnership contract; it charged unfair competition and asked that he be forced to remove his name from the new casino.

Firing back with a countersuit, Trump claimed that Harrah's "amateurish" management had besmirched his name almost beyond redemption. In a four-page letter to Harrah's Chief Executive Officer, Philip G. Satre, filed in court, Trump cracked: "The Trump name has been so badly bloodied by your management of the facility that hopefully Trump's Castle Casino Hotel can do something to bring it back."

Trump's complaint read like a Madison Avenue brochure. It described him as "an entrepreneur who has achieved national and international prominence, reputation, and recognition as the result of the outstanding success he has achieved in conceiving, developing, and promoting various enterprises." After listing Manhattan's Trump Tower, Trump Plaza, and Grand Hyatt Hotel, the complaint noted, "the Trump name has come to be identified in the public mind with quality, excellence, achievement, and success, and Trump has been the subject of innumerable articles in the press and of substantial media attention." By comparison Harrah's parent, Holiday Inns, was described as "principally engaged in the business of operating quality but non-luxury hotels and motels."

In his court argument, Harrah's attorney charged that the only reason his client had agreed to remove its name from their Boardwalk casino was because "Mr. Trump kept insisting that any use of the name Harrah's would cause confusion with Harrah's Marina. He simply cannot pull the rug out from under us after he asked us to stand on it."

Judge Stanley Brotman was not impressed: "But if Holiday Inns didn't want it [the name change], it would never have happened. You're big, big boys there. If you didn't like it, you could have stopped it right there."

When Harrah's claimed that Trump was mainly known as a manager of real estate in Brooklyn and Queens before it had spent $8 million promoting his name, Brotman said he was familiar with the Trump name before the partnership was formed. "Maybe Trump came and gave your hotel something it didn't have. You're big, big companies and you're playing hard with each other. But that's the way you guys play." And when the attorneys attempted to argue that one had deceived the other when the partnership agreement was drawn up in 1982, Brotman said, "You had all the resources in the world to bargain out a partnership agreement."

Both sides hurled insults and nasty allegations. Harrah's was not all that impressed with Trump's building expertise. It indicated that Trump had none of his own money invested in the property, that he had built a facility with serious construction problems, and had interfered with the operation. Harrah's further contended that Trump, in an effort to force Harrah's to buy him out at an inflated price, had tried to hire away Trump Plaza workers for the Castle, had misappropriated lists of Trump Plaza customers and high rollers for the Castle, and had balked at constructing a long-planned parking garage for the Plaza.

And both claimed the other partner was deliberately trying to depress the value of the property for their own purposes. "Our theory," said Trump's New Jersey attorney, "is they've been mismanaging the facility trying to force Donald out."

"Trump Plaza is a cash machine for him," said a Harrah's official. "He has no cash invested in it, no obligation on the debt—all he has to do is collect. But he only gets fifty percent of the profits."

Now, they were saying, he wanted the whole loaf, with a discount. Well, isn't that also the way the big boys play?

31
The Bottom Line

The voters of Atlantic City were not the only ones unhappy with their elected officials. Casino operators were complaining that the city's government had been more of a hindrance than a help.

Although the number of gamblers visiting the Boardwalk had reached 30 million by 1985, they were still using the same three roads into Atlantic City, each the same size as before casinos. Traffic control was a nightmare, with 60,000 cars and 1100 buses on an around-the-clock schedule, spewing their exhausts into the air, snarling traffic into a gridlock that defied solution. The airport was still operating with a terminal made of trailers, without a tower, and a runway so short that it discouraged commercial airliners. The reestablishment of rail service to Philadelphia was still in the talking stage, and the convention center remained a cavernous hulk without its promised renovation.

The only first-class hotel rooms were the 6000 in hotel-casinos, fewer rooms than could be found on one corner in Las Vegas which has 53,000 rooms in 44 major resort hotels and numerous first-class motels, while accommodating a third as many visitors.

Atlantic City, once a resort with some 30,000 rooms, was stymied by its own progress. Land and construction costs made it financially impractical for anyone to build anything but casino-hotels. The cost for noncasino hotel rooms would run between $70,000 and $80,000 per unit. The scarcity of hotel accommodations was the area's greatest drawback to long-term growth.

As for the gamblers, life was hell in the casinos during peak hours, with every seat at every $5 and $10 table taken and lines forming at the slot machines. With their money burning holes in their pocket, the day-trippers had to wait for gamblers to go broke before they could have their chance with Lady Luck.

Business was so terrific that casino builders were queuing up for a shot at the Boardwalk. There was Nathan Jacobson and his proposed Camelot casino. This was the same Jacobson who with Jay Sarno had created Caesars Palace, the Las Vegas casino that had been such a boon to so many Mafia families. And it was the same Jacobson who had gone from Caesars to the Bonanza, escaping months before it had gone belly-up, only to surface with King's Castle at Lake Tahoe, another financial fiasco absorbed by the Teamsters pension fund and taken over by the Pritzkers. On the heels of his entry into Atlantic City was a complaint from the Securities and Exchange Commission charging that the underwriters for Jacobson's American Leisure Corporation had fraudulently handled a $25 million stock offering in violation of antitrust and securities laws. The agency also charged that "untrue statements" had been made in selling the securities, including assertions that the stock would double or triple in value shortly after the offering due to the company's purchase of land for the Atlantic City hotel-casino. Jacobson denied the charges.

Bass Brothers Enterprises of Fort Worth were proposing a complex of five casino-hotels and a convention center on the site of a former municipal dump in the marina section—to be called Golden Pyramids.

San Diego developer Jack Bona was proposing to build the Dunes, "one of the largest casinos in Atlantic City." It would mean tearing down the Mayfair Apartments and displacing hundreds of tenants, but not to worry: Bona had promised to build a 300-plus-unit high-rise housing complex. "We have developed plans that take into consideration the needs of the people we will serve, our neighbors in the area and the city," Bona said in a prepared statement. "We have been sensitive to all these needs at the same time that we have planned a casino-hotel project that is truly unique in many ways."

The Mayfair tenants had rushed to Bona's support at council meetings, praising their hero and booing the proponents of a rezoning plan that could have killed the project or at least stalled it indefinitely. Reacting to their enthusiasm, the council dropped the rezoning measure, but a year later Bona's tenants were no longer calling him an "angel" and "godsend." They were complaining about the building being filthy and rundown, and plagued by endless problems with heat, elevators, and lack of security. When they went to Bona, his answer was: "Move if you don't like it." But move where? Certainly not to Mayfair II—that was still on that big drawing board up in pie heaven.

Developer Jack Blumenfeld wanted to build the resort's largest casino hotel. His Carnival Club would squeeze in a 40-story building with 1070 rooms and a 90,000-square-foot casino on three acres, but the planning board made him scale it down to 675 rooms, lopping off 60 feet from its original 400-foot height. "They took a building that was monstrous even by Jabba the Hutt standards and made it workable," said the city's planning director.

Showboat, Inc., of Las Vegas was planning something truly unique, a casino-hotel in the shape of an ocean liner. When bleary-eyed gamblers woke up in the afternoon, they could stumble to portholes to peer out at the ocean, because each of its 504 rooms would face that beautiful sea. It would be christened Ocean Showboat. The land on which it would anchor its Showboat was the 8-acre parcel it had leased from Resorts International for 99 years, at $6.4 million per year.

Tony Torcasio had been waiting since 1978 for Bob Guccione to come up with enough millions to finish his Penthouse Boardwalk Hotel Casino. Anxious to assume his role as chief executive officer, Torcasio was "raring to go. I'm like a lion in a cage here. I'm dying for the opportunity to show people that we have the team and the expertise to be a top-running casino." This is the same Torcasio who had boasted to Abscam undercover agents that he could skim vast sums of money from the Penthouse casino without Guccione being aware of it.

Golden Nugget had set aside its plans for a new casino in the marina area when it made its bid to buy out Hilton. But Resorts International was moving ahead with its 1250-room hotel-casino on its Uptown Urban Renewal Tract site. Caesars, Tropicana, Bally, Atlantis, and the Sands were expanding their facilities. Gross earnings were $2.2 billion in 1984. It was estimated that by 1987, with the advent of at least four more casinos, earnings would rise to $3 billion and exceed $5 billion by 1991—with 40 million annual visitors.

The way it looked, there was no end to the progress Atlantic City could look forward to in the future. Members of the division and commission would be kept busy checking out prospective casino operators willing to gamble on the future.

Billions upon billions were there for the taking. The boom was big enough to satisfy the greediest of entrepreneurs. Twice as many casinos would mean twice as much money, twice as many rooms, twice as many buses and cars rumbling through the narrow, crowded streets, twice as many cushy jobs for retired politicians and bureaucrats.

Of course, it would mean twice as many jobs for qualified outsiders willing to move to the area, most of them settling in suburban towns and busing to the casinos like day-trippers. It would mean more tax dollars for the state and more "promised" assistance for the elderly and disabled.

Figures indicated that part of the 8 percent tax on gross casino profits was providing annual utility credits of less than $200 to about 300,000 recipients, many of whom had probably plunked far more into casino slot machines. Whether they came to win or to while away a few remaining hours of a winding-down life, or for whatever reasons, the fact was that they came in droves. On weekdays the slot machine areas look like geriatric conventions.

As a parting gesture of goodwill from the governor's office, Brendan Byrne shifted $80 million from the casino fund into the general budget, a move that senior citizen groups saw as a final act of betrayal. The new governor, Thomas Kean, looking forward to a repeat performance at the polls, restored $50 million and promised to replace the rest in the near future.

More casinos meant more street crimes, more prostitutes, more loansharks, more mobsters working the edges, more workers joining corrupt unions, more drugs on the streets, more high-school students trading their allowances for gambling chips, more shoplifting, more burglaries and robberies, and more arson.

How could it be otherwise? Thirty million gamblers flooding a small town of 37,000 mostly poor people. Prostitution was a thriving industry. The whores and their pimps had taken over Pacific Avenue, which, only one block from the Boardwalk, offered the best opportunity for a car pickup. Others roamed the Boardwalk and the casinos. The youngest and prettiest belonged to escort services that supplied them to casinos.

From time to time, there were swift police forays that filled the local jail for the night, but on the whole the resort police and the streetwalkers managed to stay out of one another's way, in what was characterized as an "uneasy truce" by the *Press*. The forays, though, have been more interesting than the truces.

Three cops, posing as Arab sheiks, lured 51 whores and pimps into their limousine as they cruised Pacific Avenue for a few hours, finally having to call off the sweep when the city jail was full. The next month, two cops, disguised as Vietnam veterans, one posing as an amputee confined to a wheelchair, bagged 18 whores and one pimp.

The FBI joined the state police in a crackdown on escort services. Called Operation Condor, the joint venture resulted in the arrest and conviction of Joseph Altimari, a Scarfo soldier who used extortion and threats of violence to control prostitution rings. Included in the rings were four escort services: Lucky Ladies, Tigress, Dial-A-Date, and Good Time Girls. The investigation detailed a series of meetings between Altimari and co-conspirators in which Altimari "was to receive a weekly fee of at least 50 percent of the money from all the businesses."

Transcripts of taped conversations showed that Altimari and five of his bodyguards and drivers demanded more "action" and warned that "downtown ain't too happy with what's going on because they're not making enough money." Operators were told to do "whatever must be done to make things happen," including the use of violence.

A corpulent man in a black suit, with diamond rings on both fat pinkies, Altimari called his 50 percent cut a "protection" fee. "Now, if it's a problem that somebody big comes into him, that's uh, that's affiliated with someone else, don't worry about it," he told one operator the police had wired for sound. "It'll be straightened out. They'll be told and you'll never hear from them again. If it's a tough guy that's giving you a hard time, I'll send in. I'll straighten that out."

A year prior to Altimari's arrest, the executive director of the state police, Lieutenant Colonel Justin Dintino, had told the Senate Judiciary Committee on Organized Crime that Altimari was in charge of gambling networks in Philadelphia and Bucks County for the Scarfo family. "Altimari's involvement in other illicit activities includes narcotics and prostitution," Dintino had said, "and information indicates that permission from Altimari was needed to open an escort service in Atlantic City."

In March 1984, Altimari, his stepson, and two others were convicted of conspiracy and promoting prostitution. Altimari received the stiffest sentence, 2½ years, which meant that he would be out on the street in about a year's time.

Another involved in prostitution was Barry Rosenstein, a former assistant Atlantic City municipal court prosecutor. He was convicted of two counts of promoting prostitution by providing call girls to casino high-rollers through his escort service, Elegant Escorts. Because of a prior conviction for credit card theft, he was sentenced to six months in the county jail.

Streetwalkers in Atlantic City, as elsewhere, were at the mercy of their pimps, who beat them frequently, often just to remind them of their place. While on the street they could talk only to their "wives-in-law," whores in the same pimp's stable, and were expected to be thieves. While call girls working casino lounges and hotel rooms received hundreds of dollars for leisurely sex, the streetwalker was expected to perform quickies and bring home wallets. One of the oldest ploys was to slit a john's wallet pocket with a razor blade while distracting him with tricks of the trade.

Besides the prostitutes, pimps, toughs, and the lunatics released in droves from Ancora State Psychiatric Hospital in recent years, Pacific Avenue has parking garages and lots, tired motels, abandoned buildings with boarded-up or soaped windows, the flashy backs of casinos—only two have doors that open on the avenue—sleazy coffee shops, an adult bookstore, a fortuneteller, and a slew of pawnshops with proprietors waiting behind walls of bulletproof glass. Once it had elegant hotels, jewelry stores, fine restaurants, and famed jazz clubs. The rich and celebrated of another era strolled its clean and safe sidewalk.

Now couples scurry from the parking garages and lots with heads down, women desperately clutching their purses—with good reason. In 1984 there were 19,000 reported pickpocket incidents inside casinos as well as in hotel areas. For the first six months of 1985, there were 15,016 reported incidents. Statistics showed that only a fraction of the incidents were reported to police. "A lot of people think they report it because they go to a security guard," said Detective Sergeant Steve Mangam, "but it's not officially reported until they come to the police department. A lot of people just take the loss."

Before the couple scurrying from the parking lot reach the casino of their choice chances are they will run into a hotdog vendor. For a long time there was an outside chance they might witness a battle in the raging "weiner wars," described as the Mafia's effort to take over choice locations near casino entrances in the $6 million-a-year business.

Peter Spalluto, owner of Hot Digity Dogs, charged that police confiscated his carts while ignoring the carts of competitors guilty of the same violations. Brought before Judge Steven Perskie on 20 counts of health code violations, Spalluto was fined $2000 and finally driven out of the pushcart rental business. The war, which had flared sporadically for several years, came to an end after the FBI got into the picture. The result of their investigation, a joint effort with the state police, was the indictment of 16 people for attempting to take control of the casino produce and hotdog vending businesses in Atlantic City. Charges included racketeering, conspiracy, bribery, and extortion.

In an effort to give a company called Island Vets control of the choice pushcart locations (a key spot can gross $100,000 during a busy summer), the defendants had tried to force Hot Digity Dogs out of business by damaging carts and physically attacking Hot Digity owners and vendors. They also demanded 50 percent of Hot Digity's profits and threatened to have city health officials and policemen prosecute Hot Digity for violating ordinances. Included among the defendants were police sergeant Joseph LaMaina and Scarfo's close friend Rick Casale. While threatening Spalluto, Casale had ominously reminded him that he was "a longtime friend of Scarfo."

Vice, drugs, and street crimes have become a second industry. After years of agitating for more police officers, Police Chief Joseph Pasquale was permitted to hire 35 recruits. What he came up with were 11 who were relatives of city and police officials, and several who had police records, including his own son Joseph, Jr. In 1977 Joseph, Jr., pleaded guilty to one count each of possession of a weapon without a permit and malicious damage—a woman was injured by a shot allegedly fired from a car in which he was a passenger. He served two months in the county jail. In 1982 he was arrested for assaulting a police officer, resisting arrest, and other assault and disorderly conduct charges. The more serious charges were dropped and he pleaded guilty to a single disorderly conduct charge and was ordered to pay $300 in fines and court costs.

Between 1977—the year before the first casino opened—and 1983, indexed crimes (murder, rape, robbery, aggravated assault, burglary, larceny/theft, motor vehicle theft) leaped 252 percent. For a town of

37,000 population, Atlantic City reported 15,480 indexed crimes in 1983.

By 1984 crime statistics had Police Chief Pasquale fighting mad. Reacting to an FBI report showing steep rises in burglaries, arsons, and thefts during 1983, Pasquale blamed the casinos. "It's the same problem," he said. "It includes the casinos, and that skews the hell out of it. We have no control over the casinos. They have their own security forces and the state police. We don't have anything to do with it." Perhaps, but one-third of Pasquale's force was moonlighting in casinos, doing security and traffic work.

Pasquale issued his own statistics, showing that anywhere from 20 to 50 percent of the crimes reported by the FBI occurred in casinos and casino-hotels. Chief Pasquale's figures showed that of the 6365 thefts reported to police in the first six months of 1984, 3658 had occurred in casinos-hotels.

(Before being sentenced for some early morning burglaries, the "Bedtime Bandit" had told the judge that one way the court could help reduce burglaries was for the court to see that something was done about improving door locks at casino-hotels, which he demonstrated could be easily circumvented by a small screwdriver. One call girl became known as the "Kissing Bandit" because she slipped a knockout drug into the mouth of her victim while kissing him. One incident involved three men she met in Resorts' Rendezvous Lounge. Later, in their tenth-floor rooms, she put all three to sleep with her kisses and made off with $3000 in cash and $8000 in jewelry. Her kissing spree netted her over $50,000 before she was caught.)

Chief Pasquale was right. It was as dangerous inside the casinos as outside, yet the penalty for getting caught stealing inside could be a lot stiffer. Two men who robbed a couple at the Sands, roughing them up in the process, were each sentenced to life, plus an additional 31 years for one, and 44 years for the other, which meant that they would serve a minimum of 40 years, a sentence six times as great as most murderers serve.

When sentenced, one of the defendants unburdened himself to Superior Court Judge Arthur V. Guerrera: "Because of the many injustices that I have pointed out, I can't help but wonder if you are connected somehow with the Sands Casino." "No, I'm not," Guerrera laughed, "but sometimes I think I wish I were."

On the other hand, as of this writing, nothing but administrative charges have been leveled at Caesars and nine of its high-ranking officials, including President Peter Boynton, who were charged by the gaming division with violating 29 gaming regulations when they assisted a bank manager in gambling away more than $10.2 million he had embezzled from the Canadian Imperial Bank of Commerce in Toronto, most of which he lost at Caesars' tables. Between February 1981 and April 1982 Brian Molony came to Caesars 49 times and on two occasions lost as much as a million in a single night.

The gaming division charged that Caesars told Molony how to deposit money secretly and directly with the casino by placing it in a Canadian bank account of the California Clearing Corporation, a dummy corporation set up "so that patrons could pay gambling debts without expressly writing checks to Caesars Palace or Desert Palace, Inc., thus avoid identifying these payments as gambling debts." Molony was provided with this arrangement after visiting the casino with a large amount of cash. His first transfer was $3.6 million, deposited under the name of Alphonse Ruggiero, a known bookmaker, and twice casino officials flew to Toronto to get Ruggiero to sign away money so Molony could continue gambling at Caesars.

On April 27, 1982, Molony returned to Toronto on Caesars' private jet and was met at the airport by police. He pleaded guilty and was sentenced to six years in prison.

The division charged that Caesars, in addition to violating state gaming regulations, also violated its own internal controls, noting that it failed to report that it gave Molony an $8500 Rolex watch. And the gaming panel faulted Caesars for "failing to take into consideration the fact that compulsive gambling is an illness," charging that "they were interested only in helping him gamble away his money."

Although Caesars officials denied they knew the source of Molony's money, and protested they didn't want to invade Molony's privacy with a lot of questions about his background, under gaming credit regulations they were obligated to find out.

It was the same story with Gaetano Caltagirone, an Italian industrialist who was later accused of defrauding the Italian government of 200 billion lira, equal to $245 million. Caesars executives were so eager to separate Caltagirone from $1.2 million of his ill-gained fortune that they allowed him to break a whole series of gaming regulations. Caesars was later fined $257,000 for the infractions.

Similarly, the Sands and Atlantis were fined for breaking gaming rules to accommodate 32 Oriental gamblers who arrived from Hong

Kong with $2.95 million in cash and checks. Neither the Italians nor Orientals could speak English, but they had little trouble making their wishes known.

In all fairness, how could a casino know if money had been embezzled? For all they knew Molony and Caltagirone could have been wealthy drug dealers who happened to be compulsive gamblers. After all, criminals of all persuasions use casinos to launder their dirty money. In testimony before a House committee in November 1983, Justin Dintino said that a survey of Atlantic City casinos earlier in the year had shown cash deposits of $33 million in May and $31 million in June. "Members of organized crime, drug traffickers, and some legitimate businessmen made these deposits."

Criminals deposited cash—usually in $5, $10, and $20 bills—from robberies and drug deals in the casino cages for a line of credit. Some gambled a few hours and some waited several days before returning to retrieve their money. Because of the constant flow of cash at the casinos, the criminals received new $100 bills when they picked up their deposits. "We found some hit men with over $1 million deposited," Dintino said, identifying one of them as Joseph Pedulla, who had become a state witness after he was convicted for his attack on Salvatore Testa.

In May 1985 a federal indictment charged that nine reputed organized crime figures had laundered at least $3.5 million obtained from the street sale of heroin at four Atlantic City casinos in December 1982. Most of the money—$2.5 million—was deposited on three separate days at the Golden Nugget. In one day, Anthony C. Castelbuono, a New York lawyer, deposited $1,187,450 at the cashier's cage in the Golden Nugget in denominations of $5, $10, and $20 bills—a bundle of cash weighing 280 pounds and stacking nearly 6 feet high.

At first, "every alarm and buzzer and bell went off," Steve Wynn told the President's Commission on Organized Crime. "We don't make change." But Wynn became convinced Castelbuono was legitimate when he began gambling "feverishly and steadily."

In less than 24 hours Castelbuono lost about $300,000 at the tables and left with $983,000 in $100 bills. Five days later one of Castelbuono's accomplices deposited approximately $1 million into an account at the Credit Suisse Bank in Switzerland, a bank also used by the Pizza Connection heroin ring to launder money. Nor did Wynn find it suspicious that Castelbuono opened accounts with the casino under the fictitious name of Tony Cakes, because, he told the commission, it is not uncommon for some patrons to seek anonymity while gambling. In fact, Wynn said he visited Castelbuono at his New York office and on Castelbuono's advice even invested $50,000 in silver through a firm Castelbuono also used, an investment which he lost.

The other casinos involved in the laundering scheme were the Tropicana, Bally, and Caesars. But the casinos were not implicated in the criminal indictment which stemmed from a two-year investigation into heroin smuggling by the President's Organized Crime Drug Enforcement Task Force.

According to the indictment, the case "began in October 1982 when DEA agents in New York seized 15 kilograms of Far East heroin" supplied by a Thai national to Antonio Turano, an Italian national. Five months later "Turano's bullet-ridden body was found in the marshlands in Queens." The smugglers, based in Sicily, were moving 80 kilograms of heroin every two weeks.

Also indicted with Castelbuono was Gaetano Giuffrida who in June 1985 was convicted in Italy of attempting to ship 80 kilos of heroin to the United States. The heroin was seized in Florence, Italy, on January 21, 1983, less than five weeks after the Golden Nugget transaction.

In explaining the laundering process, Thomas Sheehan, an investigator with the President's commission, testified that organized crime groups are willing to suffer losses just to launder their illicit money. He pointed to the Pizza Connection heroin traffickers who "laundered $13.45 million through E. F. Hutton in New York for transfer to Switzerland. There, as with Atlantic City casinos, millions of dollars in small bills were brought in. E. F. Hutton testified that the Pizza Connection traffickers apparently lost over $10.5 million in precious metals trades. Put another way, the Sicilian Mafia was apparently willing to gamble $13.45 million to legitimize less than $3 million, in the process paying a laundering fee of over seventy-five percent."

Augustino Ferrone, a member of the LaRocca Mafia family of Pittsburgh, ran a bookmaking operation from his free suites at Caesars, which came equipped with six telephones. Ferrone and five associates were arrested on bookmaking charges, and the day he was released on bail he was back in his complimentary room.

During Caesars' license renewal hearings in November 1984, the casino's attorney successfully blocked attempts by the division to introduce any information dealing with the Molony matter. The division's attorney had pointed to the casino's "troubled past," also mentioning that a state grand jury had recently indicted a number of people, some linked to organized crime, who had conspired to control junkets of wealthy gamblers to Atlantic City casinos, including Caesars. Caesars' attorney said he was "astounded" that the division attorney would mention the Molony case and the junket indictment in his opening statement and asked the commission to strike them.

Commission Chairman Walter N. Read agreed that the comments were "inappropriate at this time." Several of the commissioners spoke harshly about the division's tactics and later voted unanimously to renew the license. The Molony case, it decided, would be reviewed at a later time, when all the facts were known.

As for the junkets, they too were linked to organized crime. New Jersey Attorney General Irwin I. Kimmelman estimated that illegal junket operators—in the business of delivering gamblers to casinos by air and buses—controlled some $20 millions ("just the tip of the iceberg") in trade from 65 cities.

"It was only a matter of time before this highly lucrative business captured the attention of organized crime interests bent on getting their share of the action," Kimmelman told the gaming commission in February 1985. "Operating under imaginative but highly structured schemes designed to circumvent the regulatory process, these interests soon succeeded in diverting millions of casino dollars to those not licensed to participate in this privilege. These arrangements are fraught with abuse and scams, involving such things as kickbacks, phantom gamblers, falsified player-rating schemes, and unlicensed operators as fronts."

The way the law read, junket operators could be in business up to 18 months with a temporary grace period while their applications awaited investigation. As many as 600 applications were pending at a single time. Others circumvented the investigation process by using a "front" for the license. "If you couldn't get a license and you had a list of high-rollers, the ideal thing to do is ask the housewife next door to apply for a license," a division agent told the commission.

After a two-year undercover investigation into the junket industry, the New Jersey state police reported that about 45 percent of the 200 licensed junket operators flying gamblers to Atlantic City were associated with organized crime. And it revealed that members of the

Colombo family had once plotted to hijack a Cosmopolitan Airlines flight carrying high-rollers from Republic Airport in Farmingdale, Long Island, to Atlantic City. According to the gaming division, "At least eight organized crime groups [families] have some semblance of control or influence junkets in Atlantic City." Many licensed junket operators were forced to pay a kickback of $35 per customer to a network of unlicensed operators controlled by organized crime. Then the kickback was raised to $75 so that a larger portion could be passed on to casino executives.

"We want people in the junket business who aren't going to rip off the junketeers and who will deal honestly with the casinos," said James Flanagan, the gaming division's deputy director.

But they were ripping off the casinos. What made junkets so attractive to organized crime was that casinos paid commissions and premiums to junket operators based on a patron's losses. One junket operator was indicted on charges that he bribed three Tropicana employees to inflate the amount of money reported lost in the casino. In its investigation, the division uncovered "a systematic use" by the Tropicana of unlicensed persons in the daily operations of its junket program.

In 1984 11 individuals and three junket companies were indicted on 89 counts of defrauding Caesars, Sands, Tropicana, and the Claridge, including $1.6 million from Caesars' superbus junket operations. The charges included racketeering, conspiracy, theft by deception, tampering with witnesses, and perjury. Gaming division director Thomas O'Brien called the junkets an aberration. "Junkets as we know them today should be abolished," he said.

Caesars was having all kinds of problems. While employed as its purchasing agent, Carmen Bannon allegedly accepted bribes to turn over confidential "bid sheets" that listed how other produce companies had bid on various items. Cash and gifts were given to personnel at other casinos to procure the wholesale produce business, but Caesars was the only casino named in the indictment. To strengthen their argument for securing produce contracts, the defendants threatened to exert their influence over unions involved with casino operations and construction.

Ten thousand vendors were selling about $300 million a year in goods and services to the casinos and the rule was that a vendor doing $50,000 in business with a casino, or a total of $150,000 with all casinos, had to be investigated by the gaming division before being licensed by the state on a yearly renewal system. The problem with the regulation was that the division had no way of knowing who to check out unless notified by the vendor or casino. Seventeen investigators were assigned to carry out the investigations, which involved checking financial records and background checks of owners and principal employees, and in the first six years about 1000 were processed and licensed, with the remaining 9000 continuing in business, waiting for the division to catch up with them.

Ernest DeMasi was a compulsive gambler who embezzled $416,000 and pled guilty before Judge Guerrera. Prior to sentencing, a team of four doctors examined DeMasi. All concurred that he was suicidal and that the suicide would "most likely occur if he is sent to prison."

Prosecutor Jeffrey Blitz recommended a seven-year prison term. DeMasi's attorney pleaded with Guerrera for probation monitored by a licensed psychiatrist and community service.

Asked by Guerrera if he had anything to say, DeMasi said, "Just sorry that I messed up my family's life. That's all."

Only a handful of spectators were in the courtroom, including DeMasi's wife, Bonnie, when Guerrera began reading his sentence. Saying that this would be a difficult case for any judge, but pointing out that the difficulty had been caused by DeMasi's embezzlement, Guerrera said, "I read the medical reports very, very carefully, and I am afraid the suicide ideation is brought about because of your fear of being incarcerated." This gave Guerrera a great deal of trouble. "If that were the case, everybody who is incarcerated, if they have that fear, could potentially commit suicide."

While the judge droned on, DeMasi removed a handkerchief from his pocket and wiped his face.

"The seriousness of the offense, I believe, clearly outweighs any other consideration. I think . . ."

Before the judge could finish the sentence, DeMasi uncovered a small handgun concealed in his handkerchief and sent a bullet into his brain. He left behind five sons and three daughters between the ages of four months and 16 years. A week later Bonnie DeMasi was arrested for having passed two bad checks earlier in the year.

In March 1984, FBI special agent Anthony J. Civitano was arrested in the Golden Nugget when he was caught using a counterfeit credit card to get cash. Civitano was later arraigned on charges of solicitation of a bribe, extortion by an officer of the United States, fraud by wire, interstate transportation of a counterfeit credit card, and violation of Hobbs Act extortion statutes.

Money is the name of the game and high-rollers come in all types of packages. Money has only one color no matter where or how it is acquired. As long as the high-rollers are willing to gamble with it, the casinos will not only gladly oblige them but will go to most any length to lure them into their golden cocoons. Nothing is too good for high-rollers, called whales, who become prized catches. They are flown to New York and Philadelphia in private customized jets, some with 14-carat gold hardware, where they are bundled into luxury helicopters for their trip to the resort, greeted at the airport by beautiful hostesses, chauffeured by stretch limousines to the casino footing the bill, and ushered into $1000-a-night suites. The casinos are spending $80 million a year on complimentary services, all tax-deductible.

This is where competition is the most intense. Some casinos shower their whales with gifts of jewelry, luxury cars, Super Bowl tickets, ringside seats at championship fights, Caribbean cruises on private yachts—it all depends on the size of a whale's credit line.

All casinos rate their whales. It takes a minimum credit line of $5000 to start receiving comps. That minimum line will get the player a free room, food, and beverages. About a million gamblers received free rooms in 1984 and about six million free meals were served. The cost of free liquor is astronomical because all gamblers, except slot players, receive free drinks at the tables.

A $15,000 credit line will also get the player free transportation, plus quick or slow sex—though this is vehemently denied by hotel executives.

The big whales start at the $50,000 line and swiftly spiral up to a million plus. Here the sky's the limit. Lavish parties are given with superstars in attendance, and each whale is personally greeted by the hotel's owner or chief executive who smoothly points out the virtues of his operation over that of his competition.

How a whale picks one hotel over another is what makes the game so expensive for the casinos. Aside from the comps, what attracts a whale to a certain casino can be anything from a friendship with a casino manager or pit boss who understands his special needs to the size of the credit line the casino is willing to grant. Popular casino executives, like superstar athletes, offer their services to the highest bidder. The moves from one casino to another are so frequent that an observer needs a scorecard to keep track. When Billy Weinberger went from Caesars to Bally, it was probably as much for his school of whales as for his managerial ability.

Competition for hotel rooms is nonexistent in Atlantic City. There is no occupancy problem in a city with 30 million visitors and some 6000 first class rooms. Reservations for weekends and holidays have to be made a year in advance. The price is $120 per night and up, whereas in Las Vegas, major hotel-casinos advertise rooms for as low as $10, double occupancy, and offer package deals that include airline transportation, free meals, and free supper shows.

To gamble is a whale's function in a casino. "If a man is a $15,000 customer and he doesn't gamble, he's reminded he gets all those gratuities because of his gambling," says Morris Shenker, owner of the Las Vegas Dunes. "If he doesn't patronize the casino sufficiently, he will have to be charged."

On a far lower scale are the high-pullers, day-trippers who play slot machines without interruption for the six or eight hours they are in town. The Golden Nugget founded a club exclusively for them. Members are wined and dined by the casino and the slots spew out coupons that can be redeemed for bonuses. At Resorts International high-pullers belong to the Superstar Club. Inducements include free trips to the Bahamas, unlimited free parking, free drinks, and food. All casinos fight for bus passengers, who are rewarded with $10 or more in gambling chips, free drinks, discount lunches, and coupons that can be redeemed on the next trip.

Ever since Bugsy Siegel opened his fabulous Flamingo on December 26, 1946, with Jimmy Durante and Xavier Cugat's band, a casino's showroom has been a powerful marketing tool in the casino business. It is a greater lure than a hotel's decor. It brings in the little fish as well as the big ones.

Yet entertainment, at both ends of the country, features the same acts year after year. The visitor who missed Phyllis Diller, Red Buttons, Engelbert Humperdinck, Tom Jones, Don Rickles, Liberace, Johnny Mathis, Shecky Greene, Vic Damone, Charlie Callas, or any of a hundred other performers in Las Vegas can always catch up with them in Atlantic City. The same faces and voices that play to half-empty showrooms in Las Vegas are booked solid in Atlantic City.

With business booming, entertainers, like casino executives, have learned it pays to move around. Steve Lawrence and Eydie Gorme worked Resorts International, the Sands, Atlantis, and the Golden Nugget. When Joan Rivers got hot, she switched from the Sands to Resorts International. Susan Anton went from Caesars to the Claridge to the Tropicana. For the casinos, it's a frantic musical chair's game that has them locked into a costly "Talent War." By now casino executives know exactly the kind of business an act will draw at the gaming tables and slot machines and the price goes up correspondingly.

"The better you do your job, the higher the expectations and the more spoiled the customer becomes," says the Golden Nugget's Steve Wynn. "You begin to compete with yourself and that's where the trouble begins."

Yet in the Talent War, Wynn is the general with the most decorations. His conquests go beyond young rising star and older superstar. He travels in the private universe of megastars, who for the most part, perform solely for whales and their friends. When Diana Ross, Willie Nelson, Frank Sinatra, Kenny Rogers, and others revolving in that celestial firmament appear at the Golden Nugget, a little sign on the lightboards says Sold Out.

At first their presence in the showrooms was kept secret—when Bob Hope played a one-nighter in the Golden Nugget's showroom for Wynn's invited guests, there were no lightboards, no newspaper ads—but in time Steve Wynn saw the extra benefits to be gained for his vast expenditures by letting the public know what a great showman he was.

The shows are it in Atlantic City. Except for going to the beach during sunny days of the three short summer months, there is nothing to do in Atlantic City. It is strictly a gambling den and doesn't pretend to be anything else. It is not a place for a family vacation.

And if all gamblers were as easily plucked as the day-trippers, the casinos could even do away with the entertainment. Herded on buses, all they care about are the slot machines, gaming tables, and the bargain lunch. Except for what they can see from the window of their bus while it's in a holding pattern for an hour or so with hundreds of other buses buzzing around the casinos for their turn to unload, they know nothing about Atlantic City and for the most part couldn't care less.

*　　*　　*

As it approached its first decade as a gambling mecca, Atlantic City was becoming the focus of criticism from politicians and public officials who had opposed or supported casino gambling during the 1976 referendum.

For gaming commissioner Joel Jacobson, gambling is "an industry motivated by greed" and Atlantic City is "a place where ten Taj Mahals flourish in the midst of a war zone."

For gaming commissioner Carl Zeitz, "It is a place where it takes you twenty minutes to go four blocks in a car, because after seven years the city government hasn't been able to synchronize the traffic lights on a computer, a place where once stable, fine neighborhoods have become collections of scattered, barren, littered lots, a place where public ego takes precedence over public accomplishment, a place, in sum, that is a sorry testament to the supposed advantages of public and private partnership."

For former gaming division director Mickey Brown, the state was sold "a bill of goods that the streets would be paved with gold and everyone would have a warm house and two cars in the garage."

For Mayor James Usry, the pro-gambling proponents "wouldn't dare put it up for referendum again."

For professor Jack Samuels, the city was still a "glorified bingo hall" where people came for a few hours to gamble and then went home. Less than 20 percent of the visitors stayed overnight.

For Robert M. Klein, a counselor at Atlantic City High School, "My survey found that students are gambling, and students are being identified as potential and active compulsive gamblers." Children as young as 14 were playing hooky and sneaking into the casinos to gamble, even though the legal gambling age was 19. About one-fifth of the students polled said they had gambled their weekly allowance and had even shoplifted to gamble at casinos. The high school was in walking distance of the Boardwalk and Central Junior High School was less than one block away.

For Jaycees president Nicholas Russo, "This city is a toilet. We've got vintage trash in the streets."

For Councilman James Whelan, "The first place you look is in the mirror. We're not doing what we're supposed to be doing down here. I wish I knew the answers to getting us to do what we're supposed to do."

For Women's Chamber of Commerce President Georgia Paxson-Steinfals, the "people of Atlantic City have had just about enough from this city government.'' The people were ''promised good government and yet have received nothing but bad politics from a self-serving crowd of selfish power seekers.'' On another occasion, Georgia Paxson-Steinfals said of the City Council, ''It is difficult to soar with eagles when you have to work with turkeys.''

For State Senator William Gormley, the city's besmirched reputation was a major block to its economic potential in years ahead. ''Old money,'' he said, shakes its head over Atlantic City and says, ''We understand about down there.'' Atlantic City held unequaled economic potential, but ''the reality is that we have a town in the tank.''

For Mayor Usry, ''I don't know what makes people think Atlantic City is in this position because it wants to be. We have problems with the city. That's why we are raising so much heck about why we don't have the casino reinvestment fund to help us.''

For Councilman Gene Dorn, ''The ambiguity built into the law has permitted casinos, eight years up the road from the advent of casino gaming, to have done nothing for the citizens of Atlantic City.''

For Joel Jacobson, ''Stated very bluntly, if Atlantic City is unable to extricate itself from the bureaucratic folly which has surrounded the spending of this comparatively paltry sum of money [Resorts' $1 million to the Housing Authority], what will be its record of success as it contemplates the expenditure of almost $1 billion in the future?''

For Cora Boggs, ''They [casinos] want to take over the whole city. I think they're trying to prolong the agony of the people of Atlantic City. They're hoping we're going to move out.''

For Carl Zeitz, gambling ''is regressive taxation. It brings crime, compulsive gambling and dislocation. I voted against the referendum. But now the decision is made, and it is irrevocable. You can't undo 36,000 jobs. We've got it and we have to live with it.''

For former U.S. Attorney and gubernatorial candidate Robert Del Tufo, ''We have two governors in New Jersey, two state governments, and two administrations. The one administration is that elected by the people. The other administration is that designated by the leaders of organized crime.'' He accused the Kean administration of being soft on the Mob. ''It is a government that lives off blood money and drug money and rules from the alleys and back rooms and the shadowy places you and I never go. No party—and no candidate— can lay legitimate claim to the first government of New Jersey until it deals with the second.''

For U.S. Attorney W. Hunt Dumont, Atlantic City is one of the state's major heroin markets and "New Jersey is a residence for many organized crime figures who use the state to either store or transport heroin."

For New Jersey State Police Superintendent Clinton L. Pagano, "We have found a substantial increase in illegal sports bookmaking in Atlantic City, involving members of crime families from Pennsylvania and New York and Massachusetts." These people actually conduct "their illegal sports bookmaking operations in and around casinos."

For FBI Special Agent Frank Storey, as many as ten Mafia families are involved in unions, junkets, and other ancillary businesses serving the casino industry in Atlantic City.

For Ron Lane, an undercover cop, who has been beaten, robbed, and stabbed in the line of duty, "You walk one block in either direction from a casino and you're in a high-crime area. That's a bad thing for out-of-towners who don't know it. A lot of people are getting mugged and no one is doing anything about it."

For Resorts president I. G. "Jack" Davis, Jr., the casino industry needed more freedom from rules in areas affecting profits. The industry needed fewer restrictions in areas such as extending credit to gamblers, promotions, and internal management if they were to improve profitability and contribute more to the New Jersey economy. "There's a market out there that wants to come spend money in Atlantic City," he said. "That market can double."

For Casino Association President Thomas Carver, "We are in the process of creating a new metropolitan area firmly based on the entertainment industry in southern New Jersey." The casino industry will play a role as the economic "foundation for the future," but it will "no longer accept indiscriminate kicks in the groin" by those who blame it for all ills. The state's "overregulation" of the industry was dangerous. Annual regulatory costs had risen from $4.3 million in 1978 to $49 million in 1985. "We may have a failure if government continues to insist on the theory that casinos are cash cows, that all they have to do is come to Atlantic City and get more money." The next month—July 1985—the 11 casinos set a record for the biggest win ever, with revenues of $224.2 million for that month, or about $7.2 million a day.

For casino commissioner Valerie Armstrong, casinos wanted to reduce regulation so they could "gouge out bigger and bigger profits without addressing the societal needs of Atlantic City. Instead of plans for the rebuilding of Atlantic City, we hear complaints about overregulation and excessive costs.''

For Carl Zeitz, on the casino industry's proposal that a new commission be created to review the state's casino law and regulations, "I've never heard of a highly-regulated industry, particularly one that is illegal in 48 states in this country and 566 of the 567 municipalities of this state, deciding when and under what terms the regulatory agencies that have oversight over it will be reviewed.''

The *Press,* being the local paper, is often of mixed opinion. But when Governor Kean got carried away at the 1984 Republican National Convention in Dallas and talked about Atlantic City hosting the event in the near future, the *Press* moved quickly to quash the idea. "We have to wonder where they would all stay. Where would they eat? Where would they shop? How would they get here? On casino buses? What would they think of the city's spreading slums, its rundown business district, its jammed streets? Sure, Atlantic City has ten shiny new casinos and there will be more in the next few years. But it still has the many failings that almost destroyed the city's image when the Democrats convened in the resort in 1964.''

In a letter to the *Press* on November 29, 1983, Albert Nelson, a resident of Ventnor, a community only a stone's throw from the Boardwalk, summed up what he called the "benefits" of the casino era to date: "We have corruption in unions, scandals, inflation, and pollution. An incredibly high crime rate, inadequate public transportation, dire traffic conditions, and limited parking.

"There is virtually no new housing, but we have the continued demolition of whatever livable units remain. We have further destruction of landmarks, increased prostitution, drug traffic, and alcoholism. More political corruption, law perversion, character deterioration, family disruption, and compulsive gambling.

"A 'family resort' characterized by casino-hotels, pornography shops, eroded beaches, urban blight, police brutality, discrimination, and arcades that stimulate aggression and a propensity to gamble in the young. . . .

"As for New Jersey, anyone can see that when presented with the figures, annual tax revenues are practically nil when compared to daily wins, and that, consequently, there have been no major improvements for the elderly, for the handicapped, or for the people throughout the state. Human welfare . . . does not depend on self-serving groups who, through any number of ways, wish to gain control of a city or state at the cost of constituent populations.''

Compared to the state's annual budget for 1984–85 of $7.67 billion, casino revenues were a minuscule $204 million, while the state-sponsored lottery brought in $340 million. The lottery paid out 50 percent in prizes, retained 40 percent for public purposes, and spent 10 percent on administration, whereas the casinos paid 8 percent in taxes, less the 4 percent allowed for bad credit, and retained 92 percent. The total amount of taxes paid by casinos in the first six years was $436.4 million, not exactly a bonanza for the price it has exacted.

The fact that about half of the casinos' patrons are from New Jersey creates another form of income redistribution, with many of the elderly and disabled getting back from the state only a small fraction of their gambling losses. As for the state, its cost for human services in 1984–85 was set at nearly $1.5 billion.

Gambling is a parasitic enterprise that thrives on the weaknesses of people. It leaves in its wake corruption, debasement, despair, and the subversion of moral authority. That is the real bottom line.

Index